An Anthology of Vietnamese Poems

An Anthology of Vietnamese Poems

From the Eleventh through the Twentieth Centuries

Edited and translated by Huỳnh Sanh Thông

Yale University Press New Haven and London

Designed by Sonia L. Scanlon
Set in Bodoni type by Asco Trade
Typesetting Ltd., Hong Kong.
Printed by Vail-Ballou Press,
Binghamton, New York.

Library of Congress Cataloging-in-Publication
Data

An anthology of Vietnamese poems : from the
    eleventh through the twentieth centuries /
    edited and translated by Huỳnh Sanh
    Thông.
        p.   cm.
    Includes bibliographical references.
    ISBN 0-300-06410-1 (cloth : alk. paper)
    1. Vietnamese poetry—Translations into
English.   I. Huỳnh, Sanh Thông, 1926–
PL4378.65.E5A57   1996
895.9'221008—dc20   95-37761
                                        CIP

A catalogue record for this book is
available from the British Library.

The paper in this book meets the guidelines for permanence and durability of
the Committee on Production Guidelines
for Book Longevity of the Council on
Library Resources.

10 9 8 7 6 5 4 3 2 1

The muse lends me her lyre of myriad tunes,
her brush of myriad tints—I want to play
a wizard working wonders, magic tricks
with all the sounds and colors of the earth.

—Thế Lữ

Contents

preface ix

acknowledgments xi

introduction 1

1. Vietnam and China 27

2. The Buddhist Ethos 61

3. Responses to the West 84

4. After the Russian Revolution 153

5. Men and Women 211

6. Life and Art 296

7. The Passage of Time 316

8. Peasants, Merchants, and Scholars 352

9. War and Peace 378

index of poets and poems 419

bibliography 427

Preface

In 1979 Yale University Press published *The Heritage of Vietnamese Poetry*. Although that collection of premodern poems has gone out of print, there is renewed demand for such an anthology on the part of instructors of courses on Vietnamese history, the Vietnam War, Southeast Asian and East Asian literatures, Asian-American studies, and women's studies.

Not only to meet the needs of those academic constituencies but also to provide for Vietnamese throughout the world and their international friends an omnibus of Vietnamese verse in English translation, I have prepared *An Anthology of Vietnamese Poems*. This book consists of 322 works by about a hundred fifty poets, celebrated, obscure, or anonymous. It includes 125 poems (many revised) from the 1979 volume, as well as two long narratives written before the twentieth century: the *Bích câu kỳ ngộ* ("The marvelous encounter at Blue Creek," Poem 209] and the *Trinh thử* ("The constant mouse," Poem 210). Besides those two, this book numbers five other traditional poems of above average length: the *Chiêu hồn* ("Calling all souls," Poem 45) by Nguyễn Du, the *Cung oán ngâm khúc* ("A song of sorrow inside the royal harem," Poem 44) by Nguyễn Gia Thiều, the *Chinh phụ ngâm* ("The song of a soldier's wife," Poem 322) by Đặng Trần Côn and Phan Huy Ích, the *Trê cóc* ("Catfish and Toad," Poem 37), and the *Lục súc tranh công* ("The quarrel of the six beasts," Poem 302). Significantly, the new anthology omits most of the poems written in Chinese and instead features hundreds of works composed during the twentieth century. The new introduction, an emended and expanded version of the introduction to *The Heritage of Vietnamese Poetry*, takes such changes into account.

All the poems, ancient and modern, are grouped under nine headings meant to suggest the various ways in which, for a thousand years or so, the Vietnamese people collectively or individually have responded to either cultural pressures or military and political changes and have debated in their minds such universal issues as the relations between men and women, the role of art in life, war and peace, conflicts between the social classes, and attitudes toward time, change, old age, and death. Because history is not created—nor its burdens borne—solely by the powerful and famous, I have made room in this anthology for poems by ordinary, uncelebrated persons: they have something to say and thus earn their place in a book that is meant to contribute toward understanding the Vietnamese experience. The omission of works by many far better known poets by no means implies that I consider them unworthy of inclusion.

Translating poetry has always enjoyed a place of honor in Vietnamese literature. As heir to that tradition, I have attempted to the best of my ability to meet the three criteria observed by successful translators in the past: fidelity *(tín)*, expressiveness *(đạt)*, and elegance *(nhã)*. I hope that my work does not fall too short of standards once set by such poets as Phan Huy Ích and Tản Đà.

Acknowledgments

An amateur loves not wisely but too well. Since the early 1970s, I have enjoyed the good fortune of finding in academia scholars with such openness of mind and largesse of heart that they have glossed over all my eccentricities and shortcomings and welcomed me as one of their own. For offering me the chance to dream of a book like this and then to see it achieve realization in print, I honor the memory of the late John M. Echols and of the late John K. Musgrave; and I wish to thank Oliver W. Wolters, James C. Scott, Alton L. Becker, Eric Henry, Alexander B. Woodside, David G. Marr, John K. Whitmore, David Chandler, Gerald C. Hickey, Keith Weller Taylor, Stephen O'Harrow, Kristin Pelzer, Marion W. Ross, John C. Schafer, David W. P. Elliott, Nguyễn Khắc Kham, Nguyễn Đình Hòa, Hồ Huệ Tâm (or Hue-Tam Ho-Tai), Công-Huyền Tôn-Nữ Nha-Trang (or Nha-Trang Pensinger), Lucy Nguyễn Hồng Nhiệm, Trần Văn Dĩnh, and Trương Bửu Lâm.

At the request of Yale University Press, two of those scholars (who prefer anonymity) set aside their personal concerns and read the manuscript with care. Their judicious comments resolved most of my perplexities, helping me to temper my excesses and decide on the final shape and size of this book. As it still leaves much to be desired, I take full blame for all its flaws and infelicities. Kim Ninh and Dan Duffy gave me recent materials from Vietnam, and I gratefully acknowledge their assistance.

To the John D. and Catherine T. MacArthur Foundation I am grateful for a generous fellowship, awarded in 1987: it has freed me from financial pressures and let me focus both time and energy on this project and on several others, too.

The book has benefited in no small measure from the suggestions of Susan Abel, the manuscript editor, and I deeply appreciate her professional skill and devotion.

As a token of my love and gratitude I dedicate this book to my wife, Yên, who, in the heroic tradition of Vietnamese womanhood, has put up with me for forty years.

An Anthology of Vietnamese Poems

Introduction

The strikingly worded and artfully measured utterance, whether it takes the form of a saying, a riddle, or a song, has doubtless enlivened the speech of Vietnamese peasants from time immemorial. But not until Vietnam had been exposed for many centuries to Chinese writing and literature did Vietnamese oral poetry come to be set down on paper and become a favorite and highly regarded pursuit of the educated class. *An Anthology of Vietnamese Poems* gathers in translation a varied and representative sampling of works composed by Vietnamese poets over the past thousand years, both in Vietnamese and (occasionally) in Chinese. (Italics for the title of a poem indicate that it was originally written in Chinese.) All the poems, whether they were created by consummate artists or by dilettantes, provide instructive glimpses into Vietnamese experience and history.

The poems composed before the twentieth century, in particular, reflect Vietnamese society and culture from the vantage point of the dominant group: the ruling kings and mandarins, along with those whose influence derived from their scholarly training and expertise. A study of those poems may answer some questions about Vietnamese ambivalence toward Chinese culture, and about the dual process of cultural borrowing and cultural resistance in Vietnam. How did transplants from China, the seedbed of all East Asian classical civilizations, fare in Southeast Asian soil? To what extent did they manage to survive more or less intact in the tropical climate? To what extent did they have to change and adapt? Here I seek to trace the birth and growth of a national poetry, which at its most mature reconciled and wedded into a harmonious whole two disparate, even antagonistic elements: the "little," or oral, folk tradition of the Vietnamese village, and the "great," or written, learned tradition from China.

When Ngô Quyền won his battle on the Bạch-đằng River and independence for his country in 938, Vietnam had gone through a little more than a thousand years of Chinese domination, from the Han to the T'ang dynasties. The refusal of the "Southern" people, after ten centuries of "Northern" influence, to allow the Chinese empire to assimilate them, and their demand for a separate existence, demonstrate an almost obsessive sense of ethnic and cultural identity, a self-affirmation tantamount to xenophobia. Therefore, at first blush, it may seem perverse that as soon as they had thrown off the Chinese yoke, native Vietnamese rulers would methodically proceed to reimpose on their people a structure of social and political control patterned on the Chinese model. This paradox, more apparent than real, can be explained by the uniquely vulnerable position into which both geography and history had thrust Vietname vis-à-vis China. Here was a land that in size, population, and resources was overshadowed and dwarfed by its gigantic neighbor to the north, which never willingly curbed its appetite for expansion and always kept an eye out for the first chance, the flimsiest excuse, to march south again in the name of a civilizing mission. Even as today many non-Western peoples all over the world have chosen deliberate Westernization as an alternative to colonialism and imperialism, Vietname's leaders preferred to sinicize the country selectively and voluntarily, rather than allow it to be sinicized totally and by force. When some northern visitor inquired about local customs, Hồ Quý Ly replied as if he had been challenged to defend his country against a charge of barbarism (Poem 14 in *The Heritage of Vietnamese Poetry*): "The Quiet South boasts polished ways./Our King and subjects heed Han laws./Our caps and gowns obey T'ang rules."

The need to "civilize" their country themselves and forestall Chinese conquest lay behind Vietnamese monarchs' decision to borrow from Sung China the neo-Confucian ideology and its institutional apparatus. Imitation of the Chinese model, moreover, had a profound impact on Vietnamese society in two ways: classical Chinese was adopted as the language for official business; and through the system of civil service examinations, literature was elevated to a preeminent status among all pursuits. Because those examinations required the writing of verse as a crucial exercise, poetry—which had been thriving in the oral tradition—now came to occupy a central niche in the written culture imported from China, as well. If before, farmers had won admiration at village festivals for their skill in improvising rhymes and ditties, now scholars too were expected to rise to any occasion—an academic contest, a reunion of friends, a farewell party—and compose serviceable poems, if not masterpieces, in classical Chinese. Throughout the millennium of Chinese domination, Vietnamese men and women were in all likelihood schooled in the script of the conqueror and encouraged to put it to poetic use. The earliest extant specimen of Chinese verse written by a Vietnamese, however, dates from the waning decades of the tenth century, when Vietnam had already driven its conquerors out ("Farewell to Ambassador Li Chüeh," by the monk-diplomat Khuông Việt, Poem 1 in *The Heritage of Vietnamese Poetry*). Once integrated into the civil service examination system, verse writing in classical Chinese grew to be a major concern of all Vietnamese scholars and persisted as such for nine hundred years, until French colonialism toppled the whole neo-Confucian setup toward the end of the nineteenth century.

Vietnamese literati who wrote in classical Chinese employed verse forms that were the stock-in-trade of Chinese poets: they either followed the "old style" *(ku-feng)* with its few requirements or tried to observe the stricter rules of T'ang prosody, those pertaining to the "regulated poem" *(lü-shih),* sometimes conveniently defined as an eight-line "sonnet." It came as no surprise that the latter ended up dominating the scene, because it was the touchstone on state examinations for a candidate's versificatory know-how. With its bewildering requirements and intricacies packed into a narrow compass (the use of rhymes at the end of alternate lines; syntactical and semantic parallelism in the two middle couplets; fixed patterns of tonal contrast in all couplets; avoidance of eight specific defects, such as the "wasp's waist," the "crane's knee," and so on), the regulated poem epitomized the virtues in which students eager to join the political establishment should be trained: the cult of punctilios, a reverence for authority, and an aversion to heterodoxy. Nevertheless, some poets did not regard the Chinese norm as sacrosanct; they tried to innovate and introduce features of Vietnamese folk prosody into the writing of Chinese verse. Some experimenters, like Nguyễn Huy Oánh in the eighteenth century and Đinh Nhật Thận in the nineteenth, even went so far as to produce extensive poems in classical Chinese, adopting the Vietnamese "six-eight" *(lục-bát)* and "double-seven–six-eight" *(song-thất lục-bát)* meters, respectively. But given the length and weight of the learned tradition, those tinkerings with Chinese verse remained isolated instances of quixotism.

It may appear self-evident that a foreign language ill qualifies to be the midwife of a national literature. And yet Chinese did in fact make the birth and growth of literature possible in Vietnam by supplying the script in which the vernacular could be recorded. Vietnamese scholars selected Chinese graphs for either their semantic equivalence or their phonetic similarity to Vietnamese words and, through various combinations, devised a writing system that they named the southern script *(chữ nôm)*. As an instrument for representing the sounds of Vietnamese, the southern script suffered from many limitations and defects. Of course, because of the peculiar manner in which it was put together, it presupposed a considerable knowledge of Chinese graphs on the part of both writers and readers. Then, too, it was never rigorously standardized but remained dependent on the skill and whim of anyone who chose to write in it; its inconsistencies and obscurities bedeviled anyone who tried to decipher it. For all its shortcomings, it was a momentous invention. It freed Vietnamese poets from complete reliance on an alien medium and allowed them to speak in their own voice at last.

A latecomer to the lists where prospective bureaucrats tilted their writing brushes, verse writing in Vietnamese started under a handicap. Still, its position was rather that of a younger sister or favorite concubine than that of a stepchild or poor relation. It was true, on the one hand, that scholars being groomed as leaders composed Chinese poems as part of their professional training and in that sense were playing a game of national survival according to rules laid down by the Chinese colossus. On the other hand, outside the province of duty and career, reading and writing poetry was something that Vietnamese scholars cherished and pursued by inclination in their own language, without ulterior motive, any thought of preferment or gain. They wrote Vietnamese verse in the morganatic sense, for love and not for reasons of state. Indeed, sovereigns were known to practice the craft diligently and to pride themselves on an expert appreciation of it. As proof of his active interest and patronage, the fifteenth-century king Lê Thánh-tông assembled an important body of poems written by either himself or his court ministers, *The Hồng Đức Anthology of Verse in the National Language* (*Hồng Đức quốc âm thi tập*, referred to henceforth as *The Hồng Đức Anthology*). In the nineteenth century, King Tự Đức admired Nguyễn Du's masterpiece *The Tale of Kiều* enough to forgive the sentiments of lèse-majesté lurking therein; he simply edited some lines to suit himself. Vernacular verse enjoyed such esteem among scholars that they made a point of translating or adapting into Vietnamese any Chinese poem that caught their fancy. If successful, a translation or adaptation might surpass the original in popularity. The Phan Huy family excelled in that cross-cultural role. Like several other scholars and with greater success, Phan Huy Ích rendered "The song of a soldier's wife" (*Chinh phụ ngâm*, Poem 322) by Đặng Trần Côn into "double-seven" quatrains. Either his son, Phan Huy Thực, or his grandson, Phan Huy Vịnh, performed the same metamorphosis for "The ballad of the lute," by Po Chü-i.

The southern script was the brainchild of scholar-poets who had been tutored exclusively in Chinese versification. They used it first to domesticate that type of Chinese verse with which they felt most at home: the *lü-shih*, or regulated poem. Although the process must have enlisted the efforts of many, credit for it goes to one man, Nguyễn Thuyên, who wrote during the second half of the thirteenth century. He was one of the heroes whom the Vietnamese people honored for having effectively incorporated into their culture valuable elements of Chinese civilization. It is alleged that on being ordered to repeat the feat of Han Yü (Hàn Dũ in Vietnamese), he penned an ultimatum and flung it at the crocodiles in the Lô River, thus chasing the monsters away: an impressed sovereign renamed him Hàn Thuyên. It is also claimed that he emulated such luminaries as Sung Chih-wen and Shen Ch'üan-ch'i and incorporated elements of T'ang prosody into the composition of Vietnamese verse. The precepts he proposed gained acceptance and currency as "Hàn [Thuyên]'s metrics" (Hàn-luật). Within the context of victories over Mongol troops dispatched by the Yüan court, Hàn Thuyên's well-received attempt to Vietnamize the regulated poem could be interpreted as a gesture of southern assertiveness, as a declaration of greater independence from the northern model. Poems that he and his contemporaries wrote in the vernacular should serve as precious indices of those exhilarating times. Unfortunately, all such works were lost in the early part of the fifteenth century; during that holocaust, the Ming occupation, the avowed policy of the Chinese emperor Ch'eng-tsu was to destroy Vietnamese culture through book burning and other means.

The transfer of lü-shih requirements from Chinese to Vietnamese could be brought about with few hitches, since the two languages share major traits. Both are predominantly monosyllabic. Both include two categories of tones that can be set off against one another for musical effect: the "flat," or even, level, which is constant in pitch (called p'ing in Chinese, bằng in Vietnamese), and the "sharp," or oblique, which is deflected, changing in pitch (called tsê in Chinese, trắc in Vietnamese). Both languages are blessed with supple, economical syntaxes that can do without empty (or merely functional) words and pare a sentence or line down to muscle and sinew. It is remarkable, then, that the regulated poem in Vietnamese took quite a long time to assume the shape it would have from the eighteenth century onward. It would seem that Vietnamese poets were not content to abide by lü-shih rules; they wanted to play fast and loose with them, bend them to fit different practices of native oral verse. Sometimes they displaced the medial caesura in the seven-syllable line of a regulated poem—a liberty they had taken with that verse form in Chinese. More often, they substituted a six-syllable line for that seven-syllable line—another bias of folk prosody, which favored the even number over the odd number. In the long run, the Vietnamese ear grew attuned to the peculiarities of T'ang metrics, and such breaches were recognized as infelicitous and were abandoned; by the end of the nineteenth century, the rigidly built poem of "eight seven-word lines" *(thât-ngôn bát-cú)* had established its dominance in Vietnamese poetry. The Chinese ideal had to compromise with Vietnamese reality on one point, however: the preferred number of syllables in a *lü-shih* line became seven, not five. Most Vietnamese poets judged the poem of "eight five-word lines" *(ngũ-ngôn bát-cú)* to be too confining a vessel for their vernacular, which, though pithy, could not match the lapidary quality of classical Chinese.

On its southward migration, the Chinese regulated poem maintained its outward structure virtually unscathed. But in the hands of Vietnamese poets, the very nature of the poem underwent changes so profound that they altered it beyond recognition. In its original habitat it remained an aristocratic medium, the embodiment of Confucian decorum and restraint. Over and above the explicit rules governing its formal construction, it obeyed an implicit etiquette that not only controlled style, diction, and subject matter but also tended to detach the poet from the toiling masses and their mundane cares and isolate him in the most rarefied of atmospheres. In Vietnam, by contrast, the regulated poem shed its haughty reserve and fastidious aloofness and went native—it fell into such laxity that even the blithest spirit among classical Chinese poets would have disowned it. It lifted all taboos and welcomed any word, however vulgar, that circumstance might justify. In "Carrying a cangue around the neck" (Poem 46), Nguyễn Hữu Huân, soon to face the executioner, hurled in his righteous wrath an obscenity at the fellow countrymen he despised for collaborating with the French. The verse form accommodated any topic or theme, from the most solemn to the most ridiculous, any poetic fancy, from the elegist's to the limerick-monger's. The regulated poem became a vehicle for all purposes: descriptive, lyrical, expository, satirical, didactic, and even narrative. (Stories were told in long sequences of "regulated" octaves.)

Purists might frown on such a plebification of the regulated poem, yet it was actually carried out under the most unplebeian auspices: already, there were abundant signs of the tendency in the oldest works that have come down to us in Vietnamese, from the fifteenth century: poems by Nguyễn Trãi, a paragon of neo-Confucian learning and rectitude, and by King Lê Thánh-tông or members of his court. In thoroughly domesticating *lü-shih*, those patricians veered away from slavish worship of foreign culture and took a giant stride in the direction of ethnic originality. Others who wrote verse went further yet: they wielded the southern script not only to propagate Confucian doctrine among the populace but also to rediscover and celebrate their ancestral roots. Now more and more they would lend their ears to the melodies and lyrics, naïve but hardly lacking in charm or wisdom, of a poetry cultivated by their own people in the mud of their fields. Nguyễn Du, whom the Vietnamese hail as their greatest poet, wrote: "Folk songs taught me hemp and mulberry lore. / Poor peasants' cries told me the tale of war." A classicist who composed many brilliant poems in Chinese, Nguyễn Du was and is acclaimed above all for vernacular masterpieces written in two folk meters, "six-eight" *(lục-bát)* and "double-seven–six-eight" *(song-thât lục-bát)*.

In the last analysis, both verse forms can be traced to two basic meters that reproduce the common cadence of Vietnamese speech, a rising rhythm—the iamb (a group of two syllables with the stress on the second syllable), and the anapest (a group of three syllables, with the primary stress on the last syllable and sometimes a secondary accent on the first). Vietnamese sayings and proverbs are often folk poems in miniature; they combine two iambs, two anapests, one iamb, and one anapest, or varying numbers of both. A line of folk verse tends to be made up of an even number of syllables, a series of

	1	2	3	4	5	6	7	8
I		F		S		F↕		
II		F		S		F↕		F

Figure 1

iambs in particular, when there is an odd number of syllables, the line usually ends with an iamb, not an anapest. That double propensity of folk verse accounts for the practice, persistent in the past, of replacing the normal seven-syllable line (four | three) of a regulated poem *(lü-shih)* with a six-syllable line or with a "three | four" line. The constituent unit of six-eight *(lục-bát)* verse is a couplet in which the first line has six syllables and the second line eight syllables. Usually, both lines consist of iambs, and the stress falls on each even-numbered syllable: in such a case, they can be described as iambic trimeter and iambic tetrameter, respectively. On occasion, the first line departs from the norm and comprises two anapests, instead: two equal, balanced hemistichs divided by a medial caesura (three | three). The last (or sixth) syllable of the first line rhymes with the last-but-two (or sixth) syllable of the second line (or, as an archaism, with the fourth syllable). What stamps six-eight verse with individuality, however, is its pattern of euphonic requirements, an ingeniously plotted alternation of "flat" *(bằng)* and "sharp" *(trắc)* tones. The scheme, as observable in a typical couplet, is diagrammed in Figure 1: the double-headed arrow indicates rhyming, an open space represents an unstressed syllable, and *F* and *S* stand for flats and sharps. It will be noted that the tonal rules apply only to accented (even-numbered) syllables; that the same type of tones is assigned to syllables taking up the same position in both lines (flats for I–2 and II–2, sharps for I–4 and II–4, and flats for I–6 and II–6); and that flats predominate: they flank a single sharp in each line and monopolize the rhyme-fellows (I–6 and II–6) as well as the last two stressed syllables of the second line (II–6 and II–8). There

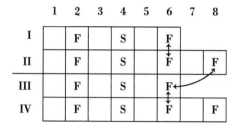

	1	2	3	4	5	6	7	8
I		F		S		F		
II		F		S		F		F
III		F		S		F		
IV		F		S		F		F

Figure 2

is another prescription, not specified in the diagram: both II–6 and II–8 carry level tones, as shown, but they must be different; "monotony" is thus avoided or at least alleviated. (There are only two flat, level tones in Vietnamese, as compared with four sharp, oblique tones.) Also, flats for syllables in the second position (I–2 and II–2) are recommended though they are not mandatory.

Six-eight verse amounts to a concatenation of such couplets. A simple device provides the needed linkage: the last (or eighth) syllable in the second line of one couplet rhymes with the last (or sixth) syllable in the first line of the next couplet. The way two consecutive couplets look is shown in Figure 2, which makes it clear that in six-eight verse, rhymes work according to a consistent yet varied arrangement, in two distinct fashions: internally within each couplet (I–6 and II–6, III–6 and IV–6), and at the end between couplets (II–8 and III–6). Each line rhymes with the next, but a new, different rhyme appears in every other line, in every couplet.

A six-eight couplet can stand by itself as a poem, and it often does in folklore. The following is a riddle about the chicken: *Có chân mà chẳng có tay, / có hai con mắt, ăn mày dương-gian.* ("It has legs and yet no arms; / it has two eyes and lives on alms from the world.") Here is a bit of folk astrology: *Tháng mười coi cái sao tua, / khi nằm khi dậy làm mùa mới nên.* ("In the tenth month watch the stars of Orion, / when you lie down or wake up, if you're to get a good harvest.") This is how a lad attempts to strike up an acquaintance with a lass as both work at night in the rice fields: *Hỡi cô tát nước bên*

đàng! / Sao cô múc ánh trăng vàng đổ đi? ("Hey, young lady, you
who are bailing water by the road! / How come you scoop the golden
moonlight and pour it all off?") Two lines can wrap up a philosophical comment inside a vivid image: *Đố ai lặn xuống vực sâu / mà đo
miệng cá uốn câu cho vừa.* ("I dare anyone to dive into the depths /
and measure a fish's mouth for a hook that will fit.") These examples
suggest the possibilities of a six-eight couplet: to state a fact, paint a
scene, or voice an opinion or sentiment.

The six-eight couplet executed those functions even better when
poets used it as a link in a chain—a chain that they could make as
short or as long as they wished. In fact, the six-eight verse was ideal
for storytelling. A competent storyteller could spin out a yarn at
prodigious length and yet induce no tedium in the listener or reader:
the iambic rhythm (with few interruptions) would impart a steady
thrust to the narrative; and at the same time, the joint recourse
to internal and final rhymes (occurring by turns and constantly
renewed), along with the periodic contrast between flat and sharp
tones, provides adequate diversity within the predictable continuum.
In the hands of an inspired craftsman and storyteller, six-eight verse
was destined to give Vietnamese literature its own flawless gem, *The
Tale of Kiều*, by Nguyễn Du.

Nonetheless, some of the qualities that endeared six-eight verse to
tellers of long tales made it less desirable to poets who wanted to
convey a welter of feelings and emotions. Six-eight verse emphasized
uniformity, as a neutral background against which incidents of any
sort could unfold, whereas the lyrical poet needed a medium better
suited to expressing psychological moods and nuances. He or she
remedied deficiencies in the six-eight couplet by appending a comple-
mentary doublet, the "double-seven" *(song-thất).*

Each line of the doublet has seven syllables: an anapest followed
by two iambs (three | two | two). The disposition of rhyming syllables
and prescribed tones is shown in Figure 3. The double-seven doublet
resembles the six-eight couplet in that the last syllable of the first line
rhymes with the penultimate stressed syllable of the second line. In

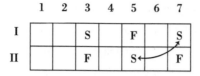

Figure 3

everything else, the double-seven is the opposite of the six-eight. Each line has an odd number of syllables. The rhyme-fellows carry sharp tones. Odd-numbered syllables are accented and embody a tonal scheme which, significantly, contradicts that of six-eight verse and no longer favors flat tones: three flats are balanced by three sharps. Furthermore, sharps and flats rotate exactly and occur in reverse order in the two lines: two sharps (I–3, I–7) flank one flat (I–5) in the first, and two flats (II–3, II–7) flank one sharp (II–5) in the second. In addition to rhythmic identity and tonal contrast, there is syntactical and semantic parallelism (combined with antithesis) between the lines of the doublet.

Unlike the six-eight couplet, which can stand alone, the double-seven doublet rarely does so, though a folk saying may adopt this form. Its skewed rhythm and harsh dissonance go too much against the grain of Vietnamese speech, and in particular, the oblique tones of its rhyme words leave the impression of something unfinished, unresolved; a poem that combines the couplet and the doublet invariably ends with the couplet. But the doublet supplies those very qualities which the couplet lacks. The couplet and the doublet can join in three combinations. First, a long six-eight poem can be randomly interspersed with double-seven doublets for variety's sake. Second, a poem may start out with a couplet and continue with a regular alternation of doublets and couplets. Third (and this is the most common pattern), a poem may consist of a regular alternation of doublets and couplets: it is then called double-seven six-eight *(song-thất lục-bát)* verse or simply double-seven *(song-thất)* verse.

In any of those combinations, whether a couplet precedes or fol-

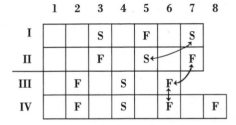

	1	2	3	4	5	6	7	8
I			S		F		S	
II			F		S		F	
III		F		S		F		
IV		F		S		F		F

Figure 4

lows a doublet, there is always rhyming between the last line of one and the first line of the other. If a couplet precedes a doublet, the last syllable of the couplet rhymes with the fifth (or less frequently the third) syllable of the first line of the doublet. If a couplet follows a doublet, the last syllable of the doublet rhymes with the last syllable of the first line of the couplet. All this rhyming system will be illustrated and become apparent in the two diagrams of double-seven–six-eight verse.

Basically, the constituent unit of double-seven–six-eight verse is a four-line stanza in which a double-seven doublet is followed by a six-eight couplet. Figure 4 represents the double-seven–six-eight (or, for short, double-seven) quatrain—the doublet and the couplet are joined by the rhyme-fellows II–7 and III–6. It should be noted that II–7 and III–6 carry flats; as a result, such tones still predominate within the rhyming scheme of the double-seven quatrain, although sharps more than hold their own in the first two lines: they equal flats in number and appropriate the rhyme syllables (I–7, II–5).

The double-seven quatrain, ending with a six-eight couplet, could theoretically lead an autonomous existence. In practice, however, poets vastly prefer to treat it as a constituent unit, a building block. Double-seven verse consists of such quatrains superimposed on one another and interlocked chiefly by a method already encountered within the six-eight couplet and the double-seven doublet: by having the last syllable of one quatrain (the eighth syllable in the second line of a couplet) rhyme with the penultimate stressed syllable in the first

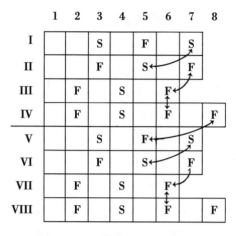

	1	2	3	4	5	6	7	8
I			S		F		S	
II			F		S←		F	
III		F		S		F←		
IV		F		S		F		F
V			S		F←		S	
VI			F		S←		F	
VII		F		S		F←		
VIII		F		S		F		F

Figure 5

line of the next quatrain (the fifth syllable in the first line of a doublet). Those key rhyme syllables carry flat tones (IV–8 and V–5 in
Figure 5). Lines of three different lengths arrayed in an asymmetrical
but regular configuration; flats and sharps fused in a tense yet happy
marriage between euphony and dissonance; internal and final rhymes
woven into a tapestry both complex and uniform—all those features
seem to resolve chaos into order: no doubt they make double-seven–
six-eight verse one of the most expressive vehicles for poetry in the
world. Many poets even applied it to short tales, little homilies, and
so on. But its great strength is the rendering of feelings and emotions
in all their complexity, in long lyrics. Its glory rests chiefly on three
works (ranging from 46 to 102 quatrains): "A song of sorrow inside
the royal harem" (*Cung oán ngâm khúc*, Poem 44), by Nguyễn Gia
Thiều, "Calling all souls" (*Chiêu hồn*, Poem 45), by Nguyễn Du, and
"The song of a soldier's wife" (*Chinh phụ ngâm*, Poem 322), Phan
Huy Ích's rendition of a work in classical Chinese by Đặng Trần Côn.

Regulated, six-eight, and double-seven poems all conformed to
fixed requirements. Poets who could do with a less regular, more
flexible scheme often resorted to the "sing-and-speak" (*hát nói*)
poem. A subtype of "sung verse" (*ca-trù*), it reached its highest level

of subtlety and sophistication in the nineteenth century. Though still subject to certain structural requisites, it was freewheeling in several respects. The length and number of lines could be varied at will, but a recurrent pattern featured an uneven number of lines (usually eleven), with the odd first line of a six-eight couplet dangling at the end. The heterogeneous meter mixed components from both Chinese and Vietnamese prosody. A couplet in Chinese often added a dash of classical bravura. This eclectic form cut a fresh, engaging figure in Vietnamese poetry, accustomed as it had been to rigid frameworks. Despite its disheveled, uninhibited air, sing-and-speak succeeded only when employed by such sensitive practitioners as Nguyễn Công Trứ and Cao Bá Quát. Because sing-and-speak was meant to be sung or chanted by professional singing-girls *(ả đào)* in brothel-like dens, it took on a certain naughty quality and acquired a soupçon of disrepute among straitlaced Confucianists. Morality aside, *hát nói* begot poems less likely than traditional verse forms to display received opinions or artificial feelings. With a singing-girl as his confidante, his kindred soul, the poet could reveal sentiments he would hide from the world at large, where they were apt to shock humdrum careerists. It was no accident that Nguyễn Công Trứ chose the sing-and-speak form when he proclaimed his unbureaucratic outlook on life in "A hero's will" (Poem 32) or when he acknowledged the diversity of female beauty in "Ode to all flowers" (Poem 207).

Both the Chinese and the Vietnamese ruling classes agreed on the efficacy of poetry as an educational tool, and they could invoke no less an authority than Confucius himself in their support. But whereas the Vietnamese were to broaden its scope to reach the unlettered multitude, the Chinese reserved versification for the training of an elite. After Chinese poetry left the swamps and fields, it disowned its humble origins. Confucius and later the Music Bureau (Yüeh-fu) collected peasants' songs; by installing rustic poetry at the head of a literary tradition, however, they cut it off from its humble roots. The imposition of T'ang prosody on even folk poems completed the break. (For example, the injunction against *feng-yao*, the "wasp's waist," seemed aimed at the penchant for internal rhymes, which were found frequently in folk songs collected during the Han period.) Chinese poets were taught to consider their vocation something that enabled them to transcend the vulgar herd. Po Chü-i was among the few to advocate a return to the people, but his new Yüeh-fu movement got nowhere. He often would elicit the reactions of his servants to what he had written, to ascertain that his poems made sense to them. Such a reasonable act passed into legend. His peers deemed him an eccentric: whether hoi polloi understood the poems should have been the least of his concerns! Another poet was chided for discussing Kuan Yü in verse: that stalwart, whose devotion to his friend and lord Liu Pei fulfilled the strictest criteria of Confucian ethics, might appear as a folk hero in plays or prose fiction but not in poetry, since he did not figure in the official hagiography. For many centuries, Chinese poets inhabited the closed, inbred world of the "great" tradition; they disregarded the "little" tradition, which might have transfused new blood into it.

In Vietnam, poetry among the literati took the opposite course: it gradually climbed down from its early place on the heights and made itself at home in the lowlands. The descent, by no means easy and smooth, may have been inevitable: a fundamental contradiction within Vietnamese society had to be mediated, if not entirely re-solved. The great tradition, which enjoyed the ascendancy in books from abroad, came into conflict in remote villages and hamlets, with the little tradition that flourished there. Chinese culture imposed a code of behavior based on respect for authority, whereas the native Vietnamese culture urged peasants to regard any source of power or authority as suspect: "Win and you become a king; lose and you become a bandit." *(Được làm vua, thua làm giặc.)* With its "three bonds" *(tam-cương)* and "five norms" *(ngũ-thường)*, the Confucian straitjacket was not tailored to a body politic accustomed to the mercurial ethos of Southeast Asia. For the sake of ideological appear-ances, the ruling class gave precedence and paid homage to the great tradition, but it could not afford to ignore the little tradition and so reluctantly came to terms with it. As the oft-quoted adage had it: "The king's laws yield to the customs of the village." *(Phép vua thua lệ làng.)* And one of the customs most firmly ensconced in the village was the use—and misuse—of verse.

Moderate literacy, the ability to write and read a fair number of Chinese or even "southern" graphs, was perhaps more widespread in the period before French rule than has been generally assumed. Almost every village was likely to harbor some scholar able at least to drill the rudiments of Chinese into the sons of farmers ambitious to see them pass the civil service examinations and enter officialdom. But even if villagers could read, they might not find reading material. Restrictions—a threadbare economy, underdeveloped printing technology, official control of publications, and so on—severely limited the supply of books and other printed material. In their absence, verse came to play a vital role, as a mnemonic device, among other things: composed in catchy folk meters, memorized, and recited, it served as the most common vehicle for news and opinion. Six-eight verse was the overwhelming favorite: its special qualities made it the easiest to memorize and recite. (In these days when the oral tradition is nearly extinct, not a few people still know by heart all or most of the 1,627 couplets of *The Tale of Kiều*.) Ideas counter to Confucian tenets, when passed around in the form of six-eight verse, were capable of undermining the authority of the ruling elite. The latter realized the seditious purposes that folk rhymes could serve, as this saying implies: "The southern vernacular fathers knaves and rogues." *(Nôm-na là cha mách-qué.)* Some critics or historians have claimed that the men in power felt utter contempt for their native tongue and worshipped classical Chinese. Although the saying does not corroborate this, it dramatically illustrates how much these rulers feared the potential mischief of antiestablishment diatribes in folk verse, whether spread by word of mouth or through the southern script. Some rulers banned oral dissemination of such dangerous material and destroyed books containing it. But folk verse, so deeply rooted in village culture, resisted and survived the interdict; other rulers therefore tried a more positive approach: they commissioned favorable propaganda in six-eight. It was under such sponsorship that in the seventeenth century a scholar wrote the *Thiên Nam ngữ lục* ("The Chronicles of Heaven's South"), a folk history of the country slanted to show the Trịnh regime in the best light. Its 4,068 couplets make it the longest extant poem in six-eight.

The Vietnamese poet's motley background—foreign and indigenous, learned and popular, East Asian and Southeast Asian—was displayed to best advantage in the vernacular. He or she recognized no hard and fast boundaries between genres and types. Chinese prose stories or novels might have their southern avatars in a series of regulated poems or, far more often, as romances in six-eight: narrative verse came to play a star role thanks to that folk meter, which lent itself to the composition of both relatively short poems like "Catfish and Toad" (*Trê Cóc*, Poem 37) and fully developed works like *The Tale of Kiều*. The *lü-shih*, or regulated poem, the pride of aristocratic Chinese literature, crossed the border to frame the picture of a village crier (Poem 18) or an unwed mother (Poem 204) as becomingly as it did King Lê Thánh-tông's self-portrait (Poem 10). At its normal length of eight lines or as a "stop-short" quatrain, it was also called on to perform functions usually expected of folk rhymes: to set forth proverbial truths, propound riddles, or even tell jokes. While Confucian decorum tended to banish the comic muse from Chinese poetry, mirth and satire triumphed in Vietnamese verse, aided and abetted by the peasants' gift of laughter and their refusal to feel awe for pomp and grandeur: a poet could attack specific targets, as Hồ Xuân Hương satirized religious sham in "Poking fun at a bonze" (Poem 205), or could aim broadsides at a range of personal and social foibles, drawing ammunition from a combined arsenal of folklore and book learning, as in "The quarrel of the six beasts" (*Lục súc tranh công*, Poem 302).

The same earthy humor and iconoclastic wit helped to introduce into Vietnamese poetry a subject that poets of the classical tradition considered beneath their notice: sex. Lady Pan's plaintive poem about a fan, appreciated in summer and tossed aside in autumn (see note to Poem 65) has clear sexual overtones. Yet male writers always feigned to see in the disgraced Han queen's fan a political allegory —see Nguyễn Trãi's "For years you wallowed in the scholar's world" (Poem 22) and Nguyễn Khuyến's "To a discarded fan" (Poem 65). Not until almost ten centuries after Lady Pan did anyone confront the sexual imagery of the fan. Hồ Xuân Hương, a Vietnamese woman brought up in a folk tradition that did not mince words, composed a hymn to womanhood, "Lords cherish, kings adore this single thing." Though she wrote "Ode to the fan" (Poem 202) and other poems on the sexual theme according to T'ang prosody, they might have closer kinship with the folk rhymes known as dirty riddles with clean answers *(đố tục giảng thanh)*, in which innocent objects are described in suggestive terms. Hồ Xuân Hương reversed that process, depicting sexual objects as if they were innocuous things: her poems could be called clean riddles with dirty answers *(đố thanh giảng tục)*. As she handled it, however, sex was no mere excuse for prurience but a weapon against male arrogance and hypocrisy.

The hallmarks of Chinese verse are often greatly transformed when adapted to native Vietnamese verse. The austere structure of a regulated poem exacts concentrated images in both Chinese and Vietnamese poetry, but images in Vietnamese poems are generally more vivid and appeal to the senses with less reserve. Poets who chafed at the parsimony of images forced on them by T'ang metrics turned for inspiration to Vietnamese folk poetry, which prized "too much" above "too little" and encouraged virtuoso performance and rhapsodical abandon. In this passage from *The Tale of Kiều* (lines 1047–1054), Nguyễn Du reproduced with uncanny fidelity the feel, tone, and spirit of descriptive folk poetry in six-eight:

She sadly watched the harbor in gray dusk—
whose boat was that with fluttering sails, far off?
She sadly watched the river flow to sea—
where would this flower end, adrift and lost?
She sadly watched the field of wilted grass

the bluish haze where merged the earth and clouds.
She sadly watched the wind whip up the cove
and set all waves a-roaring round her seat.

"The song of a soldier's wife," which Đặng Trần Côn had written in classical Chinese, could pass for a compendium of classical scholarship, yet it was in other respects so akin to Vietnamese folk poetry that a superb vernacular poet like Phan Huy Ích could adapt it into idiomatic double-seven verse that often betrayed no trace of its erudite sources (Poem 322—see, for example, lines 125–132).

Because Confucian decorum shrank from an overt show of emotion, Chinese poetry valued reticence, allusiveness, and self-effacement and disapproved of passion, effusion, and confession. Nguyễn Gia Thiều, writing in the vernacular, felt no check on his sensibilities. His quatrain "Secret love" was a *cri de coeur*: "Can't spit it out, can't gulp it down. / My love chokes me—what should I do? / Would I could scream one long, loud scream! / Oh, it hurts so! Does someone know?" If the regulated poem dammed up feelings and emotions, six-eight verse, by contrast, allowed the blind poet Nguyễn Đình Chiểu's anger and despair at the loss of his country to the French to flow freely (see Poem 53).

Vietnamese poems written before the twentieth century, whether in the vernacular or in Chinese, have come down to us in sufficient number to offer an accurate reflection of almost a thousand years of Vietnamese experience. In some way, that experience paralleled those of Japan and Korea; all belonged to the East Asian classical culture whose hub or fountainhead was China. In other ways, Vietnam's situation was unique. First, Vietnam faced the continual necessity—and exerted unrelenting effort—to avoid annexation by an unneighborly giant. Confronting the Chinese under one dynasty or another (Sung, Yüan, Ming, and Ch'ing), the Vietnamese swung back and forth between diplomacy and war to defend the principle that Marshal Lý Thường Kiệt formulated in the eleventh century (Poem 1): "The Southern emperor rules the Southern land. / Our destiny is writ in Heaven's Book." Second, in Vietnam and nowhere else in Southeast

Asia, native rulers tried to put neo-Confucianism into effect by imposing drab conformity and stern discipline on people who preferred to bask in the tropical sun and colors, who thrived on meridional exuberance. As a result, strain may have bred—beneath apparent submission to authority and law—a restive, defiant individualism, evident in the work of such poets as Hồ Xuân Hương, Nguyễn Du, Nguyễn Công Trứ, and Cao Bá Quát.

That wayward streak perhaps partly accounts for Vietnam's long record of internal division and civil turbulence. After fighting off and on for hundreds of years with the Trịnh lords in the North, the Nguyễn lords in the South defeated the Tây-Sơn rebels, who had briefly ruled the country. The Nguyễn lords unified it and established their own dynasty in 1802. That period saw a florescence of Vietnamese verse that was to make the nineteenth century the most brilliant period in Vietnamese literature.

But the Nguyễn reign did not last much beyond mid-century and soon collapsed under assaults from the West. Once again, it devolved on poets—Nguyễn Đình Chiểu, Nguyễn Khuyến, Trần Tế Xương, and others—to bear witness and register, in personal as well as social terms, the seismic tremors caused by French colonialism. The French ushered in the era of the Latin alphabet, which marked the end of the millennium during which the "Confucian scholars' script" (chữ nho) had held sway. With bitter irony, Trần Tế Xương reported the shift in this quatrain (Poem 71): "What earthly use are these Confucian graphs? / Masters and doctors lie curled up and wilt. / Why not take lessons and become a clerk? / At night champagne, at break of day cow's milk!"

The poet typified all those educated and trained in the old school who either would not or could not adjust to the "tide from the West" (Tây-trào) and accept the supplanting of the Confucian scholars' script by the romanized script (known in Vietnamese as quốc-ngữ, "the national [written] language"). But many thoughtful leaders acknowledged the inevitable and would now promote "modernization" (duy-tân) among the populace, often using simple verse to achieve that goal. From the early years of the twentieth century has survived a snatch of doggerel urging men to cut off their long hair, the traditional image of Confucian manliness: "One hand holds a. comb, / one hand holds a pair of scissors. / Heigh-ho, clip! Heigh-ho, clip! / Go slow and do a skillful job. / Cast off all this stupidity, / cast off all this foolishness . . . . / This time we cut the hair— / tomorrow we'll shave the beard." Of course, the "modernizers" would advocate transformations far more profound than haircuts. The Vietnamese people have been cursed with too much history since 1900; their poets, meanwhile, have confronted the ordeal of change or responded to the European and American challenge by creating some of the most memorable works of Vietnamese poetry in its thousand-year history.

Literary Vietnamese have not failed to notice the transition from old prosodic practices based on folk verse meters and on Chinese patterns to the "new poetry" *(thơ mới)* inaugurated under French auspices: new first of all because it tended to depart from time-hallowed forms, but more significantly because it encouraged a freer and fresher, less stereotypical expression of an individual's inmost feelings. Some critics have judged the first hesitant step along this road important enough to commemorate it with a precise date: March 10, 1932. That was when a women's magazine printed Phan Khôi's poem "An old love." Rather unremarkable per se, his short piece achieved instant notoriety, due to both its unorthodox shape and its nature: as a personal confession of love for a woman, it must have struck some readers as scandalous and others as admirable, coming as it did from the pen of an elderly man (the author had been born in 1887) respected for his Confucian and sinological background. But as prophet and poet of the brave new age, Phan Khôi never achieved much beyond that *coup d'essai.* For its real guru, the new poetry had to wait for someone tutored in French romanticism on the bench of a Hanoi lycée to publish its manifesto—Thê Lữ with "The lyre of myriad tunes" (Poem 224): "The muse lends me her lyre of myriad tunes,/her brush of myriad tints—I want to play/a wizard working wonders, magic tricks/with all the sounds and colors of the earth."

Before the Vietnamese came under French rule and influence, the Confucian scholars trained and recruited to serve as "fathers and mothers of the people" *(dân chi phụ mẫu)* had taken for granted the central role in the world of poetry as a didactic instrument. Now poets, marginalized and denied any function, had to define their status in a society controlled by foreigners. Some succumbed to the temptation of art for art's sake *(nghệ thuật vị nghệ thuật)*, described in Xuân Diệu's "Foreword to a book of poems" (Poem 228): "I am a bird from mountains you don't know./My throat feels itchy—so I start to chirp/when sings the morning wind among the leaves,/when dreams the moon at midnight in the blue./Perched on a branch, the bird longs for its brook—/it will break into song and not know why./Its ditties cannot make the fruits grow ripe;/its carols cannot help the flowers bloom./It's profitless to sing, and yet the bird/will burst its throat and heart to sing its best." Not surprisingly, on the subject of love between the sexes, Xuân Diệu was to create works that surpassed in both number and quality the poems which that most human of all sentiments had inspired Vietnamese poets to compose before.

But few poets aware of the underground struggle against the French colonial administration, however, could adopt pure aesthetics as their creed. Nam Trân would waver between the pursuit of beauty (Poem 229) and the need to "stand up and rid your lyre of doleful airs" (Poem 230). After the Vietnamese Communists succeeded in capturing the leadership of the independence movement, Trường Chinh, their commissar in literature and the arts, would single out Xuân Diệu as the target of his censure and dictate the Communist ideal of what a poet should be (Poem 231): "A poet has a soul that soars to heights,/a will of steel, a noble mission too./He writes and sings of freedom, progress, love/(love for peace, justice, and humanity)./He lifts his voice intoning hymns to praise/heroes who loved our land and risked their lives." The Marxist-Leninist doctrine of "art for human life's sake" *(nghệ thuật vị nhân sinh)* really carried on the Confucian tradition of didacticism. In fact, the birth of the new poetry hardly meant the death of the old poetry. Oblivious to trends, nationalists like Phan Bội Châu, Tản Đà, and Trần Tuấn Khải kept conveying their anti-French message and even introduced such notions as democratic rights (Poem 95) in prosodic forms familiar to those who had never attended French schools. Official persecution of the Vietnamese, both nationalist and Communist, who were fighting for independence was the impetus for a special genre of verse—prison poetry. With poetic justice, just as it was from inside a French jail that Tô Hữu smuggled out his first poems, which helped to spread his fame as the bard of Vietnamese Communism, so too it was inside the various "reeducation camps" where Nguyễn Chí Thiện spent more than twenty years of his life that the anticommunist activist composed in his head those "flowers from hell" which have now established him as a poet to be reckoned with.

The Vietnamese diaspora began on April 30, 1975, as the Communists were poised to seize Saigon and conquer the South. Again, it fell to writers like Mai Thảo (Poem 170) and Viên Linh (Poems 172 and 173) to record that event. In many pieces, poets such as Nhật Tiến (Poem 171) and Hà Huyền Chi (Poem 169) bore witness to the flight of the boat people, with all its tragedies in high seas. Settled in the United States and other countries, refugees from Vietnam would use verse to describe and reflect on how they coped, or failed to cope, with their new environment. Quite a few older refugees found salvation or at least solace in poetry, which helped them make some sense of their twilight years on alien soil (Poems 282, 283, and 284). Among the younger poets, Lê Tất Điều, a distinguished writer of prose fiction living in California, "changed his skin" *(đổi lốt)* and became Cao Tần, who wrote poignantly about himself and his fellow expatriates (Poems 177 through 179). Back in southern Vietnam, life after 1975 was portrayed in pieces by Bàng Bá Lân (Poem 183), Định An (Poem 182), and Yên Ba (Poem 184).

While twentieth-century attempts to deal with intrusions or influences from the world beyond the seas have brought many cultural edifices down in ruins, what has remained standing is the heritage of verse. It will endure as long as the Vietnamese commemorate their past and sing, playing the lyre of myriad tunes.

1. Vietnam and China

1. *The Southern emperor rules the Southern land*
Lý Thường Kiệt

The Southern emperor rules the Southern land.

Our destiny is writ in Heaven's Book.

How dare ye bandits trespass on our soil?

Ye shall meet your undoing at our hands!

Note: According to tradition, Marshal Lý Thường Kiệt read this poem to his troops in 1076, exhorting them to resist aggressors from China.

2. *The Bạch-đằng River*
(King) Trần Minh-tông

Blue peaks are swords and lances thrust at clouds.

The dragon swallows waves and spews white spray.

After spring rain, flowers deck the earth like gems—

in chilly winds, pines hum and stir the sky.

Open your eyes, admire your timeless land:

bow and recall the strife of Việts and Huns.

Down goes the sun—the river's flowing red:

is that the blood, undried, of those war killed?

Note: The Bạch-đằng River flows to sea through the district of Yên-hưng in Quảng-yên Province (northern Vietnam). It was the theater of decisive Vietnamese victories over Chinese invaders: in 838 Ngô Quyền killed the Han general Liu Huang-ts'ao, in 980 Lê Đại Hành killed the Sung general Hou Jen-pao, and in 1288 Trần Quốc Tuấn (also celebrated as Prince Hưng Đạo) captured the Mongol general Omar alive. The Vietnamese used the tactic of secretly planting sharp, heavy stakes and spikes in the bed of the river and luring Chinese war boats into pursuit of fleeing Vietnamese vessels at high tide. When the tide receded, the invading boats were trapped and wrecked by the stakes.

3. *Farewell to two envoys from the Yüan court*

(King) Trần Minh-tông

Post-horses galloped through miasmal wilds.

You brought your star to light this seaside realm.

A hero's will can face the world at large;[1]

a sovereign's heart should treat all men alike.[2]

Yüeh hills and streams give poets peerless lines:[3]

Chou rain and dew pour from the emperor's writ.[4]

Tomorrow, we shall sunder South and North;[5]

today, do not turn down this cup of wine.

Note: King Trần Minh-tông wrote this poem saying goodbye to two envoys from the Yüan court of China in 1332. Some forty years after the death of Kublai Khan, his successor had grudgingly agreed to leave Vietnam alone and sent an embassy, instead of troops, to establish more amicable relations.

1. This line ostensibly compliments the envoys on their diplomatic skills, but it also implies Vietnam's determination to resist foreign attacks.

2. This is a veiled warning to the Yüan emperor not to adopt high-handed methods in dealing with Vietnam.

3. Yüeh: Việt, Vietnamese.

4. Chou rain and dew: favors from the Chinese emperor.

5. This line hints at a fundamental cleavage between Vietnam and China. Traditionally, the Vietnamese regarded their own country as the South and China as the North.

4. A womb's own flesh and bone—strong brotherhood

Nguyễn Trãi

A womb's own flesh and bone—strong brotherhood.

From one root spring all branches, north and south.

Don't covet more rice fields than you can till.

Let not the lowly climb and sit on top.

Chopped off, an arm or leg will not grow back—

torn up, a shirt and skirt can be replaced.

Learn to give way and yield—all will go well.

Know both when to act hard, when to act soft.

Note: This poem is Nguyễn Trãi's call to various factions to settle their differences in a fraternal spirit and not to form alliances with outsiders against their own kind: your compatriots should be cherished like your own arms and legs, but foreigners should be treated as shirts and skirts that could be discarded at will.

5. The Bạch-đằng River

The Hồng Đức Anthology

Blue, limpid water smoothly flows, like oil.

A thousand tributaries feed this stream.[1]

Those fools from Wu have all been washed away;[2]

vassals of Việt have all been cleansed of dirt.

The throne stands strong, high-soaring like Mount T'ai.[3]

Where has it wandered off, Omar's lost soul?[4]

The world's at peace—all sharks lie still as rice.[5]

Let's take our ease and cast our nets or lines.

Note: Bạch-đằng: see the note to Poem 2, "The Bạch-đằng River" by King Trần Minh-tông.

1. Besides its literal sense, this line has a metaphorical reading, in conjunction with the fourth line, which carries a double meaning: once the Chinese occupation forces had been eliminated from Vietnam, neighboring tribes acknowledged the Lê king as their sovereign and harbored no more intent to revolt.

2. Those fools from Wu: the Chinese. The mildly pejorative term *Wu* (Ngô in Vietnamese), as applied to the Chinese, dates from the deeply hated Ming occupation of Vietnam in the early fifteenth century: the founder of the Ming dynasty came from Wu, an area of the Yangtze Valley that included Chekiang and extended north and south.

3. Mount T'ai: the most sacred Chinese mountain in Shantung Province.

4. Omar: the Mongol general captured by the Vietnamese in 1288.

5. The word *kình* (*ch'ing* in Chinese) refers to sharks and whales, which eat smaller fish. Traditional Vietnamese poets have used that term to refer to predatory conquerors. "Quiet and still as rice paddy in the bin" (*im-ìm như thóc trong bồ*) is a folk saying.

6. Homage to the Trưng queens

The Hồng Đức Anthology

To slay the people's foe and wreak revenge,

two sisters took up arms for their just cause.

One battle put Su Ting's scared wits to rout;

a hundred tribes rose up to guard Lingnan.[1]

They climbed the throne—large bounties they bestowed.

They donned their crowns—sweet blessings they conferred.

While streams and hills endure, their shrine shall stand,

a monument to peerless womanhood.

Note: In the first century of the Christian era, Vietnam was known as Chiao-chih (Giao-chỉ in Vietnamese) and was part of the Han empire. The tradition goes that the Chinese governor Su Ting (Tô Định) killed Trưng Trắc's husband, Thi Sách. After that incident, the widow and her younger sister Trưng Nhị led a revolt that succeeded in toppling Chinese rule. The two women reigned briefly, from 40 to 43. Defeated by China's legendary Marshal Ma Yüan (Mã Viện), they either drowned themselves or were captured and executed, according to various accounts.

    1. Lingnan ("south of the mountain range"): an old Chinese name for the area that included Kwangtung, Kwangsi, and northern Vietnam.

7. The old banyan tree

Nguyễn Trãi

It finds a home amid the woods and brooks.

When springtime comes, it dons the green of spring.

Not good enough for pillars and for beams,[1]

it shelters common folk beneath its shade.

Note: Nearly every village in Vietnam has its banyan tree, an object of folk worship because it is believed to be the abode of spirits. But it serves in this poem as a Confucian symbol for an old village schoolteacher who serves as the moral leader of his community.

    1. The pillars and beams are ministers of state or high court officials.

8. He tends the tree who wants to eat the fruit

Nguyễn Trãi

He tends the tree who wants to eat the fruit.

Peruse your books and soon or late you'll know.

A broken rope can't hold the fiery horse—

high office will not seek a stupid man.

To rule the realm, first straighten up your heart.

Let water mirror radiance from the moon.

Ungifted, you are not called on to serve:

don't say the sovereign has forgotten you.

9. *The conduct of kings*

(King) Lê Thánh-tông

Ponder the Ruler's Way with utmost care.

Feed men on earth, fear Heaven throned above.

Protect the realm—walk in the ancients' steps.

Cleanse cravings from the heart—go on no hunt.

Wide choice of talents spreads the scholar's faith.

Weapons in plenty build the soldier's pride.

Light your jade torch and see your subjects' needs.

May we and all our neighbors live at peace.

10. A king's portrait

(King) Lê Thánh-tông

The people's welfare is his first concern.

High Heaven's mandate he dare not neglect.

Drums beat a night-watch shift—he still reads books.

The sun is going down—he yet holds court.

In crisis able men reveal themselves.

To circumstance wise policies adapt.

Don't say the gold-robed person does no work—

reports on all state matters reach his ear.

11. King and subjects

The Hồng Đức Anthology

Of all five norms observed from first to last,[1]

the code of king and subjects stands supreme.[2]

Ranks high and low reflect the cosmic plan.

To land and people give your love and care.

By virtue Shun enlisted Kao and K'uei.[3]

With kindness T'ang recruited Yi and Chung.[4]

Make cheer! Sage-king and loyal subjects meet.

Your common glory shall endure and shine.

    1. According to Confucian ethics, the "five norms" (*wu-ch'ang*, or *ngũ-thường* in Vietnamese) constitute ideal relationships between ruler and subject, between father and son, between husband and wife, between elder brother and younger brother, and between friends. In other contexts, the expression can also apply to five cardinal virtues: humaneness, righteousness, decorum, wisdom, and good faith.

    2. In this poem, the word *subjects* more specifically designates ministers who serve the king or emperor.

    3. Two worthies assisted the mythical sage-king Shun of ancient China: Kao Yao and K'uei, a musician.

    4. King T'ang, legendary founder of the Shang (or Yin) dynasty, could enlist the talents of Yi Yin and Chung Hui.

12. Staffs and hats

The Hồng Đức Anthology

They're paltry objects when denied their roles,

but they work wonders, put to rightful use.

In peril upright staffs defend the lord;

from weather broad-brimmed hats protect all men.

A staff keeps peace and plenty through the land;

a hat gives shade and shelter to the world.

They make all marvels happen when at work:

the hand wields power, the head directs and leads.

Note: The staff and the hat, as humble equivalents of the scepter and the crown, can readily be visualized as emblems of royal or imperial power. More specifically, the staff represents military force, and the hat, civil authority.

13. Ode to the toad

The Hồng Đức Anthology

From birth he's worn a home-spun cotton shirt.[1]

He sits in his deep sanctum all alone.

He briefly lifts his arms—all tigers cringe.[2]

He often clicks his tongue—all ants withdraw.[3]

He's glad to see his children land for warmth.[4]

He may yet wed the beauty in the moon.[5]

His temple rings with his imperious voice—

he saves the people from the blight of drought.

Note: Folk legend would have us believe that before King Lê Thánh-tông was allowed to ascend the throne, he was required to demonstrate his fitness for the supreme office by composing a poem about the toad, something not unlike this piece. According to peasant superstition, the toad can make Heaven send down rain whenever it grinds its teeth. Thus, in this poem, the ugly but awe-inspiring toad is to be seen as a powerful emperor of humble origins who is responsive to the people's needs and wants. Even though Lê Thánh-tông was a son of King Lê Thái-tông, he was born to a disgraced concubine and brought up among the common folk. Once on the throne, he made his Hồng Đức reign the most prosperous and peaceful in all of Vietnamese history. It is noteworthy that popular tradition also associates the toad with another ruler of lowly background: the peasant Nguyễn Huệ, who led the Tây Sơn revolt and rose to be King Quang Trung. Legend has it that at a banquet celebrating his victory over the Chinese, Quang Trung ordered his ministers to compose a poem about the toad. Read Huỳnh Sanh Thông's essay, "Toads and Frogs as Vietnamese Peasants," in the *Vietnam Forum* 1 (Winter-Spring 1983), published by the Council on Southeast Asia Studies at Yale University. See also Poem 37, "Catfish and Toad."

1. The toad is notorious for its rough skin and warts.

2. This line alludes to a folktale in which the toad outwitted the tiger and forced the fierce beast to accept its leadership. Together with another animal, they went to heaven and complained about the drought on earth, demanding rain: they wrought such havoc up there that Heaven had to comply.

3. The toad, feeding on ants and other insects, metaphorically represents a ruler successful in eliminating bandits and rebels.

4. This line, which in the original contains an untranslatable pun, says literally that the toad "is glad to see the children come out for âm." Since the commonest meaning of âm is "warmth," the line refers first of all to the fact that tadpoles eventually become toads and leave the cold water to live on warm land. But âm (Chinese yin, "shade, shelter, protection") also denotes the hereditary ranks and privileges that a king bestows on his sons or on those who serve him well.

5. According to Chinese myth, the goddess Ch'ang O lives in the moon with a three-legged striped toad.

14. Ode to the watermelon

The Hồng Đức Anthology

As sweet as jackfruit, cool like coconut juice,

a melon's unsurpassed for slaking thirst.

Its subtle scent is loved by everyone;

of its rare flavor all the world is fond.

Red heart—it never fails to serve the lord.[1]

Green coat—it brings rich bounty on the clan.[2]

Grown in good earth, it bears abundant fruits—

its offspring will forever wax and thrive.

Note: A thirst quencher with a red heart and a green coat, the watermelon symbolizes the model Confucian scholar-official who helps the people; whose learning and integrity win admiration; whose devoted services to the sovereign earn honors and emoluments and redound to the benefit of his whole clan and of all his descendants.

1. "Red heart" (*lòng son*) signifies unfading, steadfast loyalty and allegiance.

2. Green represents prosperity; *lục* (Chinese *lü*) sounds more or less the same as *lộc* (Chinese *lu*, "gift, favor, official pay"). According to a Vietnamese proverb, "One man becomes a mandarin, and the whole clan gains." (*Một người làm quan, cả họ được nhờ.*)

15. Ode to the betel palm

The Hồng Đức Anthology

The lord has raised and nursed it all along.

Its trunk shoots up, grows taller every year.

Uncounted sons and daughters bless its home.[1]

Warm-greeted guests and callers throng its house.[2]

Many rain-laundered girdles deck its waist.[3]

A lofty parasol protects its head.[4]

Proud pillar, it stands straight beneath the skies.

Let windstorms rage—it never lists and falls.

Note: With its slender, soaring trunk and its crown of leaves, which look like a parasol or a ceremonial umbrella, the areca (or betel) palm (*Areca catechu*; *cây cau* in Vietnamese) cuts a striking figure in the Vietnamese landscape. In this poem, it stands for the upright scholar-official who faithfully serves his king, even in the most difficult conditions.

1. The betel palm bears bunches of drupes known in English as either areca nuts or betel nuts (*quả cau* or *trái cau* in Vietnamese).

2. Wrapped with some slaked lime in a leaf of the betel vine (*Piper betle*; *giầu* or *trầu* in Vietnamese), the astringent seed of the betel nut when chewed produces a mildly narcotic effect. In traditional Vietnamese culture, a betel quid (*miếng giầu* or *trầu*) was offered to guests as a gesture of hospitality and goodwill. Betel leaves and betel nuts also served as ritual gifts for betrothals and weddings.

3. This line calls attention to the many rings around the trunk of the betel palm: they evoke the girdles that mandarins used to wear.

4. Parasols or ceremonial umbrellas, used only by kings and mandarins, were emblems of political authority.

16. Ode to the sewing needle

The Hồng Đức Anthology

Well-tempered, it stays straight and will not warp:

don't try to bend it into some vile hook.

With skill it interweaves five hues of thread;

to beauty it can add four seasons' flowers.

It's fondled by soft hands in halls of state;

to feasts it sends fine guests adorned with silk.

It sews the dragon-robe—its task supreme.[1]

In service it's unmatched by Chung Shan-fu.[2]

Note: This poems pays homage to women who with Confucian rectitude and devotion serve their masters: men.

    1. The dragon-robe: the royal robe or gown.

    2. Chung Shan-fu was the indispensable minister of King Hsüan of Chou.

17. Three ranks of men, three grades of things

Nguyễn Bỉnh Khiêm

There are three ranks of men, three grades of things.[1]

It's wise to know that flowers now bloom, now fade.[2]

A feast is spread, awaiting worthy guests:[3]

the seats of state wait ready for high skills.

Must we let vulgar hands draw Heaven's sword?

Should wicked scoundrels hone the crescent ax?[4]

All-seeing majesty shines there on high:

need any person cry and hawk pure gold?[5]

Note: Nguyễn Bỉnh Khiêm may have written this poem before he was invited to serve at the Mạc court.

    1. This is a folk saying: *Người ba đẳng, của ba loài.*

    2. A person's fortune waxes and wanes.

    3. Only qualified scholars should occupy high positions in society.

    4. The sword and the crescent ax were emblems of authority awarded to mandarins.

    5. A worthy scholar need not advertise his merits: they will in themselves attract the attention of a wise ruler.

18. The village crier

Anonymous

His voice rings loud and carries far.

He dawdles not but swiftly acts.

His drum resounds throughout the world;

his bell chimes forth to every place.

Both young and old heed his appeal;

the entire realm obeys his word.

Once duties are assigned to all,

he sits at ease on his own mat.

Note: In this poem, the humble village crier (*thằng mõ*) stands for the sovereign ruler, an absolute monarch who shares power with no one, as the last line suggests.

19. In praise of the hat

Anonymous

It's round, full round, yet not a hollow thing.[1]

It shelters and protects on all four sides.

Left there, it looks just like a parasol;[2]

once on, it will defy both sun and rain.

It covers every head and favors none;

from dawn to dark it staunchly serves the chief.

Aloft it sits, positioned at the top:

a grateful world takes refuge underneath.

Note: Traditional attribution of this poem to King Lê Thánh-tông is now doubted by most scholars. *Nón* is the familiar conical hat usually made of palm leaves and worn by people from many walks of life, most often by peasants working in the fields. It allegorically represents the ideal Confucian scholar-official as a servant of the sovereign and protector of the people.

1. The hat's round shape suggests associations with heaven, imagined to be round, like the womb, and feminine. From heaven the sovereign obtains his mandate to rule on earth, which is conceived of as "square" and male. Such a theory of divine kingship, once accepted by the Chinese and others, implies the presence on high of the Great Mother, who will delegate her powers to her Son and to his ministers here below, where they serve as her vicars.

2. The parasol or ceremonial umbrella is an emblem of political power and official authority.

20. In praise of the broom

Anonymous

It stoops to labor at the lord's behest—
named marshal, it must sweep all dust away.
A single hand stirs windstorms in the sky;
in all four quarters, thorns are cleared from earth.
Still days—it hangs in mansions like a cloud;
clear nights—it sleeps in towers beneath the moon.
Its heart of straw and fiber frays in time—
a girdle it still keeps, though worn to shreds.[1]

Note: The humble broom is the loyal military commander who rids the realm of bandits and rebels (dust and thorns) and serves his sovereign till his strength fails him.

1. The girdle, worn by both civil and military mandarins as part of their formal attire, here refers to the string that ties straws or twigs together into a broom.

21. Ask to be put in charge of streams and hills

Nguyễn Trãi

Ask to be put in charge of streams and hills!
For you know naught about the world of men.
Pick firewood near the clouds—bamboo galore.
Hear music in the wind—sweet hum of pines.
By day, leave doors unlocked, watch flowers drop.
At nightfall roam the grove and welcome birds.
Hide out like one who fishes or cuts wood.
Stop speaking of the country—is it yours?

Note: Judging by the bitter irony of the first, second, and last lines, it is fair to assume that Nguyễn Trãi wrote this poem after Lê Lợi had virtually dismissed him as minister of the Board of Civil Office: the suspicious king had turned against his most trusted adviser during the long struggle for independence from Ming China.

22. For years you wallowed in the scholar's world

Nguyễn Trãi

For years you wallowed in the scholar's world.

Much time you wasted telling *dolts* from *fish*.[1]

Beware your mouth and stop it like a jar;

conceal a heart as hollow as bamboo.[2]

The swallows have deserted Wang and Hsieh;[3]

a fan in fall means grief for Lady Pan.[4]

Better withdraw and mind your own affairs.

Reform your ways—leave books and such alone!

1. Because of the similarity of the two graphs 魯 (*lu*, "coarse, stupid") and 魚 (*yü*, "a fish"), careless or incompetent students mistake one for the other.

2. The bamboo symbolizes Confucian integrity. A "heart as hollow as bamboo" is free of worldly ambition and greed.

3. Under the Tsin dynasty in China, Wang and Hsieh were two aristocratic clans that produced many chief ministers, those who wore black coats. In a quatrain titled "Black-Coat Lane," the T'ang poet Liu Yü-hsi (772–842) described social and political upheaval as follows: "In the old days the swallows lived in the halls of Wang and Hsieh. / Now they have flown into the huts of boors and louts." Swallows, with their black plumage, are metaphors here for high court officials. By his allusion to Liu's poem, Nguyễn Trãi obviously deplores the rise at court of plebeians whom he deems unworthy or even dangerous.

4. Displaced by a cunning rival as the favorite consort of Emperor Han Ch'eng-ti, Lady Pan (Pan Chieh-yü) wrote a poem comparing herself to a fan, appreciated in summer and discarded in fall. Nguyễn Trãi likens his disgrace at court to Lady Pan's plight. Read Huỳnh Sanh Thông's essay, "The Fan in the Battle of the Sexes," in the *Vietnam Forum* 2 (Summer-Fall 1983), published by the Council on Southeast Asia Studies at Yale University. See also Poem 65, "To a discarded fan," by Nguyễn Khuyến, and Poem 202, "Ode to the fan," by Hồ Xuân Hương.

23. Among the great, no smooth and open world

Nguyễn Trãi

Among the great, no smooth and open world.

At home, a lord enjoys his mums and pines.

Desponding like Shao-ling, you have turned gray;[1]

blithe as Pei-hai, you can yet fill your cup.[2]

Don't touch plum trees and mar their jade-like buds;

mulch your bamboos and raise their dragon-shoots.

The public welfare still concerns your heart:

a restless sea, it surges day and night.

1. Shao-ling: Tu Fu, the T'ang scholar, admired by the Chinese not only as a great poet but also as a great patriot.

2. Pei-hai: K'ung Yung, a Han scholar who loved wine and company.

24. Tired legs won't climb the high road of blue clouds
Nguyễn Trãi

Tired legs won't climb the high road of blue clouds.[1]

Go back to quiet scenes of your old home.

No smell of rue when autumn spreads its chill.[2]

A boat lies on white sands as dips the moon.

The king once lavished love and care on you.

One slip—the race for honors comes to grief.

Your debts to king and father you still owe—

they keep you wide-awake all through the night.

1. The "high road of blue clouds" is the career of prominent officials close to the sovereign.

2. Rue was used to keep fish moths or other insects from books and papers in government offices.

25. Both favor and disgrace you have full known
Nguyễn Trãi

Both favor and disgrace you have full known;

now you walk free of what men think and do.

Those in high posts are sages; idlers, fools.

Grieve not at loss, nor gloat at gain.

Content and safe from danger, stay at home;

refrain from offering your Twelve Points for Peace.[1]

Is there a kindred heart that feels with yours?

Above the western hills, a lonesome moon.

1. Tu Yen once offered a twelve-point plan for peace to Emperor Sui
Wen-ti.

26. Clouds float through dreams

Nguyễn Bỉnh Khiêm

Clouds float through dreams, are nowhere to be seen:

you've borne and shed the load of rank and wealth.

Stars shift, things change within the realm of kings;

streams flow, flowers drop outside the gate of lords.

Life is a game of chess played here and there:

men's hearts are seas with shallow waves and deep.

Speak out or not—what difference does it make?

Keep brooding and your head will soon turn white.

27. Time and again you've seen them win or lose

Nguyễn Bỉnh Khiêm

Time and again you've seen them win or lose;

for leisure you've exchanged their hectic world.

You take your own sweet ease at the White Cloud,[1]

so loath to plod your way through dust and mud.

They visit you till dark—the flowers, your guests.

It sees your heart at night—the moon, your lamp.

Don't glance past things—look closely; you can tell:

vermilion will stay red, and ink pitch-black.[2]

1. The White Cloud symbolizes the hermit who spurns the busy human
world and prefers a life of leisure close to nature. *Bạch Vân* (White Cloud)
was the style name that Nguyễn Bỉnh Khiêm gave to himself and also the name
he gave to the hut where he chose to live upon retirement from office.

2. With some discrimination, you can tell loyal people from opportunists and traitors.

28. Before the world of power you'll fold your arms
Nguyễn Bỉnh Khiêm

Before the world of power you'll fold your arms:
you'll gladly spare yourself so many griefs!
Plum blossoms dim as moonlight shines too bright;
bamboos cast shadows, swaying where wind blows.
You don't forget your past concern and love:
of present rights and wrongs you shall not speak.
You've traveled through the human realm and learned—
how many pitfalls lie along the road!

29. Advice to students
Phùng Khắc Khoan

Through your own efforts learn, and Heaven helps.
Let's save old books and study them with care.
To read proves quite an act in these foul times:
even wise heads have found it hard to teach.
By knowledge freed, the mind flows like a stream;
with few desires, the body fears no threat.
Purge man of greed, and Heaven's truth will shine:
must scholars think of stipends and naught else?

30. Exhortation to learning
Anonymous

The court holds open contests for good men;
my son, apply your mind and study hard.
Three meals a day—your father plows and plants.

Four seasons' clothes—your mother sews and mends.

Learn lines of verse and rhythmic prose by heart.

Keep histories and classics near at hand.

Some day, your name shall top the honor roll:

you'll be your parents' pride, your teacher's joy.

31. Officialdom
Nguyễn Công Trứ

In age I boast not many scores of years,

yet I have witnessed changes through three reigns.[1]

In life's arena, fame dwells next to shame:

born into dust, you cry before you laugh.

With past events I've surfeited my eyes:

on things to come I shall not waste my breath.

Such is the high road of the world—I know:

a man does what he must, to be a man.

1. Nguyễn Công Trứ's official career began in 1819 under King Gia Long and continued under Minh Mạng and Thiệu Trị.

32. A hero's will
Nguyễn Công Trứ

To roam the universe in length and breadth!

To pay a man's full dues and be a man!

To work one's will north and south, east and west!

To fare and fight one's way across the seas!

Who lacks a trade on earth? But how to live

and leave on history a heart's red stamp!

Who yet can tell true glory from crass fame?

How many see a hero still unsung?

The time shall come when, fighting mists and waves,

his hand will steer the vessel through a storm.

He will fill rivers up, cut mountains down,

and all the world shall know of his high deeds.

At leisure, he will stroll the royal road

and clap for joy, his debts at last discharged.

Unfettered idler, he will tend

his bag of verse, his gourd of wine.

33. Drink and drown your cares

Cao Bá Quát

Thirty-six thousand days—how long is that?[1]

To watch a moth's brief pageant makes you laugh.

Why stir and ask for mischief from the world?

Toss off a cup or two and drown it all.

To chase away life's cares, there's only wine:

a hundred schemes can't match one idle hour.

Under the autumn hedge, gaze toward South Hills:[2]

when you glance back, the nine-sphere realm looks small.[3]

Present and past swirl through the universe:

your flesh and bones appear to disappear.

Who needs a thousand rigs, ten thousand pecks?[4]

1. Thirty-six thousand days make up the optimum span of human life.

2. An allusion to lines from a poem about wine by the Tsin recluse T'ao Ch'ien (365–427): "I pluck mums under the east hedge; / I gaze afar toward South Hills." South Hills represents escape from the world of human hustle and bustle.

3. The "nine-sphere realm" is the earthly domain of a king who has received his mandate from the Great Mother in heaven. In symbolism the world over, nine represents the female principle; seven, the male. See note 1 to Poem 19, "In praise of the hat."

4. "A thousand four-horse rigs and ten thousand pecks of grain" (*thiên tử vạn chung*): great success in the world, marked by wealth and rank.

34. Good luck, bad luck

Cao Bá Quát

Good luck, bad luck are both the Maker's works:
wise men and fools can both instruct the world.
Brood on what's past and you will dull your wits:
sharpen your mind and cut all sorrows off.
Lulling your wife to sleep, lie idle and hum verse;
watching your children play, sit stock-still and drink wine.
Teach a few boys who yet can't wipe their snoots;
make sport with girls who have just learned to sing.
Let anyone call you by names he cares to choose:
"A horse? An ox? Yes, I'm a horse, an ox!"[1]
Indeed, who's better than the rest?

1. This line refers to a passage in the *Chuang Tzu*, a Taoist classic.

35. The bird in a cage

Anonymous

In all the world one cage holds this small bird
whose eyes once roamed the space of winds and clouds!
But why, oh, why did I get snared and caught
to brood, to moan, to mourn my gift of flight?
I used to preen my feathers, flap my wings—
and now I sing of freedom, in a jail!
Orioles dip and dart by the north hedge;
phoenixes chirp and coo on the south branch.
Let carpers, east and west, all wag their tongues:
at my first chance, from bondage I'll break loose.
Straight-winged, I'll soar and race toward yonder blue;
I'll smash my chains and visit that sun-crow.[1]
Upon this earth, who knows my heart?

Note: Some scholars speculate that this poem was composed in prison by
Nguyễn Hữu Chỉnh while he was awaiting execution. Popularly known as

Prince Porpoise (Quận He), he led a peasant revolt for five years against the Trịnh lords in the North and was captured in 1751.

    1. According to Chinese myth, there is a golden crow in the sun.

36. Last words

Anonymous

Today, your servant will give back his head.
Let him bequeath some lines to all the world.
You'll see his towering body cut quite short—
yet for a thousand years his name shall live.
His crimson blood will stain the stage of kings—
one stroke of red crossed out all his grand dreams.[1]
Beheader, will you chop his head clean off?
He'll pay you for your service afterward.

Note: This poem is sometimes attributed to Cao Bá Quát (1809–1853) by those who believe that the rebel poet was captured and sentenced to death, not killed in battle.

    1. One stroke of red: the king's signature in red ordering the death penalty for a captured rebel.

37. Catfish and Toad *(Trê Cóc)*

Anonymous

Of old and now, the world has tales to tell,
strange stories making plain the universe.
And animals who hardly know one whit
will argufy the cause and end of things!

Long, long ago, He-Catfish and He-Toad   5
once quarreled and provoked a bitter feud.
He-Toad had his own burrow by a lake
but proudly haunted halls and seats of power.
Now, when his pregnant wife had reached her term,
she hopped into a pond where fish did live,   10

and there she spawned. She feasted her fond eyes
upon her brood, then to her den retired.

He-Catfish chanced to come along and found
the school of tadpoles in a noisy romp.
When he caught sight of them, his heart rejoiced: 15
there was no doubt—they looked like catfish babes!
He took them home—he loved and cherished them,
adopting them as his own flesh and blood.

But next, to view his offspring came He-Toad
when taboo-observation time was past.[1] 20
With bated breath, he looked and looked about:
the pond was hushed and bare—no sign of life!

He bottled up his anger and hopped in
to paddle round and search for his lost tribe.
By midnight he was still there churning mud. 25
Disturbed, He-Catfish surfaced and inquired.
He saw He-Toad in ambush on the bank,
and straightaway he raised a hue and cry:
"Hey, Toad, it's night! Why are you prowling here?
To plan a theft or work some lewd design?"[2] 30

"Look who's the mischief-monger!" croaked He-Toad.
"You're guilty of a horrid crime yourself.
I've braved the dark for my dear brood you stole.
If not, would I have stooped to visit you?"

He-Catfish, smarting from the taunt he heard, 35
pricked up his whiskers and reviled He-Toad:
"Why, Toad! How bold and impudent you are![3]
And what a handsome figure you all cut!
Your kind will never mend—once smeared with lime,
you'll take your acrid temper to the grave![4] 40
To one theft victim, ten will look like thieves.[5]
How do you know who did it? Why blame me?
Stop trying to match wits with me, my friend.
Go back and squat yourself beneath some bed!"

Angry He-Toad bugged out his eyes and growled: 45

"Though smart, you're stuck inside a stagnant pond!

I may be short on brains, but I frequent

those stately mansions where the mighty live.

I move amid the purple and the gold

or roam the kingdom at my own sweet will.   50

Each time I grind my teeth, I shake the skies[6]

and strike the souls of men with darkest fears.

But what are you good for, you smelly fish?

Once boiled, you'll yield a ladleful of broth!"

    And choked with helpless rage, He-Toad went home.   55

Husband and wife took counsel night and day.

She said, "The children are quite small and young.

Away from us, how can they bear the cold?

Forget about the means to win a feud—

let's pay whatever price and buy them back."   60

"Your head spins such bright notions!" he replied.

"Why should we put ourselves to such expense?

What does a shallow woman really know[7]

to meddle and suggest this scheme or that?

He-Catfish covets our own flesh and blood: 65

I'll sue him, then—let's do or die in court!

While you were lying in, some fish saw you:

Tench, Bass, and Carp all witnessed the event.

I'll carry to the yamen my complaint,

and when the case is tried, the truth will out!"   70

    The prefect-judge perused the plaintiff's bill,

then summoned all his staff of clerks and scribes:

"I've read He-Toad's complaint from first to last:

to steal somebody's children is no joke!

I've yet to ascertain the hidden facts,   75

but it looks like a pickle as of now!

Go draft a warrant and arrest the knave,

and haul all witnesses before the court."

With due instructions scribes and clerks went out
and made He-Toad cough up the usual fees.   80
The drafted summons was approved and signed—
a bailiff was dispatched to serve it soon.

Now brandishing his warrant of arrest,
the bailiff swaggered off, bound for Clear Pond.
Once there, he ordered village chiefs to catch   85
and fetch the suspect—Catfish was his name.
Greeting the man who came to question them,
all gathered, spread the table, poured much wine.
The bailiff said: "Like thunder is the law,
so where it's told to strike, right there it strikes![8]   90
He-Catfish perpetrated his foul deed,
and all of you have lent him help and aid!
If I obey my orders to the full,
your flesh and bones will fall to bits and shreds!
But mercy is the other arm of law—   95
take care to gratify my softer side.
As long as judge and clerks are still far off,
don't anger me, or strokes shall rain on you!"

He-Catfish reared his head and pleaded hard:
"Why would this churl have dared to flout the law? 100
Some liar's pinned a bogus charge on me!
Please help me, uncle. As the proverb says,
'One day in jail, a thousand years at large!'[9]
I beg to pay, no matter what the sum.
I have two friends and neighbors, Carp and Tench—   105
both can be counted on to back me up.
For our good magistrate, I'll purchase gifts:
what need be done, I promise, shall be done!"

Those words were music to the bailiff's ear.
He led them all to the abode of law.   110
Before the judge he dropped a bow, then said:
"At your behest, I've bid them all appear!"

The judge held court and tried the case forthwith:
"You, Catfish, dared commit the vilest crime!
The plaintiff, Toad, who's kneeling there, asserts   115
you kidnapped all his children: yes or no?"

    He-Catfish first kowtowed before the judge,
then, perking up, he told his tale at length:
"He-Toad must bear full blame for this affair.
At night he came and squatted by my pond.   120
So, raising the alarm, I gave a shout
and plainly saw him scamper through my hedge.
Afraid I would expose his foul offense,
he covered it all up with his false charge.
For if indeed they were his flesh and blood,   125
would he have dumped them there, in my cold pond?
We little folk live lives as cheap as dirt!
Please spare me gross injustice—weigh the facts!"

    "No more of your pert talk!" the prefect snapped,
then summoned fish to take the witness stand.   130
Tench, Bass, and Carp—all three came forth at once
and prostrated themselves before the judge:
"We all are simple folk—we mean no harm.
A poor, clean living's all we have eked out.
Others may want to venture down the stream—   135
we are content to dodge those nets and traps.
Who knows what Toad or Catfish brewed and hatched,
yet with complicity we now stand charged!
May Heaven's lamp cast light on right and wrong!
The wall's caught fire—should fish die in the moat?"[10]   140

    Before the court He-Toad now put his case:
"They all are kith and kin, as thick as thieves!
Their water and our land are worlds apart—
how are dry toads to fare among wet fish?
Before Your Highness, may I bow and pray?   145
From hapless exile save our children, please!"

"Well, let He-Toad go home," the prefect said.
"For further hearings bolt He-Catfish in!"
The zealous bailiffs did as they were told
and promptly clapped He-Catfish into jail.   150
Alas, they kept him under lock and key:
ten men closed in—on one—and bled him white.
From mandarin to bailiffs orders flowed:
they cangued his neck by day and chained his legs
by night; they cut his hide to rags and shreds,   155

    His wife watched his ordeal and sorely grieved.
To save him she would spare no costs or pains.
She wandered over hill and dale to find
somebody with the answer to her prayer.   160
She heard a bravo's name—through go-betweens,
she reached Stargazer's lair for his advice.[11]
In detail she told him what troubled her:
"I'm married to He-Catfish—his chief wife.
Because He-Toad has lodged a false complaint,   165
my husband's landed in a prison cell.
A foolish woman only bungles things—
please figure out some way to set him free."

    "I'm willing to oblige," Stargazer said.
"But I need not go plead with anyone.   170
For I've got Pike, a village mayor back there—
he's my own man: my wish is his command.
A holy terror for all his born days!
You're in a fix—I'll have him succor you."

    The bravo's word transported her with joy—   175
she hurried to find Pike and woo his aid.
She came before him bearing lavish gifts:
prawns, squids, and dainty bits, the tongue's delights.
"I know what makes them tick, those yamen chaps,"
said Pike, "those foxes clad in tigers' coats![12]   180
You wish to win your lawsuit with all speed?

I'll have you talk to Shiner, their head clerk.
If things are to come off without a hitch,
you also must grease well all yamen palms!"
    Once Pike had seen the judge behind closed doors,   185
the female catfish went to his court hall.
Down on her knees, she pled: "With our respects,
accept these gifts and pity my poor clod!
He-Catfish twice was nabbed and thrown in jail
because the facts were twisted out of shape.   190
He thinks straight thoughts, he dared no crooked schemes.
Please open wide the merciful T'ang net!"[13]
    "Since you're beseeching me," the judge declared,
"I shall not poke beneath the hair for scars![14]
As far as I can see from all the facts,   195
He-Toad may lack firm grounds for his complaint.
Let the accuser face him he's accused,
for I must hear both sides to know the truth."
    He-Toad, who was then crouching by a wall,
dashed out at that pronouncement and burst forth: 200
"Dame Catfish, no fast talk! I would not fear
winged tigers, let alone the finny tribe!
Your husband stole our children in broad day,
and he's charged me with trespassing at night!
Does he expect to live forevermore   205
and see his serpents swallow up a whale?[15]
They can teach monkeys how to climb a tree,[16]
they goad one side, they egg the other on.[17]
Those altar rats or rampart foxes strut
and flaunt their borrowed power to hurt the weak.[18]   210
Whose hand will kill the deer and win the day?[19]
The fight is on: birds' beaks against rats' fangs!"[20]
    "None of your lip, Sir Toad!" the prefect roared.
"You need not mouth it so to state your case.
Here, bailiff! Tell the clerks to go and make   215

a thorough inquest—gather all the facts.
If they establish guilt and foul intent,
He-Catfish shall be punished by the book."

The clerks obeyed their order, hit the road—
all in a body hastened toward Clear Pond.   220
Arriving there, they summoned village chiefs
to show them round and help them learn the truth.
They found those tadpoles in a frisk and romp
quite near the surface—little swarthy ones.
"No shadow of a doubt!" the clerks agreed.   225
"From head to tail they look like catfish, yes!"
After recording what they had observed,
they hurried back, submitted their report:
"Before your lofty virtue we bow low!
We made a careful inquest in your name.   230
He-Catfish was accused on no good ground,
a fact the village chiefs themselves confirm."

The prefect had He-Toad hauled in and said:
"You, brazen rascal, filed a perjured charge!
Now my inquirers have come back and cleared   235
He-Catfish of the crime you laid to him."

He-Toad kowtowed and told the magistrate:
"To shield He-Catfish, clerks and scribes have lied!
He's crammed so many goodies down their throats—
no wonder what they say does stink of fish!"   240

The charge incensed those yamen hands—they begged
to clap He-Toad in jail and serve him right.
"The case must be retried," the prefect said.
"Pending a verdict, lock in this He-Toad!"

Now huddled up, He-Toad just sighed and groaned,   245
seething with righteous wrath against the world:
"Heaven above, would that you knew my plight!
I'll gnash my teeth, then you'll hear me, perhaps.

If they malign me and will cause my death,
may your celestial thunder strike them down!"   250
    To her poor Toad, who tossed and turned all night,
the wife proposed a course she had thought out:
"Let me consult a doctor of the laws
and quickly learn how to proceed in court.
If we just try to measure wits with them,   255
it will not work and we may come to grief.
Please let me go and do what need be done.
I shall not quit until revenge is ours!"
    She-Toad set forth to roam and rove afield,
crossing from Bufoland to Ranaburg.   260
She'd wade this stream and climb that hill; she'd search
deep wells and thickets, anguish in her heart.
One day, as she trudged on through wind and rain,
she spotted someone in a field: He-Frog.
    He had been squatting there, at pleasant ease,   265
when he laid eyes on her, so up he hopped.
He asked her, "Where did you come from, my dear?
But you don't seem to wear your freshest looks!
Is something ailing you? What is amiss?
All frogs and toads are kin—you can speak out!"   270
    "There's nothing wrong with me," She-Toad replied.
"But I must save my husband and my home!
He-Catfish is an arrant thief and rogue!
He stole our brood, then slandered my poor Toad.
He oiled the palms of mandarin and clerks—   275
it followed that my Toad was sent to jail.
I've traveled hills and streams to come this far.
I pray you—rescue us from our dire pass!"
    "Bare field, plain water—here's my home," he said.
"Loud though I croak, my voice is empty air.   280
Among famed doctors of the laws there's one
who doctors them expertly: our Tree Frog!

He knows the yamen well—the ins and outs.
He breaks its statutes, juggles with its rules.
You want to see your troubles all resolved?   285
Go track him down and ask for his advice!"

    After she heard the Frog explain all things,
She-Toad then rushed back home to start again.
Across the realm, through silent groves and woods,
she tramped the lonesome trail on tireless feet.   290
Then, as a pretty scene came into view,
she stopped her quest and tarried in the shade.
A gentle rain was falling on the grass—
she glimpsed a little sprawler: that Tree Frog!

    "I welcome you, my sister," greeted he.   295
"What prompted you to come and seek me out?
Your distant home's a thousand miles from here—
how did you know your way to make the trip?"
"I thank you for your kindly words," she said.
"What would I not go through for my loved ones!   300
It so enrages me to talk of him—
He-Catfish caused us all our griefs and woes.
We've suffered countless wrongs without redress
and held our anger till we're fit to burst.
They throw their weight around and crush the weak;   305
they tamper with the laws and wreak such harm!
From mandarin to clerks, they all are crooks.
For long they have tormented my poor Toad—
mere thought of it just rankles in my soul!
I knew of no one who could counsel me.   310
I took He-Frog's advice—I did not dread
the far, rough trek and found my way to you.
Whatever action wisdom might suggest
to save my Toad and toadlings, tell me, please!"

    The Tree Frog laughed: "A woman's rigmarole!   315
But you don't know a thing about the world.

We share a common fate—we all shall die.
Why fight and war with our own kind? What for?
He-Catfish is an utter, hopeless fool—
he's gone clean daft with greed, can't think too deep.   320
Well, cease your squabbles and disputes at law.
Your brood is in their pond—what can you do?
Just let that dumb He-Catfish nurture them.
It's best to wait till they've all shed their tails—
then by themselves they'll find their way back home!   325
The case can then be settled with no fuss:
petition for full custody—a cinch!
If you still wish to pick a bone with him,
against He-Catfish file a countersuit!"
With eagerness She-Toad concurred and said: 330
"I'll make him feel the sting of all my spite
and teach him not to bluster any more!"

    She-Toad now bowed her thanks and took her leave.
Back to the yamen she was quick to trot.
She told He-Toad, then at the pond she peeked,   335
and what Tree Frog had said was plain to see.

    All chat and laughter, frenzied with sheer joy,
she came before the judge with many gifts.
A written plea in hand, she entered first—
a covey of her toadlings hopped behind.   340

    In open court the prefect read her piece
and almost threw a fit. He thundered out:
"But how could this have happened, such a freak?
My orders went unheeded by those clerks!
All ye who made the inquest, come in here!   345
I should let my assistant handle this!"

    The yamen scribes craved mercy on their knees:
"At your command we went and we inquired.
With our own eyes we saw their catfish shape,
and only then did we draft our report.   350

But nature's played an impish prank on us
and, out of nowhere, darkly conjured change!
Deep in our hearts we hold to Right and Law:
how could we have presumed to tell a lie?"
    "The case remains unsettled," sighed the judge.   355
"Arraign He-Catfish, put the scamp on trial!
A twin-lash whip! A cudgel! Flog the knave,
make him own up, and straighten it all out!
He dared to toy with lives—in Heaven's sight
he robbed a couple of their flesh and blood!   360
I shall enforce the laws and banish him
to the full distance of three thousand miles.
Seize all his riches, all his worldly goods,
and go bestow them all as alms or doles.
But as for you, Dame Toad, stop squawking, pray!   365
You've got your toadlings back—complain no more.
He-Catfish did brew mischief in his breast:
I've doomed the rogue to exile—that's the end!"
    The haughty lord passed sentence with those words,
and now He-Toad hopped in, knelt down, and said: 370
"As I look up to you, Your Eminence,
your kindness stands sea-deep and mountain-high—
you shone your pity on our little toads!
We've brought some trifles, tokens of our thanks."
    "Hey, there, shut off that gush!" the prefect cried.   375
"So I've deserved a bit of gratitude!
But need you come here bearing gifts and such?
Though I esteem the thought, please take them back!"
    After more bows, He-Toad and wife withdrew,
and arm in arm, bliss-drunk, they hopped away.   380
They had no sooner left the yamen gate
than clerks and scribes snatched presents from their hands.
They set upon both toads—they groped and pawed,
claiming his flask of wine, her box of tea . . .

Thus, having won his suit, He-Toad came home.   385

Over mum wine or lotus tea, he told

his triumph to his kin, while our Tree Frog

was softly chanting verse, asprawl close by.

Then both joined in the raucous merriment

to drink their fill and sing themselves quite hoarse.   390

By lucky chance their paths had somehow crossed.

Like will to like—and thus two heroes met!

You watch the world go round and want to laugh.

It's just a comedy played out for fun.

Let these few words, embroidered into verse,   395

set forth some truths that one and all may see.

Note: The *Trê Cóc* ("Catfish and Toad") was possibly written during the
first half of the nineteenth century, under the Nguyễn dynasty. Its unknown
author borrowed the story from the oral tradition, which tells it more or less
as follows: "Once a toad gave birth to its young in a flooded rice field. A catfish found the tadpoles and adopted them as its own children. When the toad
claimed them back, the catfish would not give them up. A quarrel ensued and
had to be settled by the local mandarin. He put the case off, telling both parties to wait for the babies to grow bigger. In due course the tadpoles shed their
tails and hopped ashore to live as toads. To punish the catfish, the magistrate
ordered it bashed on the head until its head became quite flat." That skeletal
plot is both modified and fleshed out in the verse fable with many more incidents, involving an enlarged cast of characters. There are the two parties to
the dispute: on one side, He-Catfish, his wife, and other fish; on the other side,
He-Toad, his wife, and two frogs. Then, there are various representatives of
officialdom: the prefect-judge and his clerks and bailiffs. Beyond its implied
criticism of peasants' propensity for getting entangled in quarrels and lawsuits, the verse fable contains a broad attack on orthodoxy and the Confucian
establishment. Unlike the mandarin in the folktale, the prefect-judge is no
Solomon, but a bumbling fool at the head of an incompetent and corrupt
bureaucracy. In his determination to go strictly by the books, he gets caught
unprepared for the metamorphosis of tadpoles into toads. Also, within the
Vietnamese context, the prefect-judge's discomfiture may reflect the failure
of bookish and overzealous imitators of the Chinese model to take Southeast
Asian realities into account. The author thus appears to be satirizing Confucian rationalism and its limitations. Finally, the conflict between a group
of fish (which, according to East Asian myth, can change into rain-making

dragons—that is, kings and mandarins) and a group of batrachians (quasi or would-be fish) seems to echo a theme that pervades much of Vietnamese folklore: the war between the "ins" and the "outs," between the establishment and its enemies. Also read Huỳnh Sanh Thông's essay titled "Toads and Frogs as Vietnamese Peasants" in the *Vietnam Forum* 1 (Winter-Spring 1983), published by the Council on Southeast Asia Studies at Yale University.

1. After her baby is born, a Vietnamese woman traditionally observes a taboo period of seven days for a boy and nine days for a girl. See note 3 to Poem 33, "Drink and drown your cares," by Cao Bá Quát.

2. According to old Vietnamese jurisprudence, "to break into someone's house at night is to incur the charge of sexual transgression, if not of burglary."

3. In Vietnamese folklore, the toad stands for bold courage or even foolhardinesss. The epithet "toad-livered" *(gan cóc)* in Vietnamese is the very opposite of *lily-livered* or *chicken-livered* in English.

4. As a Vietnamese folk story tells it, Heaven once held a contest to recruit fish that could leap over three cascades one after another and to promote such extraordinary creatures to the status of rain-making dragons. The toad thought it could compete against the fish because it had lived in water as a tadpole. But its ugly, threatening looks disqualified the candidate: smeared on the head with white quicklime, it was driven away from the contest site, never to return. In East Asia, it should be pointed out the color white may symbolize disloyalty and treason: in the traditional theater, sycophants and traitors wear white makeup.

5. A Vietnamese proverb goes: "One loses [something], and ten will be suspected [of having stolen it]." *(Một mất mười ngờ.)*

6. In a Vietnamese folktale known either as "The toad sues the lord of heaven" *(Con cóc kiện ông trời)* or as "The toad is the lord of heaven's uncle" *(Con cóc là cậu ông trời)*, that intrepid little beast leads two other animals to the celestial spheres and complains about drought on earth. The trio makes much trouble up there, and the lord of heaven has to promise that from then on, whenever the toad grinds its teeth, rain will be sent to earth. The notion of a "lord of heaven" *(ông trời)* eventually emerged under Confucian patriarchy to contradict the far older belief that the sky, imagined to be round like the womb, was under the sway of the Great Mother, known among Taoists as the "Mysterious Woman of the Nine Heavens" *(Cửu Thiên Huyền Nữ)* and by other names. See also note 1 to Poem 19, "In praise of the hat," and note 3 to Poem 33, "Drink and drown your cares," by Cao Bá Quát.

7. The alleged inferiority of a woman's mind as compared with a man's is ironically stated in this proverbial couplet: "A man is as shallow as an open well; / a woman is as deep as a tray for betel." *(Đàn ông nông-nổi giếng khơi, / đàn bà sâu-sắc như cơi đựng trầu.)*

8. A Vietnamese proverb goes: "The Thunder God strikes wherever he's told to strike." *(Thiên-lôi chỉ đâu đánh đấy.)*

9. According to a Chinese adage, "One day in prison [seems as long as] a thousand autumns outside." *(Nhất nhật tại tù thiên thu tại ngoại.)*

10. A Chinese proverb goes: "When a city gate catches fire, disaster spreads to the fish in the moat [or pond]." *(Thành môn thất hỏa họa cập trì ngư.)* That saying deplores the fate of innocent victims in some conflicts: water is drawn from the moat (or pond) to fight the fire, and the fish perish.

11. The *quả* fish or snakehead mullet is also called "gazer on the Dipper" *(triều-đẩu)*: at night it allegedly rears its head out of the water. Various fish are called stargazers in English because they have their eyes on the top of their head and look directly upward.

12. "A fox borrows a tiger's might" to inspire fear. *(Cáo mượn oai hùm.)* The proverb comes from this fable. A tiger let a fox ride on its back, and when other beasts fled at the sight of the man-eating cat, the wily fox convinced the credulous tiger that it was he, the fox, not the tiger, who had scared them off.

13. According to Chinese tradition, King T'ang was the virtuous founder of the Shang (or Yin) dynasty. Under his rule of justice tempered with mercy, the law's net was said to be spread on one side but left open on the three other sides.

14. To describe petty faultfinding, the Vietnamese say, "to poke beneath the hair for scars" *(bới lông tìm vết)* or "to blow on the hair and look for scars" *(thổi lông tìm vết)*. Another Vietnamese expression conveys the same idea: "to part the leaves and look for worms" *(vạch lá tìm sâu)*.

15. "The little snake threatens to swallow the whale." *(Rắn con lăm nuốt cá voi.)* A conceited person takes on a much stronger opponent and is doomed to defeat.

16. "Teaching monkeys to climb trees" *(dạy khỉ leo cây)* is aiding and abetting wrongdoers.

17. "To prod the plaintiff and goad the defendant" *(xui nguyên giục bị)* is to provoke litigation or sow discord among people and exploit their quarrels.

18. This is an indictment of predatory bureaucrats and politicians entrenched in power. Despite the ravages they wreak, "altar rats and rampart foxes" *(xã thử thành hồ)* are left alone: you may upset the altar and wreck the rampart.

19. The Chinese say, "At whose hand will the deer perish?" when the issue of a struggle is still in doubt. See also note 2 to Poem 54, "The old hound," by Huỳnh Mẫn Đạt.

20. Song 17 of *The Book of Odes* includes these lines: "Who says the sparrow has no beak? / How else could it have pierced my roof? . . . / Who says the rat has no teeth? / How else could it have bored my wall?" The expression "birds' beaks and rats' fangs" *(mỏ chim nanh chuột)*, derived from that poem, is used to portray squabbles and quarrels among peasants.

2. The Buddhist Ethos

38. The hibiscus
Nguyễn Trãi

The water gleams and mirrors this red flower.
It bears no stain, for Buddha is its heart.
At break of day it blooms, by dusk it falls.
O wondrous law! A thing becomes no-thing.

Note: A Buddhist symbol of impermanence, the hibiscus is popularly known as
"Buddha's flower" *(bông bụt)* in Vietnam.

39. The monastery on Mount Hill-and-Stream
The Hồng Đức Anthology

Mountain of gods and river of fair nymphs—
together they make up the Hill-and-Stream.
Rocks heap upon more rocks, some high, some low.
Waves surge at other waves, roll after roll.
Of wealth and want the Buddha's realm steers clear.
For fame and gain, men's sails scud up and down.
Bong, bong—from far above, a bell is heard.
Beneath the cloister, wander step by step.

Note: The mountain called Hill-and-Stream *(Non Nước)*, a scenic spot in Ninh-
bình Province, is also known as the Mountain of the Five Elements *(Ngũ Hành)*.

40. On reading the Buddha's scriptures
Nguyễn Bỉnh Khiêm

The Buddha taught the Perfect Thusness Way.[1]
O blessings countless as the Ganges' sands!
The sun and moon whirl past and then come back—

all plants and blossoms thrive, to wither soon.

The richest man will never have enough—

a pauper thinks his lot the worst on earth.

Within the heart there lies a fallow field:

uproot its weeds and grow true wisdom's flowers.

1. According to the metaphysics of Mahayana Buddhism, "Thusness" or "Suchness" (Tathagatha) is a pure and integral entity existing independently of human thought.

41. Where gather mists and clouds

Đào Duy Từ

Where gather mists and clouds, a happy world.

Thick swirls of incense smoke wreathe Heaven's Gate.

The bell of Prajna chimes through vacant days.[1]

Amida's sutras drone on quiet nights.

Brooks sigh and sing like harps when rain has stopped.

Birds chirp sweet melodies as sunshine dims.

The Way lies not far off—why toil for it?

Bodhi bears fruit right here, inside the heart.[2]

1. Prajna: supreme knowledge or wisdom.
2. Bodhi: spiritual enlightenment, religious illumination.

42. The morning bell at Tiêu Monastery

Mạc Thiên Tích

The stars, about to fade, are straggling east—

a distant bell now tolls the night's last watch.

In peace the primal motive prompts the world—

across the rivers speaks a lonely voice.

Unsettled herons cry in wind-girt groves;

awakened ravens caw on moonlit trees.

In every household, folks have stirred from bed—

the cock, proclaiming daybreak, crows and crows.

43. Stepping out of the world

Anonymous

Gaze at the world—a tangled game of chess.

Gaze hard, peer closer, see more dirt and filth.

The morning bell drives off terrestrial thoughts;

the midday clapper dashes mundane cares.

Bright purple wearies eyes—coarse cloth gives warmth.

Rich fare will pall—plain salt and greens delight.

Walk up to Buddha's altar and look back:

the ocean of desire is roiled with mud.

44. A song of sorrow inside the royal harem *(Cung oán ngâm khúc)*

Nguyễn Gia Thiều

All through the moonlight sighs an autumn wind:

her dancing gown feels frigid, metal-cold.

Does Heaven hate a harem inmate so

that He'll condemn her rosy cheeks to grief?

Why has all her good fortune now turned bad?   5

How can she bear to probe and search the past?

What's happened to destroy it all midway?

She broods upon herself and mourns her plight.

As she recalls, created for the world,

she was a rosebud flaunting its fresh hues.   10

The flower has scarcely opened when it fades

like Lady Pan's white silk in autumn chill.[1]

Her cheeks, peach blossoms, wrought their spell on men;

her eyes, two restless waves, rocked city walls.

A glimpse of her fair form behind the blinds   15

would rouse the very grass and trees to lust.

Love-smitten fish would sink to ocean depths;

enamored birds would drop from heaven's heights.

Her scent divine would charm the moon and flowers,

entrance Hsi Shih, bewitch Ch'ang O herself.[2]   20

She could embroider rhymes outshining Li's[3]

or paint in brushstrokes far surpassing Wang's.[4]

What mortal rivaled her at chess or wine?

Both Indra and Liu Ling were her soul mates.[5]

She plucked the lute by moonlight like Ssu-ma;[6]   25

she played the flute in autumn like Hsiao-shih.[7]

And when she sang and waved her hands to dance,

moon fairies doffed their rainbow garb and quit.

Her gifts and looks were praised throughout the realm,

and suitors swarmed like bees outside her gate.   30

Even before they had set eyes on her,

Ch'i Hsüan's mad fever seized them like a storm.[8]

The vernal flower still kept its pistil sealed;

the autumn moon had yet to shed its glow.

Curtains like mists still screened her rosy room;   35

pure fragrance yet suffused her secret bower.

Against the peacock, archers drew their bows;[9]

upon the star young nobles trained their gaze.[10]

Her garden was still fenced from butterflies—

they saw the flower, yet found no entranceway.   40

Her heart, though not of stone, could not be moved—

mere humans should presume to climb T'ien-t'ai![11]

Her perfume was not meant for earthly dust,

and no amount of gold could buy her smile.

Why is the human realm arranged that way?   45

How can fate's red silk thread so tie your feet?[12]

Lying supine, an arm across the brow,

she ponders on what moves the world of dust.

Oh, for some drops from Kuan Yin's willow branch

to cool and quench the fire inside her heart![13]   50

Existence is a dream. The universe,

fate's engine, works in cryptic, baffling ways.

A bite of food, a sip of drink—each act,
however trivial, is foreordained.
So many, stricken by a thousand blows,   55
still walk the earth as bodies with dead souls.
No wonder that delivered from the womb,
you issue forth to utter piercing wails!
You weep in sorrow for your human plight.
Who's staged this play of fortune's ebb and flow?   60
From childhood with white teeth till hoary age,[14]
from birth to death, how often you must grieve!
Thoughts of success and failure gray the head;
to seesaw up and down inures the heart.
Sick flesh falls prey to bitter pains—the burn   65
of hunger's fire, the knife-sharp pang of cold.
Feet race for fame or gain and gather mud—
by sunscald, wind, and dust the face is tanned.
You brood on bubbles in the sea of woe,
and floating moss by shores of self-deceit   70
Life yields an acrid taste that numbs the tongue;
the rugged road you tread will scar your heels.
As waves beyond the haven surge and fall,
the skiff of foam and shadow bobs about.

A wanton boy is he who made the world!   75
For sport he'll make us reach dry land and drown.
In his huge furnace forging myriad things,
he will transmute white clouds to bluish dogs.[15]
Where dancers danced, now spiders weave, doors rot;
where singers sang, now crickets whine all night.   80
All of a sudden, thorns bestrew smooth earth—
who's dyed the human scene in shades of dusk?
Riches entice the horse-and-carriage set;
the bait of honors lures grandees and lords.
How void of substance is a Nan-k'o dream![16]   85
Open your eyes and see bare, empty hands.

A garden where the peach and plum once thrived
now runs to waste, all carpeted by moss.
Above a yard where urns and bells once stood,
the moon now comes to rest in drowsy haze.   90
Those who must sail the sea of gain and fame
are buffeted like toys by wind and waves.
Heaven has grasped all powers for weal or woe,
allowing none a snippet of free choice.
The world is spun to turn as Heaven bids—   95
men grope their way like toddlers in the night.
All trees and rocks are marked and marred by time;
all birds and fish must dread fierce wind or rain.
All flesh must share the common, dismal lot
of transitory hills, of short-lived flies.   100
A lonesome bridge still squats on its old banks;
an inn, forlorn, looms stark in autumn gusts.
Raw wind and weather tell on hills and brooks;
no leaf, no flower escapes decay and fall.
A shadow play's unfolding there on stage: 105
it hurts to watch the fleeting show of life.
Of your full hundred years what will be left?
A mound of earth all smothered by rank weeds!

The road of life is paved with griefs and woes:
why gladly hug your ties to dust or dirt?   110
The mortal drama plays for all to see:
why not through Dhyana seek release and cure?[17]
Cross Buddha's gate and wander free at last.
Sever for good the seven passions' bonds.[18]
Why shoulder loads and carry burdens still?   115
What joys in human love can you expect?
For friendship, take pure moonlight and cool breeze;
for love, adopt the Udumbara flower,[19]
and raise the torch of Prajna. Leave the world:[20]
stay free of things and be a god on earth!   120

She wished to dodge the Potter's grasping hand
and somehow wriggle through the marriage noose.
But Heaven would not let her have her way—
round the peach blossom twined the red silk thread.
A debt contracted in some earlier life?   125
A fruit whose seed had long ago been sown?
Or had she once in Heaven's palace done
some deed she now must expiate on earth?
All living creatures, even birds and beasts,
insensate beings, tangle in love's toils.   130
Female and male as *yin* and *yang* unite—
both earth and heaven will in wedlock merge.
The Maker wants the sexes to conjoin:
how can a human shy from human love?
Stop struggling! Look away, don't murmur—wait   135
and see where destiny will set you down.

How careless was that Old Man of the Moon![21]
He let his red silk thread wind round her feet.
What was that night, the night she met her lord?
Over a rose in bloom the sun went down.   140
A thirst-scorched peony waited for the rain;
a spell-bound orchid waked and dreamed by turns.
In the spring night, the spring-born blossom smiled
and welcomed caresses from the east wind.[22]
Her rainbow skirt lay tattered, wind-exposed;   145
her feather jacket gleamed beneath the moon.
The flutes and singers sang sweet melodies—
Hsi Shih climbed step by step up Ku-su Tower![23]
The halcyon couch gave off faint whiffs of musk;
the moonlit jewels shimmered round her neck.   150
From clouds, in rites of love, raindrops poured down
to bless the peony there in Scentwood Hall.[24]
Clear notes of lute inside the sky-blue room;
soft moans of flute throughout the crimson yard.

The music grew, enrapturing her soul;   155
it surged and soared—her heart went numb with bliss.
Moth-eyebrows brushed against the dragon's face:[25]
they formed a perfect couple, side by side.
Upon the queen of flowers the king of men
conferred the world's rewards to beauty due.   160
She nestled to the sun enthroned above;
she waited on his pleasure night and day.
They loved each other—fire and incense glowed:
no need to strew mulberry leaves for goats![26]
On moon-bright balconies they hugged and kissed;   165
in sunny maple groves they laughed and played.
Her fresh pear-blossom face bewitched his eyes—
he cherished her unpainted, unadorned.
The flawless gem that flashed a hundred sparks
was fondled, pampered by a king in love.   170
A woman's beauty! Soul-entrancing drug,
toppler of kingdoms, shaker of the world!
They listened to "Clear Moonlight" at West Park;
they heard "Fair Harem Flower" up in Spring Tower.
By royal grace, she shared his bed till dawn—   175
jade and vermilion glimmered through the dark.
To lie inside those curtains of brocade
and snuggle close to him, the lord supreme!
Offer to pay a thousand coins, in gold,
and try to purchase one such spring night's dream!   180
Now she would smile, now she would purse her brows
when teased about her golden-lotus feet.[27]
She flounced and flirted with consummate art
as would befit a goddess born to earth!

Some orchids grow unnoticed in the wilds,[28]   185
their scent not treasured by a prince or duke.
But fickle destiny had chosen her
and given her a king to love and serve:

her parents who had tutted at her birth
forgave her now for being just a girl! 190
Paintings of lovebirds flying wing to wing,
of flowers that bloom on intertwining boughs:[29]
she etched those union symbols in her heart
and vowed eternal troth on Seventh Night.[30]
A drop of rain had fallen, by sheer luck, 195
into a stately mansion—she rejoiced
that fish and water, meant to meet, had met.
She relished her position more and more,
delighted with her fortune and well pleased
her hand had dipped in royal indigo.[31] 200

Some years went past—his ardor slowly cooled;
the wellspring, somehow, started running dry.
Heaven will shift—one morning she woke up
and found the sovereign's love for her had died.
If royal grace and justice be a torch, 205
let it shine forth and reach the farthest nooks!
A thousand roses vie in color—yet
the lord will choose and pluck those near at hand.
When many anglers angle for one fish,
the glutted fish stops nibbling at the bait. 210
When many swallows flock to one lone tree,
how can a branch be found whereon to perch?
She'd hoped to fare far better than the rest
and last—instead, the Maker played a prank:
no sooner had the sun bestowed warm light 215
than this deep grotto plunged back into dark.

Inside the silent chamber, all alone,
she's waiting hour by hour the livelong night.
Why act so wantonly, O Lord of Spring?
You play with flowers, but leave before they fade. 220
Here on this tower where once they watched the moon,

she stirs and frets away a night of rain.
Beside the terrace where they breathed the cool,
she lies awake while howls the autumn gale.
Her room feels metal-cold—broken in two,   225
their phoenix mirror; split, their common sash.
Mornings and nights, she broods and dreams of love
like one who slumbered under that plum tree.[32]
Or she imagines she's a butterfly[33]
that flutters to and fro like some lost soul.   230
Her alcove's hushed and still—through crimson doors
winds pierce, to ivory blinds dew clings.
The phoenix coach, the goat-drawn cart are gone—
they've left grass-covered tracks, moss-speckled ruts.
The harem lies immersed in autumn dusk—   235
her mat and pillow freeze in solitude.
All day she waits for news—no wild goose comes;
all night she hears bells toll—no other sound.
It's cold to sleep alone as incense wafts
and lamplight flickers in the shadowed night.   240
Portraits of beauties she admires no more—
gray eyes she fastens on the royal hall.
All by herself, unseen, she grieves and mourns,
complaining to the moon, sighing with flowers.
A hundred torments gnaw within her heart;   245
beset by care, she staggers in a daze.
How can the butterfly forsake the flower
and let her petals fade, her pistil wilt?
Deep into night, she gazes at the moon.
Who has invented this, the grief that kills?   250
No whetted sword is used to kill the girl—
she's killed with sorrow: what a cruel way!
Why spin your thread, Old Codger of the Moon,
if you don't bind two lovers hard and fast?
She would as soon yank loose the red silk thread,   255

kick down the harem gate and flee outside.
They strolled here in this garden where, years past,
he plucked the red peach blossom in its prime.
Up Phoenix Terrace, down Oriole Bower,
twin pillows lie where both dreamed wondrous dreams.   260
But now contempt has settled in his heart—
he lets her wilt like grass and fray like silk.
Sun king of love, why do you feel no love?
The flower regrets lost spring as wanes the moon.
Where is the royal hall of yesteryear,   265
when he broke off the tender willow spray?
Behind pearl-studded veils and ivory blinds,
her bridal gown still bears the marks of love.
But now he's cast her from his fickle heart
to let the blossom float and drift downstream.   270
Creator, why play these capricious tricks?
The pallid moon sets on a life laid waste.
A flower adrift beneath the waning moon—
the smoldering fire of twilight burns her soul.
More twilight, yet more twilight looms ahead—   275
she sorrows for the flower and for the moon.
Who cares to glorify a waning moon?
Who bothers to admire a fallen flower?
In cheerless nature grief finds no reprieve—
grief mirrors nature, nature mirrors grief.   280

While leaves are rustling, stirred by gusts of wind,
she thinks she hears faint voices from afar.
His coach is coming! Hurriedly she burns
stale incense and perfumes her musty robe.
Alas, the voices heard are crickets' cries,   285
sad autumn's whispers to all lovelorn hearts.
No tidings break the hush—bone-chilled, she waits;
by her cold window, fireflies flit about.
When over her high roof the moon slopes down,

she thinks she hears a call that summons her.   290
He's sent a page for her! With moldy powder,
she quickly touches up her withered cheeks.
Alas, she's heard a cuckoo's stubborn wail—
it mourns all widows and defunct spring joys.
She feels so cold—no one is hugging her.   295
Bleak sorrow floods the yard where blossoms fall.

In Halcyon Palace, laughter turns to tears:
all pomp and glory dazzle but soon dim.
Dry rot eats gates of power—if she had known,
she'd have preferred the simple, humdrum life.   300
Had she suspected Heaven wished her ill,
she'd have rebuffed the lure of gold itself.
She broods on destiny, and she despairs.
The flower has left its branch—what can be done?
Rich viands, fit for princes, will soon pall: 305
plain greens and beans taste bland, yet always please.
To live together under one thatch roof
with children big and small—that's happiness!
Had she but known what fate reserved for her,
would she have acted proud and hard to please?   310
She would have settled for some country lad
and quashed all dreams of grandeur from her soul.
Her haggard face is like to that gaunt moon;
her glassy eyes resembles this dim lamp.
She wants to laugh and sing her grief away—   315
her laughs all sound like sobs, her songs like moans.
The heart's dull fire has parched her lovely brows;
the tears of blood have washed rouge from her face.
Her sorrow mars or kills all little joys:
tea freshly brewed, fine incense, or rare scent.   320
He lives close by, yet seems a world away.
Why such a destiny? She fares far worse
than do the Herdboy and his Weaver Maid:[34]

they see each other every autumn once.
Endowed with charm and beauty, she must wait   325
year after year inside her empty room.
Is she not meant for him? Oh, for red dye
to dye again the faded thread of silk!
The royal flowers smile to greet the sun—
who would forbid the bee to come their way?   330
A shallow stream keeps her and him apart—
he's over there, she's waiting over here.
A languor blurs her senses, eyes, and ears.
The vacant chamber rouses thoughts of love.
In dreams she lives those nights of long ago—   335
she yearns and thirsts for raindrops after drought.
Upon his lofty throne is he aware?
A woman's left forlorn and cold, unloved.
East wind, why scorn the peach bloom and veer off,
to let her pine and wither in her nook?   340
The Maker wields a wayward hand—for fun
he's locked her in a prison made of gold!
As she sits here and broods about the world,
she feels like bursting into one long scream.
She's cold, left by herself—they lie near him!   345
Yet has she lost all beauty and all charm?
You play such jokes, Old Codger of the Moon!
From strong red yarn you've spun a thin, pale thread.

Her weary soul is deadened to all things—
her anguished thoughts all snarl like sleaves of silk.   350
Upon the lamp that lit their nuptial night,
twin flowers of wedded troth still bloom, intact.
Have many state affairs so troubled him
that he's expelled her from his mind and heart?
Why has her servant failed to bring her plight   355
to his full notice, seeking some redress?
Night, wind, and rain—a woman, cold, alone.

Raindrops tap plantain leaves to beat each watch.

A few fireflies wink feebly by the wall,

now clouded by dawn's mist. The lamp's grown dim,   360

the clock's dripped low: she has not closed her eyes.[35]

This melancholy view—she hates it so!

What name to give this sadness? In one night,

how many scenes recalled and seen again!

Fleet time, white stallion, gallops past her blind:[36]   365

when will they ever end, her pain and grief?

Perhaps, her plaint will move the sovereign's ear—

oh, may her face stay fresh as in those days!

Note: The *Cung oán ngâm khúc* ("A song of sorrow inside the royal harem") is Nguyễn Gia Thiều's best-loved work. It laments the common fate of many royal concubines who once the king tired of them were condemned to solitude and neglect inside the harem. The poem, which can also be figuratively construed as the veiled complaint of a courtier once high in favor and now disgraced, shows strong Buddhist and Taoist influences. Its wealth of recondite allusions makes it a scholar's delight but renders it less accessible to many less educated readers.

1. Supplanted by a rival concubine in her Han emperor's affections, Lady Pan wrote a poem in which she compared herself to a white silk fan much appreciated in summer but laid aside in autumn. A translation of her poem appears in the note to Poem 65, "To a discarded fan," by Nguyễn Khuyến.

2. Kou Chien, king of Yüeh, sent the beautiful Hsi Shih as a gift to his rival, King Fu Ch'a of Wu. The latter fell so completely under her spell that she was able to bring about his downfall. Ch'ang O is the Chinese goddess of the moon.

3. Li Po (699–762) is considered one of China's greatest poets, perhaps second only to Tu Fu.

4. Under the T'ang dynasty, Wang Wei (699–759) enjoyed equal fame as a landscape painter and as a poet.

5. Indra, the Hindu deity, is worshiped as the god of chess in Vietnamese folk tradition. Liu Ling was the great drinker of a group of Taoist anarchists who called themselves the Seven Sages of the Bamboo Grove in the early period of the Tsin dynasty.

6. The Han writer Ssu-ma Hsiang-ju played the lute on a moonlit night and conquered the heart of Cho Wen-chün, a young widow.

7. According to Chinese legend, Hsiao Shih (the "Flute Master") played the bamboo flute so entrancingly, making it sound like the mating call of a

male phoenix, that Nung-yü, the beautiful daughter of Duke Mu (ruler of Ch'in) fell in love with the musician and married him. A phoenix terrace was built for the couple, and there he taught her how to play the flute and attract phoenixes as he did. One morning, both were carried away by a phoenix and became immortals.

8. King Ch'i Hsüan, who ruled during the Warring States period in Chinese history, could never resist the charms of a woman.

9. Tou Yi, to choose a son-in-law, had suitors shoot arrows at a peacock painted on a screen. The young man who hit the bird's eye and won the daughter was later to mount the throne of China as the founder of the T'ang dynasty, according to legend.

10. Traceable to *The Book of Odes*, the phrase "to gaze on the stars" means to look forward to marriage.

11. Mount T'ien-t'ai in Chekiang Province is the Chinese Olympus.

12. According to Chinese myth, the Old Man of the Moon picks men and women, whose feet he ties in marriage with a red silk thread. Understood broadly, the red silk thread represents fate as a hindrance to free will. Although the concept of a male deity or spirit of the moon emerged under patriarchy, nowhere has it ever quite supplanted the older tradition of some lunar goddess as the patron of love and marriage: in fact, the Vietnamese call that deity *Bà Nguyệt*, or Lady Moon.

13. Kuan Yin, the Chinese goddess of mercy in Mahayana Buddhism, is often portrayed with a willow branch, sprinkling drops of magic water on a world consumed by the fire of the seven passions. See note 18.

14. In old Vietnam, childhood was marked by white teeth; later, the boy or girl was required to blacken his or her teeth through a lacquering process, as an initiation rite.

15. This metaphor comes from a poem by the T'ang poet Tu Fu.

16. Li Kung-tso, a minor T'ang official, wrote a tale titled "The dream of Nan-k'o." It is about a man named Ch'un-yü Fen who fell asleep under a *huai*, or pagoda tree *(Sophora japonica)* and dreamed a life of glory in the kingdom of Huai-an ("Sophora Peace"), where he married the king's daughter and became governor of Nan-k'o Province. When he woke up, he found only an ant hill at the foot of the tree, and Nan-k'o turned out to be the south branch of the tree under which he had slept. The story concludes with this quatrain: "They've climbed the highest peaks—wealth, rank and fame. / Their power lays waste all cities and all fields. / A wise man casts one glance and merely says: / "Forever bustling, don't they look like ants?"

17. *Dhyana:* meditation or contemplation; Buddhism in general, and especially the Ch'an (meditative, or intuitional) school founded in China by Bodhidharma.

18. According to Buddhism, the seven passions are pleasure, anger, sorrow, joy, love, hate, and desire.

19. Buddhist myth claims that the Udumbara tree *(Ficus glomerata)*, supposed to bear fruit without flowers, does flower once every three thousand years to hail the advent of a Buddha.

20. *Prajna:* supreme knowledge or wisdom, according to Buddhism.

21. The Old Man of the Moon: see note 12.

22. The east wind blows in spring and therefore favors love.

23. Fu Ch'a became so madly enamored of Hsi Shih that he built a special palace for her: Ku-su Tower. See note 2.

24. Scentwood Hall: the T'ang emperor Ming-huang loved to spend his spring nights with his favorite consort, Lady Yang, in a palace built of sandalwood.

25. "Moth-eyebrows" are a beautiful woman's eyebrows, as fine and delicate as the antennae of a silkworm moth.

26. Emperor Tsin Wu-ti went visiting within his far-flung harem in a light carriage drawn by goats. His competing concubines would scatter mulberry leaves in front of their doors to attract the goats and bring the emperor to their chambers.

27. "Golden-lotus feet" were women's bound feet, once aesthetically appreciated by men of the elite in China.

28. In classical East Asian literature, "wild orchids" often stand for high-principled Confucians who live in obscurity and whose talents go to waste, as in the poem "On finding some wild orchids," by the T'ang poet Ch'en Tzu-ang (662–702): "Through spring and summer, in the wilds, / these orchids stay so fresh and green. / They live alone in sunless woods. / Their crimson flowers cap purple stems. / Then one by one, clear days take leave. / The autumn wind begins to blow. / All the year's blooms now droop and fall. / What's to become of all that scent?"

29. These two lines allude to the passionate love affair between Emperor Ming-huang and Lady Yang as described by the T'ang poet Po Chü-i in "A song of everlasting sorrow."

30. According to Chinese myth, once a year, on the seventh night of the seventh moon, the Herdboy and the Weaver Maid are allowed to meet on a bridge of magpies across the Silver Stream (the Milky Way). They once lived together as man and wife, but they were so wrapped up in each other that they neglected their respective duties and were separated, as a punishment. Tradition claims that Emperor Ming-huang and Lady Yang gazed at those stars on the seventh night of the seventh moon and swore eternal love to each other.

31. "To have dipped one's hand in indigo" *(tay đã nhúng chàm)* is a Vietnamese proverbial phrase meaning "to have done something that cannot be undone, have taken some irreversible course of action."

32. Under the Sui dynasty, Chao Shih-hsiung dreamed he met a beautiful girl whom he invited to join him at an inn, and together they drank and made love. When he woke up, he found himself lying under a plum tree on Mount Lo-fu, the abode of nymphs and spirits.

33. A well-known passage in the *Chuang Tzu* reads: "Chuang Chou once dreamed that he was a butterfly, fluttering to and fro and enjoying itself. Suddenly he woke up and was Chuang Chou again. But he did not know whether he was Chuang Chou who had dreamed he was a butterfly, or whether he was a butterfly dreaming that it was Chuang Chou."

34. For the Herdboy and the Weaver Maid, see note 30.

35. The timepiece mentioned here is a clepsydra, or water clock.

36. In the *Chuang Tzu*, fleeting time is likened to the glimpse you catch of a white colt galloping past a crack in your window.

45. Calling all souls *(Chiêu hồn)*

Nguyễn Du

Throughout the seventh month, rain sobs and wails.
The chill of wind gnaws into aged bones.
An autumn evening—what a dismal scene!
Reeds drown in silver, plane trees strew gold leaves.
Among the poplars twilight lingers still.   5
Upon the pear trees, drop by drop, dew falls.
Whose heart would not feel sorrow at this sight?
And if the living mourn, what of the dead?

Out of the darkness shrouding sky and earth,
let specters, ghosts, and phantoms all appear!   10
All creatures of ten classes, pity them!
Lost, lonely souls, they wander in strange lands.
They find no home where votive incense burns—
forlorn, they prowl and prowl from night to night.
They once sat high or low—what matter now?   15
Can you now tell the sages from the fools?

As autumn starts, let's set an altar up.
Pure water sprinkles from the willow branch.[1]

May Buddha's mercy heal those suffering souls,
save them and guide them toward the Promised West.[2]   20

There were proud men who followed glory's path—
they warred and hoped to conquer all the world.
Why talk about the heyday of their might?
Remember their decline, their fall, and grieve.
A storm broke forth—their roofs came crashing down: 25
could they trade places with the meanest boor?
For pride and pomp breed hatred and revenge—
blood flowed in streams, bones crumbled into bits.
Killed young, they've left no heir—they drift unmourned
as headless ghosts that moan on nights of rain.   30
Defeat or triumph lies in Heaven's scheme—
will ever those lost souls escape their fate?

Where are those ladies, veiled by flowered drapes,
who reigned supreme in cassia-scented bowers?
Once more the realm changed masters—hapless leaves,   35
did they know where they'd go, swept off by winds?
From lofty towers they toppled into waves—
the hairpin snapped in two, the pitcher sank![3]
A merry court had flocked round them in life—
once their eyes closed, none gathered up their bones.   40
Alas, no incense burns to keep them warm:
they hide in thickets, or they skulk near brooks.
Oh, pity their soft hands, their tender feet!
They wilt night after night, rot year by year.

Those who once wore tall hats and waved broad sleeves   45
meted out life and death with their red brush.
To rule—they did know how; their pockets stuck
with statecraft handbooks like so many knives:
they'd read Yi Yin, the Duke of Chou by day,
study Kuan Chung or Chu-ko Liang at night.[4]   50
Higher they climbed, more hatred they inspired,

creating all round more tombs, more ghosts.
No gold on earth can ransom back their lives.
Their halls lie shattered where gay songs once rang.
No kinsfolk stay close by to offer them 55
a bowl of water or an incense stick.
Deserted souls, they stagger here and there,
far from salvation, loaded down with guilt.

There were those who mapped plans and marshaled troops.
They rushed to battle, seized batons and seals. 60
They raged like windstorms, roared like thunderbolts:
many laid down their lives for one man's sake.
Stray arrows, errant bullets spelled their doom—
they squandered flesh and blood on battlegrounds.
Stranded and waifed upon some distant shore, 65
where could they find a grave, poor bones none claimed?
All through the sky's abyss, rain wails, wind howls:
the mists of darkness blur and dim the world.
Forests and fields wear mourning shades of gray—
the cast-off dead receive no sacrifice. 70

There were those who once hankered after wealth.
They traded, losing sleep and appetite.
Estranged from kith and kin, they had no friend:
to whom could they bequeath their hard-earned goods?
Who would be there to hear their dying words? 75
All earthly riches come and go like clouds—
now dead, they could not take one coin with them.
The neighbors, squeezing out some ritual tears,
dumped them in coffins made of banyan wood
and buried them by torchlight after dark. 80
Bewildered, at a loss, they roam the fields—
where is an incense stick, a drop of drink?

There were those scholars chasing post and rank—
they'd all trek into town and try their luck.

In fall, they would pack up and leave their homes   85
to go and measure pens with fellow scribes.[5]
But was officialdom, their cherished goal,
a cause worth risking soul and body for?
When they took sick, bedridden at some inn,
they lacked their wives' and children's loving care.   90
Without ado, they were consigned to earth,
while strangers, and no brothers, would look on.
Far, far away from their ancestral soil,
their corpses dot unhallowed burial grounds.
Unwarmed by fire and incense, exiled souls   95
must shiver as winds blow beneath the moon.

There were those travelers roving streams and seas,
whose sails unfurled and dared the east's fierce gusts.
A tempest rose and struck them in midcourse—
they met their end inside the maws of sharks.   100
There were those who strolled round and peddled wares,
their shoulders mangled by the carrying pole.
As they fell victim to harsh sun or rain,
where did they wend their way, souls turned adrift?

There were those who, enlisted by main force,   105
left their beloved to go serve the state.
With water scooped from brooks, rice kept in tubes,
they trudged along rain-swept, wind-beaten trails.
In wartime human life is cheap as trash—
stray bullets and chance arrows smote them down.   110
Will-o'-the-wisps, they flutter to and fro,
as night skies echo with their piteous moans.

There were poor girls whom fortune failed in need:
they sold their charms and threw their youth away.
Old age caught them alone and desolate—   115
unmarried, childless, where could they seek help?
Alive, they drained the cup of bitter dregs;

and dead, they eat rice mush from banyan leaves.[6]

How sorrowful is women's destiny!

Who can explain why they are born to grief?   120

There were those wretches tramping all the year—
a bridge served as their roof, hard ground their bed.
They too belonged to humankind—alas,
they lived on alms and died beside back roads.
Some got locked up in jail for no offense—   125
they languished, clad in tattered mats, and died.
Their bones were tucked in nooks of prison camps.
When will they ever have their wrongs set right?
Some children, newborn at a baleful hour,
had to forsake their parents and pass on.   130
Who's now to hold them, walk and play with them?
Their strangled cries and wails distress the heart.

And there were those who drowned in streams or lakes,
those who climbed trees and fell when their foot slipped.
Some tumbled down deep wells when their rope broke.   135
Some washed away in floods, some burned in fires.
Some perished by wolves' fangs or elephants' tusks,
a prey to monsters of the hills or seas.
Some women bore a child, but left it soon;
and some, alas, miscarried of their babe.   140

Along the way, all tripped and fell head first
to cross the Bridge of No Return, one after one.[7]
Those persons bound for separate destinies,
stray souls and vagrant ghosts—where are they now?
They crouch against a dike, behind a bush.   145
They dwell where rivers spring, where earth meets sky.
They lurk in clumps of grass, in shade of trees.
They hover near this hostel, haunt that bridge.
They find asylum at some shrine, some church.
They make abode in market towns and ports.   150

They clamber up and down some mounds or knolls.

They wade all through the mire of bogs or swamps.

After a life of agonies and woes,

bowels and guts have shriveled, numb with cold.

For scores of years they've suffered gales and storms;   155

moaning, they eat and sleep on dirt or dew.

By cockcrow frightened, they all flee and hide—

at sunset they all venture forth again.

In rags they all slink out, hugging their young

or steering by the hand their tottery old.   160

All wandering, damned souls, both old and young!

For your salvation come and hear a prayer.

May Buddha rescue you from life and death

and ferry you to his Pure Land of Bliss.

Let his effulgent light dispel such gloom   165

as clouds the mind in ignorance and sin.

Then over all four seas his peace shall reign

to soothe all griefs and purge all enmity.

May Buddha's power send the Wheel of the Law

through all three realms, to all ten cardinal points.[8]   170

The Burnt-Faced King shall raise his holy flag[9]

and lead all creatures on their joyous march.

May Buddha work his magic and awake

all beings from the dream of self-deceit.

All creatures of ten classes, are you there?   175

Women and men, you young and old, all come!

All enter Buddha's house and hear his word!

This life is just a bubble or a flash.

O friends, make room for Buddha in your hearts,

and you'll escape the cycle of rebirths!   180

At his behest, we set a bowl of gruel

and incense candles on the hallowed board.

We offer paper gold and paper clothes

to help you speed your heavenward ascent.

All who have come, be seated and partake: 185
spurn not these trifles, gifts of our goodwill.
By Buddha's grace they'll grow a millionfold,
and all of you shall get your even share.
To all he brings compassion and release:
no longer fear the curse of life and death.   190
Buddha, the Law, the Order—all be praised![10]
Glory to those who sit on lotus thrones!

Note: This poem is known either as "A song calling back dead souls" *(Chiêu hồn ca)* or as "A dirge for all ten classes of beings" *(Văn tế thập loại chúng sinh)*. The best known of Nguyễn Du's works next to *The Tale of Kiều*, it is associated with the folk custom of offering ritual food and other gifts on the full-moon of the seventh month to "lost souls" *(vong-hồn)*—those wandering spirits who are denied a regular family cult because they died without heirs or perished in inauspicious circumstances. The poem seems to make veiled reference to the social turmoil and tragedy caused by the Tây Sơn rebellion and also by the subsequent victory of the Nguyễn lords, with its vengeful bloodbath.

1. Kuan Yin, the Chinese goddess of mercy in Mahayana Buddhism, is often pictured with a jade vase, holding a willow branch that scatters drops of healing water on a sick world.

2. The Promised West: the western paradise of Amida Buddha.

3. "The hairpin snapped in two, the pitcher sank": two metaphors used together for the sudden death of a wife or ladylove.

4. Yi Yin of Shang, the Duke of Chou, Kuan Chung, and Chu-ko Liang were all renowned statesmen of ancient China.

5. "To measure pens with fellow scribes": to compete against other scholars in civil service examinations.

6. Rice porridge is offered to "lost souls" in banyan-leaf containers at small open-air shrines.

7. The Bridge of No Return: the bridge that leads across the Buddhist Styx, to the netherworld.

8. "All three realms": the world consists of sensual desire, form, and pure spirit, according to Buddhist metaphysics. "All ten cardinal points": the eight points of the compass plus the nadir and the zenith.

9. The Burned-Faced King is a deity of the netherworld: with his grim face and long tongue, he is much dreaded by ghosts and spirits, according to Buddhist belief.

10. The Buddha, the Law (or *Dharma*) and the Order (or *Sangha*) are the "three jewels" *(tam-bảo)* of Buddhism.

3. Responses to the West

46. Carrying a cangue around the neck
Nguyễn Hữu Huân

Folks on both sides, see what I'm bearing here?

A moral burden, yes, and not a cangue![1]

Beneath its weight, the scholar's shoulders stoop;

around its neck, the hero flaunts his pride.

I'll die and go up north: my name will shine.

You live and stay down south: it's your disgrace.[2]

One wins or loses—Heaven take the blame.

Fuck you base traitors who dare laugh at me!

Note: A leader of the resistance movement in the South, Nguyễn Hữu Huân wrote this poem and then bit his tongue, dying in 1875 before he was to be executed by the French.

1. A cangue, a wooden framework, was fastened around the neck of an offender as a portable pillory. It was a symbol of infamy.

2. The North was still under Vietnamese control, while the South (Cochin China) had been in French possession since 1867.

47. Fleeing from bandits
Nguyễn Đình Chiểu

The market breaks at sound of Western guns.

Just one false move—the game of chess is lost.

Children flee home to scurry here and there.

Birds leave their nests to flutter back and forth.

Calf Haven's riches wash away like foam.[1]

Deer Field's roof thatch and tile go up in smoke.[2]

O turmoil quellers, are you hiding now?

Why let the little people bear this scourge?

Note: This poem must have been composed around 1859, when the French began to attack Gia-định in the south.

1. Bến Nghé (Calf Haven) is an old, colloquial name for the area around Saigon, including Gia-định Province.

2. Đồng Nai (Deer Field) is a common name for southern Vietnam (as distinguished from central and northern Vietnam).

48. The storm
Nguyễn Đình Chiểu

Where do you keep your armies, O Wind God?
Unleash your might, and tumble ocean waves.
Whip, whip—blow down all temples and all shrines.
Roar, roar—bring down all forests and all hills.
Beneath Mount Lu did Shun desert his path?[1]
Upon the Sui, Liu Pang found his escape.[2]
May Heaven storm and sweep our kingdom clean,
then put it back within its rightful bounds.

Note: This poem calls for a general uprising against the French.

1. Before turning the throne over to Shun, the sage-king Yao tested him by sending him alone into the wilderness. At the foot of Mount Lu, Shun was caught in a dust storm—he weathered it and found his way home.

2. In his power struggle against Hsiang Yü for hegemony in China, Liu Pang (the future founder of the Han dynasty) once ran the danger of being captured on the Sui River; a providential storm rose up and saved him.

49. Elegy for Trương Định
Nguyễn Đình Chiểu

His fame rose like a billow in the south.
Gò-công in battles echoed with his feats.
His bullets made white devils' warships throb;
his sword cast glory on the Golden Gate.[1]
The flag of justice Heaven's yet to fell—

the captain's seal lies buried under earth!

Why must brave men break down and shed salt tears?

A murmured prayer is offered to his soul.

Note: This is one of a series of poems which Nguyễn Đình Chiểu composed to mourn Trương Định, a leader of the anti-French resistance in the South, who was betrayed and killed in 1864.

    1. The Golden Gate is the entrance to the royal palace.

50. Waiting for the east wind

Nguyễn Đình Chiểu

All plants and flowers yearn for their east wind.

O Lord of Spring, do *you* know? Where are you?

No sign of geese through the cloud-hung north pass;

swallows' hushed cries in twilit southern woods.

To strangers our old realm is parceled out—

must we and they live under this same sky?

Wait till our holy sovereign's grace shines through—

a shower of rain will cleanse all streams and hills.

Note: The east wind blows in spring. The poem expresses Nguyễn Đình Chiểu's forlorn hope that somehow a wise, strong king could emerge to save the country from the French and like a spring shower, cleanse it of foreign influence.

51. The loyal horse

Nguyễn Đình Chiểu

Su-chuang, a horse, won fame throughout the world.

By scoundrels caught, it knew a woeful fate.

It stamped its foot, refused to eat Sung hay;

it turned its head and neighed for its Liang stall.

It would let no new master ride its back—

it wanted its own king to hold the reins.

A loyal horse remembered its old home:

should men forget the country of their birth?

Note: Su-chuang, a horse belonging to the Liang king, was captured by the
founder of the Sung dynasty in China. It refused to serve the new master and
starved itself to death.

52. A fisherman speaks his mind

Nguyễn Đình Chiểu

Wise men of talent, now and in the past,

have never let ambition seal their doom.

High-placed, you're still no better than a slave—

a plowman's buffalo, a rider's horse.

In evil times avoid officialdom

and spare yourself some pitfall or some net.

Those who serve tigers, running as their hounds,

will feed the tigers when no hare is left.

Beyond harm's reach persist in your own sphere—

some stream or sea none covets or disputes.

Plying a paddle, row your wicker boat

and catch a livelihood from dawn to dusk.

Weave your own way through rivers' zigs and zags,

with fishing line and rod made of bamboo.

Befriend the moon by night, the wind by day—

sing a gay tune, enjoy a jar of wine.

Drift past where cranes resort, where oysters haunt.

In nature take delight, at ease and free.

The fish and shrimp, by Heaven sent, abound.

You eat your fill—for what else could you wish?

Note: In this excerpt from the *"Dương Từ Hà Mậu"* ("Dương Từ and Hà
Mậu"), Nguyễn Đình Chiểu preached the ideal that he practiced: absolute
noncooperation with the French colonialists.

53. A blind poet looks at the world outside

Nguyễn Đình Chiểu

I'll try to look and see how far they'll go
in tearing up, in carving up this realm.
They all run hustling after wealth and rank—
lackeys at dawn, by nightfall petty lords,
they strut it, speaking daggers with their eyes.   5
The people are squeezed dry, impressed by force
to build their mansions or to polish guns.
All rogues and toadies jostle as they hail
those heathens who encroach upon our shores.
Rice fields are littered with our battle-killed—   10
blood flows or lies in pools, stains hills and streams.
Troops bluster on and grab our land, our towns,
roaring and stirring dust to dim the skies.
Clouds glower, winds howl—the ordered earth upheaves,
with summer snows and winter thunderclaps!   15
These days when light recedes and darkness spreads,
all three bonds and five norms in disarray[1]
are nothing but a raveled skein of silk.
Were Yi and Fu to live in these warped times,[2]
they would be hoeing gardens, plowing fields.   20
A scholar with no talent and no power,
could I redress a world turned upside down?
Stopped short in midcareer, I've spent my nights
dreaming and praying for a Yao, a Shun.[3]
I've failed the people—yet, deep in my heart,   25
I yearn to help them in their hour of need.
Before the country I must stand disgraced—
my vow of public service I've betrayed.
When I pronounce these words, my tears well up—
when will my sorrow ever know an end?   30
I've read the Scriptures of the Unicorn;[4]
Heaven's decree I'll heed and shan't appeal.

Better to have both eyes obscured by mists

than to sit here and see the kingdom's foes.

Better to curse the void before your eyes   35

than to sit here and watch the people's hell.

Better to have a desert for your eyes

than foreign conquest and defeat at dusk.

Better to have both eyes in pitch-dark night

than warfare drowning this dear land in blood.   40

Sooner be blind and honor your home cult

than see no worship of your ancestors.

Sooner be blind and keep from foul repute

than have both eyes and feed on putrid meat.

Sooner be blind and to yourself stay true   45

than keep both eyes and tamper with your hair.[5]

Why see and ape those creatures garbed in wool[6]

and swagger, bowing to no lord above?

Why see and, stirred by gold and flesh,

unleash all lusts inviting Heaven's scourge?   50

Why see and race against the madding throng?

Today's reward will be tomorrow's shame.

Why see and throw all ethics to the winds,

spurning old virtues, flouting Heaven's laws?

I've seen what's happened to the world outside—   55

inside I shall preserve my heart and soul.

Note: This is an excerpt from the "*Ngư tiều y thuật vấn đáp*" ("The dialogue between a fisherman and a woodcutter about the healing art").

1. The three bonds *(tam-cương)*: the network of relationships between king and subject, between father and son, and between husband and wife. The five norms *(ngũ-thường)*: in this context, the five Confucian virtues of humaneness, righteousness, decorum, wisdom, and good faith.

2. Yi Yin and Fu Yüeh were paragons of statesmanship in ancient China.

3. Yao (Nghiêu) and Shun (Thuấn) were the mythical sage-kings of China.

4. The "Scriptures of the Unicorn" are the "Spring and Autumn *[Ch'un Ch'iu]* Annals," one of the five classics of Confucianism. Usually attributed to Confucius, the work chronicles events in the state of Lu (722–481 BCE).

5. Almost as a religious duty, Vietnamese men kept their hair long.

6. Since wool and fur came from beasts, men who wore such materials were viewed as barbarians.

54. The old hound

Huỳnh Mẫn Đạt

Three virtues always grace the canine breed.[1]
Still, when his teeth fall out, a dog's grown old.
Chasing the deer of Ch'in, his knees wore out.[2]
Scowling at apes from Ch'u, his skin grew limp.[3]
No one will stop the foxes loose up north.
Few can deter the bandits rife out west.
Once spry and strong, he used to roam the world:
decrepit now, he sallies forth no more.

Note: This is an allegory about a patriotic soldier too old to keep on fighting against the French.

1. A dog is endowed with three virtues: ability to guard his master's house, willingness to risk his life for him, and loyalty to him.

2. When the Ch'in dynasty in China collapsed, people said that it had lost a deer that anyone was now free to capture or slay. Capture of the deer of Ch'in metaphorically represents political dominion over a country.

3. Hsiang Yü of Ch'u (who fought against Liu Pang for control of China after the disintegration of the Ch'in dynasty) was derisively portrayed as "the ape who wears a cap"—a witless brute. Huỳnh Mẫn Đạt used the phrase *apes from Ch'u* as a subtler disparagement of French soldiers than the stereotype *white devils.*

55. The old whore becomes a nun

Huỳnh Mẫn Đạt

The brothel echoes with the chime of bells—
you twist and turn in bed; then you wake up.
Your boat of love will cross the sea of lust;
your beauty's waves must reach the Dhyana grove.[1]
Grab Wisdom's sword and cleanse your filthy heart;[2]

tell Bodhi beads and weave your karmic fate.[3]

Your temple's nice and cool, with moon and wind:[4]

no Buddha yet, you live a god's good life!

Note: Tôn Thọ Tường (1825–1877) worked for the French and reaped hand-some benefits from them. In his old age, he wished to express repentance with a poem titled "The old whore becomes a nun." Huỳnh Mẫn Đạt used the same title and attacked the collaborator in this sarcastic reply.

   1. Dhyana: meditation, contemplation; the Ch'an school of Mahayana Buddhism.

   2. A Buddhist sutra includes this line: "Take Wisdom's sword and smash the fortress of cares and woes."

   3. Bodhi: Buddhist enlightenment.

   4. The expression "moon and wind" *(trăng gió)* suggests illicit love.

56. The rice mill

Phan Văn Trị

For merit here below, who equals it?

To grind our rice, all call upon the mill.[1]

Dauntless, it copes with storms of wind and dust;

unshaken, it will take a hundred spins.

To serve its lord, it must wear out its teeth.

Who made it so it chokes within its throat?[2]

It cares not if its stones have both worn down:

because the foe's still there, it must fight on.

   1. The rice mill represents a man who sacrifices himself for his country.

   2. A rice mill sometimes gets jammed—a metaphor for the patriot who chokes and grieves inside as he helplessly watches the enemy rule and exploit his country.

57. The mosquito

Phan Văn Trị

Mosquito, you are blessed with all nice things!

What do you lack? Why buzz still and complain?

You've rested on jade mats and ivory beds;

you've stroked and kissed rouged lips and powdered cheeks.

You've not spared children, you indulge your tastes;

you've stung poor people, filling up your paunch.

When a good swatter someday comes to hand,

I'll pay you for your crimes without a blink!

Note: The mosquito symbolizes the collaborator serving the French and sucking the blood of his fellow countrymen.

58. Opera actors

Phan Văn Trị

Some rub their shingles, others scratch their mange:

a shabby lot, for all their fine array.

A loyalist's red face displays white eyes;[1]

a sycophant's black beard sports scraggly hairs.

Though under rooftops, they boast parasols;[2]

astride no horse, they brandish and crack whips.

Thespians, folk say, make up a faithless lot:[3]

they daub their faces, then trade knocks and thumps.[4]

Note: This is an attack on those Vietnamese who joined and served the French colonial administration as officials without real powers.

　　1. In traditional opera, "red" symbolizes loyalty and "white" treason.

　　2. Parasols were ceremonial umbrellas and emblems of political authority.

　　3. A proverb says: "Opera actors are faithless." *(Bội là bạc.)*

　　4. Collaborators forgot their origins and turned against their own compatriots.

59. On hearing the rail cry

Nguyễn Khuyến

Your voice, grief-laden, lingers in the air.

Were you the king of Shu who died long since?[1]

Your blood pours out on quiet summer nights;

your soul takes flight as moonlight fades at dawn.
Are you bemoaning spring, now past and gone?
Or is it your lost land you're dreaming of?
Whom are you calling, crying through the night?
You make a wanderer brood within his heart.

1. According to Chinese legend, the king of Shu lost both the woman he loved and his realm—he died in exile and turned into a nightjar or rail, forever crying disconsolately. Nguyễn Khuyến uses the well-known tale to convey his sorrow over the demise of national sovereignty under French rule. The Vietnamese name for the nightjar is *cuốc*, which sounds like *quốc*, "homeland, nation." See also Poem 114, "The rail and the bullfrog," by Tản Đà.

60. To a statue
Nguyễn Khuyến

But what are you, Sir Statue, doing there?
You're standing still as rock and firm as bronze.
For whom must you keep vigil day and night?
How does our homeland fare? Or don't you know?

61. The French national holiday
Nguyễn Khuyến

Hail peace and joy on earth! Firecrackers snap.
They've hoisted flags, they've hung gay lanterns out.
Big dames peer down their snoots at some boat race;
small boys, hunched up, catch glimpses of a farce.
Trusting its strength, girls wigway on the swing;
for money, fellows climb the greasy pole.
Praise those who stage this merriest of shows!
The merrier, the sorrier, alas!

62. At an exposition

Nguyễn Khuyến

The fair displays a hundred goods and wares.
Uncanny crafts! Undreamed-of novelties!
Not long ago they dug and bored through earth.[1]
Here you behold the cosmos in its spring.
From distant lands, strange artifacts for garb.
Out of deep forests, fabled birds and beasts.
Our wretched country shows one work of art:
a wooden mandarin, all capped and gowned.[2]

    1. This line probably refers to the start of coal mining by the French in northern Vietnam (then known as Tonkin).

    2. Nguyễn Khuyến seems impressed with Western civilization and technology and deplores his own country's backwardness. For a different perspective, read Poem 75, "Looking far ahead," by Trần Tế Xương.

63. The comedian gets a curtain lecture

Nguyễn Khuyến

An actor lived in the East Ward.
One night in bed, he asked his wife:
"I play a mandarin on stage—
why don't I seem to awe the world?"
Her anger broke—she scolded him:
"You're old enough, but still a fool!
No one has heard you, thank the gods,
or I could never show my face!
The world's no dupe—it only fears
power of life and death, not mere pretense.
How could your feeble make-believe
impress one single soul on earth?
You're just a pauper, don't forget—
you scrape along by playing roles.
A king means little on the boards—
stage mandarins are mere buffoons."

Note: This poem is believed to be a personal attack on Hoàng Cao Khải, who rose to high office by catering to all French wishes and harshly cracking down on those of his compatriots who fought against foreign rule. Compare this with Poem 115, "The canary in a cage," by Tản Đà.

64. The widow's reply to a matchmaker
Nguyễn Khuyễn

I've lost my man—I lie bereft of joy,
bereft of him who fed me, kept me warm.
A neighbor plays matchmaker and suggests
I start my life afresh with some young lad.
A youngster, full of spirit, may run wild—
how can a woman, getting old, keep pace?
Try as I would, I could not please him long—
our union, soon or late, would split apart.
A widow weds again for roof and board—
if he took off and left me bare and starved,
what a disgrace! My parents warned me, once,
to shun back-alley trysts, which would make talk.
My friend, is that the way you pity me?
You kindly wish to help, but that won't work.
If you love me, then lend me rice and cloth—
don't ask me, please, to take another man!

Note: On behalf of the French authorities, Vũ Văn Bảo, Nam-định province chief, once approached Nguyễn Khuyễn with a job offer and was rebuffed.

65. To a discarded fan
Nguyễn Khuyễn

After three months of autumn chill,
you're lying tucked away, unused.
Your bones and muscles, though age-worn,

can still stir up a storm, can't they?
This season's ruled by waxing *yin*—
all's in abeyance and must wait.
When the red sun shines forth once more,
the world will then bid you come out.

Note: Displaced by a conniving rival as the favorite consort of Emperor Han Ch'eng-ti (33–7 BCE), Lady Pan (Pan Chieh-yü) wrote this poem of self-lament: "Fresh-woven silk, white silk of Ch'i, / as pure and clear as dew or snow. / From it was made a Shared Joy fan, / as round and full as the bright moon. / It was picked up by the King's hand. / Fluttered, it roused a gentle breeze. / It trembled so when autumn came, / when coldness triumphed over warmth. / Into a chest he cast it off, / abruptly ending love halfway." Nguyễn Khuyến borrowed the discarded fan metaphor and turned it into a political allegory: he hoped that French rule would pass and that a rightful monarch would return who would require the talents and services of unemployed Confucian scholars. Nguyễn Trãi made a similar use of the metaphor in "For years you wallowed in the scholar's world" (Poem 22). A woman's fan, either the kind that is round like the full moon or the type that folds and suggests the "delta of Venus" when spread out, has always represented the female sex. For a frank treatment of the fan as a female sexual symbol, read Poem 202, "Ode to the fan," by Hồ Xuân Hương.

66. Shrimp

Nguyễn Văn Lạc

They are no lords, no marquesses or dukes,
yet they all brandish swords and sport long beards.
They splash in water, popping their red eyes,
quite unaware their heads are full of shit.[1]

1. Given their peculiar anatomy, shrimp are said to carry their feces in their heads. In this poem, they represent those scholar-officials who worked for the French and combined the worst defects of their class: arrogance and lack of wisdom.

67. To a dead dog in the river

Nguyễn Văn Lạc

Alive, you caught the hares and made them cry—
now down the river your dead body bobs.
Some streaks still faintly show upon your coat—
a stench is all your name has left behind.
Lamenting at your wake are fish and shrimp;
escorting your remains are crows and hawks.
Wait till a storm comes up and whips the waves:
your flesh and bones will crumble into bits.

Note: The target of this attack must have been some dead collaborator who
had helped the French hunt down his own compatriots.

68. Tomorrow, should I fail ...

Trần Tế Xương

Tomorrow, should I fail, I'll go away.[1]
In future, folks, remember our feast days.[2]
I've studied till rice boils yet won't get cooked—
exams taste hot like chilies in the mouth.
To you, my sons, I'll leave my lamp and books;
I'll count on you, their mom, to fill their pot.
Kung-hsi! Merci! I know all foreign tongues:
if not to China, I'll run off to France!

1. In 1906 Trần Tế Xương tried for the last time to win the elusive *cử-
nhân* (or master's) degree.
2. As the eldest son, the poet was normally responsible for the family cult
and observance of feast days or death anniversaries.

69. New-style examinations

Trần Tế Xương

They're said to hold new-style exams this year.[1]
You old-school fogies, take and pass 'em quick!
No stone-carved glory, but the world will talk.[2]
For their lead pencil throw away your brush!

1. As of 1900, the French introduction of *quốc-ngữ*, or the romanized script of Vietnamese, into the civil service examinations, marked the beginning of the end for the traditional system based on knowledge of Chinese characters and on the use of the writing brush, rendered obsolete by the lead pencil.

2. In the old days, the names of *tiến-sĩ* (or doctoral graduates) were engraved on large stone tablets for posterity.

70. No, thank you!

Trần Tế Xương

My wife, you claim that French is mere child's play:
you'll give me money, pack me off to school.
No, thank you! Thank you with *cinquante* bows!
There's no lead pencil in my forebears' graves.

71. What earthly use are these Confucian graphs?

Trần Tế Xương

What earthly use are these Confucian graphs?[1]
Masters and doctors lie curled up and wilt.
Why not take lessons and become a clerk?
At night champagne, at break of day cow's milk!

1. Chinese characters were known as the Confucian scholars' script (*chữ nho*).

72. Lamenting the state of Confucian scholarship

Trần Tế Xương

It makes me sick, the state of schooling now:
of ten who learned Chinese, some nine have quit.
Salesgirls at idle bookstalls nod and doze;
tutors in private households squirm on mats.
Like chickens, scholars quail before the fox.
Writers take blows—and all to eat steamed rice.[1]
I'm not maligning fellow villagers!
I mean the headman and his deputy.[2]

1. To take blows and eat steamed rice *(cô đấm ăn xôi)*: to subject oneself to ill treatment and humiliation for the sake of earning a livelihood.
2. The last two lines take a dig at some scholars who rose to high office by selling out to the French.

73. Actors

Trần Tế Xương

You're good for nothing, actors all!
You scream and shriek, you mouth and mug.
None but the children can you fool,
sad humbugs under masks of chalk.[1]

1. In traditional opera, white makeup is reserved for actors who play sycophants and other treasonous characters.

74. Poor and happy

Trần Tế Xương

On this whole earth who can compare with him?[1]
He's worldly-wise and plays the fool.
Ashamed to live in these foul days,
he holds his peace and hides a hero's hand.
Obscure, he comes and goes at will.

He craves no wealth, he eyes no rank.

Sometimes he sports a tuft of hair,

sometimes he shaves his head.

All by himself he sings wild songs,

half in Chinese, half in our tongue.

He wears no hat, lets sunshine tan his skin.

He leaves his teeth undyed and white

to flash them at the world and laugh.[2]

He lets 'em bow and scrape through gates of power—

who knows that, bridle-shy, he's free as air?

Hemming and hawing, he acts deaf and dumb.

Joy bubbling up in him escapes as song.

How many understand him here below?

1. While pouring scorn on fellow scholars who worked for the French, Trần Tế Xương saved his admiration for a Nam-định butcher known simply as Mán, praised in this poem. It is likely that Mán took part in clandestine activities, perhaps serving as an occasional courier to carry messages back and forth between those who at home opposed colonial rule and those abroad, like Phan Bội Châu.

2. In old Vietnam, tooth lacquering was a must, and failure to have one's teeth blackened was a disgrace excusable only by dire poverty. The fact that Mán kept his teeth white was an indication either of extreme indigence in his youth or of unconventional behavior.

75. Looking far ahead

Trần Tế Xương

Through five night watches I've stayed wide awake.

I'm looking far ahead—I feel a jolt.

To ancient wisdom people have gone blind.

The human race may vanish, quite wiped out.

Hills mined for wealth will someday crumble down.

Seas opened up for trade will tilt, in time.

Once hollowed out, the earth will fade away.

They say a comet's started whirling round.

Note: Contrast Trần Tế Xương's pessimism about Western technology and economic exploitation with Nguyễn Khuyến's attitude in Poem 62, "At an exposition."

76. Drought

Trần Tế Xương

These days the sun could melt both gold and stone.[1]
The people, wild and frantic, pray for rain.
In happier times, carefree, they ate and slept—
now, waterless, they tremble for their land.[2]
Glad buffalo don't have to plow cracked earth;
aghast, the fish leap out and flee dry ponds.[3]
Each one must cope with drought in his own way:
a makeshift fan I'm fluttering by myself.[4]

1. Gold *(vàng)* and stone *(đá)*, being durable substances, symbolize staunch loyalty. This line suggests that foreign rule puts patriotism to a severe test.

2. The drought *(hạn)* metaphor, readily understood by wet-rice farmers anywhere as grievous misrule or tyranny that injures the people, can acquire an extra dimension in Vietnam and imply loss of national sovereignty or foreign domination, because the word *nước* means both "water" and "homeland, nation"—hence the poignant ambiguity of the fourth line. It literally reads: "Now they do nothing but worry about *nước-nôi*"—and *nước-nôi*, a reduplicative form, can be variously translated as "water," "homeland," or "water and homeland," depending on the context.

3. The fifth and sixth lines implicitly depict colonialism as an evil because it upsets the natural order of things.

4. The last line may be interpreted as an expression of the poet's disgust with himself, with his own inability to fight against foreign conquest and occupation: to "flutter a makeshift fan" by onself is a selfish and futile gesture in coping with drought.

77. A man has lost his way

Trần Tế Xương

He's standing here alone—a stray, a waif.
He's waiting—will he meet a friend or guide?

The streams and hills are empty of all life.[1]

Some strangers shuffle past, forlorn and wan.

He's seeking men but only sees blue clouds.[2]

He'll tarry for the tide till he grows gray.

Who will show him the path through this vast world?

How long, how long must he stand here and wait?

Note: This poem epitomizes the plight of all Vietnamese like Trần Tế Xương—those who hated foreign rule but lacked either the will or the opportunity to do anything against it and were reduced to wishing for the advent of some charismatic leader.

    1. The third and sixth lines make use of the equivocal meaning of the word *nước*, which in this context can be rendered as either "homeland, country" or "water, streams, rivers, tide." See also note 2 to Poem 76, "Drought."

    2. Since blue clouds symbolize officialdom in traditional Vietnam, this line may imply the poet's disappointment at seeing around him not "men" willing to fight for their country but only opportunists eager to promote their own careers as mandarins under the aegis of the French colonial administration.

78. Best wishes for the New Year

Trần Tế Xương

Hear 'em exchange best wishes at New Year's!

They'll live to be a hundred, grow white hair.

I'll sell 'em betel mortars and get rich—

too old to chew, they all will grind their quids.

Hear 'em! They wish each other lofty rank.

They'll purchase titles and official posts.

This time I'll go and sell 'em parasols:[1]

I'll curse, and cry my wares, and they will buy.

Hear 'em again! They wish each other wealth.

Where will they hoard their bulging millions, though?

This time, the chickens will be money-fed:

they'll peck at silver coins dropped here and there.

They wish each other many sons and heirs:

by fives and sevens children will be born.

More folk and yet more folk will choke the streets:
with babes in arms they'll migrate to the hills.

I'll join well-wishers and convey my wish.
I'll wish all people of the world one thing.
May kings and mandarins, may each and all
learn how to live such lives as men should live.

    1. Parasols were ceremonial umbrellas. As emblems of official power and authority, they were used for kings and mandarins only.

79. The Lake of the Returned Sword

Anonymous

The tower's reflection swims amid the waves.[1]
A little bridge rests on a hillock's slope.
Clear water—of the magic sword, no trace.[2]
Broad path—from Buddha's shrine one relic's left.
For then and now a picture hangs on view.
Things shift and change—a flash, and twilight falls.[3]
The lake's still there to mirror ebb and flow.
When will the waning moon wax full again?

Note: The Lake of the Returned Sword *(Hồ Hoàn-kiếm)*, also known simply as Sword Lake *(Hồ Gươm)*, is in Hanoi. According to legend, it was here that King Lê Thái-tổ (or Lê Lợi) returned to a golden tortoise the magic sword that Heaven had lent him to drive the Ming occupation forces out of the realm in the early part of the fifteenth century.

    1. Near Sword Lake there used to stand a magnificent Buddhist temple, of which only a stupa is left—a fact alluded to in the first and fourth lines.

    2. This poem may have been composed by someone discreetly bemoaning French rule and hoping for the appearance of another Lê Lợi with a magic sword and for the recovery of national independence (a wish hinted at in the last line).

    3. This line seems to lament the sudden loss of the country to the French.

80. Flood

Anonymous

Rains pour shower upon shower, winds blow by gusts—
the rivers and the mountains lie submerged.
Ants, good for nothing, wash away in droves;
driftwood, unused, floats downstream like a raft.
You hear birds peep and cry in lonesome woods;
you see dogs climb and lord it on high beds.[1]
How can you bear to watch the people drown?
O King Hsia Yü, flood tamer, where are you?[2]

Note: This poem has been attributed to either Nguyễn Đình Chiểu (1822–1888) or Nguyễn Xuân Ôn (1825–1889). Rather reminiscent of the former's style of composing verse, it laments (in the third and fourth lines) the failure of the Huế court to resist French conquest and castigates those who collaborate with the enemy for high positions, while their compatriots suffer (fifth and sixth lines). Compare this with Poem 76, "Drought," by Trần Tế Xương, and Poem 104, "Dogs in the loft," by Phan Chu Trinh.

1. A "flood" *(lụt)* is a frequent metaphor in the Vietnamese tradition for some political and social crisis during which unworthy, unscrupulous individuals take advantage of the turbulent situation and rise to the top. As the proverb goes: "When there's a flood, dogs will jump onto the altar." *(Lụt chó nhảy bàn độc.)*

2. Yü was the mythical founder of the Hsia dynasty in ancient China. He succeeded in draining the waters of a great flood that had been afflicting the land.

81. Prison life

Dương Bá Trạc

I've knocked about the world, worn out my legs:
to let me rest, kind Heaven keeps me here.
Where is the homeland? Does it still exist?
What is this place? I stand and sit by turns.
Some three square meters—air enough to breathe.
Four walls around—the moonlight wriggles in.
There's freedom in my little true-red heart.
Put me in chains and shackles—I don't care.

82. On Poulo Condore

Trần Cao Vân

I

Why have you landed on Poulo Condore?
By your jail door, gaze at the vast, vast sea.
A man has yet to pay his manly debt—
a filial son thinks of his living sire.
Letters that cross the sea reveal the heart—
waves roar beneath the sky and wake the soul.
Invoke those kings who built the realm of Việt—
now swear you'll never live without this land.

II

A plan's not yet laid down—the heart still churns.
You've hoarded all your fervor for long years.
If to this isle of bliss you had not come,
how could you know the world has perfect skies?
Let us leave off bemoaning our ordeal—
the Maker in the blue decides it all.
Find here the stuff of heroes and great men:
uncommon plights will form uncommon bonds.

Note: Poulo Condore is a group of islands off the south-eastern coast of Vietnam. There the French colonial authorities maintained a penitentiary notorious for its harsh treatment of political prisoners, whether nationalist or communist.

83. It's mere child's play to die

Trần Cao Vân

It's mere child's play to die—who'd care to try?
To die a patriot's death is Heaven's grace.
I'll have my body crushed and die a man.
I'll let my head fall off, and die upright.

Who dies for justice wins the world's respect.
Who dies to serve his king forever lives.
To die this way will be a sheer delight.
Hey, do you hear? I'm not afraid to die!

Note: Trần Cao Vân composed this poem just before he was guillotined by the French in 1916.

84. The long night
Từ Diễn Đồng

Why does the night drag on and on, pitch-dark?
When ever will it end and day begin?
A baby whimpers, waking from its sleep.
An elder hacks and hawks to nurse his cough.
The light, which warns off burglars, still burns low.
The dog, suspecting thieves, still loudly barks.
Who has awakened in this neighborhood?
Please raise your voice and rouse our scholars up.

85. To a piggy bank
Tôn Thất Diệm

One thing you know is money—not much else.
Your belly's big, your mouth's a thin, mean slit.
You stretch it open, eat, and never stop.
As long as I feed you, you will keep mum.
No hero, have you ever done some deed?
A slave, you hug your riches for dear life.
After so long, I shake you—you sound full.
Shaken and sounding full, you'll get smashed up!

86. Neither fish nor fowl

Nguyễn Hữu Chu

I am one-half Chinese and one-half French:[1]
as neither fish nor fowl, what should I do?
I'd till the soil but don't know how to plow.
I'd hold high office but have flunked from school.
I'd buy and sell but run quite short of cash.
I'd ply some trade but haven't learned a skill.
Well, I'll put up with being such a flop.
This flop's worth more than all of you, rank knaves!

1. One-half Chinese and one-half French: influenced in an ambiguous, contradictory way by both civilizations; uneasily caught between East and West.

87. Prison impromptu

Nguyễn Đình Kiên

We've met in here—we know each other now.
It hurts to ruminate, to voice these thoughts.
The West's great culture? Criminals and thugs.
Children of gods and dragons? Jailbirds all.[1]
They're not our betters—they hold guns in hand.
We're dumb and base—our pockets boast no sou.
The world is whirling—men are sound asleep.
I feel so mad, I'd crumple up the earth.

(1929)

1. The expression "children and grandchildren of dragons and gods" *(con rồng cháu tiên)* comes from a myth that traces the origin of the Vietnamese people to the union between the Serpent Lady (Âu-Cơ), a goddess, and the Vietnamese culture hero, the Water Dragon Lord (Lạc-Long-Quân).

88. Back in prison

Nguyễn Đình Kiên

Light flickers on my shadow and myself.
My thoughts snarl up about this thing or that.
Imprisoned twice or thrice, I shall live long.
Forty to fifty years—I'm still quite young.
My mind roams far and wide—the world's too small.
Struggling with storm and dust, I'll pass my days.
To all our hills and streams I swore an oath—
I wait for cockcrow, pillowed on my lance.[1]

1. Under the Tsin dynasty in China, Liu Kun and Tsu T'i would sleep with their weapons under their heads and wake up at cockcrow to go after the enemy.

89. In a Canton jail

Phan Bội Châu

I

I'm still a man, still free to be a man.
I've run and tired my legs—in jail I rest.
Without a home, I once roamed all four seas—
a prisoner now, I have to face the world.
My outspread arms embrace a statesman's lot.
My open mouth can laugh all hatred off.
While I'm alive, my purpose stays alive—
what matter if I must incur grave risks?

II

It would be fine if I could up and die.
Since I am meant to live, how should I live?
Heaven will not lock up a holy cause.
Has earth no path for gifted men to tread?
Bail out the ocean, plying your smooth tongues!
Cut down the forest, swinging both your arms!

All brothers, persevere, try harder yet—
no monument gets built in just one day.

90. Mourning Nguyễn Thái Học and Nguyễn thị Giang
Phan Bội Châu

I. SHE MOURNS HIM

A bolt of lightning struck out of midair.
I'm choking on my love—what can I say?
Clouds dim amidst the blue—the sky stays dark.
Teardrops are drenched with red—the sea runs blood.
Your golden body they consigned to earth—
my snow-pure heart I'll leave beneath the moon.
In the hereafter we may meet again—
among the shades shall we two someday smile?

II. HIS SOUL REPLIES

As I see you, my darling, I feel shame.
Who made you come and meet with me so soon?
We pledged we'd have each other, first and last;
we swore to live together or to die.
The world of dust keeps changing—weal or woe?
A true-red heart stays firm as stone and steel.
The rainstorm raves and rages—let it storm.
We'll take our grief to Heaven's court of law.

We'll take our grief to Heaven's court of law—
we'll calm the waves of outrage in our hearts.
Your drops of blood still tinge the stream with red—
my hands yet stink of debts unpaid to life.
I swore I'd never live beneath their skies—
this body Mother might have failed to bear.
My darling, don't you feel unhappy so—
our souls stay strong, our spirits still wield power.

Note: As leader of the main nationalist party, the Việt Nam Quốc Dân Đảng, and as organizer of the abortive Yên-báy mutiny, Nguyễn Thái Học was arrested by the French and executed on the guillotine on June 17, 1930, along with his comrades. Nguyễn thị Giang, his lover and fellow revolutionist, would not live without him and committed suicide. See also Poem 131, "The day of mourning at Yên-báy," by Đằng Phương.

91. The alarm clock
Phan Bội Châu

Lest sluggards loaf in bed and oversleep,
it will awaken them by day or night.
Of heaven's time it duly marks twelve hours;
a magic work, it runs with one sole spring.
The bell chimes now and then and folks will rise.
The earth, not stopping for a minute, turns.
Our people are sound sleepers, are they not?
It shrilly rings and not a soul will stir.

92. To a cuckoo
Phan Bội Châu

This nest is none of yours, O cuckoo bird!
Why did you barge in here and call it home?
My wife and I took pains to build our house.
You and your kind, don't sit so brazen there.
I thought you'd spend two days or three with us.
Who knew you'd stay for a whole week or more?
How in the world can such a freak occur?
Unasked, you came—unwanted, you won't leave!

Note: The cuckoo is notorious for its habit of laying eggs in the nests of other birds and letting them hatch its eggs. In this poem it represents the French colonialist who has overstayed his welcome.

93. Human nature

Phan Bội Châu

On the outside, in shape,
people are much alike.
Endowed with human traits,
they form a breed apart.
Fierce tigers and fair swans
are splendid in their way.
Because they lack a soul,
they're known as beasts and birds.
Our nature's Heaven's gift—
we're made humane and wise.
Humane, we love our kind;
and wise, we learn from saints.
We're rich in courage, too—
we don't take fright and quail.
Who has all virtues shows
humanity at its best.

94. Character

Phan Bội Châu

Man's nature shows no shape
till it's informed with heart.
When heart prevails and rules,
it's then called character.
All acts need character
as soldiers need a chief.
If that chief's strong and brave,
the soldiers follow him.
The chief must prove himself
and lead his men to fight.
Who are the foes to fight?

Know them by their true names.
They all indulge the self,
awaken greed and lust:
to eat and dress too well,
to vie in outward show,
to crave for wealth or sex,
to serve your private ends.
The flesh may work much harm—
man's nature may get lost.
That foe, if not put down,
will slay the chief called heart.
If wisdom is your goal,
you must correct your heart.
Who fights and conquers hearts
earns glory as a chief.

95. Rights

Phan Bội Châu

How straight is Heaven's Way!
How just is human law!
Your duties you have done—
don't you deserve some rights?
The mouth must utter words.
The brain must think and judge.
The feet must walk and run.
The hands must push and pull.
The eyes must watch and see.
The ears must hear and learn.
In countries near and far,
people may move about,
write essays, publish books,
plying the pen at will.
To reach their common goals,

they may form groups and meet.
Workers, for mutual help,
form unions and found guilds.
Merchants on land and sea
may freely circulate.
Look at their codes of law—
in all enlightened lands,
clearly defined are rights
a citizen may enjoy.
Where civil rights prevail,
there benefits abound.
More duties you perform,
more rights you must obtain.
It's only fair and square
that interest's paid on loans.
They're there for all to see:
compatriots, know your rights!

96. You eat the figs, so sit beneath the tree

Phan Bội Châu

> You eat the figs, so sit beneath the tree.
> All right, I'll wed him but shan't sleep with him.

Forced by circumstance, I'll feign to be his wife—
I've wedded him, yet hardly sleep with him.
I'll play him out of all his silver coins,
but let nobody kiss my rosy cheeks.
I smile forced smiles while hiding half my face;
I weep in secret, being of two minds.
When my true lover comes and takes his place,
together we'll scoop dry the eastern sea.[1]

Note: Phan Bội Châu wrote this poem implying that as far as Vietnamese
nationalists were concerned, any alliance with the Japanese occupation forces
in French Indochina was no love match but at best a marriage of convenience,

a strictly temporary arrangement while Vietnam waited for independence. The epigraph, a couplet from folk verse, reads in Vietnamese: *Ăn sung ngồi gốc cây sung. / Lấy anh thì lấy nằm chung không nằm.*

1. The two last lines allude to a well-known proverb: "Wife and husband, at one, can scoop dry the eastern sea." (*Thuận vợ thuận chồng tát biển đông cũng cạn.*)

97. Epitaph for my dog

Phan Bội Châu

Men who are quite humane
often lack wits.
Men who boast wits
are often inhumane.
Those who have wits and are humane
one seldom meets.
Who would believe that Ky, this dog,
had both those qualities?
When you all serve one lord,
treat one another as close friends;
never behave like cats and dogs.
That's how you prove humane.
When he you serve is not your lord,
treat him as your own foe,
let no choice morsel lure you on.
That's how you prove your wits.
To have sharp wits and be humane,
to be humane and have sharp wits—
of all those creatures whose brute strength man dreads,
my dog, you were the first
to show both qualities.
Why did you hasten off and die?
O God, O God! Ah, how it hurts!
Listen, you men who are like beasts!
Gallant, he risked his life and fought.

Loyal, he stayed with his own lord.
To talk is easy, but it's hard to act—
a human finds it so, still more a dog.
O brindle dog, you had both qualities,
unlike some men
whose human faces hide
the hearts of beasts.
One aches to think of them—
let me set up a tombstone to my dog.

98. My shadow and I

Phan Bội Châu

It's night—I'm dangling here beneath the sky.
I've asked some questions—Heaven, though, keeps mum.
The moon, the stream—between, there's only I:
to my own shadow let me say some words.
Ah, what a quick-tongued chap my shadow is!   5
At once he opens his big mouth and speaks:

    "Where can you find so true a friend as I?
Sit down, stand up, walk out—I'll follow you.
Yet, for some reason, you still look quite sad,
and so you make me feel unhappy too.   10
Is something rankling there, inside your breast?
Unburden all your thoughts and let me hear."

    "I did want to, but in the dead of night,
I feared a lengthly speech might bore you stiff.
Wasn't it strange that Heaven's wife would choose   15
to drop down here a fellow like this man?
The earth rang with a whine—the race of gods
and dragons overnight got one more son:
a pair of gleaming eyes, perceptive ears,
a handsome body, rather tall and stout;   20
a nice, round head that holds a deep, deep brain;

a beard and brows such as become a man.
Were Europe and America short of space?
I was plunked down in this, Vietnam's midpart.
Why wasn't I born deaf and dumb as well? 25
Why have I always taken burdens on,
trying to kick at heaven with bare feet,
striving to move the hills with naked hands?
Doesn't my tongue get jaded clattering so?
My heartstrings I keep spinning, but what for? 30
And is my body made of stone or steel,
to serve as target for the shots they fire?
My heart and soul, unyielding, firm as rock,
haven't they had enough of dust and storm?
What thoughts or whims keep churning day and night 35
within my core, bewildering my poor brain?
Why persevere at what serves no clear end?
Why stick with it and win not one success?
Is it another's fault, or is it mine?
If I am blameless, then who is to blame?" 40

    My shadow hears me out, then sighs and says:
"From first to last, my friend, it's all your fault.
The world's forked tongues drip venom sweet as mead—
why do you lend a ready ear to lies?
You don't think matters through, you lightly treat 45
a lifetime task as if it were a game.
You take all human hearts to be like yours,
quite unaware that high roads crawl with snakes.
The guileless you suspect—you give your trust
to fiends who spout the Buddha's holy word. 50
Thickheaded, you stay clean in this foul crowd;
insane, you stay awake while others sleep.
But don't you see that glory in these times
means horse and carriage, mansions, real estate?
Eat well, dress warmly—that's the sense of life! 55

Who cares for what takes place outside the home?
About our history who will give a damn?
Of shame and honor they take no account—
why grapple with what's none of your concern?
Yes, under Heaven, you're the champion fool!   60
Invite Miss Moon down here—ask what she thinks
and see if I've told you the truth or not."

    I've heard those words—admonishing myself,
I vow I shan't repeat my old mistakes.
O shadow, tarry here and help me out—   65
stay by my side and be my bosom friend.
The moon's just dipped behind those western heights—
the east will shine again on you and me.

Note: Phan Bội Châu expresses the loneliness and discontent he felt when he lived in Huế as a virtual prisoner of the French, in the years following 1925.

99. Impromptu
Phan Chu Trinh

A windstorm's turned the country upside down.
How could high Heaven weave this noose for us?
Chew over your own duties—bitter tang.
Open your bag of literature—dank mold.
Those scoundrels play and dally fighting fire—
waifs wander, mourning fathers in distress.
Hight hills, vast seas—the land lies broad, immense.
Climb peaks or swim the deep—do all you can.

100. Ode to the candle
Phan Chu Trinh

Work it, knead it—the wax won't fall apart.
Sing of the candle—patient, it persists.
Some inches long, its wick stands straight and true.

How many times its body rolls around!

Its head's on fire to brighten up the dark;

its bosom burns because it cares for light.

Who's left the door ajar? The wind slips in.

For whom does it shed tears all through the night?

101. Breaking rocks on Poulo Condore

Phan Chu Trinh

A man stands tall upon Poulo Condore—

he makes a din that makes the mountains shake.

Hammer to shatter heap on heap of rocks.

Break stone by hand to hundreds of small chips.

To granite turn your body day by day.

Can sun or rainstorm daunt an iron heart?

When they're laid low, those who will save the world

endure and let no trifle bother them.

102. A game of chess

Phan Chu Trinh

Within the palace sits a mangy king.

Elephants and knights stand idly by, won't fight.

Off in the corners lie two duds, the guns.

Along the river slump five sickly pawns.

A pair of baffled nags trot back and forth.

Twin chariots hurry-scurry to and fro.

Who's lost his wits and thrown this game of chess?

Perhaps some god will come and save the day.

Note: The lost game of chess was the failure of Vietnamese leaders to prevent French conquest. In literal terms, chess in this poem is Chinese chess *(cờ tướng)*, which includes the following pieces for each side: a general or king *(tướng)*, two knights or ministers *(sĩ)*, two elephants *(tượng)*, two war chariots *(xe)*, two cannons *(pháo)*, two horses *(ngựa)*, and five plain soldiers or pawns *(tôt)*. On the chessboard, the space between the two sides is called the "river."

103. Opera actors

Phan Chu Trinh

War drums and cymbals clash, offend the ear.

What, is it just you bastards and your clan?

Three senile actors, mugs perked up, slouch there.

Arms folded, famished extras, hang around.

You flounce in flowing robes like Chinamen.

You brandish swagger sticks like Western lords.

Kowtow and scrounge some coins for meat and wine.

You need not know what happens with your host.[1]

Note: This is an attack on the Vietnamese in high or low positions who collaborated with the French—and in particular on Bảo Đại's court at Huê.

    1. A person could hire a theatrical troupe and host a performance. Here, of course, the "host" is the French colonial government.

104. Dogs in the loft

Phan Chu Trinh

For heaven's sake, behold that loft!

The country's flooded—dogs have leapt up there.

In troubled waters, precepts wash away.

By chance, curs strut and lord it overhead.

Bustling and hustling, they lick feet and rumps.

All in a dither, they glance up and down.

After the flood, things will fall back in place;

whipped dogs will scamper, tails between their legs.

Note: Compare this with Poem 80, "Flood."

105. The comedy of the world

Huỳnh Thúc Kháng

The world's aswirl with fun and games galore.
On stage unfolds a farce with many parts.
Loud drums and rattles deafen earthly ears.
Bright flags and banners dazzle Heaven's eyes.
Half scoops of water fight a roaring fire.
Ten elephants yield not one bowl of broth.[1]
Curtains—let each feel his own pocket now:
a hole's burned there—alas, your penny's gone!

Note: After Léon Blum and the Socialists came to power in France in 1936, cosmetic reforms were carried out in French Indochina, and elections were held. Huỳnh Thúc Kháng treated it all as a farce and a fraud.

1. The line is a folk proverb about grand promises made with no intention to keep them. In Vietnamese: *Mười voi không được bát nước xáo.*

106. A farewell song

Huỳnh Thúc Kháng

On high, the moon must wax and wane by turns—
down here, how can we humans shun hard times?
A man will take what happens with due calm—
when in distress, he will confront distress.
Heaven has eyes to watch our road ahead—
now exiled, we shall someday yet come home.
After these years, we all shall still be young.
Here flows the rive Đà, there stands Mount Ấn.[1]
Our land is waiting—we shall deck it out.
Now we must part, but shall join hands again.
That gaffer lost his horse—was it bad luck?[2]
Tomorrow, as the Maker will arrange,
we shall return from all four seas and meet.
Within this world there must be room for us.
The hills may fall, the seas may rise;

the sky may tilt, the earth may heave—

our hearts of stone and iron shall stay true.

The moon that's waning shall wax full again.

Note: At a farewell party given by his friends in Hội-an (Quảng-nam Province) before he was exiled to Poulo Condore, Huỳnh Thúc Kháng recited this poem.

　1. The "river Đà" is the Đà-nẵng River, better known as the Cẩm-lệ. Mount Ân stands between the districts of Quế-sơn and Duy-xuyên in Quảng-nam Province.

　2. According to a Chinese fable, when his horse went astray, a wise old man said, "This may well be a blessing in disguise." Indeed, a few days later, the horse came back, bringing another horse.

107. A ricksha man's impromptu
Phan Trọng Quảng

Born of good parents, you're a filial son.

Alas, your country knows its darkest hour.

The wheels of history stoop your back and pull;

try hard to climb the uphill road ahead.

The wind and dust may tan your soft-skinned face—

no thorns or spikes can pierce your iron will.

The world goes through a play of change and flux—

this human horse may turn a dragon yet.

Note: It was not unusual for anti-French conspirators to work as ricksha men because they wished to move about freely without attracting notice. See also Poem 120, "The ricksha man," by Phan Văn Hy.

108. A sense of history
Nhượng Tống

Three regions—one long strip of hills and streams.

White bone and crimson blood have built Vietnam.

Let Heaven stage the play of flux and change—

on earth our forebears' heritage endures.

We have a land, a people—spurn them not.

Who would survive should struggle, should compete.

Recall the past long gone and feel a jolt:

Champa was once no weakling but a power.[1]

1. Once a powerful kingdom, Champa virtually ceased to exist after 1471, under expansionist pressures from the Vietnamese. See Poem 266 through 269, by Chế Lan Viên.

109. Mourning a hero

Nhượng Tống

Under the foreign yoke, they lived in shame.

He loved his kind—could he just stand and watch?

He threw his pen away and turned to guns—

a man, he would not bear the country's shame.

His body perished, but his soul still shines.

He tried and failed, yet through his crime he served.

His words at parting I remember now.

Over some midnight wine, we smiled and wept.

Note: Nhượng Tống was a close friend of Nguyễn Thái Học, the patriot doomed to pay with his life for the abortive Yên-báy uprising of 1930. See Poem 90, "Mourning Nguyễn Thái Học and Nguyễn thị Giang," by Phan Bội Châu, and Poem 131, "The day of mourning at Yên-báy," by Đằng Phương.

110. The tattered map

Tản Đà

Stand there and have a look at that poor map.

Its streams and hills make sorry butts for jokes.

You know how long it took to draw the map?

Why is it now all tattered and torn up?

Our fathers purchased it, left it to us—

how dare their children make a toy of it?

Oh well, it's no use blaming juveniles.

Let's all do what we must and mend the map.

111. The ship An-Nam

Tản Đà

Four seas, five continents—the world's astir.

Behold our ship, O fellow countrymen!

Her hull has proved its mettle—watertight.

Her whistle sounds the call to streams and hills.

The winds and storms are raging—friends, make haste.

How vast the skies and oceans! Head for sea.

Europe, America—where are their ports?

Now start the engine—let us venture forth.

Note: When the Chinese ruled Vietnam they called it *An-Nam* or "the Pacified South," an appellation which the French colonialists also favored and used.

112. The barber

Tản Đà

A man still lacks a scheme to save the world—

with his short razor he must earn his keep.

Far from the madding throng he hones his blade:

in town, it's shaven many faces smooth.

Note: The humble barber stands for a patriot who is lying low and "honing his blade" as he waits for his chance to rise up against the enemy.

113. Dark night

Tản Đà

A howling wind blows hard from west to east.

Look out—the night is dark, an eerie night.

Creation, minus hands, can still create—

earthlings, endowed with eyes, yet fail to see.

How many people slumber in some dream!

Who is to save our lovely streams and hills?

Let's light a torch and search all through the land:
where must we go to spy a hero's face?

114. The rail and the bullfrog
Tản Đà

Beside the pond, a rail roosts on a bush,
and there's a bullfrog dwelling in the pond.
They share the neighborhood—both often cry:
one cries for grief, the other cries with glee.
The bullfrog croaks, so happy it gets rain—
the rail, though, wails, complaining spring is gone.
Two animals inhabit pond and bush:
they live together, yet feel far apart.

Note: Because the cry of the rail (or *cuốc*) sounds like the word *quốc*
("homeland, nation"), the bird symbolizes the patriot mourning the loss of his
country. The bullfrog is the opposite: it represents a collaborator well pleased
with the benefits he receives from his foreign master. See also Poem 59, "On
hearing the rail cry," by Nguyễn Khuyến.

115. The canary in a cage
Tản Đà

    Canary-bird, who painted you?
You sport a handsome look, you sing sweet songs.
    But who was it that brought you here?
Clear water and white rice—each day you gorge.
    At leisure in your crimson cage,
you hop and skip, you have the grandest time.
    You think you've lucked on your main chance:
your greenwood, bird, do you miss it or not?

(1921)

Note: This poem is an attack on Hoàng Cao Khải, viceroy of Tonkin and notorious collaborator. His family name, Hoàng, can mean "yellow," the color of a canary. See also Poem 63, "The comedian gets a curtain lecture," by Nguyễn Khuyến.

116. To a scarecrow
Tản Đà

Forlorn and lost, who's standing by the field?
On earth have you made friends with any soul?
Beaten by rain and storm, your wood lies bare.
In all four winds your shirt flaps like a flag.
You're pleased with little, don't know how to plow.
You put on airs, won't answer when you're called.
Long since, the world acquired enlightened ways—
after some thousand years, you'll stay the same?

117. The state of the world
Tản Đà

It blows and rains enough to make you sick.
And thinking of the world, you feel damn sad.
Dung stinks in baskets—lasses carry it.
Coins smell like garbage—fellows covet them.
Chinks grope in girlies' pants and paw soft thighs.
Bushmen, amid green woods, climb cassia trees.[1]
What's going on in cities that's great fun?
Some farces—comics don their caps and gowns.

1. Lines 5 and 6 allude pejoratively to foreign men who use their money and power to seduce and debauch Vietnamese women. *Bushmen* refers to coarse, brutish Frenchmen.

118. The troth between the hill and the stream

Tản Đà

The stream and hill once swore their solemn troth—
why has the stream flowed off and not come back?
The hill remembers well the troth they pledged
and stands there waiting, while the stream's away.
And standing tall, the hill just stares and waits,
hoping for months, its spring of tears dried up.
Its handful of frail bones have worn away—
its clouds of hair are capped with frost and snow.
The sun is sinking in the west, while jade
is turning pale and gold is fading out.
The hill, still young, feels lonesome for the stream,
but has the stream forgotten it, the hill?
Though stone wears down and water may dry up,
the troth between the stream and hill endures.
Green hill, do you know this? Gone out to sea,
the stream comes back to its own source as rain.
Yes, stream and hill shall always meet again—
advise the hill, and it won't feel so sad.
Although the stream's away, mulberry groves
are thriving, lush and green—O hill, cheer up!
For hill and stream have pledged eternal troth—
the oath between the two shall never break.

Note: The expression "hills and stream" *(non nước)* means "the country, the homeland, the nation." The poet Nguyễn Khắc Hiếu (whose pen name, Tản Đà, combines a mountain, Tản, and a river, Đà) probably meant "the troth between the hill and the stream" to be a sworn determination of all Vietnamese patriots to work for independence from the French. The hill stands for one who stayed at home, and the stream represents one who had to go far away to accomplish that end.

119. The Fourteenth of July

Anonymous

All flock together, revel, celebrate!
Proceed, French civilization—teach us clods!
Gents gorge and swill and fool around with dames;
children, agog, lick pans and climb greased poles.
For fame and gain they sell their country out;
in dust and dirt they jostle, peddling power.
A stone-blind minstrel, who sees not that farce,
keeps drumming thump-thump-thump and fiddling on.

120. The ricksha man

Phan Văn Hy

The ricksha man does quite a simple job:
he who can hardly walk pulls him who can.
He'll fake the slave for now and bide his time:
he may yet throw the bigwig who sits there.
He fights his way through streets against the cars;
the wind blows dust and smudges up his face.
Both he who pulls and he who's pulled are men:
between the two the difference lies in luck.

Note: This thinly disguised attack on French colonialism almost cost Phan Văn Hy his job and his freedom. Influential friends in Huê saved him. See also Poem 107, "A ricksha man's impromptu," by Phan Trọng Quảng.

121. Zoo cages

Hải Âu Tử

Some rows of cages under those green trees,
and in each cage, a breed of birds or beasts.
King Tiger, surfeited, just sleeps and snores,[1]
but helter-skelter run his hungry deer.

Monkeys, well fed, are up to tricks and pranks,
while parrots, squawking, put on shows or skits.
There is a pack of wolves and jackals, too:
over a batch of bones they fight and feud.

(1932)

1. In 1932 Bảo Đại ("King Tiger") came back from France and assumed
the nominal throne of Annam at Huế, under French tutelage.

122. Our land, our home
Trần Tuấn Khải

Nguyễn Phi Khanh's parting words to his son Nguyễn Trãi

Over the northern pass, dark clouds spread gloom;
under the southern skies, sad winds sigh grief.
Birds cry and tigers roar on every side—
the landscape stirs such outrage in the heart.
The country's soul soaks up each drop of blood—   5
a worn-out man must tread the long, long road.
I look at you, and tears keep pouring down—
my son, mark well the words I'll say to you.
As Heaven has ordained, our Lạc Hồng race[1]
has for millennia gone through ups and downs.   10
We've always owned this southern land, our home:
great men and women have we ever lacked?
Alas, our homeland in a time of flux
let Ming aggressors grab their chance and come.
The flames of war are blazing everywhere—   15
in forests bones heap up; blood flows with streams.
The townsfolk see their roofs and walls collapse;
the countrymen lose children, part from wives.
All means are used to break us, wear us down—
how can they care for us, a different breed?   20
To lose our homeland—woe no words can tell!

I watch our realm and feel torn up inside.
To Heaven I complain yet hold my tongue;
inside, I mourn the sorrow of our race.
Mists on Mount Nùng look like a tower of wrath;[2]   25
the Dragon River roils as if in grief.[3]
My son, it hurts so when I speak of it—
who is to save our children from this plight?
I'm sorry: now I'm just a weak old man—
in my misfortune I'm tied hand and foot.   30
But ought a lowly eel to mind the swamp?[4]
To save our homeland! Shoulder that great task.
Remember our ancestors—in times past,
they often struggled for our country's sake.
China and they fought over this our land—   35
blood stains our independence banner yet.
Lo, two Trưng sisters steered the ship of state[5]
against a storm, frail women that they were.
They killed the foe, avenged a husband's death—
forevermore, their names shall live and shine.   40
Lo, when the realm was threatened, Prince Hưng Đạo[6]
fought savage, mortal battles for our race.
On the Bạch-đằng he crushed Yüan troops—his sword
proclaimed our righteous cause, our country's might.
Read history books—his sword still glows today.   45
Glance at the map—his realm's not vanished yet.
This land's still ours—but, as the herd breaks up,
how will the calves survive? Who'll capture them?[7]
My son, you're of this country, so you must
bear firm in mind two thoughts: our home, our land.   50
A man fights for his purpose in the world—
don't tarnish it, the mirror of Lạc Hồng.
The times bring forth their heroes—that's the truth:
why bother with cheap things like wealth and rank?
Those gallant men and women of the past   55

all put their country's fate above their own.

You're in the prime of youth—let no one, son,

outvie you in devotion to our realm.

You must care for all members of our race—

don't covet wealth and rank or cool such love.   60

Those toadies gorge and feast but swallow shame—

free spirits starve, yet walk with head held high.

Never forget the family honor, son—

to future times leave not a tainted name.

Don't ever imitate that breed of slaves   65

and sell our fathers for a livelihood.

A servant's lot is pain and infamy—

why bear so much and earn the world's sly sneers?

A life so lived is life demeaned, abased—

so why live on and merely crowd the earth?   70

Far better, then, to call it quits and die—

what can one hope for from a dog, a pig?

Besides, you've gone to school, you've read and learned

that humans must think through their every deed:

how can they bring themselves to bow their heads   75

and toil like beasts of burden with no pride?

Such are my inmost thoughts, straight from my heart—

that's all the counsel you'll receive from me.

My son, if you're a human being, then

defer to me and act on my advice.   80

I've suffered so much tragedy in life—

to speak of it is torture to my heart.

Toward the horizon ripples wilted grass—

I sorrow as I gaze on our old realm.

Etch deep my words of counsel in your bones: 85

no peril should deter you from your vow.

Unsheathe your sword—to Heaven swear your oath:

with blood you shall acquit your debt on earth.

You shall stand firm and keep a valiant heart—

true men will make their country their own home.   90

They'll merge themselves with all their streams and hills:

stone tablets and bronze statues they shall win.

Later, once you have slaughtered all our foes

and wiped your sword quite clean of blood's foul stench,

after you've done the heaven-shaking deed,   95

your land, your home shall have their finest day.

Your double duty will you bear in mind?

Do see to it that both ends shall be served.

Though I may leave my bones in alien soil,

my soul won't mourn when looking back this way.   100

Remember these two words: our land, our home.

Note: Nguyễn Phi Khanh (1336–1408) served Hồ Quý Ly in a high post and
shared his fate when Hồ was toppled by the Ming invaders and taken as a
prisoner to China in 1407. Legend has it that his son Nguyễn Trãi (1380–1442)
wanted to accompany him into exile, but Phi Khanh told him to stay home and
work for national liberation. Nguyễn Trãi was destined to become Lê Lợi's
strategist and the architect of their ultimate victory over the Chinese in 1428.

1. One of several traditional names for the Vietnamese people, "Lạc Hồng"
refers to their mythological origins. The Water (Lạc) Dragon Lord (Lạc-Long-
Quân), a descendant of dragons, wedded a goddess named the Serpent Lady
(Âu-Cơ), who gave birth to one hundred eggs. From them hatched one hundred
boys: fifty followed their father to the seacoast, and fifty went with their mother
to the mountains. The eldest son became King Hùng I, founder of the Hồng
Bàng dynasty and ruler of Văn Lang, the legendary cradle of the Vietnamese
nation.

2. Mount Nùng: the best known of the four hills around West Lake in
Hanoi.

3. The Dragon River (Red River) flows through the City of the Soaring
Dragon (Thăng-Long), which was the old name for Hanoi.

4. See line 1148 in *The Tale of Kiều*: "How can an eel mind muddying its
head?" *(Thân lươn bao quản lấm đầu?)* The line has acquired proverbial
status and means that a poor, helpless person may have to endure humiliation
and indignity to save him- or herself and survive.

5. The Trưng sisters: see Poem 6, "Homage to the Trưng queens."

6. Prince Hưng Đạo was General Trần Quốc Tuấn (1232–1300), who
engineered two victories over the Mongols in 1285 and 1288.

7. This refers to a proverb: "Removed from the herd, the calves perish."
(Sảy đàn tan nghé.)

123. Opium

Thê Lữ

Dark smokes ascend, dark smokes ascend—
drunk eyes alight upon the dim oil lamp.

All mists and clouds—the world of Nil?
The ice-cold moon is lurking somewhere near.

I'm lying here, but where am I,
lost in indifference, clasped by loveless arms?

Around me, intimates and friends
I seem to see, but are they really there?

All cares and griefs have left the heart—
the body's fled, is floating, floating free.

The mind sinks low, the soul soars high—
I glimpse a thousand peach-red gowns of nymphs.

Dark smokes rise up, dark smokes rise up—
the dream blends gray and scarlet hues in fumes.

The air is drenched with fragrant scents—
look, myriad shapes and forms, entranced, bewitched!

A ruby hall where glitters gold,
where fairy maids appear and disappear.

I float and drift, now near, now far—
jade sings ten thousand melodies, unheard.

In silence, pearls drop one by one
in a clear lake, pristine beside the steps.

Two nymphs come sliding down to lie—
two nymphs stand there with incense, on both sides.

Dark smokes ascend, dark smokes ascend—
the boat is bobbing: where're Peach Blossom Springs?[1]

1. Peach Blossom Springs: wonderland, paradise on earth. A prose story
written by the Chinese recluse-poet T'ao Ch'ien (365–427) tells of a fisherman
from Wu-ling who lost his way and wandered with his boat into a Shangri-la
through a crack in the side of a hill, near where peach trees were in full
bloom. After he returned to the world and reported his discovery, no one was
able to find that blissful realm again.

124. Far away

Vũ Hoàng Chương

Anchors aweigh! O boat, please let the waves
push your frail hull and drive us east or west.
Far off from land, between the sky and sea
our bitter loneliness may slowly ebb.

We here are five or seven, all lost souls
our fatherland rejects, our race disowns.
Why take our bearings on the boundless sea?
Go with the wind, O boat, and drift away.

We've wrongly picked the age in which to live—
we're men forlorn, bewildered, steeped in gloom.
A puffed-up world will bide no simple soul—
O boat, stop at some humble port of call.

The wine has taken—let's await dark night.
We'll hoist the sails as we all cry heave-ho!
The wind has risen, wafting in the dusk.
O boat, submit and yield—go with the wind.

125. Bread

Huỳnh Phú Sổ

Does our own soil produce the bread they sell?
We hear them hawk it, and feel hurt inside.
Each loaf or crumblet reeks its foreign smell—
rice in the bowl tastes of our fathers' blood.
New culture everywhere flaunts empty crusts—
from deep within our entrails tears well up.
Recall what happened scores of years ago:
so many sold their homeland just for bread.

Note: Huỳnh Phú Sổ, a nationalist, was the charismatic leader of the Hòa Hảo
Buddhist sect in southern Vietnam. In 1947 he disappeared in mysterious
circumstances, reportedly killed by the Communists.

126. They starved, they starved ...

Bàng Bá Lân

Remember that third month, the year Ất-dậu.
The Lạc Hồng race endured its direst woe:[1]
tottering specters roamed the roads and streets,
then dropped from hunger, not to rise again.
They starved from Bắc-giang to Hà-nội;   5
they starved from Thái-bình to Gia-lâm ...

Along the highways, famished corpses moaned,
curled up in sun-drenched filth and dust.
Amid those rags the hollow eyes alone
still harbored sparks of soul soon to be quenched.   10
Gaunt arms would jerk and wave and grope around
as if to grasp at what you could not see.
Beneath the thatch of tousled, matted hair,
a layer of ashen skin encased the skulls.
Teeth jutted grinning, as out of death's-heads,   15
and deeply scored the wasted, sunken cheeks.
No telling man from woman, young from old—
all looked the same, as corpses look the same,
some skin still clinging to the skeletons,
reeking of death, though not quite dead, as yet.   20
It was the strangest smell, both faint and rank,
that turned the stomach, caused the flesh to creep.
(The stench persisted and would haunt the nose
and spoil the appetite for many months.)
Those walking corpses, one by one, would slump   25
and sprawl in twisted shapes with staring eyes,
and pupils where remained a hint of tears,
with mouths awry as if half moaning yet.
Some bodies, dead for days, would lie there still,
while flies from all the world would flock to mourn.   30
Then, by the road, a casual hoe would dig
the shallow graves to bury them in haste.

They starved from Bắc-giang to Hà-nội;
they starved from Thái-bình to Gia-lâm ...

Dispersed along the road, those secret tombs   35
were marked by riotous weeds and swarming flies.
Those corpses not interred quite deep enough
exhaled a fetid odor to the skies.
A heavy rainfall drenched their flesh and bones,
leaving uncovered remnants strewn about.   40

And day by day, toward cities, toward Hà-nội
more corpses, yet more corpses dragged themselves,
trailing their strand of flies, the flood of smells,
then crumpled up along some street or lane.
When gingerly at dawn you cracked your door,   45
you'd check if there were someone dead outside.
Each morning oxcarts, creaking on their wheels,
would go around and pick the corpses up.
The heaps of bodies seemed like garbage dumps,
and out of each would stick the bone-dry feet,   50
the shrunken, scrawny arms, all black and blue,
aquiver as if fumbling in the air
or waving for your notice, for your help.
You'd hear an indrawn breath still throb with life,
a body stir or gasp ... and teary eyes   55
watched humans bury humans not quite dead.
Four suburbs opened rows and rows of graves,
which corpses in unbroken ranks would fill,
and clouds of flies would darken all the land.
They died and died—two million people died.   60

They all were sons and daughters of Việt soil
who labored hard in rice or manioc fields.
Rice grew so lush, well watered by their sweat—
we all lived off the sweat our peasants shed.
That year, when both the French and Japs held sway,   65

both vied in robbing us of all the rice.
Rice went, then yam, cassava, maize, banana roots ...
Nothing to gnaw on till the harvest came:
when hunger burned our stomachs, we would chew
areca spathe or duckweed, swallow straw.   70

They starved from Bắc-giang to Hà-nội;
they starved from Thái-bình to Gia-lâm ...

They left their land and mutely dragged their heels
all through the country, wandering back and forth.
Whole families prowled together, since they hoped   75
they somehow could subsist, outlast those days,
while waiting for the rice ears to get ripe:
another month, they'd go back home and live.
Alas, it was an idle dream! They left,
believing someday they could all return—   80
they never made it, though, as one by one
they slumped along back streets, near market stalls.

Meanwhile, along those selfsame busy roads,
convoys of trucks would carry golden rice,
the grain of peasants who were starving then,   85
the grain colonialists had robbed them of.
Part of that paddy would be spilled and lost,
and in the warehouse, part of it would spoil.
Ah, woe of woes, what men had never borne,
what through all time had never come to pass!   90
Two million people left the land they loved,
met with such wretched deaths along the way,
while on their native soil, across vast fields,
luxuriant rice was coming into ear
to yield a bumper crop of golden grains,   95
whose scent should augur plenty, warmth, good life.
But those who left could not come back, alas—
no one was left to reap ripe, drooping ears.

That time of darkness let's remember well.

Can we forget those alien robbers's crime? 100

Can we forget they did the foulest deed?

Can we forget two million starved and died?

Remember that third month, the year Ất-dậu.

The Lạc Hồng race endured its direst woe

as tottering corpses roamed the roads and streets, 105

then dropped from hunger, not to rise again.

They starved from Bắc-giang to Hà-nội;

they starved from Thái-bình to Gia-lâm . . .

Note: The famine of 1945 (known in the Chinese calendar as the year Ất-dậu) killed millions of peasants in northern Vietnam.

1. Lạc Hồng: see note 2 to Poem 122, "Our land, our home," by Trần Tuấn Khải.

127. Revolutionary youth

Hồ Văn Hảo

O months and years, why hurry so? Slow down
and linger now and then on fragrant paths.
Let youths take time and pluck the flower of life,
oblivious still to wrinkles and gray hair.

Here sunshine's warm and bright, here blow cool winds;
here colors glow, here scents intoxicate.
Pour spring's sweet brew and let it overflow,
so youth at will may raise the cup and taste.

Fainthearted youth belongs to yesteryear—
all those lost generations why recall?
Today a symphony of joy and zeal
is rising up from millions of new hearts.

The hush of every classroom harbors this:
young minds are nursing dreams of gallant deeds.

And who are they, now marching on the road,
singing the victory hymn of fighting men?

Chests swell and still can't hold that breath of life.
Arms flex their brawn, each muscle hard and firm.
The young look toward tomorrow's world ahead,
and to a fresh, strong beat their hearts all throb.

(1944)

128. A deathless autumn
Ái Lan

Blood flowed on Vietnam's soil as we rose up:
a deathless autumn under southern skies.
We broke the bonds and chains of eighty years:
Vietnam was making history there and then.

My memory will forever hold the scene:
men surging forward like the ocean's waves,
storming like waters through a broken dike;
and flags, our emblems, darkening the earth.

We shouted mottoes that proclaimed high deeds;
like charging cavalry we sallied forth.
The air resounded with an awesome cry:
the faith of millions who would be set free.

All lungs, wide open, take in heaven's breath.
All arms stretch out, embracing freedom's hour.
Oh, wild and drunk, and shouting, we all swore:
we'd write this page of history with our blood.

That autumn shall defy decay and death.
An autumn which all Asian lands could claim;
an autumn that sent echoes round the earth:
that autumn shall live on, shall never die.

(1947)

Note: In September 1945, as the French tried to reconquer southern Vietnam with the help or connivance of British troops (which had come ostensibly to disarm the Japanese), fighting broke out in Saigon and soon spread to other parts of the country: that was the start of the First Indochina War.

129. Wrecking the statue of Paul Bert

Thiên Thê

Paul Bert stands tall—a statue in the park.
Look at his mug: it makes you sick, his smirk.
Freedom? Equality? A gang of rogues.
Fraternity? The brotherhood of thieves.
They've sucked our blood—an open secret now.
They've robbed and murdered—no more cover-up.
These days colonialists are doomed to go—
how could they dodge and miss our hammers' blows?

(1945)

Note: Paul Bert (1838–1886): the French "resident general" for Annam (central Vietnam) and Tonkin (northern Vietnam) in 1886.

130. Independence Day

Phan Trọng Bình

For eighty years we lived the fate of beasts,
with burdens weighing down our heads, our necks.
Our people now have broken all the yokes
to stand up straight as humans on this earth.

The banner glows—red blood, the gold of flowers:
unfurled, it proudly flies across our land.
As citizens, we own our country now.
The nation has her masters: we are they.

Vietnam! Vietnam! O glorious fatherland!
The name's agleam with crimson and with gold.

The latest map depicting our whole world
now shows, in splendor, new and stately lines.

(1945)

Note: In 1945, the Việt-Minh (controlled by the Communists) seized power in
Hanoi and proclaimed national independence on September 2.

131. The day of mourning at Yên-báy

Đằng Phương

To the memory of those heroes
who lost their lives in the Yên-báy revolt

"Long live Vietnam! Long live Vietnam!"
In that hushed dawn enshrouded in chill fog,
thirteen loud shouts from thirteen valiant men
would stir awake all people on Việt soil.

A wind of wrath, a storm of roars and moans—   5
white mists from heaven hung a mourning pall.
The light of dawn, a glimmer faint and wan,
diffused its gloomy silence on Yên-báy.
Between the rows of bayonets, thirteen
walked slowly up to Honor's stand of death.   10
Amid the crowd of heads bowed low in grief,
some elders, silver-haired and drenched in tears,
let out a cry, "O son!," then swooned and slumped.
A hint of sudden sorrow flashed through eyes
that always had made light of pain and hurt,   15
the eyes of heroes soon to leave this world.
A second later, though, the radiant look
appeared again on faces that breathed strength.
Those who would for their country give their lives
must disavow their love of kith and kin.   20
Alas, to serve their homeland, all those men
had trampled on so many cherished hearts.

But now the sacred moment had arrived—
they cast a farewell glance at hills and streams,
then coldly, one by one, strode up the steps,   25
and with defiance loosed the gallant cry.
"Long live Vietnam!" The severed head fell off.
Another man stepped forth. "Long live Vietnam!"
and Death respectfully carved in stone the names
of those who for their land laid down their lives.   30
After Đức Chính, now came Thái Học's own turn.
He bowed before the bodies of his friends,
then with a smile looked up. He watched the throng
of spectators on hand, then took his leave
of comrades, of all those who shared his dream.   35
The cry again resounded through the air.
At once he was pushed forward. Guillotine,
poised bolt upright, saluting, dropped her blade—
his head fell off as red blood splattered round;
he was no more, the champion of Vietnam.   40
The Frenchmen traded glances as if pleased
they had shrugged off all worries in the world,
and sighing with relief, they rubbed their hands.
Lost in the crowd of men with tear-filled eyes,
suppressing all the grief which rent her heart,   45
Thị Giang stood dazed beside Hữu Cảnh. The wind
of fury swore an oath to martyrs' souls,
and all across the tortured land of Việt
it carried echoes of those awesome shouts
from men who died so their own race might live.   50

"Long live Vietnam! Long live Vietnam!"
Dissolving in the wind which shrieked and wailed,
thirteen loud shouts from thirteen valiant men
would stir awake all people on Việt soil.

Their bodies came to nothing in those woods—   55
their battle cry still echoes hereabout.

Fifteen long years now since that day of woe,

the race of gods and dragons has stood up[1]

to chase those plunderers from its hills and streams.

Red blood has bathed Việt soil these past two years,   60

yet fighters with one heart and mind still fight,

swearing to struggle till the land of Việt

is free and clear again of foreign rule.

The blood that spurted forth beneath gray skies,

one day at dawn fifteen long years ago,   65

did paint a scene those heroes pledged to paint.

They hoped to lift the darkness from their land—

forevermore, all people of Vietnam

shall in their hearts etch deep that fateful day,

alas, the day of mourning at Yên-báy.   70

"Long live Vietnam! Long live Vietnam!"

Ripping the veil of mist, the pall of hush,

thirteen loud shouts from thirteen valiant men

did stir awake all people on Việt soil.

Note: Read the note to Poem 90, "Mourning Nguyễn Thái Học and Nguyễn thị Giang," by Phan Bội Châu.

    1. The race of gods and dragons: see note 1 to Poem 122, "Our land, our home," by Trần Tuấn Khải.

132. The hero of our times

Kiên Giang

We're twenty, young—our hearts are twenty, young:

we're grain in flower, heaven at the dawn.

Stars glimmer in our eyes—the will to live

is shining through our hair, aglow with youth.

Our slums and alleys, where thick shadows lie,

look bright to us, and we still hold them dear.

A splendid body is no splendid thing
if it lacks spirit, has no soul, no heart—
it's just a bag of rice, a rack for coats;
then life can't soar or rise above the mire.

The hero need not ply a sword or gun
and build the world on blood, on dead men's bones.
Create out of your heart, your brain, your guts—
a world of grace and splendor will arise.

The flesh will shrivel, muscles will decay,
but age can triumph over callow youth.
Let's take the road and sing our hymn to life,
and our proud song will even shake the sun.

The hero of our times: a Vietnamese
who'll strive and fight not with his brawn alone,
but with his brain, with all his heart and soul.
O Vietnamese, be heroes of our times!

(1956)

133. Verses for the end of an era
T. P.

> *Bidding farewell to the French expeditionary corps*
> *and commemorating Vietnam's hundred-year ordeal*

Over a new horizon glows the dawn—
the flames of war have sputtered out.
This afternoon,
some men are going home.
Deep down, what are they feeling? Joy or pain?   5
This afternoon,
the bugle chokes as it blares forth—
its brazen voice stirs up the hearts

of soldiers far away from home.

This afternoon,   10

their cemetery boasts a squad of their best troops.

With drooping flags and guns at rest,

they stand in silence, bow their heads.

They stifle sobs as they take leave

of all their dead,   15

those who laid down their lives

on alien soil, in distant climes.

Their flesh and bones have crumbled into dust,

their souls bemoan defeat—

forever they will nurse their grief,   20

within the world of shades.

Men of the expeditionary corps!

This afternoon,

all board your warship, please,

and steam back home.   25

The warship whistles now!

The warship whistles now!

The waves are churning now at Hàm-tử Port.[1]

All souls are hovering now on the Bạch-đằng.[2]

You'll leave here, finding your way home.   30

That day, you came unasked—

today, you'll leave unmissed.

One thousand nine hundred and fifty-six—

one thousand eight hundred and sixty-two.

As I count on my fingers, what a jolt!   35

The nightmare lasted for a hundred years.

The day you came,

your cannons shot Đà-nẵng to bits—

to ashes turned a gallant man, Đinh Lý.

To save Gia-định, Duy Ninh   40

would sacrifice himself—
hugging the kingdom's flag,
he died when caught amidst the siege.

He swallowed shame and grief,
mixing his poison, Phan Thanh Giản,   45
because the conquerors would have
him cut a parcel off this land.
And in Thăng-long, blood soaked the earth:[3]
the fortress fell—Hoàng Diệu collapsed
on corpses littering the ground.   50
Alas, blood flowed and bones heaped high—
you landed in this country dealing death.
With swords and guns in hand,
you'd strut and swagger everywhere.
You made arrests.   55
You stabbed.
You crushed.
You killed.

You banished people to Bà-rá, Côn-nôn.
You tortured people at Sơn-la, Lao-bảo.   60
You robbed us of our rice, our cloth.
You snatched the silver, grabbed the gold.
You chopped off old men's heads,
hung them on view at butchers' shops.
You slit up young men's livers for their bile   65
to drink it on the battlefield.
You pummeled babies, smashed their brains.
You slaughtered pregnant women, too,
and fed them to red coals.
Mothers and children had to part,   70
husbands and wives went separate ways.
The trees lost all their leaves,
the houses turned to empty shells.

So many sank into the ocean depths,
so many washed up on the river shore,   75
so many fell among the hills,
so many perished in the wilds. . . .

Here was Cà-mau, there was the China Gate—
alas, my fatherland, Vietnam,
you grasped and squeezed in your foul hands.   80
In that old realm of mine reigned peace and joy,
with fragrant jackfruits, honeyed pomelos.
Rice flourished on the land,
potatoes liked the soil.
Why did you feel no love?   85
Instead, you maimed and killed.
Gritting our teeth, we all bore our ordeal.
Stroking your beards, you all lived off our toil.
You wished to split us, South from North,
divide the rich and poor.   90
All those above served you as slaves,
all those below served you as beasts.
You wrecked this country, turned it upside down,
roused enmity, dared homicide.
You took a man and made a wretch in rags;   95
you threw his sons in jail.
And you produced those "high-class" gents
who'd sneer at all our "dumb, malodorous clods."
Yes, treated like dumb clods, they played dumb clods,
and all through life their children played dumb beasts.   100

But that's enough.
After so many years of war,
we've understood each other well.
What's cruel and unrighteous goes against
the people's wish and Heaven's will.   105

No tempered steel, no battle-seasoned troops
can overwhelm the human heart.

It's right and proper that you're steaming home.
Go now—the world will all think well of you.
What rankled me,   110
what I despised
I shall forgive—let bygones be bygones
now that you board your homebound ship.
Forever I'll admire
la Belle France,   **115**
Paris, the City of Lights,
where civilization shines,
the Côte d'Azur's attractive crowds and sights,
Marseilles, a jewel of your land ...
The spirit of your streams and hills   120
has bred your heroes, your great souls,
such patriots as Joffre and Joan of Arc.
I still recall that day in '89
when you rose up and struck the Bastille down.
You liberated your own land   125
and let your people live
under the Fourth Republic as proud men.
You laughed and cheered,
you sang and danced—
and I, a foreigner far away,   130
rejoiced with you on your all-glorious day.

Back in your distant France,
never shall you forget
the roads and rivers here,
the names of places in Vietnam: 135
Yên-thê where streamlets roiled with wrath,
Thái-nguyên, whose angry earth upheaved,

Tháp-mười, whose waters raged below,

U-minh still seething after many storms . . .

My country is Vietnam.   140

Deep streams, vast fields;

lush fruits, bright flowers.

Hà-nội, the capital

where wars were fought and won.

Sài-gòn, the market town   145

aglow with talents, with keen minds.

Phú-xuân, the mirror for all patriots,

for those who love and want to serve their land.

My country is Vietnam.

The old and young,   150

women and men—

we all would sooner die

than bow to foreign rule.

Let them beware,

all those who'd covet and invade this land: 155

"Come here and perish here."

My country is Vietnam.

Mulberry groves may turn to seas,

but we won't change our minds and hearts.

You may divide this land in two,   160

so in each half we mourn the other half.

You may tear out our hearts, our guts,

so friends and lovers pull away.

We'll reunite tomorrow, mark my words:

both riverbanks will then be joined again.   165

The hour has come

when you and I must part.

Leaving Vietnam, you'll feel both grief and joy.

Back home, your wives and children wait and wait,

but out of sight, fond feelings may well fade.   170
The warship's whistled once!
The warship's whistled twice!
Let's all shake hands—when you're back home
after a peaceful journey on the seas,
recall this day,   175
and please keep telling folks
not to come here again
and hurt your fellowmen.

The sun is sinking toward the west.
The wind is rising on the sea.   180
This farewell moment ends
the history of a hundred years.
Your ship is leaving my Vietnam—
now let her stay the course, head straight for home.
Don't have her stop at some North African port—   185
she'll never make it there through heavy seas.
O ship, don't go and sow the wind—
head straight toward France
and let all people sing for joy.

The warship's whistled twice!   190
The warship's whistled thrice!
Go home and *bon voyage*!
Adieu!

(Trà-vinh, April 17, 1956)

1. Hàm-tử Port, in present-day Khoái-châu, Hải-hưng Province, was the scene of a Vietnamese victory over the Mongol general Sogetu (Toa Đô, in Vietnamese) in 1285.

2. Bạch-đằng: See Poem 2, "The Bạch-đằng River," by King Trần Minh-tông.

3. Thăng-long: the "Soaring Dragon," the old name for the capital Hanoi.

134. A woman writes to her daughter who's studying overseas

Trinh Tiên

I carry that sad homeland in my soul.

On many nights I huddle here, head bowed.

Under strange skies I dream the green of grass—

when will the motherland see spring bloom forth?

—Thanh Nhung, "The sad homeland," *Phổ Thông*, no. 142, Jan. 15, 1965

Your letter crossed the ocean, bringing thoughts

to my own mind, already filled with thoughts.

Yes, fiends and demons have unleashed their storms

upon our land where fogs have gathered thick.

But war has forged the spirit in its fires—   5

the blood of sacrifice has limned in red

the glorious pages of our history book.

As bullets burst, the rivers still flow on;

while cannons roar, the mountains stand unmoved.

Gold leaves fall down and feed the motherland;   10

young buds renew the flower of our breed.

Thousands of bodies slump—our race survives.

"It's spring! It's spring!" proclaims the gay refrain.

These deaths have sown the very seed of life,

and life will breathe, inspired by death itself.   15

The mother, killed, lies there inanimate—

the baby's mouth sucks all the milk it can.

"Brave daughter!" smile our country's hills and streams.

"Undaunted grandson!" beam our fathers' woods.

If winter's waves have failed to sink the boat,   20

why brood on ruin and decay in spring?

Give love and care to your poor motherland.

Eschewing luxury, live a quiet life.

Don't let those Western snows freeze up your youth.

Over our country may these Eastern winds   25

carry and spread the beauty you'll create.

At home, your mother's like your motherland:
skinny and gaunt, I nurse my private thoughts,
quite out of place amid the tinseled world.
My soul is drenched with all that blood, those tears.   30
Consumed by care, my body wastes away.
But like our land, I boast eternal spring:
a mother's spring, her children's will to life.
I pray to Buddha, thus assuaging grief
and shame, not begging him for pots of gold.   35

Our roof of tile is cracked—cold rain floods through.
Our walls are tilting—winds blow in their chill.
And yet I deem my children blessed with luck:
so many paupers need a roof of thatch.
We daily feed on luffa broth, dried shrimp,   40
cabbage, and sesame salt—it's meager fare.
And yet I think my children overfed:
so many starve who roam the roads and streets.

You know, it's quirky, Heaven's game of chess.
Each time they build one splendid mansion up,   45
a hundred thatch-roofed hovels get burned down.
How can men live when fiends and demons shriek?
From Siam or America ships fetch rice—
our plowmen all have thrown away their plows.
Blanched rice tastes so insipid, lacking bran—   50
for crops of corpses, bombs and shells are sown.
The dailies feature ads in gorgeous frames:
those Swiss-cheese legs, curves like American hills,
Korean breasts, unclad, like snow-white pears;
lascivious music, dubbed soul-stirring sound . . .   55
Beside such pages, in fine print some lines—
death notices: "A twenty-year-old man
repaid the fatherland with his own life."
You say you're dreaming of the green of grass?
O daughter, grass is busy cloaking graves!   60

Against the swirling current I must swim—
sometime, I just can't lift my two thin arms
while struggling day by day for food and clothes.
I pray that Buddha grant me this one wish:
may he fill all my children's bowls with rice.   65
I tread the path of life, embrace His Law,
keeping my soul unstained by greed's foul slime.
On poetry's canvas of brocade, my heart
embroiders all my love for our poor land,
and over it I sprinkle beauty's scent.   70

My letter can't spell out my somber thoughts . . .
But this is spring—the world hails golden light.
Your mother sends you love, the sun of spring,
and may it thaw your spirit's frost and snow.

(Spring 1967)

4. After the Russian Revolution

135. Contrasts
Đặng Thái Thuyên

They gulp jambon, they gobble down pâté.
Your mouths just water—empty are your hands.
You get some rice for lunch—for supper none;
no wall in back, no curtain in the front.
All through the night the children bathe in tears;
from dawn to dark the fathers swim in sweat.
Unjust, unequal—that's their social scheme.
With hammers and with sickles, rise, oh friends!

(Siam, 1926)

136. International solidarity
Phan Trọng Bình

We've come from all four corners of the earth—
all slaves are brothers, gathered in one home.
Our skins are yellow, white, or black—all glow
with reddish hues beneath the crimson flag.
Of different races, we have hearts that seethe
and hate imperialists, our common foe.
Each fighter here speaks his or her own tongue—
the Internationale's our common voice.
We're in a common plight, and so we share
a common purpose, strive for common goals.
As fellow fighters, we are comrades all—
we feel so close, though continents apart.
We're meeting here for all too brief a time—
our faith and friendship will forever last.

137. Paradise and hell

Võ Liêm Sơn

I don't love paradise
nor do I care for hell.

No one's come down from paradise
to tell me what is joy or bliss;
neither has anyone come up from hell
to tell me what is grief or woe.
I have a body, am an animal—
I am a human beast with lusts.
Food, shelter, clothes, and play—all those four needs
I somehow must fulfill.
I'm dwelling on this earth—
I must consume enough to be content.
Why should I hear all that mind-numbing rot
from those who'll grab the lion's share,
robbing the ones who have dozed off?
Just think it over, friends.
Since time began, mankind from east to west
has won or lost, has waxed or waned,
smearing all history books with blood—
and yet it's never solved
the problem of a livelihood.
Up to the present, men still die
from hunger and sheer want,
from strife and war,
from servitude,
from work and toil.
The dead have solved their problems—but the quick
mix rice with teardrops and still starve.
Where's hell? It's hell right here—
who'll gainsay me and claim it's not?
But nowadays,
as life's become so harsh,

the problem of a livelihood
must needs be solved.
They're rising, winds and tides of change:
class struggle's raging now.
That god called Science reigns supreme—
the truth of human life is clear as day.
The wheel of history must roll on.
A future world is taking shape—
the cornerstone has now been laid
to build a real, a genuine paradise.

138. Orphans

Tố Hữu

A baby bird, with drooping wings,
goes looking for its nest, forlorn,
around the silent, lonesome woods,
all wet and dripping with the rain.

The birdie sadly cheeps and cheeps;
and moved, the leaves shed tears on tears.
O Heaven, it's so sad it hurts.
O birdie, where will you go home?

The wind whips past—rain drops and drops
upon the chilly forest trail.
Where will you, little bird, go home
and dry your withered body out?

Come to my hands and warm yourself
so that your frozen heart will thaw.
Get out of where the wind goes mad
beneath a sky all dark with clouds.

The baby bird without a nest,
the orphan child without a home:

both wretches suffer pain and grief,
both strays and waifs roam here and there.

Some day, their wings will fall in shreds—
they'll slump beside the road and die.
All passers-by, with cold, blank eyes,
will cast a glance and say, "So what?"

(Huê, October 1937)

139. Since then

Tô Hữu

Since then, inside me, summer has blazed up—
the sun of truth has shone throughout my heart.
My soul's a garden full of leaves and flowers,
rich in all scents, alive with all birds' songs.

I've linked what stirs my breast to everyman
so that my love may spread, go everywhere,
so that my soul and all those suffering souls
grow close and motivate each other's life.

I've now become the son of many homes,
the friend of many lives impaired and doomed,
the brother of all little boys and girls
who roam as strays and waifs, need food and clothes.

140. The song on the River of Perfumes

Tô Hữu

"On the River of Perfumes
I let go of my pole.
The sky is clear,
the stream is clear.

I let go of my pole
on the River of Perfumes.

The moon will rise
to reach her highest point,
then she will set.
A boatmaid, I must hug my boat,
and downstream drifts my life.

My boat is torn to shreds,
and I still live alone, unwed.
I drift aboard an empty boat—
when ever could I leave
the stream of foul desire
and reach some haven back on shore?
O God, I don't know when
my body will be used
and shamed no more.
O love, such faithless love!
My boat is torn to shreds—
could it still be made whole again?"

Why not? Young woman on the riverboat!
Tomorrow, inside out you'll smell
as fragrant as a jasmine flower.
You'll be as limpid as a morning brook.
Tomorrow, fresh and strong, a wind will rise
and take you to a garden of spring flowers.
Tomorrow, clean and pure again,
you'll quit this wandering life of woe.
Tomorrow, all this dirt and filth
will vanish like tonight's dark clouds.
Young woman, life still lies ahead—
open your heart and hail a dawn to break

over the River of Perfumes.

(August 1938)

141. Three sounds

Tô Hữu

Three sounds sum up the sense of life.
The motor grumbles on and on.
The bell in church serenely chimes.
The prison gong will shout and clang.
A voice is heard within each sound;
a speech is heard within its voice.

The motor orders: "Work and sweat,
or let your eyes pour bitter tears.
Work all your fingers to the bone—
that's what you'll do throughout your life.
Keep working—work, then work some more,
and don't you take a moment off."

The bell will coax with soothing words:
"My child, accept your wretched lot
and gain salvation for your soul,
since fortitude means paradise.
Hatred is hell—just laugh things off
and let the wind blow all away."

The gong will utter threats: "Sit still!
You must bend low your head and bow ...
Here are jail doors and prison walls;
here are our truncheons and our guns.
Don't ask for life or you shall die!"

The prison gong will shout and clang.
The motor grumbles on and on.
The bell in church serenely chimes.
Three sounds sum up the sense of life.

(Qui-nhơn Prison, August 1941)

142. A cradlesong

Tô Hữu

A honey-making bee loves flowers.
Fish swim, love water; birds sing songs, love air.
People, O child, if they're to live,
must love their comrades, love their friends.

One star does not light up the night.
One stalk of rice won't yield a crop of gold.
One person's not all humankind
but just one spark of fire and life.

A mountain rises high, held up by earth—
scorning low earth, where would the mountain stand?
Ten thousand streams pour into one deep sea—
scorning small streams, how would the sea stay full?

An old bamboo cares for young shoots
as mother loves her young, year in year out.
My son will someday rise above his dad—
you, children, in both arms will clasp the globe.

143. Prison thoughts

Tô Hữu

How lonely it can be in jail!
Ears open wide and heart athrob,
I listen—with that vibrant life,
how happy they must be out there!
It's dark in here—faint rays of sunset light
can hardly infiltrate through window bars.
It's cold within four dismal whitewashed walls
and on a wooden floor with dirt-gray planks ...

How lonely it can be in jail!
Ears open wide and heart athrob,

I listen—with that vibrant life,
how happy they must be out there!
I hear birds sing of flood tide on the wind,
a bat flap wings, aflutter in the dusk,
a horse with tinkling bells stop by the well,
some wooden clogs walk home down that long road . . .
Oh, why today do such familiar sounds
seem pregnant with the sap of life itself?

The wind is lashing at the trees, the leaves—
I hear creation's power quite unleashed.
I fancy all the world on the outside
is throbbing under heaven's vault with joy,
is sucking honey from the flower of life,
is breathing freedom's scent forever now.

Oh, sheer delusions of a fuddled mind!
Can I forget dire woes are rife out there?
The world's a prison, dooming countless souls
to grief and torment in abysmal pits.
Confined, with rancor in my heart, I'm one
of victims in the millions on this earth.
I'm just a little fledgling who's cooped up
in this small cage within a larger cage.
To answer freedom's call and change the world,
I'm one among a host of fighting men
who still walk tall along a blood-stained road,
too proud to ever backtrack or retreat.

For now I'm being held far from the flag—
the fighting spirit animates me still.
Who says Dak-pao, Lao-bảo, Poulo Condore
are exile hells and valleys of despair?
I'll smile a true believer's smile and keep
my soul immaculate amidst the filth.
I'm not yet dead—that means my hate still lives.

That means the age-old shame is not yet cleansed.

That means I'll have to struggle on until

we have wiped out the breeds of snakes and wolves.

Far off, upon the wind, a whistle shrieks.

(Cell 1, Thừa-thiên Prison, April 29, 1939)

144. The cuckoo calls its flock

Tô Hữu

The cuckoo calls its flock—it's when the rice

begins to ripen, fruits are growing sweet.

The garden's ringing with cicadas' hums.

Gold maize aplenty strews the sun-red yard.

The sky, so blue, seems vaster, higher yet,

and whistle-kites turn somersaults in space.

O summer, as you stir within my heart,

I rage and feel like kicking down these walls.

It's stifling in here—I will choke and die.

Meanwhile, outside, the cuckoo's call still rings.

(Huê, July 1939)

145. You cannot lock up the mind

Xuân Thủy

Imperialists jail us—we are not jailed.

We have our mind still—so we feel no fear.

Lock up our bodies, tie us hand and foot,

you can't prevent us, though, from thinking free.

Time and again you've tried to crush our heads—

our heads stay whole, and longer we shall live.

In our long lives, we shall devise the schemes

to knock you down and lay you in the pit.

We lead our lives along a single path.
Toward all the world's four corners go our thoughts,
to reach secluded hovels, prison cells,
to call on human souls and salve their wounds.

Hey, you imperialists! Do you know?
You've grown decrepit—we stay young and strong.
The earth you held you can no longer hold—
we aim at heaven, reaching for the moon.

Aging imperialists, you're on the wane.
This earth, this country, give it back to us.
Closed doors, tall walls may close in everything—
we still can see the firmament's vast sweep.

We contemplate tomorrow hunger-free—
no poverty, no jail, no wretched life.
All peoples will be brothers in the world—
O fair spring garden for their days and nights!

(1938)

146. A prison cell

Nguyễn Văn Năng

This Buddha-land has iron doors, high walls—
the clink locks up a monk with shaven head.
Thin fare cools bowels, helps forget foul life;
jail garb clothes flesh, shields it from earthly dust.
Read sutras—conjure up your race's soul.
Chant scriptures—hope to cure your country's ills.
In chains and shackles humankind still writhes:
from Buddha's realm let's head for that One World.

147. I shall not die

Nguyễn Văn Năng

Am I to die? I feel atrocious pain—
a head that reels, a heart that must have stopped;
both arms and legs benumbed: a cripple's limbs.
I'm lying in a graveyard, as it seems—
my brain's a screen on which flash bygone days.
What pity, O my God! What terror, too!
My chest feels crushed beneath the weight of stones.
My eyes see nothing but a dark, black mist.
My ears hear only toads and frogs—their thrums
and croaks sound like the moans of all damned souls.
The sky is hushed and still and thick with gloom—
must I let soul and body turn to naught?
No, no! Though swords and guns are aimed at me,
I shall not die—forever shall I live!
I shall not die!

        It's just one setback, this—
the tide has ebbed, but it will surge again.
Some leaves have dropped—the tree still stands, unmarred:
it's hoarding sap and will sprout forth strong shoots.
The stream that's flowing through a jungle neck
will swell and merge with this unbounded sea.
Here at Bắc-mê all perils threaten me:
I shall not die—forever shall I live!
And I shall live among exuberant souls
who will, together, reconstruct our life.
The garden will, tomorrow, glow with flowers—
of their bewitching fragrance I'll partake.
The body's nothing if the soul's expired—
false life fades out, but genuine life abides.
My own true life, despite all threats and blows,
I shall keep living, I shall love to live.

And I shall live in rhythms of my verse—
my poems voice great sorrow, epic will,
bespeaking infinite strength and no despair.
I keep on living, go on living yet
with ardent faith in common people's strength.

Bong, bong! The gong rings faintly in my ear—
waving my arms, I give a kick, spring up.
A ray of light beams in from far away,
then follow squawks and screeches of wild fowls,
a chorus of bright birdsong ripples forth—
the chirping birds demand that there be light . . .
I have just seen a whole expanse of gloom
clear off and then a glare of red burst forth.
With all my friends I want to dance and shout:
"I shall not die—forever shall I live!"

(1942)

148. The song of a cotton yarn
Hồ Chí Minh

My mother was a cotton flower;
stark white and wholesome, I'm a cotton yarn.

I used to be so frail and weak:
crumpled, I'd break; and shaken, I'd fall apart.

And once I had become a yarn,
I'd fret and fidget, being puny still.

What power had a little thread?
What fate would Heaven hold in store for it?

A longer yarn gets brittler yet:
who in the world would give a thread respect?

I leaned on countless comrades, though:
we came together, woofs and wefts galore.

We formed a piece of lovely cloth—
stronger than silk, and prized above tanned hide.

Let no one try to tear it up:

there lies our strength; there shines our glory too.

O children of the Hồng Bàng race,[1]

let's all unite and act without delay.

Love one another—heed these words:

hurry, O friends, and join the Việt-Minh League.[2]

(April 1, 1942)

1. Hồng Bàng: one of several traditional names for the Vietnamese people.

2. Việt-Minh League: the League for the Independence of Vietnam (Việt
Nam Độc Lập Đồng Minh Hội), formed by Hồ Chí Minh in May 1941.

149. What's my crime?

Trần Huy Liệu

You've bolted me in prison—what's my crime?

I love my country—do I break some law?

A furnace tempers iron into steel:

fire tests true gold and leaves no room for doubt.

The tiger waits his chance to flee the cage;

the dragon bides his time to break the lock.

Pull any dirty trick you may devise—

just try and shake my purpose—I dare you!

150. A down-and-out fighter and the spring nymph

Trần Huy Liệu

Amid tall hills and stretches of white sand,

no single patch of shade, no clump of flowers;

four lookout posts, two rows of thatch-roofed huts,

all prisons for a herd of homeless men.

The boom of guns sounds faintly in the ear;   5

the trumpet blares in battle, east and west.

Gritting his teeth and swallowing his rage,
the man so craves the joy of running free.

On evenings when dusk covers all the sky
and of his distant home he gets no sign,   10
within his chest he feels a ferment, where
brew many feelings, rankle many thoughts.

Then days keep passing by like falling leaves—
the same procession of monotonous days.
Waiting forlorn, sustained by futile hope,   15
he lets his youth drain off, day after day.

It drizzles—winter winds slip through the bars:
alone, he turns and tosses all night long.
His blanket gapes. Quite often he wakes up—
his skin feels cold, and colder feels his heart.   20

How can he know today a new dawn breaks?
Green hills on the horizon stand out clear.
Mists lift, revealing glimpses of the blue—
sparrows together chirp their harmonies.

The sunshine scatters warmth across the land.   25
A wind, too, spreads the gentle glow abroad.
The man himself feels restless—he sits up,
his body all aquiver with desires.

Then suddenly, music dances in his ears—
as he looks out the window he can see   30
a maiden lissome as a willow branch,
so lovely in her gown bedecked with flowers.

With throbbing heart he smiles and greets the nymph:
"Fair maiden, tell me, where do you come from?
You look familiar. Are you real? A dream?   35
But didn't you and I meet somewhere once?"

She says, "Oh, you've forgotten—I am Spring!
I seldom come around, just once a year.
Wherever I do call, I freshen things,
to sow delight and joy among all men.   40

Today I chance to travel through these parts—
I stop by this shut-in, oppressive place
and tell you all who've been imprisoned here
that life is beautiful—keep loving it.

At present, storms are raging overseas,   45
black clouds are spreading thick across the skies.
And yet, rejoice and be prepared to hail
the radiant sun—tomorrow it shall rise.

But now I come to offer you a smile,
a little kiss, as tokens of new life,   50
to dress those wounds a hero's suffered while
fighting a battle he's already won.

And so, my man, give me a fit reward.
What matter if there are locked doors, high walls?
Within the next few days I shall come back   55
and bring you news of victories over there.

That day shall come, a day not too far off,
when all the world lights up with vernal hues.
Together, joyously, we two shall live
and reminisce about a Bá-vân Têt."   60

(Bá-vân Camp, 1943)

151. Dropping by the guava graveyard in Sơn-la
Trần Huy Liệu

I come to visit here this afternoon—
a sky with mud-gray clouds, a soft, sad breeze.

Along the brook, a jumbled crop of tombs,
which on the hills spread shadows like dark drapes.

I've heard that, at this spot, in days long past,   5
you could see guava trees wave their green leaves.
Today, they're gone, replaced by mugwort weeds:
they cloak the tombstones, blurring all the words.

Let's count the men who're lying in black earth:
there're forty-three, all fighters, known, unknown.   10
These heroes fought till their last breath
before they would lie down and rest in peace.

Some were mere striplings in the flush of youth
who'd passed their time with books beside a lamp.
When winds and tides of change swept them along,   15
one day they left their school bench for the fray.

A few of them had worked as writers once,
committed to a literary path.
But their red blood boiled over in a fit—
they flung their pens away and joined the fight.   20

A few of them had led adventurous lives—
they had braved perils and endured travails.
But then a gallant purpose roused their will—
they'd shatter now the world they hated so.

Some had inhabited the realm of crime,   25
breaking the law and reckless of themselves.
But then they saw the light, reformed their ways:
they joined the masses, struggling for their cause.

Some had been members of the working class,
selling their labor for starvation pay.   30
One day, they felt impelled to claim their rights:
they would resist all those who preyed on them.

Some had been peasants, tillers of the soil,
oppressed by all, landowners, mandarins . . .

One day, they got together, raised their flag   35
to fight imperialists and feudalists.

Some had been members of the middle class—
hard times had slowly pushed them to the wall.
One day, as all their wealth and fortune crashed,
they joined the peasants and the workingmen.   40

Some had once been the poorest of the poor—
high levies, heavy taxes they had paid.
One day, they could no longer bear their woes—
they smashed the chains and shackles they had worn.

All these brave men who're sleeping underground   45
fell victim to the system now in place.
Their bones have found a home, these hills and woods—
their grievances still live as time goes by.

On days when fogs spread thick across the hills,
they look like dark effluvia from wronged souls.   50
On nights of rain when winds howl through the woods,
they sound like strangled gasps from those down there.

But listen, fellow fighters, mark this well:
your sacred mission you have all fulfilled.
We've followed on your heels, along your path,   55
to go where sunrise floods the skies with light.

And someday soon society will change:
the road of life will brighten up with flowers.
My friends, this spot records so many griefs,
yet you'll be smiling under all these trees.   60

(Sơn-la, 1940)

Note: Sơn-la: a highland province in northern Vietnam. There the French
maintained a prison for political offenders, many of whom died and were
buried at the "guava tree [gốc ổi] graveyard."

152. Prison dreams

Trần Minh Tước

A beautiful dream was on when I woke up—
delicate scents still linger in the soul.
Rushing past iron bars, a gust of wind
sends shivers through the prison's gloomy depths.

The bitter soul must wallow in real life,   5
hear mournful night tell tales of pain and grief
through that soft breathing, all my comrades' breath,
or in the wind which darkly knocks on walls.

Sprawled here and there upon the ice-cold floor,
my prison mates like corpses lie quite still.   10
Kind darkness spreads a blanket everywhere:
to dreams it lulls my friends—what sort of dreams?

There are sweet dreams where sunshine gives much warmth,
alive with birdsongs heard in happy youth.
Near coral lips you whisper words of love,   15
as wine excites and romance turns the head.

But all such dreams too quickly float away,
as lips that smile start quivering with dire fear.
A million sparks of red flare up at once—
like some hot torrent seethes another dream.   20

The earth resounds with men who demonstrate—
from myriad hearts, wills surge in furious waves.
Armies of fighters, strong as tempered steel,
bear torture as bones crack and blood spurts forth.

The dream goes on ... but then abruptly stops   25
because a chilly gust of wind whips past,
rousing the weary soul from scenes of blood,
and harsh reality stares you in the face ...

The tower drum sounds the hour all through the night—
it keeps count of so many fleeting hours,   30
it nips so many days off your one life,
the petals of your rose, the human heart.

Stand up, you shivering souls in prison cells!
Banish sad dreams, and in defiance laugh.
Amid dark shadows lurking in your minds,   35
unfurl the flag that glows with crimson blood.

A clarion call drives off all shades of night
as hammers pound and sickles cut their swaths.
The glorious sun has pierced the fence of steel—
a violent morn is dawning: all rise up!   40

(Sơn-la Prison, 1940)

153. At Condore Port

Đào Duy Kỳ

This afternoon, at Condore Port,
high heaven and vast ocean lull my soul.
    The breakers crash, the whirlwinds howl—
my spirit swells with sea and soars with sky . . .
    There's no one else in this lone cell—   5
through iron bars, squalls blow the breath of wrath.
    Here fleece-white clouds conceal the wilds,
and sands have leveled off the heroes' tombs.
    A few green bramble shrubs stand still—
no waves or winds can fade the true heart's blood.   10
    My friends are gone, my will remains:
it stokes my heart's hot fury day and night.
    I swear this oath to sky and sea:
I'll break out of this cage and go my way.
    This evening, propped against the bars,   15
I think of gallant men, and my heart seethes.

I swear this oath to my dead friends:
I'll smash my chains and from this hell escape.

A swallow's flying in the sky.
Listen, O bird, and take this message back: 20

"Condore—how many have returned
from here to know again the joys of home?

Today, I'm trapped inside this cage—
tomorrow, I'll run free through streams and hills!"

Here sunshine burns and singes clouds;   25
it casts a glow on faces weather's tanned;

it scorches sand, it parches dew;
it bakes and broils the prison at Condore.

Here many corpses lie interred
in fragile tombs on beaches of white sand.   30

Survivors, haggard-faced, pale-skinned,
hide wasted bodies under blue attire.

Weighed down with irons, bound with chains,
we must spend days of gloom inside dark cells.

Our hearts still drink up life's strong wine—   35
as we compress our lips, we sneer at woes.

So many loves still stir our breasts,
and faith can soothe all sorrows, pains, or griefs.

We want to leave—our legs won't move:
let geese bear this our message through the air.   40

Our eyes gaze far away toward home:
blue sky, green ocean, winds and waves that roar.

The days resound with our war songs
against imperialists and feudalists.

The nights are peopled with our dreams—   45
the gecko cries "Go home!" within our souls.

Condore's a string of leaden days—
we brew our brew of hate with anger's yeast.

Here wind gusts shriek through clouds of sand—
our wasted bodies lie within tall walls.   50

Here chains and irons weigh us down;
gun butts and rattan whips numb us with pain.

But these wild billows, these fierce storms
will only further temper wills of steel.

Despite all trials and travails,   55
the flag glows red, more gold shines on the star.

The world's a tide that ebbs and flows:
we'll have our day tomorrow, vow our hearts.

We shall break free, and on our road
we'll hone our swords for battle, whet them sharp.   60

We'll cleanse our shame with enemy blood—
all life will gleam with our high-flying flag.

(1944)

154. A fallen fruit

Bùi Công Trừng

A fruit falls off, and that's when it's all ripe.
A flower fades, and then we miss its scent.
Why give a damn if *they* love us or not?
They'll weep for us once we are dead and gone!
To say goodbye—does it mean "nevermore"?
A sprouting seed encloses pain and grief—
the fact of life and death is nature's rule:
breakage occurs and only then comes change.
Look at all things as they evolve and shift:
what dies today will feed tomorrow's life.
In sorrow we need not shed tears, O friends!
The seeds lie ready—strew them on the earth;
with all our strength, let's sow them on the wind,
and deep within our breasts let's tell ourselves:
"The ripest fruit tastes sweeter, skin and all.

Seeing a fruit fall off, don't weep for it:
as one fruit falls, a hundred trees spring up."

(Trà-khê Prison, 1943)

Note: Bùi Công Trừng composed this poem to mourn Nguyễn Đình Trúc, a communist cadre and fellow prisoner who had committed suicide.

155. It's me, your son

Hồng Chương

Mother, I know that now you're suffering much,
waiting for news about your cherished son.
In anguished hope, you're sitting at the loom,
your scarlet breastcloth drenched and stained with tears.

I know that soon or late you'll fail in health,
wasting away with waiting; with your hand,
wiping your dark-ringed and beclouded eyes,
you'll lie in agony upon your bed.

But Mother, I had sworn a steadfast vow.
I left when sunshine faded on the hills—
I weighed a son's due love, a patriot's debt:
which should have tipped the scales, O mother mine?

Beneath the banner I set forth to fight;
you worried thinking I'd be all alone.
After I was released from your soft hands,
I had more loving hands to welcome me.

Somewhere along the road, so many times,
living a soldier's life away from home,
I've met those mothers who, with open arms,
have clasped me to their bosoms, giving love.

So, as it sometimes happens, in this world,
you'll chance upon some distant spot and meet

men who are fighting, dazed with battle smoke.
Please hug and kiss each one: it's me, your son.

(Quảng-trị, 1940)

156. A fighter's thoughts of spring
Lê Đức Thọ

Inside my heart it's changed, what spring once meant.
No longer do I sing of flowers as fresh
as a fair maiden's lips that flash a smile,
coquetting with the eastern wind in love.

The flowers blooming now to welcome spring
are all the people's hearts throughout the land,
all bunched together here in my mind's eye
to deck the land anew as spring comes back.

Inside my heart it's changed, what spring once meant.
No longer do I sip a glass of wine
and drunken, dream of nymphs as fresh as spring,
letting the years of youth all go to waste.

This year's salute is not that of the past.
The toast to springtime is a shout of hate—
we fighters revel on the battleground
to make our cherished dreams come true at last.

Inside my heart it's changed, what spring once meant.
No longer do firecrackers burst with joy
and their red shreds hail springtime at the gate,
as if to welcome home a much loved bride.

Firecrackers nowadays are sputtering guns—
those of guerrillas on the battlefield,
tearing the foe to bits in morning mist
and leaving scarlet blood on many trails.

Inside my heart it's changed, what spring once meant.
O comrades, all those idle dreams of yore
I've buried in oblivion's grave, deep down:
my oath to this our country dare I break?

(Spring 1945)

157. The two wooden men

Huy Cận

Let me retell a story, rather old,
a story I once heard while in the South.
I don't think it an idle exercise
if in our lifetime we retell a tale
that carries hope for change, a better world.   5
My friend, a writer in our southern half,
told me that story many years ago—
now is he still alive, or is he dead?
I'm angry with a nation cut in two:
to reach compatriots, we address the clouds.   10
Plain news or confidences, literature—
all choke up in the throat. White paper, then,
will do, as I record what I've to say.
It was a bitter story that he told—
I'll try to reproduce the bitter taste.   15
The difference is, now that I write it down,
I don't feel bitter as we both felt once,
when he, a slave, told me, a fellow slave,
the tale that caused such bitter pain to us
who, feeling flayed and bare, walked through the world   20
and empathized with those two wooden men.

It happened in a city of the South.
There lived two schoolboys who were bosom friends:

they shared their joys, their anger, and their pain,
shared everything in life—in fiction, too.   25
(Children, like slaves, are not insensitive
to all the grief pervading their real world.)
When homeward bound from school, they took a street
and on it saw each day two wooden men.
They were two columns of a stately house,   30
atlantes fashioned out of ironwood,
who on their shoulders and with might and main
upheld the massive balcony above.
They seemed about to yield their very breath
as in their shoulders they put all their strength   35
to bear the balcony, with its large roof,
like all the weight of pain and woe on earth.
Their shoulder muscles bulged and formed great lumps
against their throats, lumps that would never shrink.
That was not all—young pranksters often climbed   40
up there to daub their faces up with dirt or mud.
Well, our two schoolboys, who were bosom friends
and sensed the grief pervading their slave world,
kept seeing those two figures shoulder up
their load of shame—how could they stand the sight?   45
(Those figures were not men of flesh and blood,
nor were they characters in storybooks,
yet deeply they impressed the two young souls.)
The boys held secret talks and laid a plan
to right the wrong. But how can we detail   50
their preparations and their probes,
count all the trips they made to map the streets?
Top secret! No third person was to know.
They must take care, design each single step—
to right a wrong was not a marbles game   55
out in the schoolyard, or a classroom drill.
Matchboxes they collected, our young knights—

the strips of sulphur they'd tear off and save,
and after school, each day, they'd go and check:
could those two captives last till they got freed?   60
Well, straining all their sinews, both bore up
while in their hearts our schoolboys agonized.
But bravely they'd cheer on the wooden men:
"Be patient—wait a little longer yet!"
Their pocket money didn't go for snacks;   65
instead, they'd buy firecrackers for a fuse,
and on a day near Tết they'd pull their coup.
One Thursday evening, they both groped their way
lugging two boxes (filled with all their hopes).
They reached the mansion, hid behind a bush,   70
rolled powder up in paper for a fuse.
They set the boxes up against the wall,
and both contained explosives and hot zeal.
Their hearts throbbed fast, their souls were catching fire—
they'd soon wipe out that haunting scene of grief.   75
The sacred moment came—they swapped a glance.
The wooden men looked to them from far off
like suffering souls who pleaded to be saved.
With everything in place, they struck a match
and lit the fuse—"Quick, run, let's flee from here!"   80
The two young friends together fled before
the building could collapse and crush them both.
The wooden men, the slaves, would be set free!
O holy moment! Sakyamuni once[1]
found out the cure for sorrow in the world—   85
did he then feel as happy as our boys?

But why did no explosion come about?
Next morning, on the quiet, our two friends
returned and took a peek at that big house:
the wooden men still shouldered their huge load.   90
The youngsters felt a pang inside their hearts—

poor fellows, their first dream was quite destroyed.
They looked for their explosives, and they found
the boxes in the gutter. Heavenward
they raised their eyes—they were not beaten yet.   95
Then they picked up the fuse—it was intact:
the fabric of their lives stayed whole, uncut.
To all who suffered they both made a vow:
"Today, we've failed to save the wooden men.
Tomorrow, when we're grown, we two shall work   100
together harder—we shall save the world."

Dear southern friend, I've now retold at length
the tale you once told me. Beneath the skies
where are you now? Are you alive or dead?
When you first told it, you felt melancholy still,   105
so you concluded on a bitter note:
"No doubt those boys would later on forget
their sacred pledge to work and save the world!"
My friend, those two young schoolboys have grown up
and kept the solemn promise of the tale.   110
Hundred and thousands of young men have fought
and are now fighting on so many fronts
to save life and to save the light of day:
they are those boys—they have your spirit, too.
Times have quite changed since you told me your tale—   115
the world's become a brighter place. That tale
can motivate our youth—so, on this day
when sunshine sparkles, I've told it again.
I'm sending you a message from afar:
your spirit, much of it, inspires my verse.   120

(Cẩm-phả, January 1959)

1. Sakyamuni: one of the names for Gautama Buddha.

158. New tiles

Xuân Diệu

On roads I've trodden, everywhere,
I've heard their whisper of sheer joy,
        "New tiles!"
On streets and alleys I've walked through,
I've heard them sing this gay refrain:
        "New tiles!"

I've hurried past or stopped and looked—
their color's etched deep in my mind:
        new tiles.
Cool mornings, sultry afternoons—
good, wholesome pages I have turned:
        new tiles.

Amid old slums, along a lake,
in suburbs and in gardens gone to seed:
        new tiles.
High over ricelands, strewn through fields,
mingling with bushes, glimpsed in streams:
        new tiles.

O, millions of new tiles now chat and chirp,
all voices rising from the joyous earth:
        new tiles.
Oh, millions of small bits of strength
spread out through space or raised to soaring heights.

Can I forget the scene? Young stalks of rice,
so green and jostling, rippling toward the sky,
and in their midst there bloom all those red tiles.
Rice stalks and tiles compete in springing up.

Oh, roofs of markets, roofs of hospitals,
and roofs of factories and roofs of schools . . .

New tiles and open windows everywhere—
our model buildings rise and pierce the air.

I've traveled over our dear land
and seen so many of those tiles—
      new tiles.
Beneath the blue embrace this happiness!
My heart and soul may well become
      new tiles.

(September 1959)

159. What Mother told me once
Phùng Quán

I lost my father when I was just two.
My mother, for my sake,
chose not to wed again.
She'd grow mulberry trees,
raise silkworms, and weave cloth—   5
she reared me till I was grown up.
After some twenty years I still recall
that day when I was five.
It happened I told her a lie—
next day I feared she'd spank me.   10
But no, she just looked sad.
She hugged me, kissed me on the head:
"My son, before he closed his eyes,
your father said that all through life
you should remain sincere and true."   15
"Mother, what does it mean,
to be sincere and true?"
My mother kissed me on the eyes:
"My son, a man sincere and true
will laugh when, glad, he wants to laugh,   20

will cry when, sad, he wants to cry.
If you love someone, say you love.
If you hate someone, say you hate.
Someone may not entice you with sweet words—
still, don't say *hate* when you feel love.   25
Someone may grab a knife and threaten you—
still, don't say *love* when you feel hate."

Since then, when some adult asked me,
"My boy, whom do you love the best?"
remembering what my mother told me once,   30
I would reply:
"I love best one who's true, sincere."
The person stared at me in disbelief
thinking, "He's just a parrot, that young boy."
But no, for what my mother told me once   35
impressed itself upon my brain, my mind
as if on some immaculate, virgin sheet
were drawn a crimson, bright red line.

Now I am twenty-five—
the orphan has become a writer since.   40
But what my mother told me once,
when I was five,
remains intact—a crimson, bright red line.
What at the circus tightrope walkers do
is quite a feat.   45
Yet harder is what writers do
who'll walk the path of truth through life.
If you love someone, say you love.
If you hate someone, say you hate.
Someone may not entice you with sweet words—   50
still, don't say *hate* when you feel love.
Someone may grab a knife and threaten you—
still, don't say *love* when you feel hate.

A writer, I shall write the truth
and speak the truth throughout my life.   55
No sugar and no honey of success
can bribe my tongue.
Thunder that crashes overhead
can't strike me down.
And if they grab my paper, seize my pen,   60
I'll take a knife and write on stone.

(1956)

160. Looking for her

Tạ Hữu Thiện

Who, growing up, has never loved?
And who, in love, has never gone on dates?
It's nature's norm.

I've often looked for love,
and often I've despaired.   5
My heart has never cooled—
and never satisfied,
I yearn for her I'm seeking yet . . .

Is she whom I shall never meet
the one I'm clasping in my heart?   10

For half my life I've traveled everywhere
looking for her, yet nowhere finding her.
Why treat me like a stranger, O my love?
When shall I get my wish
and meet you for our date?   15

O girls whose pockets hold a looking glass,
who're dressed in dirt-brown clothes,
who toil for months and years
at hoeing hard and plowing deep!

O girls who bustle on a building site,   20
whose hands and shoulders will assist
in carrying out the Plan,
who see the future in their dreams!

O girls who push a cart or lug huge bales,
who sweep up trash or empty toilet cans   25
and flourishing on labor, boast
a filled-out chest, a slender waist!

O girls who stand at counters selling goods
that quickly come and quickly go,
whose life consists of countless reckonings   30
and shuns the tattle of the world!

O girls who sit at office desks
recording, copying day by day,
forever typing at full clip,
handling the ebb and flow of documents!   35

O girls who dance to entertain,
and in the limelight shine like nymphs
with eyes and lips that promise love,
whose world seems free of any care!

O co-eds at the university   40
who have discussed the universe with me
although our knowledge, totted up,
amounts not even to a hill of beans!

O girls whom I have met
or whom I'm yet to meet!   45
Nothing has swerved me from the party line
to make me eye some pink silk dress
and spurn a shirt that's torn and patched.
Nor do I heed those silly pros and cons
about the length of hair.   50

I feel that all you girls
who've reached a nubile age,
are lovely to look at,
each in her own way.

Bewitched, I gaze upon your lips, your eyes,   55
your swelling chest, your sloping back,
your teeth, your hair,
and dream that all through life,
we'll share one blanket, you and I.

I'm too naïve to ponder this or that   60
and know if you come from the proper class.
Neither am I a fool,
to do such useless things
as check up on your lineage, making sure
it's pure and clean.   65
Nor do I rate your virtues and your skills,
playing the chooser hard to please,
because true love is not
arithmetic.

Among you girls, is there the one   70
I've long and hard been looking for?
It's you I'm yet to meet
who are the girl I'm clasping in my heart.

Above her family line, her social class,
above her status, her good looks,   75
I value one sole thing in my dream girl—
that she can hate, can love.

161. O life I love and cherish like my wife!

Việt Phương

I once would spout words like "the most," "the best,"
and oh, poor me, believed all that I mouthed.
I didn't know what's bluer than the blue;
by passion fired, I lacked a cool, calm mind.

All comrades were good comrades, I would think:
our ranks made room for love and love alone.
We'd started on our road—who'd stop halfway?
And Moscow beckoned—paradise on earth.

A Swiss watch ranked below a Soviet watch:
that seemed a tenet of my creed, my pride.
The China moon waxed fuller than the Yankee moon:
I fancied so, raw naïf that I was.

Now five long decades gone, I've come to know
what true love is, what only maims and kills.
I've seen both crests and troughs on moon and stars;
I've seen the mud stains in the highest spheres.

Once drunk, I now stand firmer—I've waked up.
To enemies I quietly say these words:
"Give back to me what you have claimed as yours.
As yours take back what you have smeared on me."

I gilded life because I wanted faith.
Now I have faith—life needs no gilding now.
The strangest sights no longer shock my eye:
I've paid the price of pain and learned to see.

I've found those things I never dreamed I'd find.
It's not that serpents lurk beneath the flowers.
Good men, dubbed weak, are rags to throw away.
But snakes lie coiled and poised right in our midst.

Eight thousand nights at war—I thought a lot.
Fed on boiled maize, I searched and knew my heart.
From bombs and shells I winnowed happiness—
slowly my heart became a clear, pure light.

I lived those hours and minutes of stark truth,
measured our people, took the size of man.
Plain earth in all her solid beauty glowed—
valleys of sorrow went ablaze with faith.

I know who erred, I know who yet may err.
I now have grown, as Communist and man.
Unmask the idols—men show their real selves,
both front and back, both outside and within.

Quảng-bình, Vĩnh-linh shone forth in blood and fire—
I see the ugliness, yet grin and smile.
The enemy radio's on—an open door.
I trust the future—let 'em rant and rave.

It aches, it hurts, I suffer throes of birth.
O life, as close to me as my own breath!
I feel the joy and rapture of release,
O life I love and cherish like my wife!

(1969)

Note: Việt Phương is the pseudonym of a man believed to be a member of the Vietnamese Labor Party who once served as private secretary to Premier Phạm Văn Đồng.

162. The Party left me in the wilds
Nguyễn Chí Thiện

The Party left me in the wilds,
hoping my corpse would feed some manioc bush.
A huntsman I've become, and I'll emerge
bearing snake jewels, rhino horns.

The Party drowned me in the sea,
hoping I'd sink into the depths.
A diver I've become—
I'll surface sparkling with rare pearls.

The Party buried me in dark brown earth,
hoping I'd turn to mud down there.
A miner I've become—
I'll dig up precious ore, and tons of it,
no gold or diamonds for a woman's toys:
uranium ore for atom bombs.

163. A prisoner's funeral

Nguyễn Ngọc Thuận

I've taken you to your own tomb—
lie here and rest in peace.
Escaping from a prisoner's life,
you've given back their cuffs and chains.

I offer you this bowl of maize gone bad—
I failed to find an incense stick.
A mountain's pebbly soil is hard to dig:
please settle for this shallow grave.

Your coffin is a ragged mat,
your winding sheet a towel that smells.
Consider this a box of sandalwood;
consider this a shroud of crimson silk.

A stick of firewood is your tombstone, friend—
I've carved your name with this dull knife.
What's in a prisoner's name in any case?
May he be left alone and undisturbed.

Lie still and sleep a deep, sound sleep—
the winds will sing their lullaby.

The rain, when pouring down, will send
your bones and muscles on a cruise.

There's someone here to bury you—
tomorrow who'll be left for me?
They'll throw my corpse out in the fields
as fodder for wild animals.

You had your moment in the sun—
the hero of a hundred battlegrounds.
But now you've died a prisoner's death
unworthy of some bird or beast.

I'd like to weep—my tears have all dried up.
I'd like to speak—I must keep still.
Lie here and sleep in peace—
let me crawl back to cuffs and chains.

(Yên-báy, winter 1979)

164. Mother

Tê Hanh

I saw my mother after twenty years—
I spent two days with her, then said goodbye.
As liberation bubbled in the air,
she gazed at me, her son, and spoke no word.

For dinner she gave me delicious fish.
She stuffed my knapsack full of crisp dried squid.
In summer, through our seacoast sweep hot winds—
oh, how the coconut, still green, would cool!

And Mother took me to the river wharf.
The boat pulled far away—she stood there still.
I watched the water flow and flow downstream
like time, which rushes forward, never back.

We've freed our land—aggressors' shadows gone.
Mother's past eighty, Father's dead, and I,
their son, am not a youngster anymore:
half of my thatch of hair is flecked with gray.

Mother, our country's undergoing change—
these days of joy replace those years of grief.
The homeland is no longer cut in half—
I'll often come back here and visit you.

(Summer 1975)

165. Run! Run!

Lưu Văn Vong

We're free and independent—Number One!
So why are we all running for dear life?
We glimpse their blood-red flag—hair stands on end.
We peek at Uncle's photo—sweat breaks out.
Forget the fatherland, gone to the dogs.
Abandon human love, bound straight for hell.
The Kitchen God, sans pots and pants, exclaims:
"Heaven, they're coming! Let's clear out, and quick!"

166. Paradise

Lưu Văn Vong

Our people know high heaven's bliss on earth.
They live in paradise—it's no vain boast.
The child sits wide-eyed, coveting manioc.
Sore-footed, Mother queues up for her yam.
White gruel fills your stomach—half a bowl.
Black patches deck your shoulders—one T-shirt.

For "liberation" pray, untreated, in your bed,
while on the wall your Uncle waves and smiles.[1]

    1. Uncle: Hô Chí Minh (called Uncle by the Vietnamese Communists).

167. Folk songs for today

Nguyễn Tất Nhiên

My man, now you've come back without one arm—
who'll take me to the elegant soirées?
Sorry, you can't indulge me anymore—
I'd wed some foreign guy who pampers girls.

My man, now you've come back, one leg sawed off—
I love you so, but love myself still more.
Heaven, my maker, made me human, though:
I'm leaving you, with sorrow in my heart!

My man, now you've come back, both eyes snuffed out—
after the war years, lifetime in the dark.
A stone-blind husband who on earth could prize?
Don't blame the world and all its fickle ways!

My man, you're back, a crippled soldier now—
I grieve for you, your cold and lonely days.
My love, I'd stick by you until the end—
family and friends, alas, will not permit!

You're back as one of those vile "puppet" troops—
"blood debts" you owe the people you must pay.
Now you can't even lift a hoe, a spade—
I'll wed some army chap, join Uncle's clan!

168. Homecoming
Nguyễn Ý Thuần

They shared ten years as man and wife,
a closeness of so many days.
But to the victor he owed debts:
he had to pay them off in jail.

He left—their child lay in her womb.
Now he comes back—the child just stares
at that ex-counterrevolutionist,
a tattered stranger in the yard.

With scarlet polish on her nails,
she covers her shamed face and weeps.
Ten years of love as man and wife—
it goes against the present scheme.

A helmet, with its horsedung hue,
hangs brazenly upon the wall.
About his age, its owner gives
the visitor a pitying glance.

But the old dog did wag its tail,
scenting its master of years past.
It softly moans and doesn't bark,
as dumbstruck as the man himself.

169. The sea, the world, and the boat people
Hà Huyền Chi

Those boats keep rushing out to restless sea
with wind-puffed sails and souls stretched taut and tense.
In quest of hope they will go courting death,
dreaming that one day freedom will be theirs.

Those boats keep riding over turbulent waves,
defying every peril on the way.

Rather leave flesh and bones inside a shark
than rot as slaves inside a tyrant's jail.

Boat people wave to ships that will not stop—
each second of their time means life or death.
The voice grows hoarse appealing to men's hearts,
and bitter tears well up in hollow eyes.

Small children's corpses sink to ocean depths.
Young girls' pure, virgin bodies are defiled.
The ones who die cannot stay whole, unmaimed;
and drunk on blood's foul smell, the pirates laugh.

Those boats keep heading one by one toward death.
Men turn their backs and hide their cowardice.
Where has it fled, the conscience of mankind?
The world just opens wide its eyes and stares.

O ports and harbors where those boats may drift!
Unlock your hearts and let them come inside.
Give those who've lost their country, lost their all,
a chance to live out their expatriate lives.

170. Island
Mai Thảo

Well water, drawn from ocean depths,
feeds lives cut loose and cast afloat.
For many years the wind has swept these sands:
one human footprint—suddenly they're Vietnam

171. Two eyes
Nhật Tiến

When you were just a babe,
people compared your eyes

to little crystal balls
that mirrored hues and tints of life,
that shone like sunny days 5
in your fair land at peace—
the gold of splendid dreams,
the green of hope,
the flush of youth.
And when you were asleep, 10
your eyes, though shut, still sensed the lullaby
that mother hummed near you.

Later, you went to school.
The teacher taught you how
your eyes, as organs, helped you see, 15
see father and mother, see brothers and sisters,
see your sweet, cozy home,
see life as a long fleet of clouds
bound for their haven—happiness.
Two crystal eyes, two clear, pure eyes 20
not tarnished once by care or grief.

Your eyes became two witnesses when war
spread smoke across the sky
and made horizons dark.
They saw earth scorched and houses torched, 25
bomb craters pock the fields.
They saw crushed heads beside some ditch,
torn arms or legs on mountainsides,
and bodies maimed in death.
Your eyes were like two bottomless pits, 30
two gates flung open on a hell,
your native land,
which has not known one day of peace and joy.

When on the battleground the guns were hushed,
the eyes still glared with hate 35

of men for men.
The eyes were taught to hate
by doctrine,
by propaganda that deceived and lied.
The eyes lost all their tenderness,   40
were drained of human love—
instead, they flashed with spite and wrath.
And so, behind barbed wire,
still shiver bodies of mere skin and bones,
whose pain can find no vent in words.   45

During the flight across the eastern sea,
the eyes turned into frenzied cowards.
They feared the sky, they feared dark night;
they feared that clouds might harbor storms.
They hankered for the loom of land,   50
a sighting of green trees in clumps.
Despairing, they stared after all those ships
which would, unheeding, go their way
and carry off faint gleams of hope.

Then, out of nowhere came those fiends   55
with ravenous eyes—
they stormed the boat, tore it to shreds.
Their bloodshot eyes, where glowered lust,
would prey upon frail girls.
Blank eyes, cold eyes would watch   60
each person being hustled overboard.
Here on the ocean reigned primeval night,
eclipsing humankind.

But what eyes could compare with yours, O child
who drowned and perished in the sea?   65
Your eyes shut tight, achieving peace.
Your eyes took leave of life,
saying goodbye to wrath and hate,

departing from the world
that never granted you a home.   70
To you may angels lend their wings,
so you can fly and reach
the kingdom of eternal rest.

Mother once hummed and lulled your eyes to sleep.
Now let the ocean rock and sing to you.   75
To youth and innocence return them;
to your kind mother give them back,
those little crystal balls
where glimmered hints of paradise.

172. Cold season
Viên Linh

Cold season—birds all head for warmer climes.
I drown my sorrow in a tiny glass.
Oh, does some branch still host that bird from Việt,[1]
or is it lost down there, among the shades?

1. As legend has it, a rare bird from Vietnam was once given as tribute to the emperor of China. Released into the imperial gardens, it would not fly around but would perch on a southern branch and look homeward.

173. A hundred tongues
Viên Linh

Born there and scattered out to all four winds,
a hundred children speak a hundred tongues.[1]
Tomorrow, if we all should go back home,
let's hope we'll speak the common speech of tears.

1. In a poem about the diaspora after 1975, this line alludes to the mythical origin of the Vietnamese and kindred peoples. See note 1 to Poem 122, "Our land, our home," by Trần Tuấn Khải.

174. The dawn of a new humankind

Du Tử Lê

Since time began, when people leave,
each leaving represents a truth.
There can be no tomorrow if
they cower and submit.

Do you hear echoes from across
the vast Pacific Ocean, friend?
From all that land where darkness reigns
my countrymen are setting out.

Down in that ocean, for three years,
how many bodies have dissolved?
Through Southeast Asia, for three years,
how many have decayed at camps?

Just picture this in your mind's eye:
the human hair that strews the sea,
the children's corpses turned to rot,
the feasts of human flesh for fish.

And they keep leaving, nonetheless,
though humankind has looked away.
And with calm patience they persist
in going forth and meeting death.

They leave because the eastern sun
has long stopped coming up for them.
Because they want to live as men,
they may not choose another course.

How can you ever understand?
You've never lost and left your land.
All peoples share the human shape,
but human hearts don't beat alike.

Do you believe humanity
is heading straight toward its own grave?
Do corpses floating on the sea
jolt you and wake you up from sleep?

Last night a windstorm lashed the skies;
the ocean raged, the breakers roared.
In all those echoes did you hear
the howling of my countrymen?

Last night I also had a dream.
I saw the light of a new dawn:
the sun was shining everywhere,
but in the east it was pitch-dark.

Do you feel joy this morning, friend,
on finding that the world has changed?
Because I chose to stay a man,
I'm living now an exile's life.

(1978)

175. A New Year's wish for a little refugee

Trần Mộng Tú

Let me send you some words, a little wish,
on New Year's Eve, when night shrouds skies and seas.
O little child, a miracle saved your life:
aboard that boat, all perished—all but you.

Let me send you some words, a simple wish.
On New Year's Day, alone on foreign soil,
you feel just like a seaweed washed ashore—
you don't know what the future holds for you.

No lack of kindly hands to welcome you
and take you home to change what's now your name.

They'll turn you into some new human breed
that thinks your yellow skin is cause for shame.

They'll send you off to school, where you'll be taught
their own land's history, modern ways of life.
You will grow up denying what you are—
you'll never hear your forebears spoken of.

Let me send you some words, a simple wish,
for this new year, for scores of years to come.
O little child, may you retain intact
your past of sorrows, all your world of griefs.

176. Biding our time

Hậu Điền

We refugees ply all trades over here:
we'll spurn no job, however low or mean.
Hired to clean toilets, we don't wince or flinch;
told to dump garbage, we agree—Okay!
We daily sweep the floor—ah, what a feat!
We often vacuum dust—oh, such a thrill!
As we adapt and live, let's bide our time.
Is this all we deserve, this rotten lot?

177. Our friend would board the *Thương-Tín* and go home

Cao Tấn

Our friend would board the *Thương-Tín* and go home
to praise the party, struggle for its line.
Now we have heard he's buried at Yên-báy—
quell your contempt, and let him rest in peace.

He hoped to kiss his children, hug his wife,
and walk those ancient streets with tearful eyes.

He'd hug her, kiss them, see those scenes of old
just once more, then he'd gladly quit this world.

As cadres thronged around, he disembarked,
a stranger to this planet, his own land.
Then down his path of sorrows he was dragged
to fall amid the wilds without a cry.

Under vast skies he used to storm the hills,
a man who roamed the country's length and breadth.
Then suddenly, he was a refugee—
as in some dream, at camp he queued for meals.

At dawn, he'd startle, then break down and weep.
By night, he'd guzzle booze to numb his pain.
He'd dream of wife and kids and call for them;
he'd toss and turn in bed, he'd fret and fuss.

So he would board the *Thương-Tín* and go home.
His friends tried hard to talk him out of it.
He wanly smiled, a soldier off to war:
"Consider that my cursed life is shot!"

We knew the guy was finished, going back.
But we still prayed and hoped against all hope
that he'd fare well and see his wife, his kids:
"Heaven must feel some pity for the wretch!"

Fly over here and I'll treat you, O soul,
to steambaths or some flick with triple X.
Your Eden let you down, and in my own,
I too am sweating out a doggone life.

(February 1977)

178. Five crackpots got together

Cao Tân

Five crackpots got together, talked big things:
they'd take upon their shoulders state affairs.
It rather chilled the mood, the talk of war:
to boost morale, three fifths were broken out.

Combat fatigues they donned in foreign woods—
after one round, the hills began to blur.
The martial spirit soared, a towering rage:
to save the world seemed no more than a game.

One hero raised his glass and strutting, cried:
"Half of my life I soldiered, manning posts.
My days now just drag out on alien soil—
through hills and mountains I shall go back home.

Our jungles someday will all come alive.
Our tigers will all wave their claws and roar
shaking the heavens—our Vietnam will rise,
and over our fair land our flag will fly!"

Another brave had tossed six glasses off:
"Where does she stand, that Lady Liberty?
I'll climb up there and make a brand-new torch—
to shed some light, I'll set myself on fire!

She just keeps holding on to that cold torch.
Why grudge a hundred pounds of skin and bones?
I'll be the flame to search the ocean depths
for those poor souls abandoned on high seas . . ."

At dawn, a fellow came alive and saw
his friends' still bodies littering the field.
Ten bottles had struck down five valiant knights—
all quiet on this front, the exiles' world.

Sprawled on the floor lay souls that storms had roused,
huddling together with their wrath and dreams.
One, waking up, blinked at the sun and asked:
"How shall I spend the whole rest of my life?"

(March 1977)

179. The booby had a little sack
Cao Tân

The booby had a little sack—
he hid it like some treasure all year round.
His friends thought him a cheapskate hoarding cash
to spend it on himself and no one else.

One winter evening, at a loss for fun,
we jumped the guy to rob him of his sack.
The flat shook like a boat on heavy seas—
he yelled as if we aimed to take his life.

The sack was opened—out it spilled, his hoard.
Wrapped in plain paper, just an ounce of gold.
A fellow howled, "Hey, stupid, all this gold
you ought to sell. You worship it, or what?"

"Damn you, four ingots I had at the start.
I've sold off three for several hundred bucks.
But this I'll never part with till I die—
it was what Mother slipped me when I fled."

An ancient, threadbare handkerchief, as brown as dirt,
with a few words embroidered in pale blue.
"But blast you, why do you preserve this rag?"
"A keepsake from my wife when I joined up."

The sack was filled with yellowed calling cards:
names of people, places , now remote,

some hasty words scrawled for a rendezvous,
familiar streets he'd never walk again.

We all looked sheepish giving back the sack—
ashamed, he cursed us for all he was worth.
What we'd supposed must hold a miser's hoard
held cherished bits and shreds of our own land.

You, booby, threatened to murder all of us.
If only you could open up my heart,
you'd also find in there a hoard of love:
handkerchiefs, crumpled, crossed with faint blue lines,

soiled calling cards, with streets renamed long since,
numbers for homes disrupted in a flash,
dear rendezvous I never could retrieve—
all tattered lives across our fatherland.

(October 1977)

180. Washing my wife's clothes
Luân Hoán

Detergent's mixed with pinches of my love—
I wring it gently, lest I give you pain.
The cloth still sweetly smells of your own skin—
my hands, as if caressing you, feel shy.

The water in the bowl is muddy brown—
I feel so moved by all these specks of dirt.
They are the hardships you must bear alone
to feed your man, your children, month by month.

Water soaks through each fiber of the cloth
to flow and reach the bottom of my heart.
Dear, do you see the quiet tears that drop
and in the fabric merge with tender thoughts?

Now, in my forties, I learn how to wash,
and thus spend some of all my idle hours.
Should I, a man who's lost his fatherland,
stay tied down here and just complain or whine?

The world's left me without a foothold here—
but why remain forever of no use?
Well, I wash clothes, make poems, read the news—
meanwhile, around the clock I dream and dream . . .

181. The first day of school
Trương Anh Thụy

Today is his first day of school.
The child, with satchel, must go in—
wearing a face of gloom and doom,
poor boy, he looks so woebegone!

Mother will steer him to his class,
but here he balks and won't walk in.
The teacher, waiting at the door,
smiles a big smile and shakes his hand.

Against his will he follows her,
dragging his feet which feel like lead.
He turns his head and looking back,
he seems to plead, "Mom, please don't leave!"

So Mother tiptoes to a chair
and, in a corner, she sits down.
Meanwhile, the child keeps watching her
with furtive eyes that brim with tears.

For the first time he'll be away
from Mom and Dad, Grandpa, Grandma.
The child believes the sky will fall
and stars will tumble in their flight.

Recall the other day—he asked:
"But will the teacher care for me?
Who'll be my friends and play with me?
Will they look just like me or not?

"Tell me—at school what should I say
if I would like to drink or eat,
if I must go to their rest room,
if I do wrong and wet my pants?"

He knows so much for his young age!
He sees ahead and makes his plans.
Poor boy, he's just a little kid,
and Mother worries for his sake.

The child's attention now is held
by colored posters on the walls.
So toward the exit Mother slides
and disappears into the street.

But after school she does come back:
in triumph she'll escort him home.
The child clasps her and won't let go
as down his cheeks the hot tears flow.

"Mother, I won't go back to school!
There was no one to play with me.
And when I spoke in Vietnamese,
they burst out laughing—all of them!"

It breaks her heart to hear these words,
but gently she chastises him:
"You're just too spoiled, my darling son.
Watch your big brothers and behave.

You'll be taught English—you will learn;
soon you'll be making many friends.
They speak one language—only one.
Study, and you'll be speaking two!"

Tonight the child she tucks in bed
fidgets and frets and won't doze off.
Mother strokes him and softly says:
"You'll like it when you're used to school.

You're different from the other kids
because you are a Vietnamese.
Since long ago we've formed one race—
our history boasts four thousand years.

Your ancestors include Nguyễn Trãi,[1]
Lê Lợi, Quang Trung—all worthy men.[2]
You know about Hoa Lư, Saint Gióng.[3]
Such names as Trưng and Triệu still shine . . ."[4]

Suddenly the child shakes Mother's arm:
"Oh, I remember now those tales!
Reed tassels in war games were flags.
He flew to heaven, that Saint Gióng!

I'll tell those stories to my friends:
their eyes will pop out, and they'll gasp . . ."
His voice trails off and then stops short.
A steady snore—he is asleep.

1. Nguyễn Trãi and Lê Lợi: see note 1 to Poem 122, "Our land, our home," by Trần Tuấn Khải.

2. Quang Trung: the reign of Nguyễn Huệ (1752–1792), victorious peasant leader of the Tây Sơn revolt.

3. Hoa Lư: the capital of Vietnam during the Đinh dynasty (968–980) and the Earlier Lê dynasty (980–1009). A village in Ninh-bình Province, it was chosen as the capital by Đinh Bộ Lĩnh after he had triumphed over the other warlords and unified the country under his rule. *Hoa Lư* means "reed tassels." As legend has it, in his youth Đinh Bộ Lĩnh would lead fellow buffalo boys in war games, using reed tassels for flags. Saint Gióng: according to Vietnamese myth, the child hero who saved the country from the northern invaders and flew back to heaven after victory.

4. Trưng: the Trưng sisters. See Poem 6, "Homage to the Trưng queens." Lady Triệu (Triệu Ẩu): with her brother, she led a rebellion against the Chinese in 248 CE.

182. Visiting an old friend

Định An

Propped on a cane, I called on my old friend.
He and his wife, grown haggard, seemed like ghosts.
For firewood the lady combed a garbage dump.
In search of eggplants, his honor scoured the pond.
Two sons, half-naked, snooped and ambushed frogs.
A mangy dog, sound sleeper, watched the house.
My host, on seeing me, broke down and sobbed—
he found it hard to get things off his chest.

183. Mother, I am still here with you

Bàng Bá Lân

> *Burn incense, tend the fire, stay whole and true.*
> *Find out if gold and stone can stand the test.*

Each morning, it's a custom now with me:
first, breakfast, then some coffee, sipped at length.
The coffee's purchased from that shop next door—
darn little coffee, substitutes galore.
For bitter tang, mix it with betel nut.
For thicker texture, add some roasted maize.
Brown sugar will lend sweetness to it all—
enough to lull your soul, steep it in bliss.
Those ersatz cigarettes, Hoa Mai, Đà Lạt,
smell acrid, sting your mouth, and make you cough.
Ashes like blossoms sprinkle on your shirt.
Who cares? For not a soul will look at you.

Just that, and yet each morning I feel joy.
Inspired, my poems soar to reach the blue.
"My love", "my darling": passion speaks such words,

and like cascades, my thoughts and feelings flow.
Does true gold ever dread the test of fire?
I shall go nowhere, stay in our own land.
Our mother's poor—I love her nonetheless.
She's old and weak—I cherish her the more.
She's known dire woes and sorrows all through life—
and now she feels her own flesh wrenched and torn.
Mother, don't mourn for fear your son will leave.
Mother, don't weep—I am still here with you.

184. Twenty-eight lines for my wife

Yên Ba

I don't know if, when you were young,
and deep in love you had to wait,
you ever felt so desolate—
you wait for mail this morning, at the door.

It gleams in you, the ray of hope—
the mailman on his bike rides past.
Never have I seen you so crushed
as you, stoop-shouldered, walk back in.

Darling, my heart's about to rend—
for you I've never felt such love.
You need not tell me—I'm aware
how much you suffered, waiting far from me.

Your soul's weighed down with sorrows like the hills
and gnawed by infinite pains.
Our shattered livelihood, our tattered life,
the law's foul scourge, which of a sudden strikes—
you share each tear your man, your children shed:
when will your grieved compassion ever end?

A dark, bleak world like winter's dusk—
with blackened lips, with eyes gone dim,
you feel so sad, so desolate:
this morning, at the door, you wait for mail.

I understand why you're so sad,
why you've grown gaunt, your hair's grown dull.
Six long, long years of flux and change:
Hô City's meant sheer famine for us all.
This morning, it's so small, your dream of dreams:
your happiness, a package from abroad.

185. The sea and the sands
H. H. T.

The frenzied sea is roaring day and night—
the quiet sands are cowering, lying still.
The sea's fierce hands will slap and slash the sands:
waves fly apart, sands stick together still.

The sea may flaunt and vaunt its strength, its power—
it boasts a host of sharks that maim and hurt.
The sands just smile in silence and won't budge—
the sharks will die, dirt going back to dirt.

The cruel sea, with leaping billows, tries
to wash away the sands, resistant knaves.
Puffed up with pride, the sea miscalculates;
the sands ashore yet smile and mock the waves.

The sea may slowly drain and then recede—
the sands forever will endure, intact.
Wild waves, while surging high with silver crests,
will crash and break—the sands will stay compact.

The brutal sea is only tide and surf—
with no gold sands, where could it find a bed?
O sea, remember! Deep, deep lie the sands.
When burst volcanoes, you shall bow your head!

(Saigon, November 1982)

5. Men and Women

186. The shrine of Ts'en Yi-tung

Hồ Xuân Hương

I glance and see the nameboard hanging there.
The Governor's shrine is perching there forlorn.
Oh, to trade in my lot and be a man!
Was that all that a hero could have done?

Note: Ts'en Yi-tung (Sầm Nghi Đống in Vietnamese), governor of a *chou* in
China, was one of the men sent by Emperor Ch'ien-lung to Vietnam in 1789
in an attempt to reimpose Chinese rule. Nguyễn Huệ, the brilliant Tây Sơn
leader, routed the invaders, and Ts'en hanged himself to avoid capture—an
incident to which the last line ironically alludes. Later, in a conciliatory
gesture, the Vietnamese built a shrine on a hill and dedicated it to Ts'en.

187. Snail

Hồ Xuân Hương

Father and mother joined to breed a snail.
I grovel night and day among foul weeds.[1]
Sir, if you love me, take my breastpiece off.
Don't wiggle, please, your finger in my hole.[2]

    1. Hồ Xuân Hương comments on the position of women in a male-
dominated society.
    2. The last two lines give an accurate description of how one goes about
eating a snail. *Yếm*, a woman's breast-piece or *cache-sein*, is also the name for
the kind of "door" that a snail develops in the opening of its shell when, in
times of drought, it needs to seal itself off from the air and estivate.

188. The cake-that-drifts-in-water

Hồ Xuân Hương

My body is both white and round.

In water I may sink or swim.

The hand that kneads me may be rough—

I still shall keep my true-red heart.

Note: The "cake-that-drifts-in-water" *(bánh trôi nước)* is a glutinous rice dumpling filled with sugar or mashed beans ("my true-red heart") and served in a syrupy broth as a snack or dessert. This poem is a woman's proud assertion of her integrity in a world dominated by brutal, unworthy males.

189. Jackfruit

Hồ Xuân Hương

My body's like a jackfruit on the tree.

The skin is rough—the pulp is nice and thick.

If you love me, drive into it your plug.[1]

Don't fondle it or sap will stain your hand.[2]

Note: The jackfruit tree *(Artocarpus heterophyllus* or *integrifolia)* produces fruit with a pulp that is quite sweet and good to eat (contrary to what some English dictionaries claim, probably confusing it with the breadfruit tree, *Artocarpus incisus).*

1. The common practice is to drive a plug or wedge into a jackfruit to test it for ripeness.

2. The jackfruit is known for the sticky sap that oozes from its rough skin.

190. Scolding some dunces

Hồ Xuân Hương

Where do you think you're going, bunch of fools?[1]

Come here! Let Sister teach you how to scan.

Young wasps with itchy stings prick rotten flowers.

Horn-happy kids butt hedges full of gaps.[2]

1. Hồ Xuân Hương presumably hurled this poem at some naughty students or young men to put them in their places. They had bumped into her on purpose and tried to paw her.

2. The last two lines imply that mere boys should save their sexual advances for prostitutes.

191. Confession
Hồ Xuân Hương

Through heaven's vault it's cock-a-doodle-doo . . .
Embittered, I gaze out on every bush.
My sorrow I don't rattle—yet it claps.
Nor do I toll my grief—why does it ring?
I listen to that din—my sadness grows.
I rage against my fate—a fruit too ripe.
Talented men of letters, where are you?
Am I condemned to shrivel up and rot?

192. Elegy for the prefect of Vĩnh-tường
Hồ Xuân Hương

You're gone forever, prefect of Vĩnh-tường!
Our debt of love is now paid off and cleared.
Your talents lie beneath three feet of earth.
Your manly dreams are cast to all four winds.
The Maker's balance rod has been mislaid.
The Universal Matrix has snapped shut.[1]
Just twenty-seven months—how long was that?
You're gone forever, prefect of Vĩnh-tường!

1. In the fifth and sixth lines sexual allusions are couched in classical, nonvulgar terms.

193. On being a concubine

Hồ Xuân Hương

One wife gets quilts, the other wife must freeze.
To share a husband—damn it, what a fate!
I'd settle for just ten, nay, just five times.
But fancy, it's not even twice a month!
I take it all for rice: some musty rice.
I labor as a maid: a wageless maid.
Had I but known I should end up like this,
I would have sooner stayed the way I was.

Note: This poem is a succinct and eloquent attack on polygamy from the point of view of a concubine or second-rank wife *(vợ lẽ* or *vợ bé).*

194. The girl without a sex

Hồ Xuân Hương

Did those twelve fairies curse the gal at birth?[1]
They stole her love-thing, stuck it who knows where!
The devil take this mouse who squeaks and woos!
Let him go hang, that wasp which drones and courts!
Guess what she's got—a blossom or a fruit?
How does one tell the calyx from the stem?
No matter, really—all is for the best:
she will be spared a husband's mother's blows.[2]

    1. According to folk belief, twelve godmothers or fairy midwives *(mười hai bà mụ)* attend the birth of a baby.
    2. The last two lines reflect a frequent complaint in traditional Vietnam about the harsh treatment women would mete out to their daughters-in-law.

195. The Man-and-Wife Mountain

Hồ Xuân Hương

A clever showpiece nature here displays!
It shaped a man, then shaped a woman, too.

Above, some snowflakes dot his silver head.

Below, some dewdrops wet her rosy cheeks.

He flaunts his manhood underneath the moon.

She rubs her sex in view of hills and streams.

Even those aged boulders will make love.

Don't blame us, human beings, if in youth . . .

Note: On a journey to Tuyên-quang, Hồ Xuân Hương allegedly saw two huge rocks, one poised on top of the other, resembling a couple engaged in sexual intercourse.

196. Swinging

Hồ Xuân Hương

Let's praise whoever planted those eight posts!

Some climb up there and swing, some sit and watch.

Boys jig with egret knees, their backs hunched down.

Girls sway and twist wasp waists, their laps shown off.

Four legs of crimson trousers flap and fly.

Two rows of limbs like jade stretch pair by pair.

You'll have spring fun and games—but what is spring?

The post once pulled and gone, the hole just stays.[1]

1. The last two lines seem to suggest that men are inconstant and do not know the meaning of true love.

197. On hearing a woman mourn her husband

Hồ Xuân Hương

A woman somewhere cries—she mourns her man.

Shut up! Don't shame yourself before the world!

My little sister, someone should tell you:

"If it disturbs your blood, then swear off meat!"

198. A woman lies alone

Hồ Xuân Hương

It's getting late—the watchman's drum beats fast.
A woman lies alone in all the world.
The cup yields fragrance—drugged to sleep, she wakes.
The moon goes down—a crescent far from full.
Patch after patch, moss spreads across the earth.
Peak upon peak, rocks soar and stab at clouds.
Alas, one spring is gone, another comes.
With whom is she to share a little love?

199. A girl caught napping by day

Hồ Xuân Hương

It's summer—softly blows a southeast wind.
The girl lies down in bed and dozes off.
A wooden comb is tangled in her hair.
The scarlet breastpiece slips below her breasts.
Upon two fairy hills the dew still rests.
To those Peach Blossom Springs the way's yet barred![1]
The gentleman must wrench himself and go—
he hates to leave, but loitering there won't do!

    1. Peach Blossom Springs: see note 1 to Poem 123, "Opium," by Thế Lữ.

200. The Threefold Pass

Hồ Xuân Hương

One pass, one pass, and lo, yet one more pass!
Glory to him who carved this rugged mount!
A cherry-crimson cave—thick shrubs on top.
Some blue-gray stepstones—wisps of moss around.
Pine branches swing and sway when storm winds blast.
The willow leaves lie drenched as dewdrops fall.

What gentlemen or sages will give up?

Sore-kneed and weary-footed, they still climb!

Note: The Threefold Pass *(Đèo Ba Dội* or *Đèo Tam-điệp)* lies between Ninh-bình and Thanh-hóa.

201. The Funny Grotto

Hồ Xuân Hương

Nature has shaped this rock just like a mound.

It's split in two by—wow!—a deep, deep cleft.

Moss grows on crannies round the gaping mouth.

Pines moan when slapped by huffing, puffing gusts.

Love potion drops fall thick and fast, plop-plop.

The path of no return lies dark, pitch-dark.

Praise him who, when he chose to sculpt this hill,

cracked it ajar for many Peeping Toms!

Note: The Funny Grotto *(Hang Cắc-cớ)* is on Mount Sài-sơn in Quốc-oai District, Sơn-tây Province.

202. Ode to the fan

Hồ Xuân Hương

I

One hole can fit just any number in.[1]

But fate's glued me to you since days long past.

Stretch out three corners—creased remains the skin.[2]

Close up both sides—some jutting flesh still shows.[3]

I cool the hero's face when winds die down.

I cap the gentleman's head as rains descend.[4]

While coddling him, I'll ask the man in bed:

"Are you pleased yet with my flip-flap inside?"

II

Are you eighteen or only seventeen?[5]

Let me love you, kept always in my hand.

Slender or thick, you stretch three corners out.

Narrow or broad, you stick one rivet in.

You cool me all the better when in heat.

I fondle you at night, love you by day.

A wild persimmon lends your cheeks pink charm.[6]

Lords cherish, kings adore this single thing.

Note: The poem contains details that precisely correspond to facts about a folding fan made of paper and wood in old Vietnam. Like much of peasant verse, this poem is arranged as an exchange, a verbal joust, between a girl and her lover, with the female taking the initiative and speaking first. Also read Poem 65, "To a discarded fan," by Nguyễn Khuyến, and Huỳnh Sanh Thông's essay, "The fan in the battle of the sexes," in the *Vietnam Forum* 2 (Summer-Fall 1983), published by the Council on Southeast Asia Studies at Yale.

1. The aperture at the handle end of a slat or blade accommodates the rivet or pin, which can carry scores of blades.

2. "Creased remains the skin" because the fan, made of paper and pleated, cannot be quite smooth when spread out: the blades give it a rough, bumpy surface.

3. When the fan is folded, most of the paper vanishes from view, but some of it can still be seen.

4. The use of a fan for a makeshift hat is noted in Vietnamese folk poetry, as in this line: "This fan is for you, my swain, to cover your head with ..." *(Quạt này anh để che đầu ...)*.

5. The boy ostensibly inquires about the girl's age; the line actually indicates the average number of ribs or slats in the framework of a folding fan. A folk riddle about the fan also goes: "The lass is eighteen or twenty. / When it's hot, she's made use of; when it's cold, she's thrown away." *(Thân em mười tám hai mươi. / Nực thời dùng đến, rét thời bỏ đi.)*

6. Used as glue, sap from a wild persimmon *(cậy)* lends a reddish tint—a woman's "pink charm."

203. On picking flowers

Hồ Xuân Hương

Once you go picking flowers, you've got to climb.
Climb up and be prepared to tire your bones!
Bend 'em and lift 'em, branches high and low.
Full opened or just budding, pluck 'em all!

204. An unwed mother

Hồ Xuân Hương

Could not say no—I am in trouble now!
Do you know how I suffer, O my man?
Heaven has yet to hold its head upright—
a stroke has thrust across the willow tree.[1]
Your guilt you'll have to carry all through life;
the fruit of our old passion I shall bear.
The world will twist and slander, but who cares?
Get big without a husband—that's a feat![2]

1. The third and fourth lines contain plays on the shape of Chinese graphs. "Heaven" (天, t'ien), when holding its head upright, becomes "husband" (夫, fu); here, Heaven has yet to give the girl a husband. Liao (了, "finished, completed"), when given a horizontal bar, become tzu (子, "a son, a child"); since liao is pronounced liễu in Vietnamese and sounds exactly like the word for "a willow tree" (or, metaphorically, "a woman, a girl"), this line suggests that the girl has been made pregnant.

2. A couplet of folk verse says: "To have no husband and be with child, that's quite a feat! / To have a husband and be with child is the most common thing in the world.") (Không chồng mà chửa mới ngoan. / Có chồng mà chửa thê-gian sự thường.)

205. Poking fun at a bonze

Hồ Xuân Hương

No Chinaman nor one of us is he:

a head without one hair, an unhemmed frock.[1]

Under his nose lie three or five rice cakes;

behind his back lurk six or seven nuns.[2]

Now he claps cymbals, now he clangs the gong;

he hees, he haws, he hee-haws all the time.[3]

Keeping that up, he'll rise to be top bonze:

he'll mount the lotus throne and sit in state.

1. The first line, alluding to a Buddhist monk's general appearance, is explained by the second. Chinese men wore queues under the Ch'ing dynasty; Vietnamese men used to let their hair grow long.

2. Buddhist monks are often accused of two sins: gluttony and sexual misconduct.

3. This line is an onomatopoeic description of the way a Buddhist chants the sutras.

206. The bonze got stung by a bee

Hồ Xuân Hương

The monk does own a frock—a bonnet too.

He didn't put it on, so he got stung.

His pate is not that something of a nun.

Oh, drat the bee! It made no small mistake.

207. Ode to all flowers

Nguyễn Công Trứ

Intriguing thought—what artists dyed the flowers?

Each flower is perfect with her hue and scent.

While spring's away, they all wait for their lord

who from the east will come and reign supreme.[1]

Red peach, pink rose, white plum—all shades and tints!

Fair orchid, lovely iris—charmers all!

When kissed by wind and rain, they give off scent,

then all come out and smile upon the world.

Lovers imbibe their beauty and get drunk.

Admire a flower and pluck the lute, play chess, sip wine, hum

    verse . . .

Please, never talk of parting from your flower—

while you still can, adore her scent divine!

A flower, a man—they're foreordained to meet.

The hue he loves is fairest of all hues.

A hundred flowers in bloom! At least pick one.

    1. In the patriarchal ideology of Confucianism, the east is associated with
the sun, spring, and love—defined by the male as lord and master. For a
different outlook, from the folk tradition, read Poem 208, "Trương Chi, the
lovelorn boatman."

208. Trương Chi, the lovelorn boatman

Anonymous

Long since, there lived a boatman named Trương Chi,

ugly of face but with a golden voice.

My-Nương, the chancellor's daughter, spent lone days

cloistered inside her palace to the west.

Out on the river, he would pole his boat   5

night after night in winter, to and fro.

Through silent nights he'd raise his voice and sing—

wind-borne, his song would waft and reach her bower.

On hearing it, she fell in love with him,

but when she saw his face she turned her back.   10

Grief-stricken, Trương went home, and on his boat,

planting his pole in the water, sang a vow:

"If in this lifetime we're not meant to wed,

may fate unite us in some afterlife!"

As for My-Nương, she missed his voice and pined—   15

her looks lost freshness and her form turned gaunt.

Her appetite decreased—she scarcely touched her meals,

and failed in strength as sleep eluded her.

Her illness, caused by love, grew worse and worse—

her anxious parents worried day and night.   20

They summoned their physician, asked his help.

He took her pulse, guessed what was ailing her:

"It is the fate that for three lifetimes binds:

she longs for someone—love has made her sick.

If this disease is to be promptly cured,   25

fetch here the boatman who dwells by the stream

and bid him brew my potion for your girl:

it will work wonders, what the boatman brews!"

So from his boat Trương Chi came up and lit

a stove outside her chamber, brewed the drug.   30

Unhappy, quite forlorn, he sang his song.

My-Nương heard him—like magic she got well;

her illness seemed to have washed out to sea.

The doctor earned his fee: two bars of gold.

Trương Chi went home, securely moored his boat,   35

and threw himself headfirst into the stream.

His body drifted, floating down the stream—

his spirit entered, though, a sandal tree.

To celebrate a raise, the chancellor bought

some sandalwood: wood hewed from that same tree.   40

It was well aged—he called a craftsman in

and bade him carve a set of cups for tea.

Alone, each cup seemed plain enough—with tea,

it showed the boatman's image, sharp and clear.

My-Nương, heart-stricken, wept—her tears like pearls   45

fell on her cup: love's crystal broke, dissolved.[1]

How strange they are, the ways and wonts of love!

Who could unravel all the tangled threads?

Note: This is the verse retelling of a folk tale, probably the best known love story in Vietnamese oral tradition.

1. In *The Tale of Kiều*, Kiều says of Kim Trọng, her lover, as she is about to break her troth to him and follow Scholar Mã, the man who has bought her (lines 709–710): "Till I've paid off my debt of love to him, / my heart will stay a crystal down below." *(Nợ tình chưa trả cho ai, / khối tình mang xuống tuyền-đài chưa tan.)*

209. The marvelous encounter at Blue Creek *(Bích Câu kỳ ngộ)*

Anonymous

I

The world has always known this one word: love.

Who, here below, can slip the Maker's snare?

Now ponder on the ways and works of fate:

our Southern realm's not far from fairyland.

Think of those wondrous meetings in the past: 5

first, Liu and Yüan; then later, P'ei and Chang.[1]

And lo, somebody climbed the Tower of Yang:

his dreams of nuptial play were but a myth.[2]

II

West of the city lay Blue Creek, a scene[3]

of grass and flowers—what a charming sphere!   10

A riot of spring peach blossoms and of autumn mums;

pomegranates spat summer's fire, plums hailed winter's breath.

Green rows of willows and green groves of pines;

grass spread to herdmen's paths, moss hid woodcutters' tracks.

It was a lonesome site of hills and streams—   15

wind fluttered thin bamboos, rain fondled flowers.

Under the Lê, when peace and concord reigned,[4]

there lived a peerless youth called Trần Tú Uyên.[5]

His parents' virtues blessed him with good luck:

why, who could rival him in looks or gifts?   20

A boon from Heaven was his ready wit:

still young, he reveled in a student's joys.

He strolled about and saw a lovely scene:

a blend of wilderness and city life.

Atop a knoll, he built his study-hut: 25

old rush for walls and sparse bamboo for blinds.

Butterflies' dances and birds' songs galore;

a lamp and books, the wind and moon all round.

Where else to find such lavish wealth for all?

Hoards of mum gold and piles of lotus coins![6]   30

Compare this with all other spots on earth:

half wonderland and half a hermit's home.

Four gems enhanced his zest: he roved the sea[7]

of ancient saints and roamed the Muses' grove.

The shuttle swung—the days and months whirled round: 35

as plane trees dropped their leaves, the peaches blossomed forth.

Behind the mulberry trees the sun sank fast:[8]

his mother, then his father passed away.

Alas for him who bore this flux and change,

gazing on far white clouds, on yon blue hills.   40

Under the twofold loss his shoulders sagged—

Yen's gourd was clean and empty: nothing left.[9]

As summers went and autumns came by turns,

sun pierced the shade, frost gathered round the porch.

The skies froze at the wester's breath: plums pined   45

before the wind, the willows blanched with dew.

The roof half bristled with uneven jags:

thatch wattles stained by wind and rain-smeared limewashed walls.

The scene was other than of old: parched mums

along the hedge, foul lilies in the pond.   50

As he met woes along his road, he grinned

and hailed life's boons or setbacks with good cheer.

You win or lose as Heaven wills—he plumbed

the sea of learning, and his sorrow ebbed.

Plain rice for hunger, water for his thirst—   55

can sparrows know what dreams an eagle dreams?

His vow of yore weighed heavy on his mind:

he'd at all costs acquit his manly debt.

With brush and inkstone he spent happy hours:

he praised West Lake, he sang of Fairy Hall.[10]   60

The capital echoed with the poet's name:

he ranked with Li and Tu, matched Sun and Ts'ao.[11]

The bag of poems, slung across his back,

could hold all streams or hills, all clouds or winds!

Words decked with pearls! Thoughts blazoned on brocade!   65

Gold tinkling on the ground! Crane flashing past the boat![12]

He only loved those women met in books—

for years he had not sown the seed of jade.[13]

A hovering skiff upon the stream of love—

watching the moon, he'd clasp his lute and wait.   70

III

Jade Lake observed a rite—the Buddha's realm[14]

was all astir: now glowed the feast of spring.

It swarmed with beaux and belles—a motley throng

of wheels and horses raising clouds of dust.

Enjoying spring, Tú Uyên went for a walk,   75

his bag half filled with verse, his gourd with wine.

While he, entranced, admired the Buddha's world,

the sun descended toward the western heights.

The feast was over—one and all went home.

Pear blossoms fell, swayed by the evening breeze.   80

Beside the bridge, those groups of three or five

might hide some nymph—what earthly eyes could tell?

As he was lingering in the shadow of a tree,
a crimson leaf came flying with the breeze.[15]
He slowly read—the sense became quite clear: 85
some lines of verse, a quatrain penned by hand.
Perusing, he stayed dumbstruck for a while:
"Who sent this flirting note to tease a man?"
He was about to answer with some words
when on the wind came wafting clouds of scent.   90

He saw a damsel there outside the gate
with her cortege of waiting maids in tow.
The lady was a marvel in his eyes:
a flower unblown, a moon just waxing full.
Jade bracelets and gold hairpins shone on her—   95
a rainbow gown, a skirt of yellow silk.
The gleam of jasper, and an orchid's grace—charms fit
to drown a fish aswim, to wing a bird in flight.
She looked much fresher yet as she drew near,
strewing faint hints of fragrance in her wake.   100
Her eyes shot glints at him, suggesting spring—
one glance, one whiff, and he fell deep in love!
A youth as ardent as the student Chang,[16]
he'd met a charmer—what was he to do?
She cast a glance, a tempting wave—it would have rocked   105
a heart of iron, let alone a man's.
If Heaven had not meant Từ Thức for love,[17]
could he have strayed and reached those fairy hills?

The stranger his own heart already knew—
he walked up to the swing and courted her: 110
"Carried away by mirth, I'm making bold—
forgive this shameful conduct toward a flower!"
"This is the Buddha's festival," she said.
"In his domain, forgiveness is the rule!
The wind blows all away, both right and wrong—   115
against you, sir, no blunder will be held."

men and women 226

The siren's voice was music to his ears—
near beauty's ocean, waves of lust may surge.
"I am a man with stillborn gifts," he said.
"May Charity shed her light on my true love!   120
How can the Buddha's garden lack for space?
Open a little path and save me, please!"
She answered, "Here the Golden Cord holds sway[18]—
how dare you dally, uttering vulgar words?
Dhyana's a haven making room for all[19]—   125
its boat will ferry here benighted souls.
But what a shame that near the Bodhi tree[20]
a bee or butterfly comes hovering thus![21]
The Udumbara's hung with golden bells—
how dare a goldfinch perch thereon and chirp?"[22]   130
He listened, hushed, and heard the beauty out—
his love, around her, wrapped a shield of scent.
"Still lost on passion's sea," he said, "I shall
redeem past deeds as I amend this life.
What fate intends for us will be fulfilled—   135
may Buddha tie us with the crimson thread.[23]
Let his High Priest now wield the magic wand
and raze the tower of sorrow to the ground.
The pestle awaits the nymph of the Blue Bridge[24]—
what's for the gods may land in human hands!   140
Water and floating fern may someday meet[25]—
across the river let's now throw a bridge."

As he kept dropping hints and wooing her,
the nymph turned on her heel and mutely left.
He followed her as far as Quảng-Văn Hall[26]—   145
above the dancing branches rose the moon.
Discreetly choosing words, the youth inquired:
"Some purple mansion may be your abode.
Or is your home some stream, if not some cloud?

The winds of spring have blown you here, perchance?   150
Show me the way to go there, if you please!
Who'd reach Mount Jade and then return with naught?"[27]
Now she looked back and gave him her reply:
"Why ask about some palace on the moon?
I am so grateful for your kind concern,   155
but who can tell what's real from what's unreal?"
That said, she vanished, lost amid the pines—
her fragrance lingered, but the bird had fled.
Wind-borne, the phoenix soared to reach the skies—
the nymph went home, but love she left on earth.   160
He scanned the pageantry of rolling clouds,
spellbound, bewitched, though far from fairyland.

IV

Still dazed, he groped by moonlight his way home.
The pine-oil lamp burned low—yet he sought sleep.
Her haunting image how could he forget?   165
She lingered there, possessing all his dreams.
The lovelorn butterfly longed for his flower.
He yearned and pined—imagine, then, his gloom!
At times, he strummed the zither, but the tune
conjured up streams and hills, evoking her.   170
His hand would play "A phoenix woos his mate"—
did she, Wen-chün, feel what Hsiang-ju now felt?[28]
At times, he tried to drink peach-blossom wine—
before he'd drained the cup, it filled with tears.
And with each sip, the fumes bedimmed his mind,   175
stirring remembrance and arousing love.
At times, he sat awake as cuckoo-birds
wailed at the moon and bells tolled death of day.
They jarred his nerves and wrenched his very guts.
Could love burn out? Could lovelorn tears be stanched?   180
At times, he languished in the moonglow, as
geese sailed the night and orioles hymned the dawn.

He watched the play of nature's scenes and sounds—
to whom could he confide his secret thoughts?
Spring joy throughout the sky belonged to all—   185
spring sorrow weighed upon one man alone.
Love moved the student's hand to pen a note—
he sent his love sealed with the written plea:
"O Moon, you favor love. Pray, part the clouds—
for lovers cast a bridge amid the stars!   190
I ask to see that blossom face to face—
how can you fence a garden now, in spring?"
He dozed and prowled Mount Wu in all his dreams[29]—
a day seemed endless, longer than three years.

Among his schoolmates, one who was named Hà   195
noticed his plight and gently queried him:
"Why wear that glum expression on your face?
A lovelorn soul, you spurn your daily meals;
your study you've deserted for some time;
you seem to have turned rather thin and wan.   200
Tell what it's all about to your old friend:
perhaps I could assuage what's ailing you."

How shrewd a guess! It did strike home:
what's hidden in the heart can't fool the eye.
Though love is no one's sole preserve,   205
only the lover knows how longing hurts.
For ages out of mind both fools and saints
have all enmeshed themselves in toils of love.
But to speak out? How awkward it would sound!
And to keep still would ache and rankle so.   210
He could not lie about what caused his pain—
he took Hà's hand and told him everything:
"The more I talk, the more I yearn for her!
A woman's looks can shake a heart of steel.
The girl's perfume excites me yet—   215

my heartstrings get all tangled up in love.

My gloom is vast, one hour seems like one year:

how could I then endure, not waste away?

But all men always have experienced this:

they all have borne a common load of grief.   220

Strange that her kind should breathe forth heaven's scent!

Just try forgetting them—you never could!"

Hà heard his friend's account from first to last

and thought the story passing strange, indeed:

"If not a goddess, she must be a nymph,   225

still bound to earth by some predestined love.

The crimson leaf becomes the crimson thread[30]—

water and floating fern may sometimes meet.

A fairy tale did happen at Jade Lake.

Our emperor Lê once visited that shrine.[31]   230

In its bell tower he met a girl who sang

an eerie song and could revise his verse.

He praised her silken words, brocaded thoughts.

He loved her looks and prized a poet's gifts—

he hoped to bring her home and marry her,   235

but in a flash she vanished from his ken.

It all took place just fifteen years ago:

a trace is left—the temple named Nymph Watch."

Tú Uyên could not believe that fairy tale—

he showed the leaf, and it amazed his friend.   240

On this strange leaf Hà saw a fairy's hand

that wrote what should bewitch a mortal's heart.

"Swallow and swan are worlds apart," said Uyên.

"How could I cross all streams and get to *her*?

Despite the walls dividing east from west,   245

though she be far, one day I'll find her near.

Love's palace may be many miles away—

if fate so wills, the wind shall blow me there."

"But in affairs of fated troth," said Hà,

"love foreordained may wait till after death. 250

A futile chase, your looking for the nymph.

Which hill or stream to search in quest of her?

Which bird or fish will bear your word of love?

Go pluck the moon, a needle from the sea!

Do you know where your nymph makes her abode? 255

Why idly pine away and sorely grieve?

Don't ask for trouble falling so in love—

all nuptial matters trust to Lady Moon!³²

As one spring goes, another spring will come—

wait till next year and pick your marriage peach!" 260

In bed Tú Uyên looked back and gazed ahead,

feeling a burden lifted from his soul.

Relieved, he brightened up—he talked and laughed,

since, with his change of heart, lust turned to love.

He waited for the nymph, for news of her: 265

short days of hope deferred, long sleepless nights.

He yearned for one who stayed out of his reach—

among his books, he dreamed of fairyland.

He daily visited Jade Lake, the shrine—

when you are sad, you sadden grass and trees. 270

The selfsame sky, the selfsame streams and hills;

blue clouds and emerald waters as of yore;

peach blossoms blooming still on that same spot—

but where was she, the girl of yesterday?

The dismal breezes stirred a clump of reeds, 275

and gloom descended further in his heart.

V

Consult an oracle! He seized the thought.

At White Horse Shrine he had his fortune told.³³

He prayed, then to the western porch retired.

The candle flickered, incense sticks glowed red. 280

The moon was shining through the plane-tree leaves—
snug in his blanket, he dropped off to sleep.
He saw a figure with high bonnet and loose gown—
with iron rod in hand: an awesome sight.
He heard an order thundered from the yard: 285
"At daybreak go and wait by the Tô-lịch![34]
Need lovebirds on their own make their love tryst?
For you, East Bridge serves as the blackbirds' bridge!"[35]

Blissful, the boy awakened from his dream—
the stars had dimmed, the sky was tinged with dawn.   290
Love prodded him to sally forth in quest.
He hurried there: he could not glimpse a soul.
Clear water, lush green grass—a bridge of stone:
where was the nymph with whom he had a tryst?
Your dream is but a hoax, a mockery—   295
should he stay put and grimly hug that bridge?[36]
He watched and waited for a livelong hour—
while standing vigil, he felt like an oaf.
Tired and bored, he meekly crawled back home,
looking half sane, half mad—a butt for jokes!   300

Now he met a stranger in the street
who had in hand the picture of a girl.
At once he begged to take a look and see.
It was the portrait of a lady fair—
her face, so deftly limned in paint, seemed like   305
the face he had admired at Quảng-Văn Hall.
The more he gazed, the more he loved the art—
could a Wang Wei have made this masterpiece?[37]
He bought the picture, brought it home to hang
right in his study: a charm against his gloom!   310
He locked the door and day and night he lived
with that depicted beauty as his mate.
He brought her chopsticks, treated her to meals—

he challenged her with verse, plied her with wine.
He eyed the picture and imagined things: 315
her portrait might well be real flesh and blood!
A quiet day when autumn came around—
frost heaped cold silver, sycamores dropped gold.
A mood of longing autumn will induce—
who'll gaze down on the Hsiang and not shed tears?[38]   320
He hugged the portrait and entreated her,
telling what had befallen him, his folks:
"Since I met you, my goddess, face to face,
asleep or waking, I have dreamed of you.
You've decked yourself with powder and with rouge,   325
but let me pine and languish over you.
You never leave your bower—could your smile
be purchased for a thousand coins of gold?
For me unlock that palace in the moon:
part clouds and let me peek at Ch'ang O's face!"[39]   330
Upon her peach-red lips he glimpsed a smile—
her face a flower that hailed the Lord of Spring.[40]
Thus, passion is the norm for one and all—
not even nymphs slip through the noose of love.

VI

One day, when school was over, he came home   335
and found the board already spread with food.
He tasted—heavenly flavors it disclosed,
redolent of flowers and of scents unknown.
Was there some magic kitchen hereabouts?
He marveled at those dishes fit for gods.   340
At dawn he left for school as was his wont,
but he rushed back to spy the household out.
Wonder of wonders! He beheld this scene:
she in the picture could move to and fro!
Eyebrows like willow leaves, her face a rose: 345
the goddess he had met was present now.

As she was busy grooming, unawares
he pushed the door ajar and tiptoed in.

He greeted her—he felt the sheerest bliss,
she kept a coy reserve: both brimmed with love. 350
"I've yearned for you all these past months," he said.
"Please tell me, now I have you, who you are."
She said, "My lot's the frailty of a reed—
a woman's tied by fate's red silken thread.
I used to dwell amid the azure spheres— 355
my title is Tiên-Xu, my name Giáng Kiều.
Over three lifetimes fate has bound us two[41]—
to you this humble maiden's troth stands pledged.
For you I was predestined long ago,
and now the bond of wedlock draws us close. 360
The Wise Old Prince be thanked for what he's wrought:[42]
from now this rose shall know the Lord of Spring."
"Over too many days," the student said,
"I swallowed grief, my pillow was despair.
If Heaven will join us two with marriage ties, 365
then why subject my heart to that ordeal?"

She answered, "Yes, I'll give to you my hand.
Heaven's my witness—I do love you true.
But I care not to vie with Ts'ui Ying-ying,[43]
allowing lust to burn and love to cool. 370
She failed to guard her virtue when with Chang—
their love soon lost its glow and broke to bits.
The world still scorns their Western Chamber fling—
a mirror of misconduct for us all.
When blows the easter, naturally a flower 375
may yield her fragrance at the bluebird's call.[44]
After the storm of loveless lust has passed,
she, faded, will be spurned by other birds.

A woman's honor's fragile—if she errs,

a blatant disrepute will follow her."   380

That said, she pulled a hairpin from her hair

and made a magic sign—two maids appeared.

Abustle, they prepared a sumptuous feast:

censers all wreathed in smoke, wine cups infused with scent.

To his own ardor liquor lent more fire—   385

the boy played drunk, attempting to make free.

"We two were foreordained to wed," she said.

"If not, could I have come down here on earth?

But I have some close friends I left behind—

I have not paid them back for their kind deeds.   390

Let me first treat my sisters from Pearl Hall[45]—

for our own love there's time enough ahead!"

He heard such prudent words as pleased his ears;

he would not press his lust against her wish.

All decked with ornaments, the courtyard rang   395

with glee among the flowers, beneath the moon.

As iridescent clouds begirt the house,

the grass-thatched hut changed to a splendid hall.

An aura lit this corner of the skies—

a shower of caps and gowns, of skirts and shoes.   400

Fay spirits hobnobbed with ethereal nymphs—

each peerless maiden boasted her own charm.

With gay abandon they all talked and laughed—

they hailed their friend and toasted her new groom.

As crimson played with gold, they swayed and swirled—   405

their dance gowns winked and shimmered in the night.

They drank much wine, and when the revels peaked,

the fuddled guests excused themselves and left.

They rode in coaches headed for the clouds—

the bride-bed welcomed now the newlyweds.   410

The bridal garlands lay discarded there—

the quilt was spread, the curtain was let down.

Inside their niche they traded toasts of troth—

as blazed the nuptial torch, they dropped the shade.

The fishing boat sailed toward Peach Blossom Cave[46]—   415

clouds rolled, rains poured upon the sea of love.

How much pure gold could buy one hour of spring?

Heaven on earth, when Man and Woman meet!

For Lady Moon, once in a thousand years,

spins perfect threads and joins her chosen few!   420

It was a crimson tie of love and trust

to bind the lovers henceforth, evermore.

Since on the lute the strings had touched the frets,

after those days of longing, they knew bliss.

Cool breeze, bright moon—at all such balmy times,   425

they sipped celestial nectar, played duets.

Amid a spray of frost, a rain of flowers,

they swapped some verse or by the screen played chess.

A beautiful maiden and a handsome boy

enjoyed together all the world's delights.[47]   430

At one, a lover and his lady fair

shared nature's treasures—heaven on this earth.[48]

A happy home where gathered all his friends—

as housewife and as hostess she excelled.

VII

Year followed year: three had by now gone past—   435

almonds and pomegranates had bloomed and bloomed.

The union they had thought so perfect once

was blighted by the fate that had joined them.

After the earthly student wed the nymph,

he would indulge in wine more than before.   440

He daily staged a drunken bout or two—

to stop him then, she chidingly would say:

"By your kind leave I shall impart my thoughts.

How can you act this way and spoil your life?
But they abound, examples from the past,   445
written in stone, not soon to wear away.
Who roamed the hills with hoe to dig his grave?[49]
Who dived into a river for the moon?[50]
If you don't know the error of your ways,
let both hold up a mirror for your sake."   450

In vain, alas, did she admonish him—
her words flowed off like water off a rock.
All through the livelong day and night he drank,
consorting with Liu Ling or with Li Po.[51]
While liquor, fateful demon, haunted him,   455
his lute fell hushed, his incense burned no more.
As spirits kept his soul and wits bemused,
she tried all different ways to plead with him.
It grated on his ears and strained his nerves—
while drunk, he brutally struck and battered her.   460
He tore in two what had united them—
she'd fain have drifted, fernlike, down the stream.
The constant nymph poured tears of heaven's grief,
as she deplored the human's fickle love.
"My words exceeded what I meant," she said.   465
"please calm your wrath and deign to pardon me."

He kept carousing, happy in his cups—
his mind, bedeviled, reeled, lost to the world.
Nothing she kept repeating moved him now—
on her he heaped a drunkard's foul abuse.   470
"About our love and marriage," said the nymph,
"ah woe, spilt water can't refill the bowl.[52]
Pity the Herdboy and his Weaver Maid—
in fall, how often can they cross the bridge?[53]
Why care for this base blossom any more?   475
Why bother any more with love gone stale?

Since you intend to split two lovebirds up
and cast me from your side, I must obey.
It's over—let's pretend we give it back,
the crimson thread and all, to Lady Moon!"   480
She bowed, then out she flew and disappeared,
leaving him slumped in stupor at his desk.

VIII

Sodden and drunken, he knew not a thing—
as slowly he revived, he learned the truth.
Where was she now? And how to win her back?   485
He might see her in dreams, but nowhere else.
The fairy hills were many leagues away—
he could not send a word through those thick clouds.
He strained his eyes and scanned the great beyond:
mounds of green grass and groves of dark blue trees;   490
swirls of gold sand and silver dust far off—
mists crawled on earth, hills soared at heaven's foot.
Deep streams and seas lay past his human ken—
the way stretched forth like his own love for her.
He sadly watched the landscape robbed of life—   495
the breeze stirred leaves and frost weighed branches down.
He sadly watched the sea cove—vast, immense,
it harbored throngs of little boats downstream.
He sadly watched where Hsing-yang Town began[54]—
wild geese, dew-drenched, winged southward like a flash.   500
He sadly watched the River Tô flow on—
birds cried in bushes, buffalo roamed bare fields.
The bleak and desolate scenery touched this man
with heartstrings tangled in a web of love.
Was he Chang Shih reborn, who failed to reach   505
those fairy hills to which his wife had flown?[55]
And did she share the destiny of Ch'ang O,[56]
moon-bound and all alone on winter nights?

He mused upon his plight—the nymph had fled,
while he was left to wait and yearn for her.   510

As night and day wheeled round with moon and wind,
disheartened, he kept brooding on the world.
Why mock a human so, Old Lady Moon?
You spun a flimsy thread and tied it loose.
They lived apart—she stayed on fairy hills,   515
unlike some stream that would flow back to earth.
He watched the painting: it still looked like her,
powdered and rouged—with her the soul had fled.
He languished and despaired of everything—
allowed himself no sleep, enjoyed no food.   520
Thinner he grew: a mere cicada's shell,[57]
a gibbon's broken heart, a cuckoo's lovelorn soul.[58]
To lull his grief, ten poems he composed:
each word a tear, each line a string of pearls.

One day, Hà came to visit Trân, his friend.   525
The boy's distress moved him to give advice:
"Who knows that she's a nymph and not a fiend?
Though luck bring weal or woe, please grieve no more.
If she's a nymph, she's through with you as mate:
the pearl will not come back to your Ho-p'u.[59]   530
So make an effort, friend, and brighten up:
discard your heartache, cast it all away!
Should something happen that attracts the stare
of vulgar eyes, would it befit you well?"

Trân answered, "Once, I swore my solemn troth—   535
as firm as rock, it must now be redeemed.
I'd rather bear the world's derisive taunts
than play her false—my mate, my kindred soul.
The thread that ties us two was no mistake—
a silkworm never ceases spinning silk.[60]   540
Why trouble over what concerns you not?

men and women **239**

Wear out your tongue but you'll not shake my heart!"
Hà learned he'd spoken words to no avail—
embarrassed, he excused himself and left.

IX

The visitor regained his study room—   545
alone with his own shadow, Trần despaired.
He set his mind on scouring fairy hills—
he'd pledge his troth to her in afterlife.
Her sash of silk hung ready at his side—
he'd use it now to end both lust and love.   550

A breeze that wafted fragrance stirred the blind—
a garland scattered flowers on the sill.
While, startled, he was wondering yet, he heard
the pad of shoes and saw her reappear.
They faced each other—he was stunned and dazed: 555
awake, he thought he hovered in some dream.
Propitious fate had brought her back in time—
one minute more and he'd have killed himself.

With goggle-eyed astonishment he stared;
joy from his heart spoke words to welcome her.   560
He said, "Since I first missed your lovely face,
my soul's dwelt on the moon and roamed the clouds.
I was about to brave the streams and seas
and cross the bridge between this life and death.
I could not play you false, beloved wife—   565
I call to witness Heaven and the earth.
But why reopen bygone matters now?
To you I hereby vow my love and troth."
"The lute has found the player's hand," she said.
"You like its sound—dare I roll up its strings?   570
You did love's labor for my sake—dare I
still keep love's censer cold and light no fire?"

They swore their wedded love and troth anew—
together, they retired to their own nest.
In their spring garden, flower and bee had met—   575
after long absence, love more fiercely blazed.
For years they shared soft pillows, a warm bed—
locked room and bolted door protected love.
On its peach branch an oriole cried good news—
from that fine tree a scion had sprung forth!   580
The boy, named Trân, partook of fairyhood—
for him a scholar's glory lay in store.

X

With fervor now, Uyên burned the midnight oil,
all poised to leap the waves and ride the clouds.[61]
He'd soar and roam officialdom's high spheres—   585
but calmly she explained a thing or two.
"Look, and see through this world's affairs," said she.
"How fame and gain hold many men in thrall!
In autumn skies clouds gather and disperse;
In springtime flowers bloom and shortly fade.   590
Eighty or ninety years, that is life's span:
the colt flies past your window and won't stop![62]
The world's a sojourn for your bag of bones—
inside the Maker's furnace things are born to die.[63]
Who can escape from this terrestrial cage?   595
How many are the earthlings greed has drowned!
Wise thinkers and brave heroes of all times
have ended there to rot with weeds and shrubs.
As days roll on and months must wane and pass,
a woman's cheeks soon pale, her hair soon grays.   600
The wilds hold ancient ruins—what stands there?
The famed Bronze Sparrow Tower? Yüeh-yang Hall?[64]
The play of flux and change still runs on stage,
but iron hills have crumbled down to dust.
You'd better spend your days on holy heights: 605

there bliss reigns everywhere, all year is spring.

At will you'll rove four oceans and five lakes

or roam across three islands and ten reefs.

You'll dwell in golden domes and ruby halls—

with gourd of nectar, you'll haunt mists and streams.   610

Hamlets all snug in snow, towns decked with flowers—

pines dance to castanets, brooks sing to lutes.

One day of leisure in our wonderland

is worth ten thousand years right here on earth.

Think and conclude: Which is the happier bird,   615

a cooped-up cock or free crane in the wilds?"

He felt divided—lured by fairyland,

he was not cured of passion for this world.

He said, "A sword and books have fallen to my lot.

If I play hermit, who'll play Yi or Chou?"[65]   620

"A man who merits such a name," she said,

"keeps his own soul unsoiled by gain or loss.

Covet and get all wealth on earth—a bird

that flies and flies can't break through heaven's bounds!

Why make my fellow fairies laugh? Enjoy   625

a crane's or gibbon's life where rainbows gleam.

If to this hurly-burly world you cling,

who will inhabit those three dozen caves?"[66]

He listened, learned the cause of past mistakes—

awaked from sleep, he cleansed off earthly dust.   630

He queried her: "Like Huang-ti and An Ch'i,[67]

how can a man achieve immortal life?"

"Our magic works such wonders," she replied.

"Both Ch'iao and Sung became immortals thus.[68]

And you belong to scholardom's high spheres—   635

you're listed there, among the chosen few.

Study till you have learned the Way of Truth,

till you have grasped essential mysteries!"

She handed him a jujube and an amulet,
a crucible for pills of lasting life.   640
With pure delight the two discussed the Way—
lotus wine soothed their tongues and orchid tea their hearts.
Wind in the willows, moon on sycamores:
time flew and human bones seemed buoyed by wings.
As he was smelting ore for gold or silver,   645
he dreamed of Hsi Wang Mu, and of the Wise Old Prince.[69]
Now, out of nowhere, rainbow clouds appeared—
two cranes alit to pick the couple up.
They mounted, holding hands and full of glee—
he urged their son to keep his once-sworn vow: 650
"For you a laureate's glorious hour will sound.
Let clouds and dragon meet! You'll join us then."[70]
That said, they started on the path of clouds—
the cranes winged west and vanished out of view.

They reached P'eng-lai, a world unto itself,[71]   655
a god-wrought site: flowers for curtains, rocks for beds.
Eight wondrous landscapes ever on display—
Mount T'ien-t'ai, Lake Tung-ting they call their own.[72]
Astride a phoenix or a dragon, they rove they skies
with maids and pages, on the wind, among clouds.   660
Amid blue hills they play at chess, delight
in caves and crags, drink by some stream or lake.
They dwell in the northern sea or in T'ang-wu;[73]
they know sweet ease in Yüan-chiao or Fang-hu.[74]
Husband and wife spend joyous days and months   665
there in the infinite realm of deathless life.

A demigod, Trân triumphed as a laureate.
He rode a whale to join them in P'eng-lai.

XI

A band of folk enjoys that cloudland's bliss—
their kith and kin still live down here on earth.   670

The town still boasts the shrine of Lady Ngô,[75]

the An Quốc shrine, the Golden Turtle knoll.[76]

Blue Creek, the scene of yore, exists there still:

a book of legends tells what happened there.[77]

This tale of blessed wedlock was conceived   675

and penned as a diversion, love to chart.

Reader, may it delight you for a spell

and while away the idle midnight hour.

Note: Bích Câu kỳ ngộ ("The marvelous encounter at Blue Creek") is an
adaptation in Vietnamese six-eight *(lục-bát)* verse of a prose tale in classical
Chinese written in the eighteenth century either by the woman scholar Đoàn
Thị Điểm (1705–1748), according to Trần Văn Giáp, or by Đặng Trần Côn
(1710–1745), according to Hoàng Xuân Hãn. The identity of the person who
produced the adaptation is also a matter of dispute: Giáp attributes it to Vũ
Quốc Trân (born toward the end of the nineteenth century), whereas Hãn
thinks it the work of some descendant of Nguyễn Du, author of *The Tale of
Kiều*. In any case, the Southeast Asian roots of the tale are revealed in its
stress on sexuality and in the strong, almost dominant role of the woman,
Giáng Kiều, when she deals with the man, Tú Uyên, as well as in its implied
rejection of Confucian values and ethics, to which the male hero pays lip
service at first but which he will renounce in the end.

1. Liu and Yüan: Liu Ch'en (Lưu Thần, in Vietnamese) and Yüan Chao
(Nguyễn Triệu). Under the Han dynasty, Liu and Yüan allegedly met and fell
in love with nymphs on Mount T'ien-t'ai in Chekiang.

P'ei and Chang: P'ei Hang (Bùi Hàng) and Chang Shih (Trương Thạc).
According to Taoist lore, an unsuccessful T'ang scholar, P'ei Hang, met a
nymphlike girl, Yün-ying (Vân Anh), in Lan-t'ien, Shensi, and eventually
wedded her. Chang Shih, too, married a woman from fairyland who later left
him and went back there.

2. The Tower of Yang: Yang-t'ai (Dương-đài), the location of Mount Wu,
in a Chinese myth about divine kingship. There, King Hsiang-yang (Tương-
Dương) of Ch'u (Sở) regularly mated with a fertility goddess in his dreams.

3. The city: Thăng-long or "Soaring Dragon" (now Hanoi). Blue Creek:
Bích Câu, a suburb of Thăng-long (in the area of Hàng Bột in Hanoi).

4. The story allegedly took place in the reign of King Lê Thánh-tông (who
ruled from 1460 to 1497).

5. Trần: a family name (also designating a Vietnamese dynasty lasting
from 1225 to 1400). Tú Uyên: Tú was a title informally granted to a student

of the National College (known as Tú-Lâm-Cục under the Lê dynasty) for the political elite; Uyên was the hero's given name.

6. "Mum gold": yellow chrysanthemums as a bounty from nature. "Lotus coins": the little round leaves of the young lotus or water lily look like copper coins.

7. "Four gems": a scholar's "four treasures" (the pen or writing brush, ink, paper, and the inkslab).

8. The lengthening shadows of mulberry trees at sunset symbolize the twilight of life.

9. "Yen's gourd": a metaphor for the frugal life of a poor scholar. Confucius' favourite disciple, Yen Hui (Nhan Hồi), was so lacking in worldly goods that he drank water from a gourd and ate rice from a basket. The line signifies that the death of both his parents left Tú Uyên completely destitute.

10. West Lake: a lake located northwest of Hanoi. Fairy Hall: the name of a Taoist temple.

11. Li and Tu: Li Po (Lý Bạch) and Tu Fu (Đỗ Phủ), the two great T'ang poets. Sun and Ts'ao: Sun Ch'o (Tôn Xước) and Ts'ao Chih (Tào Thực), two famous Chinese writers.

12. "Gold tinkling on the ground": Sun Ch'o showed his prose poem to a friend and boasted, "Drop it on the floor, and you'll hear the sound of gold!". "Crane flashing past the boat": allusion to a passage from the prose poem "The Red Cliff," by Su Shih (Tô Thức), the Sung writer.

13. Tú Uyên, engrossed in his books, had never thought of meeting some girl in real life. This line alludes to a Chinese tale of magic with obvious sexual connotations. A young man in Lan-t'ien (Shensi) befriended a Taoist priest, giving him water to drink, and in return was presented with a bowl full of stones. He was told to plant the stones in the earth and they would grow into jade, allowing him to get the wife of his dreams. Later, in the capital, he met a girl he wished to marry. For the bride-price, her parents demanded a pair of white jade bracelets. He went back to the spot where he had planted the stones and found five pairs. He thus was able to wed the girl.

14. Jade Lake (Ngọc-Hồ): the name of an old Buddhist temple, once sacred to a goddess named Lady Ngô (Bà Ngô), probably a form of the Great Mother.

15. A T'ang man found a red leaf on a stream flowing out of the Imperial Palace: it carried a poem by an inmate of the harem. In reply he wrote a poem on the same leaf, and floated it back upstream into the palace; by chance, the woman found it. Later, she was discharged from the harem. The two met, fell in love, and got married, only to discover that they had written to each other before. The woman wrote in a poem: "Now we know that a red leaf makes a good go-between."

16. Chang: Chang Chün-jui (Trương Quân Thụy). Chang and Ts'ui Ying-ying (Thôi Oanh Oanh), the two most famous lovers in Chinese literature, are

the hero and heroine of a bittersweet, semi-autobiographical tale in prose by the T'ang poet Yüan Chen (Nguyên Chẩn, 779–831). It was in the "western chamber" of a Buddhist temple that Chang and Ts'ui kept their trysts.

17. At a Buddhist flower festival, Từ Thức rescued a nymph, Giáng Hương, from trouble with the authorities—by accident she had broken off a peony branch. Afterward, he wandered into a grotto of fairyland and found the girl again. Out of gratitude, her mother allowed him to wed her.

18. The "Golden Cord" is a metaphor for the Buddha's teaching.

19. Dhyana: meditation, higher contemplation; the Ch'an school of Mahayana Buddhism.

20. "The Bodhi tree": the tree under which the Buddha attained enlightenment; figuratively, a Buddhist temple.

21. "A bee or butterfly": a male who makes sexual advances; a gallant, a suitor.

22. The Udumbara tree *(Ficus glomerata)*, supposed to bear fruit without flowers, does flower every three thousand years to hail the advent of a Buddha. Hence it symbolically stands for a Buddhist temple or in general for the Buddhist faith. Tú Uyên is chided for desecrating a holy place with his banter.

23. "The crimson thread": the tie of marriage. See note 32.

24. An unsuccessful T'ang scholar, P'ei Hang (Bùi Hàng) met Yün-ying (Vân Anh), a girl as beautiful as a nymph, near Lan-ch'iao (the "Blue Bridge") in Lan-t'ien, Shensi, and wished to marry her. Her grandmother told him that he must first procure a jade mortar and pestle for grinding magic herbs. He brought the implements to the old woman and with her guidance produced a magic elixir. After the wedding, he and the girl drank it and achieved immortality.

25. "Water and floating fern": two kindred spirits meant for each other and thus predestined to meet.

26. Quảng-Văn Hall: a building erected under the Lê dynasty outside the south gate of the capital. It served as a center where official bulletins and proclamations were posted.

27. Mount Jade: the home of nymphs (whom mortal men would love to meet and marry). There dwells the Queen Mother of the West (Hsi Wang Mu), the Hera/Juno of the Taoist pantheon.

28. The Han writer Ssu-ma Hsiang-ju (Tư Mã Tương Như—his courtesy name was Ch'ang Ch'ing, 179–17 BCE) played the tune "A phoenix woos his mate" on the lute and captured the heart of a young widow, Cho Wen-chün (Trác Văn Quân). She eloped with him against her rich father's wishes.

29. Mount Wu: see note 2.

30. See notes 15 and 23.

31. Legend has it that King Lê Thánh-tông met a nymph at Jade Lake and composed a poem for her.

32. Lady Moon (*Bà Nguyệt* in Vietnamese) is the goddess presiding over love and marriage, who binds married couples with threads of red silk. But male scholars have usually preferred to treat her as a male deity called either "The Old Man of the Moon" *(Nguyệt-Lão)* or the "Lord of the Silk Threads" *(Ông Tơ)*.

33. White Horse Shrine: a temple located in the Hàng Buồm section of present-day Hanoi and sacred to an oracular god, Bạch-Mã (the White Horse).

34. Tô-lịch: a small river flowing through the western part of Thăng-long.

35. The "blackbirds' bridge" *(cầu ô)* is the means or person that brings together two lovers. The proverbial phrase comes from the Chinese myth of the Herdboy and the Weaver Maid. The Jade Emperor allowed the two lovers to wed; but once married, they became so wrapped up in each other that they neglected their duties. Angry, the lord of heaven separated them and had them live on the opposite banks of the Silver Stream (the Milky Way). They are permitted to see each other once a year, on the seventh night of the seventh moon, when blackbirds carry stones to build a bridge over the celestial river. On that occasion, the husband and wife weep so profusely that their tears fall on earth as heavy rain.

36. According to a Chinese tale, a young man named Wei, waiting for a tryst with a girl who failed to show up, stubbornly stayed under a bridge and clung to a post until he drowned in the rising tide.

37. Wang Wei (Vương Duy, 699–759): a celebrated painter and poet of the T'ang dynasty in China.

38. The Hsiang River *(Tương* in Vietnamese) metaphorically means sorrow felt, or tears of sorrow shed, by someone longing for a loved one: on the bank of that river the two widowed sisters O-huang (Nga Hoàng) and Nü-ying (Nữ Anh) wasted away as they mourned their common husband, the sage-king Shun (Thuấn).

39. Ch'ang O (Hằng Nga): the moon goddess of Chinese myth, a symbol of feminine beauty. See also note 32.

40. According to the cosmology of Chinese patriarchy, the Lord of Spring *(Chúa Xuân)* represents *yang*, or the male, as the supreme fertility principle. He is also called the Lord of the East *(Chúa Đông)*: the east is identified with the rising sun, and from that quarter in spring blows the wind that favors love and nature's rebirth.

41. Once fate has destined a man and a woman for each other, they will become mates—if not in this lifetime, then over the next two reincarnations. Bound by karmic ties *(duyên)*, they owe each other a debt *(nợ)*, which must be paid off in the course of three existences *(ba sinh)*.

42. The "Wise Old Prince" is Lao-tze, worshiped as a Taoist deity.

43. Ts'ui Ying-ying: see note 16 above.

44. The bluebird *(chim xanh)* is the herald of the Queen Mother of the West and often acts as a messenger of love.

45. Pearl Hall: the palace of Ch'ang O, the moon goddess. (Because of its shape, a pearl is often compared to the full moon and mythologically equated with it.)

46. Peach Blossom Cave: a grotto where nymphs dwell. (The phrase is used here in an erotic sense and alludes to the female pudenda.) See also note 1 to Poem 123, "Opium," by Thế Lữ.

47. "The world's delights": playing or listening to the lute *(cầm)*, playing chess *(kỳ)*, composing or enjoying poetry *(thi)*, and drinking wine *(tửu)*, the last being sometimes replaced by painting *(họa)*.

48. "Nature's treasures": the wind *(phong)*, flowers *(hoa)*, snow or frost *(tuyết)*, and the moon *(nguyệt)*.

49. Liu Ling (Lưu Linh) was the great drinker of a group of Taoist anarchists celebrated as the Seven Sages of the Bamboo Grove. In his rambles, he carried with him both a bottle of liquor and a hoe, the tool that would come in handy for digging his grave, should he drop dead while drunk.

50. According to romantic legend, the poet Li Po (Lý Bạch) died when, befuddled with drink, he mistook the moon's reflection in a river for the real thing and dived for it.

51. Liu and Li Po: see notes 49 and 50 above.

52. The Vietnamese epitomize mutual trust with the image of a bowl full of water *(bát nước đầy)*. They say: "Spilt water cannot be gathered and fill [the bowl] again." *(Nước đổ bốc không đầy.)*

53. The Herdboy an the Weaver Maid: see note 35 above.

54. Hsing-yang Town: a big market town in Hunan, south of a mountain range that the Chinese considered to be the southernmost limit of the cold country.

55. Chang Shih (Trương Thạc) wedded the nymph Tu Lan-hsiang (Đỗ Lan Hương), but the marriage did not work out, and she soon left him.

56. Ch'ang O (Hằng Nga) stole the drug of immortality from her husband Shen Yi (the sun god as the Divine Archer) and fled to the moon, where she has been living alone ever since.

57. A thin, gaunt person is proverbially likened to the shell of a dead cicada.

58. A gibbon howls to mourn the loss of its baby. The cry of a cuckoo may symbolically express sorrow over the loss of a loved one. King Wang ruled Shu (in modern Szechwan), an exemplary sovereign until he fell in love with his minister's wife and had an affair with her. When it was discovered, he yielded the throne to the offended husband and fled in shame to the mountains. He died there in seclusion and turned into a cuckoo (or some comparable bird

like the nightjar or the rail). His mournful call bewails the double loss of his realm and his love. See also Poem 59, "On hearing the rail cry," by Nguyễn Khuyến.

59. Ho-p'u (Hợp-phô) in Chiao-chou (present-day Kwangtung) was once renowned for its pearl fisheries; but, unhappy with a despotic governor, the native pearl divers fled the area. As pearl fishing decreased, people said that the pearls had disappeared. On the appointment of a wiser, kinder governor to replace the tyrant, the divers returned, and pearl fishing thrived again: people said that the pearls had come back. The saying "The pearl has come back to Ho-p'u" *(Châu về Hợp-phô)*, usually means that what was lost has been returned to its rightful owner or come back to the place it belongs.

60. A lover's true love lasts forever.

61. A fish swims upstream and leaps over three waterfalls to turn into a dragon and ride the clouds: this was once the metaphor for a scholar who successfully passed all three levels of civil service examinations and thus qualified himself to serve the king or emperor—the Son of Heaven—as a high official.

62. In the *Chuang Tzu*, a Taoist classic, fleeting time is likened to the glimpse you catch of a white colt galloping past a crack in your window.

63. The Maker: the "Great Potter's Wheel" *(Hồng-Quân)*, the shaper of human destinies.

64. Bronze Sparrow Tower: a famous palace built in Honan by Ts'ao Ts'ao (Tào Tháo, 155–22), ruler of Wei, during the Three Kingdoms period of Chinese history.

Yüeh-yang (Nhạc-dương): an area in Hunan once famous for a palace built near Lake Tung-ting under the T'ang.

65. Yi and Chou: Yi Yin (Y Doãn) and the Duke of Chou (Châu-công), two legendary statesmen of ancient China.

66. "Those three dozen caves": fairyland, the world of nymphs. See note 46 above.

67. Huang-ti (Hoàng Đế): the Yellow Emperor, the divine creator of Chinese culture and civilization. An Ch'i (Yên Kỳ): a herbalist who lived under the Tsin dynasty and achieved immortality, according to folk legend.

68. Wang Tze Ch'iao (Vương Tử Kiều) and Ch'ih Sung-tze (Xích Tùng Tử) were two Taoist immortals.

69. Hsi Wang Mu: see note 27. The Wise Old Prince: see note 42.

70. "Let clouds and dragon meet": see note 61 above.

71. P'eng-lai (Bồng-lai): the fairy island of Chinese myth, allegedly located in the eastern ocean.

72. T'ien-t'ai (Thiên-thai): a mountain range in Chekiang, reputed to be fairyland. Tung-ting (Động-đình): a scenic lake in Hunan, a favorite resort of "lake fairies," naiads, and other spirits, according to folk belief.

73. T'ang-wu (Thương-ngô): an area in Kwangsi, once considered to be the otherworld of immortals.

74. Yüan-chiao (Viên-kiệu) and Fang-hu (Phương-hồ): two of the five fairy islands (including P'eng-lai) in the Eastern Ocean, according to Chinese mythology.

75. The shrine of Lady Ngô: see note 14.

76. The An Quốc shrine: a shrine dedicated to the memory of Trần Tú Uyên, honored as a Taoist immortal. The Golden Turtle knoll: a hill shaped like a turtle, which rises above the lake at Bích-câu.

77. This line alludes to the *Truyền kỳ tân phổ (A New Record of Strange Tales)*, the collection of legends in Chinese which includes the source story of this narrative poem.

210. The constant mouse *(Trinh thử)*

Anonymous

Under the Long-Khánh reign when Trần held sway,[1]
all paid their tributes, and the realm knew peace.
In his still hermitage like Chu's Deer Cave[2]
dwelt Master Hồ Huyền Quy of high renown.[3]
He boasted knowledge of full many things   5
and understood the speech of beasts and birds.

He visited the capital one day
and stayed next door to Prime Minister Hồ.[4]
Drip-drop—the clock was marking the third watch;[5]
fretful in that strange house, he could not sleep.   10
All of a sudden, from a peach tree nearby,
he heard a dog let loose with loud, shrill barks.
Along the wall, was it not some white mouse
fleeing in panic, tail curled up in fright?

She'd found some sheltered cranny in the wall;   15
she darted in and took her refuge there.
Its quarry lost, the dog just trotted off;
but in the hole a male voice challenged her:

"Hey, who are you? We've never met before!
You've barged into my home so late at night." 20

When Scholar Hô heard those strange goings-on,
he walked up to the wall and took a peek.
He saw a rat asprawl inside his den
and prattling on like some unpracticed fool.
While he breathed his sweet nothings in her ear, 25
the scared white mouse still shivered like a leaf.[6]
When she revived, she realized her plight:
what had she stumbled into, in this spot?
Now how was she to beat a safe retreat,
an eel at risk inside a pot of crabs?[7] 30
So, making bold, she pleaded with the rat:

"My home's around the corner, hereabouts.
I lost my way and reached this neighborhood.
Misfortune had me meet a wicked dog.
But bless my nimble feet! I got away 35
and scampered to this place where I now hide.
Please let me stay and give me refuge here.
Saved from this threat, I shan't forget your help."

The female mouse's voice, so soft and sweet,
excited him, the rat, to thoughts of lust.[8] 40
"You had some nerve to rush in here," he said.
"Don't you have spouse and children? Where are they?
Alone, in these wee hours, why did you go
and wander like a bittern in the dark?
Or of some lovers' tryst did you bring word, 45
spreading a spring night's fragrance on the breeze?[9]
It happens I'm a loving-hearted rat:
what if you came across some brute, some rogue?"

After she heard him chide and remonstrate,
she told him all about herself, her life: 50
"My own abode is somewhere east of here.

As fate ordained the change, my husband died.[10]
My sorrow no lament could quite express:
I mourned him and grieved for our little ones.
Upon their mother now they all depend[11]—   55
but where to find the stuff for all their mouths?
I've spared myself no pains to scurry round[12]
and scrounge up food for them both day and night.
I heard the minister's hall stood in these parts,
a palace filled with heaps and mounds of goods.   60
Who will eat fish must dig some angleworms[13]—
through scrub and brush I dared to fight my way.
Though it was night, I boldly ventured forth
to forage here and bring provisions back.
But then I met that ruffian of a dog.[14]   65
I fled and ran off course, so here I am."

He heard the widow's tale—at once the rat
made up his mind to try seducing her:
"You've bared all your true feelings," he told her.
"Oh, how I pity you, your lonesome life!   70
I'll grant that marriage generates deep love
and staunch devotion, which I do esteem.
Our morals, though, must bend to circumstance:[15]
it's best to give your gold and jade a home.[16]
An end to care for both the widow and her young!   75
By day and dark she won't lack for a mate.
Gallants will now leave her alone—no more
must she ward off those bees and butterflies.
You're after all a woman, weak and frail—
you might chance on some cad who'd do you harm.   80
The sunflower constantly turns toward the sun,[17]
but how can she stay true and not break faith?"

The white mouse wept to hear such odious talk—
her grief gushed forth in streams of bitter tears.

She bowed her head and slowly told the rat: 85

"I'm like the willow tree the west wind blasts.

You claim to love me, so I shall speak out.

I always follow precepts from old books.

'Honor thy husband till the end,' they say.

A loyal wife must serve one man, not two. 90

Ethics may not be toyed or trifled with—

one's faith must be observed, vows must be kept.

Besides, the sun is settling on my bower—

grown older, dare I try remarriage now?

Let bees and butterflies flit to and fro— 95

I shall keep troth, unshaken and unswayed.

My summer gone, am I to hope for spring?

How often is boiled chicken boiled again?[18]

I'm doomed to emulate the widow Ts'ao,[19]

happy that in the yard sophoras thrive.[20] 100

Now that I've lost my way and reached this pass,

I carry on my head my debt to you.

You feel for me, a woman in distress,

and teach me ways and means—I owe you much!

I have spelled out what my own thinking is: 105

a flounder's glad to lie on just one side.[21]

The hills bore witness when I swore my oath:

in stone I carved a troth to stay unchanged.

Hold steadfast and endure—that's how to live:

if not, the world derides a fickle heart." 110

"You still persist in wrong ideas," he said.

"If you don't plan ahead, you'll come to woe.

Think and see through the mystery of all things:

nobody's spared the ravages of change.

You know the axiom: 'Spring doth not return.' 115

How many mornings are there in one day?

Know when you may advance, and when retreat:

better adapt than cling to chastity.

men and women 253

Let us conjoin in love as man and wife—
the anchored cypress skiff will drift no more.[22]   120
I sadly think of feelings roused in spring—
haven't you heard the proverb people quote?
'Enjoy your spring before spring goes away,
for right behind, old age comes rushing up.'[23]
The horse flies past your window in a flash.[24]   125
Hurry—cast off all cares and seize some joys.
For once the rose has faded, it's the end:
who will pledge you his vows of love and troth?
You raise your bunch of youngsters all alone,
with no one at your side to help you out.   130
There are both times of ease and times of stress[25]—
imagine us together on one mat!
We'll be a pair of chopsticks, side by side;[26]
we'll share good food, warm clothes, the sweets of life.
In half a blanket, lying mateless there,   135
you toss and turn at night—you call that bliss?
A constant widow's fame is all you get!
Weighed in the balance, which will tip the scales?
Of old and now, have those with rosy cheeks,[27]
when cold and hungry, kept their troth intact?   140
Compare them not to men in stately halls
who can afford a loyal, true-red heart!"

"A woman, I lack skills," she answered him.
"But I know right from wrong, weigh truth and lies.
Marriage, the primal bond, the general norm,   145
the world's first principle, is not a game.
Since Heaven once created this our earth,
when humans dwelt in caves or in the wilds,
they still knew how to hallow wedding rites,
and they banned lust outside the marriage bed.   150
Of wholesome ethics marriage was the source:
it's right to love my man in life and death.

Does Heaven disregard the constant souls?
Scriptures and classics have engraved their deeds.
In olden times those women who kept faith   155
all prospered, thrived, and came to happy ends.
But others veered and changed like streams or clouds,
loving a Li at dawn, a Chang at dusk.[28]
The history books record their woes in full—
my heart dare not repeat that shameful past.   160
While her own spouse was still aboveground, one
would wait for his demise while keeping trysts.
Another broke her troth and wed again
before the grass had grown on her man's grave.
Why tell who they both were? On people's tongues   165
their names live on in infamy today."[29]

He heard her out and then had this to say:
"You know a thing or two, but not enough.[30]
As your own person with good eyes and ears,
don't imitate, but follow your own lights.   170
You fish the troubled waters of this world
and catch what you can get—that's all there is.
Pick as your model one of great renown:
she might talk like a saint, live like a slut.
In fame who'd rival Empress Lü of Han?[31]   175
She dwelt with gold and purple day and night.
As soon as her Han emperor passed away,
she took a secret lover—her Hsü-chi.
Princess Hu-yang was not to be outdone:
the widow set her eyes on that man Sung.[32]   180
And Empress Wu? She proved a strumpet, too!
She hugged the dragon throne not once but twice.[33]
The moment her T'ang emperor joined the gods,
she pulled the blinds and had her love affairs.
No constant nymph was that far-famed Tiao Chan—   185
she first took up with Lü and next with Tung.[34]

Each man she happened on became her man,

yet did the world make her its laughingstock?

Ponder those facts and judge: a nobler breed,

do humans show more loyalty than beasts?   190

All winners, high in rank and great in wealth,

indulge themselves, pursue their private goals.

How can a woman from the common throng

protect her virtue, save her chastity?"

From first to last she listened, sitting hushed.   195

At times she'd look away to hide a sigh.

He thought his music had bewitched her ears.

How would his love avail her? He explained:

"I pity you for your unsettled state.

Now you must lodge with neighbors to the east.   200

A threadbare household lacking this and that—

water is scooped from streams, wood scrounged from fields.

At mealtime you eat neither meat nor fish.

No insect net or curtain shields your bed.

Wild chickens scratch the courtyard's grass to shreds.   205

Bored cats go prowling round the gate for food.

Dogs lie there gnawing on potato skins.

Thin pigs must root in dirt and gulp thin air.

The beasts your landlord keeps don't eat their fill—

how can he spare the tiniest bit for you?   210

Besides, the miser loves to scrimp and pinch:

holding a handful, he clamps tight his fist.

He'd wring a pestle's neck to get some juice,[35]

hoard food beneath a post—don't hang around![36]

One hand will squeeze, the other catches drops.[37]   215

He'll try to render crockery into fat.[38]

To starve his dog, he'll tie its neck with string.

He'll watch his bin of rice, his jar of salt.

He'll stint on heads of fish and tails of shrimp,

dole out each meager portion morn and eve.   220

men and women 256

How many grains will he allow to spill?
What's kept beneath a bowl can't be dug out.
I'm watching you and feel so sore at heart—
I'm close to tears as I think of your plight.
All my good life I owe to Heaven's grace: 225
a termite hill rose on my father's grave!
The dragon's veins run northwest to southwest;
the tiger's waters all flow east to west.[39]
My fortune, from the tea leaves, augurs well,
the powers that be will further my career.   230
For me a brilliant future lies ahead:
all ten soothsayers say the selfsame thing.
My horoscope has shown auspicious signs:
my personal star will help me rise and thrive.
Because by chance you scurried through my gate,   235
you're destined for the joys of rank and wealth.
You'll own long rows of mansions and high halls,
arbors for flowers, storerooms for your jade,
mountains of silver, hills of gold—and rice!
Enough to fill the Chou and Han grain bins!   240
Shih Sung would cluck his tongue and shake his head,
admiring so much luxury here on earth.[40]
For your own use you'll find all things at hand—
you'll live just as you please and walk head high.
Besides, we rats are gentle, kindly sorts—   245
we pray and never harm or kill one soul.
When mirthful, we do titter by the hedge,
though our housemaster makes life tough for us.
All things considered, we're quite happy here.
Our marriage, though, has given us no son.   250
The marital duty we must carry out,
so we've sought ways to help this childless pair.
We once consulted it, the tortoise shell!
Reading the future, we two tossed three coins.[41]

The Buddha's law works magic, we were told,   255
so at his shrine we begged him for an heir.
We drew black tigers in the house as charms
that might ensure the birth of healthy sons.
I saw Pien Chüeh who gave this recipe:[42]
a turtle's plastron and a horse's hoof,   260
a serpent's slough, a young deer's horn,
honey from bees, ginseng, and lotus pulp,
all to be blended with a tiger bone,
will yield a drug both spouses should ingest.
All failed to work—we would consider now   265
the need for me to wed a minor wife.
She was to have big nipples, thick ear lobes,
and eyelids of a certain size and shape.
But where to look for her? We both implored
the Oldster of the Moon to lend a hand.[43]   270
Then, yesterday, my eyelid itched and twitched!
A spider also dropped before my nose.[44]
To check those signs, I broke a chicken's leg—
the outer claws turned toward the middle one!
At Heaven's bidding, you and I have met   275
as all the omens now come plainly true.
It just so happens that my wife's gone out—
she won't be back for two or three long days.
You went off course and hither found your way,
and in your looks you equal Ts'ui Ying-ying.[45]   280
You don't hop like a sparrow, slither like a snake,[46]
and you stand peerless as a steadfast mate.
I'd build a new relationship with you.
Please let me know: will you consent or not?
A happy wind has brought you here: it proves   285
that Heaven wants to balance loss with gain.
A husband's death, and loneliness, are now
replaced by cozy union day and night.

Must we point to the hills exchanging vows?
Love from a brief encounter—that's romance!   290
Bring all your children here to stay with me,
and in a crisis I'll lend you a hand.
Let's join together sharing room and board—
you need not toil, you get good fare, warm clothes."

She listened as he murmured in her ear—   295
she told him now the tale of Hồ Quý Ly:[47]
"By nature as suspicious as a fox,
Hồ bears no love for gallant, upright men.
The puffed-up frog can splash and stir his well,[48]
but he craves power like that T'ang cat Li.[49]   300
Close to the dragon throne and phoenix hall,
he stoops to schemes promoting his own ends.
A parasite who battens on the realm,
he puts himself above the common good.
But heaven and the earth will someday quake—   305
the frog will stop his croaking and lie dead.
Fish in the ponds dread fire on city walls[50]—
those who fear for their life will up and flee.
Who's better than the landlord I have now?
A cottage with three rooms but days of ease.   310
He need not chase a hare or hunt a deer[51]—
a dragon coils and waits inside the pond.[52]
Let sharks and whales cavort with sharks and whales,
and let small shrimp seek pleasures fit for shrimp.[53]
Lo, those who'll trade a rabbit for a wolf[54]   315
get trapped like greedy pheasants lured by bait.
Better eat little crabs and snore away
than fret and fidget dining on fine beef.[55]
Shun those who sell dog meat and call it goat.[56]
Envy those cranes afield, not cooped-up cocks.[57]   320
What do I care about such hollow things?
A pauper will stay poor but clean in name.

I'm pleased with my own lot and ask no more.

Why should I heed advice from someone else?"

"You've found safe refuge in my home," he said.   325

"When danger's fled, then you'll do as you please.

Unless some urgent matter cannot wait,

why hurry off? Where will you go from here?

Signs that bode well or ill should be believed,

though Hồ Quý Ly may come to a bad end.   330

I'll ride the dragon now—all omens show[58]

a concubine will bless me with an heir.

If only I could get my heart's desire,

never would I forget this lucky hour!"

"You are too kind," she said. "But from my heart   335

how could I let a wife's devotion fade?

Though I still call this world my home, I'm like

a dead cicada or a wasting bat.

To my late lord and husband I belong—

I must stay true or I'd defile his name.   340

To join him I'd have taken my own life,

flinching at no high tower, no deep well.

But little children need a mother's care—

and first of all I have to bring them up.

If it had been inconstant like a cloud or stream,   345

would that Yüeh bird have perched on its south branch?[59]

For years I've drenched the rice in my own tears—

I've fed my little ones with broth and salt.

Would I presume to flout the moral code,

and cut the bond between husband and wife?   350

It's said, 'When husband dictates, wife obeys.'[60]

Precepts the sages taught I take to heart.

Does it look right that now I choose a mate,

I who once nursed my husband, poor and sick?[61]

I'm grateful for your aid in my distress,   355

but say no more—please stop this dalliance!"

Hearing those words, he knit his brows and frowned,
helpless to shake a constant woman's faith.
He wondered what device he should employ
to conquer her who thus cold-shouldered him.   360
He took a different tack, cajoling her
and putting her allegiance to the test:
"The butterfly is hovering near the rose.
The fisherman's boat has reached the stream—won't he . . .?
Liu wed his nymph because by fate they met,   365
and not because he had designs on her.[62]
The white she-monkey mated with young Sun,
reneging on her vows for love's sweet sake.[63]
Even if you won't tie the knot again,
don't you perceive just what I'm hinting at?   370
Two soulmates meet—who'd climb up Treasure Hills[64]
and later crawl back down with empty hands?"

Outraged by what she heard, she answered him:
"The gentleman reveals a brute's base heart!
The turtle's lust is warning for us all[65]—   375
by that commandment why don't you abide?
Ch'ang-ch'ing held secret trysts with Cho Wen-chün.[66]
His neighbor's daughter Sung, the cad, debauched.[67]
Haven't you drained vain passion from your soul,
trying to tempt a faithful wife astray?   380
If I don't keep a widow's rocklike troth,
how will you save your honor and your name?"

He heard the mouse and, smugly nodding, said:
"I am not one to relish literary fame—
don't trust what pale-faced students write of rats,   385
believe one essay and deny my worth.[68]
Have all those lecherous bees and butterflies
bored through partition screens or scaled tall walls?[69]
Filch fragrance and steal jade? That's not my aim![70]

I shun intrigues to keep my fine repute.   390

But let's suppose I harbored wanton thoughts:

would I lack lovebirds cooing in my bed?

Yes, billets-doux have come from every part

and strewn the den to tease and tempt this rat.

I've looked away and stopped up both my ears,   395

and never have I heeded such love calls.

I must think you a wife of sterling worth—

the women of these times cannot compare!

I wish for something that relates us two—

I want you, dear, not out of lust but love.   400

The queen forbids me her rose garden, but

I'll pluck one spray and please my heart's desire.

And soon we two shall go our separate ways—

in autumn could you find your spring again?

You may withhold your favors from my grasp,   405

but to the world you now look compromised! . . ."

She cut him off and told him what she thought:

"Your brazen cheek's an ugly sight to see!

In your spring garden now your queen holds sway.

Why force on me your lust like some vile oaf?   410

But walls have eyes and ears—what brews indoors

will soon be noised abroad for all to hear.

The setting moon is dipping toward the west—

let me rejoin my little ones at home.

I've far to go across the streams and hills;   415

the children, all so young, do need me still.

If, not allowed to leave, I tarry here,

your wife will find me, and there will be words.

She will cry shame on me—with loss of face,

how is a widow's dignity to stand?   420

If she suspects some hanky-panky—why,

my virtue will mean nothing to the world!"

He knew she would not let him sway her heart,
but on an off chance, he made one more try:
"To tell the truth, the mistress of the house   425
came from a clan of highborn mandarins.
Ah, she's a lady worthy of the name!
Sweet-tempered paragon! No tart-tongued shrew!
She goes along with what her husband wants—
never one peep against him, right or wrong.   430
She moves around the house, her mouth quite sealed,
doing domestic chores all by herself.
She wants somebody lending her a hand—
a turtledove, she'll treat you gently here.
For she and you will not dwell far apart   435
and will not squabble over your one man.
You'll play the ivy clinging to the tree[71]—
the bond of marriage will link her and you.
You'll be two sisters sharing this one roof,
living together—no discord at all!"   440
"That's what you tell me," she replied. "But still,
proverbs have always mentioned jealous wives.
This saw's come down to us from olden times:
'She'll share her rice, her shirt, but not her man!'[72]
Throughout the whole wide world, there is no lack   445
of beauties fit for heaven and the earth.
Why would you bother with this wilted rose
and hatch some plan or scheme inside your head?
Heaven on high hears what takes place below—
don't think nobody's there above our head.   450
If you lay violent hands upon this reed,[73]
I'll take a knife and end it all at once!"

Her threat so frightened him that he spread out
a feast by way of soothing her. He said:
"Good luck had you pay my abode a call.   455
Let's share a meal before we say good-bye.

I hope you will not mind the meager fare—
and for your little ones take home what's left!"
He called them dishes native to these parts
and served such tidbits as a dragon roast,   460
a phoenix pie, a soup of swallows' nests:
the little ones had never tasted such!
The mouse declined and said: "My family
earns an honest livelihood each day.
Our village boasts fine customs of its own—   465
the royal court admires our hills and streams.
We mice were there when Heaven made the earth[74]—
we would not let the world pour scorn on us.
With your kind leave I shall now go back home—
later I shall repay my debt to you."   470

"Today you've shown no gratitude," he said.
"What will tomorrow bring? How do I know?
Of this I'm sure: all women are alike—
all think one way, and only of themselves!"
"How cleverly you put it!" she replied.   475
"Does it become a gentleman to flirt?"
Now sore and angry in his heart, the rat
sat there in silence, brooding on his wrongs:
"You saved her life—for you that mouse should feel
eternal gratitude, if nothing else.   480
Yet she's not granted you a single wish—
you don't see her repaying what she owes.
She's smarter than most dames—though raised at home,
she can tell lies and get out of a fix.
You pitied her, a woman in distress,   485
not knowing if she had a man and kids.
She has the looks of someone meant for love,
but lacks the temperament to go with it.
A shame you'll have to let her off scot-free,
the beauty with no passion in her heart.   490

Using all arguments, you talked nonstop,

yet failed to move a virtue firm as rock.

In vain you coaxed her, hoping she would yield

and bless your home with many sons and heirs.

And you're a rat who boasts a way with words!   495

From head to tail you are a sorry fool."

Resigned, he called it quits and said some words

to exit with the smallest loss of face:

"The moon is sinking fast," he told the mouse.

"You'd better hurry back to your wee babes.   500

If I cajoled you with sweet talk tonight,

it was to test a woman's constant soul.

For I conceive no thought of love or lust—

Heaven alone can read what's in my heart.

If I were just a cad, an arrant knave,   505

would I pay court to get my way with you?

You've bested me with fancy words, but then

we've always watched *yin* wax and seen *yang* wane!

I must praise you for your staunch loyalty,

so rare in one with such bewitching charms!   510

Let's part with no ill feelings, either way:

the flower's unsoiled, for which she must thank me!"

"It was this woman's fate," she answered him,

"to owe you her escape from certain death.

Forever you have put me in your debt—   515

but I had to refute the things you said.

To pay a virtuous deed with lust would be

to burden karma further in this world.

Please think again and don't feel cross with me.

Doubt me no more—I beg to take my leave."   520

While she, the mouse, made ready to set off,

the wife, through with her errands, now came home.

She saw her rat escort a female out

and threw a tantrum as she boiled inside.

To the wroth wife the mouse gave her account,   525

explaining why and how she had come here:

"Misfortune struck me like a storm at night—

he rescued me and earned my gratitude.

If you'd been home, you would have done the same,

because all share a kind, compassionate heart.   530

You grab at shadows, making your wild charge—

to nasty gossip you thus lend yourself.

Your honor has endured for all these years—

will you let this small incident mar your name?

Am I not right? Please let me take my leave—   535

I feel concern for my poor little ones."

The mouse once gone, the rat now tried his best

to pacify his wife and calm things down.

But she declared: "All this that you've alleged

is meant to shield her, hiding your amour!   540

If there were not a thing between you two,

why trouble with a stranger and her woes?"

Then she flared up, turned crimson—down she flopped

and loudly wailing, writhed upon the ground:

"No sooner had I stepped outside and left   545

than he brought in a wench and carried on!

Let him wench all he wants if that's his wish,

but do I count for nothing in this home?

I take care of this household day and night—

if fields run dry, I scurry back and forth.   550

He eats his fill, then he starts acting up,

gets into mischief and shows no restraint.

Who'd think the jellyfish would have the gall

to bring home that boiled chicken for a feast?

A spider flees no farther than its web;   555

a frog gets spied and caught inside its well.

Just let him starve—he'll crawl back on his knees.

But feed and clothe him: carefree, he'll run wild.
He takes no pity on his hapless wife
who must go foraging from dawn till dusk.   560
When I came back and crept around the wall,
I saw a dog was lurking by the hole.
A long time passed, but I heard not one squeak,
so quiet as a mouse, I crept back here:
suspecting monkey business, I reached home   565
to find all these shenanigans—ah, woe is me!"

A jealous wife speaks nonsense; from the start
the rat told his own tale, protesting much:
"It was past midnight—sleepless, I sat there,
of course, to watch the house with you away.   570
I heard a dog's shrill bark outside the wall,
and it got closer, closer all the time.
Somebody was in trouble, so I feared,
and needed help before it was too late.
Unsure, I hardly knew what I should do,   575
as I kept wavering now this way, now that.
I poked my head out of the hole and looked—
I saw her, that white mouse, come darting in.
I was then of two minds, and while in doubt,
I took her by the hand, showed her the door.   580
But she appealed and begged a neighbor's help:
the dog was chasing her—she was at bay.
A woman all alone and in distress
entreated rescue, offering me her thanks.
A timely act of charity, 'twould be,   585
to let her cower in a nook, unseen.
She would stay here awhile, then she would leave—
no lewd intent did I have toward the wench.
Why did you have to utter such harsh words
which made no sense and grated on the ears?"   590

"But it's as clear as day!" his wife replied.
"Who's made it up, this sickening affair?
The moment his dear wife just stepped outside
he fussed and fretted waiting for the wench.
If you were such a loyal husband, then   595
why coax the strumpet into your dark room?
You twist and wriggle like a dizzy snail.
You tingle like a goat with itchy horns.
Now stop denying it and wasting words—
your elephant's hidden in a stubble field![75]   600
Who'd dare to step into a tiger's lair?
What mouse would try to catch and tie a cat?
You had it all arranged ahead of time—
would she have upped and followed you on whim?
A fly flies past and I can tell its sex—   605
my eyes don't miss what you've contrived and schemed.
I read it on your face, what's in your mind:
you eat sand crabs and try to hide your itch![76]
You hunger for a female like a cat
whose mouth will water at the sight of lard.   610
You keep your hands off neither young nor old,
just as a frog who sees a rose will pounce.[77]
Are you some dragon stranded in a pond
where you have taken after fools and dolts?[78]
Have I so frozen up in bed that you   615
must charge about just like a famished bull?
Keep socializing with exotic dames
and one day you will catch some social pox![79]
You will get your comeuppance as you moan
while you try brushing off a swarm of flies.   620
If by mistake you sleep with someone's wife,
you'll be sent down the river on a raft!"[80]

But all her words were wasted on his ears,
as he kept thinking of the youthful mouse.

He wished to see her once again at least   625

and thus assuage his longing, his desire.

If destiny had not meant her for him,[81]

why had an accident brought her his way?

Lost in a daze, he yearned and pined, eyes glazed

and staring like a shaman's slaughtered pig.   630

His wife thought him bewitched; he'd eaten up

some magic dish concocted by the mouse!

The lovelorn rat would walk about and moon.

His wife fed him a stew of eel and herbs—

she hoped to break the mouse's spell on him   635

and bid his wayward soul come home to her.

The rat, though, was past cure—no crab will leave

its hole and go to Heaven as you wish.[82]

"An eel I'm holding by the tail," she thought.[83]

"I can't divorce him on these flimsy grounds.   640

The suspect will deny the plaintiff's charge—

how can I prove what I accuse him of?

He may abscond and scamper to the woods—

who'll make him pay his alimony then?

No corpus delicti can I bring to bear—   645

I lack a case to have my day in court."

She raised an uproar, grilling him again:

"The rat has hid his head but shown his tail![84]

You still crave tender meat and fancy rice,

and you won't touch the homey fare I cook.   650

'He changes wives who's risen in the world.'[85]

This woman will not beg you for your love.

A doddering wife should be left on the shelf—

who cares for sagging breasts and shrunken frame?

None likes to eat ripe eggplant or old squash,[86]   655

and I'm well past my prime, along in years.

When there's a moon, the lamp will be ignored.[87]

They love what's piping hot, though badly cooked.[88]

I laugh so hard that I shed tears of shame.

Praise him who coined this adage in times past: 660

'While she still has her looks, they pay her court.

Her looks once gone, they leave her all forlorn.'[89]

What's new and fresh is cherished by the world—

an owl cannot compete against a nymph.

Send this old, leaky pot back to South Bridge[90]   665

and spare her more hard work, more toil and moil.

No more will she drag home a heavy egg[91]

or bustle like a gammer fighting bees.[92]

A sand crab carries sand, to no avail.[93]

Raised by a wasp, a spider gives no thanks."[94]   670

"The words you say sound rather strange," he said,

"though it's a woman's knack to nag and scold:

their sting is worse than lemon juice fresh squeezed.

Your ivy shall not conquer my whole tree.[95]

Am I a weakling you can push around?   675

I'm not a man whose mustache wilts and droops![96]

I've always tried to live and let you live,

but more and more you're baring your true face.

I've hung my head and let you tweak my beard.

I've chafed and seethed just like a cooped-up horse.   680

A donkey's used to blows and kicks, but stop[97]

your endless nagging, pick on me no more!"

She thereupon burst out in furious screams

and rolling up her sleeves, made for the door.

"Together since we were dirt-poor," she said,   685

"we two should have evolved strong, binding ties.

Instead, it now turns into this fine mess.

Well, I shall clean it up for good and all!"

Sighing and moaning, she betook herself

to that east neighborhood where lived the mouse.   690

Now she approached the mousehole—finding her,

she heaped abuse and insults on her head.
The mouse turned purple with both shame and ire.
"How dare you, ma'am, insult me here?" she asked.
"You do not know my mettle, yet you dare   695
call me these names; for that you'll surely pay!"
Sauntering around a corner of the wall,
a cat came up to arbitrate the fight.
Both parties, frightened quite out of their wits,
hopped knolls and hurdled hills to scamper off.   700
The flustered she-rat fell into a pond:
was Heaven, dispensing justice, far away?
But the white mouse got home without a hitch:
she reached her gate and gladly scurried through.

As Heaven's retribution dealt the blow,   705
our scholar Hồ was watching by the wall.
He saw the she-rat thrashing in the pond—
on shore, the cat was waiting with a grin.
Hồ waved the feline off—then, wading in,
he fished the rat out of the duckweed pond.   710
Her hair dried out, she soon regained her wits
and with bowed head, she meekly told her tale:
"I am a fool—neglected by my rat,
I traveled to these parts and met with woe.
I'm grateful that you saved my humble life—   715
how can I value your kind deed enough?
I owe it to your large and noble heart—
Heaven will not forget a virtuous man."
"Such havoc jealous mates may wreak!" said Hồ.
"You pull and tug too hard—the string must snap.[98]   720
Let me tell you what happened, make it clear.
At midnight that white mouse went hunting food.
Chased by a dog, she took her refuge here,
ready to leave once danger was no more.
As he found such a beauty in his hole,   725

was it so strange he made a play for her?

But he ran up against a constant wife—

his wooing got him nowhere, so he quit.

Then home you came—unwitting, you gnashed teeth,

and jealousy made you say vicious things.   730

The merciful Buddha, let alone your rat,

would have been angered by what you said then.

Well, think it over: whose fault was this mess?

You suffer for your act—blame no one else.

So used to braving streams and daring cats,   735

you challenged that white mouse in her own den.

You have cast ignominy on all your sex,

contemning faithful wives—is it no so?"

She listened, learning what had taken place.

"Thank you—you've let me know the facts," she said.   740

"What I said then I now recall with shame.

The moon has waned—how can I make it wax?

A fit of anger made me lose my wits[99]—

now can remorse undo what then was done?"[100]

The scholar chose his words, consoling her   745

and counseling her in every way he could:

"It's you who brought this down upon yourself.

Go back and sweet-talk him to calm his wrath.

If you want peace and quiet in your home,

the best's to get along, agree and live.   750

Who ever wears a shirt above the head?[101]

Why not think matters through before you act?

Conjugal love, how much it means and weighs!

Is marriage but a short-lived, one-day thing?

Stay out of strife—know heaven here on earth.   755

The meek and mild shall outlive shrews and brutes.

Woman and man have shared one mat, one bed—

how often should a spider spin its silk?[102]

Mull over every action like a move at chess—

using your head, do nothing in excess.   760
Don't pick a quarrel—poke at weeds or tares
and bugs come out to stink your household up.[103]
A woman's like a raindrop—where she falls
there she's to stay: she'll know no better place.[104]
However sore or furious he may be,   765
contain yourself and soothe him with soft pleas.
Spare one harsh word and earn nine words of love[105]—
never presume on what you've done for him.
Thus you'll fulfill a wife's submissive role:
yield to the man and you'll get your own way.[106]   770
When your cooked rice tastes bland and soup lacks spice,[107]
the world will sneer—a woman's wiles have failed.
A decent cat will never prowl the graves[108]—
you don't show off your treasure to all eyes!
Don't try to outtalk him and waste your breath—   775
he's your sole man, not one of three or four.
It's no disgrace to shun an elephant's path[109]—
see if a jellyfish can leap the weir![110]
Why don a croaker's face and look so grim?
Don't yank at vines or you'll shake up the woods.[111]   780
Don't swim against a hawksbill or you'll lose[112]—
how could a woman race and beat a man?
Soon mend your petulant ways, learn gentle arts—
two lovebirds will build their own nest and home.[113]
Softness becomes a woman—it's her strength,   785
or else she'll meet with sorrow and weep tears."
She heeded Hồ's advice—when she came home,
she bowed and begged forgiveness from her rat.

Back in his study, Hồ took pen and ink
and wrote the story down lest he forget.   790
Such constancy as proven by a mouse
deserves no little praise, and so it is!
If beasts keep faith, remaining staunch and true,

then why should men fall short and break their vows?

A fickle heart betrays, plays fast and loose: 795

men may be unaware, but Heaven knows.

Traitors with brazen faces, when compared,

prove not the equals of mere beasts or birds.

The he-rat won no prize as he played false

and coaxed the mouse to leave the path of right.   800

The constant mouse lived up to her ideal

although he proved himself a faithless rat.

He found a widow doing what she must

and tried to swerve her from the virtuous course.

When raucous tiffs and fights broke out at home,   805

he blamed them on a woman's jealous streak.

Praiseworthy was the mouse's steadfast troth:

temptation could not sway her true-red heart.

Though rocks may fall and mountains may wear down,

nothing can shift and change a stalwart faith.   810

If beasts keep troth, should humans do far less?

Heaven will not forsake the straight and true.

About one such unswerving, loyal soul

the tale is hereby told in chosen words.

Let those who have some leisure read all this,   815

a story spun in our vernacular mode.

Note: Legend has it that the *Trinh Thử* ("The constant mouse"), a fable in six-eight verse, was composed by a scholar-hermit named Hồ Huyền Quy, towards the end of the Trần dynasty (1225–1400), when Hồ Quý Ly had not yet usurped the throne and was still serving as Prime Minister. Huyền Quy (the "Mystic Turtle") understood the language of beasts and would often eavesdrop on what they said. In Maurice Durand's opinion, internal analysis of the text, and other considerations, suggest that although the original poem may well have been written in the fourteenth century, what we have now is a largely revised and even expanded version produced at the earliest during the latter part of the eighteenth century. A widow, the virtuous mouse, keeps faith with her husband and resists the advances of a suitor, the rat: that is a familiar theme of Confucian ethics, which imposes chastity and fidelity on wives in all circumstances. The fable may be interpreted as a political allegory for a subject who maintains allegiance to the former sovereign and will not be swayed by the blandishments of the new ruler. However its underlying message is construed, the poem can be enjoyed as a clever portrayal of human traits (here displayed by animals) and as a superb example of Vietnamese folklore: no other work in verse has made such lavish and pertinent use of popular sayings.

This translation omits about twenty-five couplets from the Vietnamese text.

1. Long Khánh: the period of King Trần Duệ-tông's reign, from 1373 to 1377.

2. Chu's Deer Cave: the retreat where the Sung philosopher Chu Hsi read and studied.

3. Hồ Huyền Quy: a scholar-recluse and mystic who, according to legend, lived towards the end of the Trần dynasty (1225–1400).

4. Prime Minister Hồ: Hồ Quý Ly, who was to usurp the throne in 1400.

5. Here the timepiece is a water clock, or clepsydra.

6. To tremble violently is "to shiver like a wet dog that is being warmed and dried at a fire" *(run như cầy sấy).*

7. "A little *cáy*-crab has strayed into a big crab's hole." *(Cáy vào hang cua.)* A weak, helpless person is in a quandary or a perilous situation. Another folk saying describes the same predicament: "The eel is dropped into a basket of crabs." *(Chạch bỏ giỏ cua.)* See notes 55 and 76 below.

8. At the sight of the she-mouse, the rat, in the original poem, is "stirred by thoughts of water and clouds" *(động tâm lòng nước mây).* "Clouds and rain" *(mây mưa)* is a common metaphor for sexual intercourse.

9. "To send word through some fish or bird" *(nhắn cá gửi chim)* is to have some intermediary deliver a message. "To greet the breeze on a spring night and go looking for fragrance" *(đêm xuân đón gió đi tìm mùi hương)* is to go out at night and arrange a lovers' tryst.

10. A "change (of white clouds) into blue dogs" *(cơ thương cầu)* is one of the many vicissitudes of human existence—separation, death, and so on. "To take to the mountain wilds" *(tếch ngàn)* is to die.

11. "The little fish (or baby snakes) follow their mother." *(Ròng ròng theo nạ.)* Children depend on their mother for protection and guidance.

12. "[To go with one] mallard foot and [one] duck foot" *(chân le chân vịt)* is to be constantly on the run, to hustle and bustle without a pause.

13. "If you want to eat blackbirds, you must dig earthworms." *(Muốn ăn hét phải đào giun.)* The birds were once caught in a trap baited with earthworms. The folk saying means "no gain without pain."

14. An untrustworthy man is a "fellow [as fickle as] the wind or the moon" *(đứa gió trăng).*

15. "It is common to have two principles of ethics, [one for] normal times [and one for] emergencies." *(Kinh quyền đôi lẽ là thường.)*

16. A woman who seeks security in marriage must "find a shelter for jade and gold" *(được nơi tựa ngọc nương vàng)*.

17. The sunflower, always turning toward the sun, or male principle, is a Confucian symbol of a woman's subservience to her husband and of a widow's dependence on her son.

18. A woman who has remarried is "chicken boiled again" *(gà luộc lại)*, according to Vietnamese folk humor.

19. In the Chinese tradition of wifely faithfulness, the widow of a man named Ts'ao, forced by her family to consider remarriage, defaced herself by cutting off her nose.

20. Under the Sung dynasty, Wang Hu, who had three sons, planted in his front yard three sophora trees, in the symbolic hope that all the sons would grow up to become ministers of state.

21. To accept one's lot in life and make no vain attempt to change it, when one is too weak or helpless, is "to resign oneself [to the fate of] a flounder [lying flat on] one side" *(chịu tốt thờn-bơn một bề)*.

22. A "cypress skiff" *(chiếc bách)* is a metaphor from *The Book of Odes* for a widow.

23. A couplet of folk verse: *Chơi xuân kẻo hết xuân đi, / cái già sồng-sộc nó thì theo sau.*

24. As a Taoist metaphor, the image of fleeting life is the glimpse you catch of "a horse [galloping] past the window" *(ngựa qua cửa sổ)*.

25. "There are emergencies and there are normal times." *(Có khi biến có khi thường.)* This is exactly the same as line 3117 in *The Tale of Kiều* (Yale University Press, 1983, p. 160).

26. "Chopsticks come in pairs." *(Đũa có đôi.)* It is natural and normal for people to be married and not to stay single.

27. Beautiful women are "those with rosy cheeks" *(khách má hồng)*.

28. The phrase "a Li and a Chang" *(gã Lý chàng Trương)* means "one man after another, with no lasting relationship."

29. "[People's] mouths still clearly recount [such cases of infidelity, as if they were engraved in] stone to this day." *(Rành rành bia miệng còn ghi đến rày.)*

30. "To know one thing and have yet ten things to learn" *(biết một chưa hay biết mười)* is to be quite wanting in knowledge and experience.

31. Empress Lü, widow of Emperor Han Kao-tsu (d. 195 BCE), allegedly carried on a secret love affair with a man named Hsü-chi.

32. Under the Han dynasty, Princess Hu-yang, a widow, wanted a man named Sung Hung for herself, but the faithful husband would not leave his wife.

33. Under the T'ang dynasty, Empress Wu was married first to Emperor T'ai-tsung and then to Emperor Kao-tsung.

34. Under the Eastern Han dynasty, Tiao Chan (Điêu Thuyền), a famed beauty, played Lü Pu (Lữ Bố) off against the older Tung Cho (Đổng Trác), causing Lü to kill Tung.

35. The expression for extreme parsimony is "wringing the neck of a pestle to get water" *(vắt cổ chày ra nước).* See note 38.

36. "The morsel of food is kept underneath a post." *(Miếng ăn đè cột.)* Extreme precautions are taken to hide one's foodstuffs or valuables.

37. To get as much as one can and not to miss anything is "to catch with the lower hand and squeeze with the upper hand" *(hứng tay dưới vắt tay trên).*

38. To "render crockery into fat" *(rán sành ra mỡ)* is to be extremely niggardly. See note 35.

39. Lines 226 through 228 all mention signs favorable according to geomancy.

40. Shih Sung (Thạch Sùng) was celebrated as the wealthiest man in China under the Chin dynasty.

41. Lines 253 and 254 allude to various methods of divination.

42. Pien Chüeh (Biển Thước) was a legendary healer of China.

43. The Old Man of the Moon is the marriage deity, according to Chinese patriarchal mythology. See notes 23 and 32 to Poem 209, "The marvelous encounter at Blue Creek."

44. Such signs announce that something (usually good) will happen soon.

45. Ts'ui Ying-ying (Thôi Oanh Oanh) was the heroine of a love story written by the T'ang poet Yüan Chen (779–831). See note 16 to Poem 209, "The marvelous encounter at Blue Creek."

46. The phrase "walking like a sparrow and moving like a snake" *(tước bộ xà hành)* describes particular kinds of gait that betray a base nature in humans, according to Chinese lore.

47. About Hồ Quý Ly, see note 4.

48. A "frog squatting at the bottom of a well" *(ếch ngồi đáy giếng)* is a self-conceited individual who has a very limited view of the world.

49. Under the reign of T'ang Kao-tsung, Li I-fu, a wily schemer, was nicknamed "Li the Cat."

50. When a city wall catches fire, water will be drawn from the moat or pond to fight the flames, and the fish may be left high and dry. The first victims of social and political turmoil are the little people, innocent bystanders hurt by the power struggle among the great. See also note 10 to Poem 37, "Catfish and Toad."

51. "To chase the hare and hunt the deer" *(đuổi thỏ săn hươu)* is to struggle for mastery. See note 2 to Poem 54, "The old hound," by Huỳnh Mẫn Đạt.

52. "The dragon, still coiled inside the pond, bides its time." *(Rồng còn*

uốn khúc ở ao đợi thì.) A great man, still unknown and living in straitened circumstances, patiently waits for his first opportunity.

53. A couplet from folk poetry, often quoted as a proverb: *Kình nghê vui thú kình nghê,/tép tôm thì lại vui bề tép tôm.* Great men and small men entertain different ambitions and have different pursuits.

54. "To sell a rabbit and buy a tiger" *(bán thỏ buôn hùm)* is to trade peace and quiet for insecurity and danger, to borrow trouble.

55. Poor peasants who can seldom afford beef catch and eat little crabs called *cáy.* A couplet of proverbial folk verse reads: "Better to eat *cáy*-crabs and snore away:/why eat beef and fidget and fret?" *(Thà ăn cáy ngáy o-o/ còn hơn ngay-ngáy ăn bò làm chi?)* Note the similarity between *ngáy* ("to snore") and *ngay-ngáy* ("to fidget and fret").

56. "To hang out a goat's head and sell dog meat" *(treo đầu heo bán thịt chó)* is to put up false pretenses, behave quite differently from what one advertises or professes.

57. A man living free and far away from the trammels of society is a "crane in the fields [or wilds]" *(hạc nội).* A prisoner of the bureaucratic life is a "chicken in a coop" *(gà lồng).*

58. "To ride the dragon" *(cưỡi rồng)* is to take a wife.

59. A bird sent from Yuëh (Việt) as tribute to the emperor of China was so homesick that it always perched on a southern branch looking homeward. The legend is often used as a metaphor for a Vietnamese expatriate's longing for his homeland. Such is the meaning of the pen name chosen by Phan Bội Châu, the patriot who went abroad (to Japan, in particular) in the early part of this century to fight for Vietnamese independence from the French: *Sào Nam* or "nesting on a southern [branch]." See Poem 172, "Cold season," by Viên Linh.

60. "The husband orders, the wife obeys" *(Phu xướng phụ tòng)*—a Confucian precept.

61. "To choose a fish and pick a soup" *(kén cá chọn canh)* is to select a mate with deliberate care or fastidious caution. "[I] used to pack cooked rice [for my husband to take with him on a journey to some faraway place where he was to sit for some civil service examination]" *(cơm nem đã trải):* "I used to work and support my husband when he was a poor student." "[I] used to hand a lime [to my husband]" *(tay chanh đã từng):* "I used to take good care of my husband when he was sick." Lime peel and lime juice are valued in folk medicine.

62. Ch'ang O: the goddess of the moon in Chinese myth; a nymph or beautiful woman. Under the Han dynasty, Liu Ch'en and Yüan Chao allegedly met and married nymphs on Mount T'ien-t'ai in Chekiang.

63. According to Chinese folklore, a white gibbon *(bạch-viên)* was transformed into a woman and married Sun Ko (Tôn Các), to whom she bore two children. The story has been retold in Vietnamese verse.

64. "Two soulmates meet." According to Chinese legend, Po Ya (Bá Nha) was a subtle lutenist, and the only man who could appreciate each and every nuance of his playing was Chung Tzu-ch'i (Chung Tử Kỳ). On Chung's death, Po smashed his lute and played no more. A kindred spirit is the "friend who understands the sound of one's music" *(bạn tri-âm)*.

65. The Chinese consider the turtle a symbol of sexual lust and lewdness.

66. See note 28 to Poem 209, "The marvelous encounter at Blue Creek."

67. Sung Yü (Tống Ngọc), a Ch'u poet of the third century before the Christian era, fell in love with a neighbor's daughter; he wooed and won her with poetry.

68. Su Tung-p'o (Tô Đông Pha), the Sung writer (1036–1101), composed an essay about the rat.

69. "To bore through partitions and climb walls" *(khoét vách đào tường)*: these feats, which are normally attributed to rats and mice, also typify the activities of trysting lovers!

70. "To filch jade and steal scent" *(thiết ngọc thâu hương)* is to carry on a secret love affair or keep a secret tryst with some woman.

71. A "clinging ivy" (from *The Book of Odes*) is a concubine who depends on her husband's chief wife.

72. A proverbial saying: "[A woman will] give [you her] rice and give [you her] shirt, but [is anyone] likely to give [you her] husband?" *(Nhường cơm nhường áo, dễ ai nhường chồng?)*

73. "To press a bamboo plant and force a plum tree" *(ép trúc nài mai)* is to molest or rape a woman.

74. The Chinese calendar cycle of the twelve beasts begins with the mouse *(tí)*.

75. "To hide an elephant in a field of stubble" *(giấu voi ruộng rạ)* is to try hiding the obvious.

76. "To eat little *cáy*-crabs and cover one's ears [where it itches]: *(ăn cáy bưng tai)*: to try to hide what one has done in a clumsy way. The brackish-water crabs may cause persons who eat them to itch.

77. A proverb about the sexual lust of males goes: "A frog will pounce on a hibiscus." *(Ếch vồ hoa dâm-bụt.)*

78. An intelligent woman yoked to a stupid man complains in this couplet of folk verse: "The golden dragon bathes in the water of a stagnant pond;/a smart person finds it irksome to live with a dolt." *(Rồng vàng tắm nước ao tù,/người khôn ở với đứa ngu bực mình.)*

79. "Scabies [brought in] by ship [from overseas]" *(ghẻ tàu)* is syphilis.

80. Village authorities in Vietnam used to punish a couple of adulterers by having the guilty woman and man tied to a raft of banana stalks *(bè chuối)* and floated down the river until they died from exposure or other causes.

81. See note 41 to Poem 209, "The marvelous encounter at Blue Creek."

82. "A crab in its hole will find it hard to go to heaven" *(Cua lỗ khó lên trên trời)*. A habit of long standing is hard to break.

83. "To hold an eel by the tail" *(bắt chạch đằng đuôi)* is to have a weak, slippery hold on something or someone.

84. "To hide the head and show the tail" *(giấu đầu hở đuôi)* is to make a clumsy attempt at hiding the truth.

85. A Chinese expression: "to change wives as one rises in the world" *(quí dịch thê)*. A Vietnamese proverb likewise takes note of male inconstancy: "[He who] gets rich changes friends, [and he who] rises in the world changes wives." *(Giàu đổi bạn, sang đổi vợ.)*

86. A woman who's no longer sexually desirable is "an overripe eggplant or an old squash" *(cà chín bầu già)*.

87. "To desert the lamp when there's a moon" *(có trăng phụ đèn)* is to leave one woman for another, be unfaithful in love or marriage.

88. When something or someone is valued strictly for novelty's sake, the Vietnamese say, "It tastes no good, but it's steaming hot." *(Chẳng ngon cũng thể sốt.)*

89. "As long as you've kept your looks, one man will greet you and another man will see you off;/when you've lost your looks, you'll be deserted and left forlorn like the temple of the Lady who Displays [her Sex]." *(Còn duyên kẻ đón người đưa, / hết duyên vắng ngắt như chùa Bà Banh.)* There used to be such a temple in the countryside, harking back to the days before the imposition of Confucian patriarchy, when the primitive cult of fertility could take the shape of a statue showing a naked woman who proudly displayed her vulva. Of course, that temple came to be proscribed and abandoned under the rule of monarchs inspired by Chinese notions of male supremacy and sexual prudery. *Bà Banh* is often mistakenly or euphemistically changed to *Bà Đanh*, a meaningless name. The Celtic counterpart of Bà Banh is Sheila-na-gig, once well known in the British Isles. During the Middle Ages, she was portrayed on walls of English churches, flaunting her pudenda as a charm against evil spirits.

90. South Bridge *(Cầu Nôm)* was the place where copper pots were made.

91. This is a proverbial reference to how hard mice work to feed themselves and one another: "[one mouse] bites the tail [of another mouse lying on its back] and drags [home] the egg [that is being held on the belly of the supine mouse]" *(cắn đuôi tha trứng)*.

92. A proverbial simile: "to hurry and scurry like an old woman fighting off bees" *(tất-tả như bà đánh ong)*.

93. A proverb about some futile endeavor: "A sand crab wastes its labor carrying sand" *(Dã-tràng xe cát luồng công)*, since it all will be washed away by the tide.

94. It's no use helping an ingrate: "How can a wasp who raises a spider

hope to get anything [in return]?" *(Tò-vò nuôi nhện há mong cậy nhờ?)* The wasp's habit of catching spiders and keeping them in its nest for food makes people believe that wasps raise spiders.

95. "The ivy spreads from branch to branch." *(Tầm-ngải lần cành.)* Give her an inch and she'll take a mile.

96. A "man whose mustache wilts and droops" *(kẻ quặp râu)* is a hen-pecked husband.

97. "Donkeys as a breed like heavy [blows]." *(Giống lừa ưa nặng.)* Unintelligent people need harsh scolding before they will behave.

98. "Pull too hard on a string and it will snap." *(Già néo đứt dây.)* A rigid, unbending attitude hurts or ruins relationships.

99. "In a fit of anger you lose your wits." *(Cả giận mất khôn.)* Anger makes you say or do foolish things.

100. "To bite one's navel" *(cắn rốn)* is to feel remorse.

101. "To wear one's shirt above the head" *(mặc áo qua đầu)* is to behave unreasonably or go against the authority of a superior or older person.

102. A woman stays married for life and should not think of finding another man.

103. "Poke at duckweed and bugs will come out." *(Bới bèo ra bọ.)* It pays to turn a blind eye and pretend not to notice certain things: if you look too closely or too critically you'll find trouble.

104. "A woman is like a falling drop of rain:/she'll take what she finds, for how can she tell where's the better place?" *(Đàn bà như hạt mưa sa,/gặp đâu hay vậy biết là đâu hơn?)*

105. A proverb about the effectiveness of soft speech or silence in maintaining good relationships: "Forbear saying one [harsh] word and [you'll get] nine statements of kindness." *(Một câu nhịn chín câu lành.)*

106. A proverb about the power of the gentle approach: "Yield to the person [who is your superior] and you'll get your way; yield to your husband and you'll get children." *(Chiều người lấy việc, chiều chồng lấy con.)*

107. A proverb about an unhappy marriage: "The rice is no good and the soup has no taste." *(Cơm chẳng lành canh chẳng ngon.)*

108. The complete proverb goes: "A good cat doesn't prowl the graves, and a good woman doesn't hang around inns." *(Mèo lành chẳng ở mả, ả lành chẳng ở hàng cơm.)*

109. "It's no loss of face to get out of an elephant's way." *(Tránh voi chẳng xấu mặt nào.)*

110. "How can a jellyfish leap the weir?" *(Sứa nào vượt qua đăng?)* Someone in a weak position [a wife or a youngster] cannot prevail against someone of greater authority [a husband or a parent].

111. "Pull hard at the vines and you'll shake the woods." *(Dứt dây động rừng.)* Pick a quarrel and you'll stir up a lot of trouble.

112. "Swim against a hawksbill turtle and you'll lose." *(Thi bơi với giải thì thua.)* Don't pit yourself against overwhelming strength or force.

113. "A swallow and an oriole" *(yến anh)* are "two lovebirds."

211. Two hearts

Nguyễn Bính

Your heart's a stall displaying wares—
the customers just stop by and then walk on.

My heart's a raft that floats along:
it goes one way while heading for one port.

My heart's the sea with its wild waves:
its vastness harbors all the tides and streams.

Your heart's a slippery taro leaf—
all water poured on it will soon run off.

My heart's a constant heliotrope:
forever it keeps turning toward the sun.

Your heart's the shuttle on a loom:
it hurtles back and forth and stays intact.

212. The girl next door

Nguyễn Bính

Her cottage is next door to mine—
a basil spinach hedge stands in between.[1]

The two of us live lonely lives—
she seems to nurse some sorrow like my own.

If that green hedge did not exist,
I would go over there and visit her.

I sleep and dream a happy dream:
a pure-white butterfly comes over here.

O butterfly, fly in, fly in!
This question may I whisper in your ear ... ?

men and women   *282*

I didn't ever see her smile
as she was hanging out wet silk to dry.

Now her sad eyes look up and gaze—
the pure-white butterfly has gone back there!

All of a sudden I feel troubled so—
I ask myself, "Am I in love with her?"

No, I can't be! My heart's grown cold
as ashes since that broken love affair.

She won't take in the silk hung out—
the butterfly keeps coming every night.

No sight of her these past few days—
if only I had silk I could hang out!

I feel a yearning—something—what?
I'm missing her? No, never could I be!

Yes, since that broken love affair,
I've yearned and pined for her I cherished so.

But rain keeps pouring, pouring down—
after today, it will have rained four days.

My lonesome heart feels sadder yet—
when ever will the butterfly come back?

Today, at last, the rain has stopped—
no silk's hung out, no butterfly's come back.

Under the eaves no sign of her—
over the desk I bow, tears welling up.

I miss the wondrous butterfly,
the golden silk—but her I do not miss!

White butterfly and golden silk,
please hurry back in time for mourning her.

Last night she died, the girl next door.
I choke with sobs and weep—yes, I love her.

O virgin soul, if still on earth,
enter a pure-white butterfly and come!

1. The Malabar nightshade (*Basella rubra*; in Vietnamese, *mồng-tơi*) is translated here as "basil spinach". The French call it *épinard de Malabar*.

213. To love

Xuân Diệu

To love is to die a little in the heart,
for when you love, can you be sure you're loved?
You give so much, so little you get back—
the other lets you down or looks away.

Together or apart, it's still the same.
The moon turns pale, blooms fade, the soul's bereaved,
for when you love, can you be sure you're loved?
To love is to die a little in the heart.

They'll lose their way within dark sorrowland,
those passionate fools who go in search of love.
And life will be a desert reft of joy,
and love will tie the knot that binds to grief.
To love is to die a little in the heart.

Note: This poem shows undisguised French influence. The line "To love is to die a little in the heart" is closely patterned after Edmond Haraucourt's "Partir, c'est mourir un peu."

214. A fool in love

Xuân Diệu

You suffer as you stray and lose your heart,
adore the wrong one, and misplace your love.
Your gold you lavish where it goes to waste;
you suffer as you beg where one won't give.

It seems so smooth, the road—who would beware?
When you come to, the thorn has stung your bone.

You loose the reins and let your heart run free—
you suffer, as you can't turn back again.

You fathom shallow eyes, discover depths;
you fancy riches stored in vacuous hearts.
Forever you'll pursue sheer mists or clouds,
intent on finding heaven here on earth.

You suffer, squeezing through a narrow gate—
the door's shut tight, so harder you will knock.
When stabbed and injured, you will keep the knife
and won't be healed of your delicious wound.

215. It's all in the heart
Xuân Diệu

It's just the wind, but on a gentle breeze
will flutter butterflies my heart sends off.
It's just the moon, but I see fairyland,
aglow with magic, for my soul's so young.
And she is just a stranger in the crowd,
with silk and perfume, with fair face and looks;
it's love, just love—but I, bewitched, admire
the cosmos in a woman's marble shape.

Life is as lonesome as a traveler's road,
and love's the roadside inn he may stop by.
Thatch roofs him, warms him in the dew-chilled night;
plain water cools him on sun-withered days.
A peasant's hut gives you no fine white rice—
lone wanderer, don't spurn a poor thatch inn.
Your only wealth you carry there with you—
amid the desert refuge is a boon.
Find paradise in your own luggage box:
for drunken rapture, pack your own strong brew;

bring your own cushion for a soft, smooth bed;
bring frankincense and music for your dreams.

I've always known how dull and drab life is:
so I have taken liquor, sentiment, and love
along to make the world a nicer place,
and tenderness, to make a man less coarse.
To light some fire and have those souls of ice
thaw out a bit, affected by my heat,
to kindle sparks from glazed or frozen eyes,
to beat a rhythm waking stolid minds,
to rouse the birdsong of desire asleep,
to sprout new wings on ruin and decay,
to welcome life with smiles and fondling arms,
I own a sun right here within my breast.

216. You must say it
Xuân Diệu

"I love you so, yet it's still not enough?
You're greedy, aren't you? You ask too much!
You know it—I've told you that I love you:
why would you have me say the same old thing?"

You love me so, yet it's still not enough
if you love me and lock it in your heart.
Unuttered love is just no love at all—
then beauty's made of marble, just as cold.

I crave the infinite, the absolute.
You know? I've always searched for it—the You.
What's true today tomorrow may prove false:
how can love ever be "the same old thing"?

You love me so, yet it's still not enough!
You must say it a hundred, a thousand times,

must keep it ever young and fresh, must fill
love's garden with spring birds and butterflies.
You must say it, say it, and still say it,
with private language spoken through your eyes,
through your eyelashes, shyly or with fire,
with some slight nod, a smile, a clasp of hands,
with silent pauses, with . . . I know not what!
What matters is, be not as cold as ice,
showing indifference near a heart that burns,
being as placid as a lake asleep.
You love me so, yet it's still not enough!

217. Distance
Xuân Diệu

Once you were sitting far, too far, from me—
"Come closer, sit nearby me," I told you.
You inched a little closer, but I sulked—
to please, you moved a little closer yet.
I threw a tantrum—with a smile you rushed
to snuggle up and coax me, "Here I am!"
I brightened then and all at once felt sad,
because I thought, "She's still too far from me!"

The eyes of her he loves—oh, two deep gulfs!
Her forehead—oh, a heaven far away!
What can he glimpse behind the lovely shape
that he grips tight, frustrated, in both arms?
We may believe we share one life, one dream—
you still are you, and I remain myself.
How ever can the fortress wall be breached
between two worlds with mysteries of their own?
Old longings have washed down the stream of days—
my love, I won't retell you of my past.

One's secret soul is darker than the night—
who else can fathom what one can't see through?
Doubting, suspecting, jealous of mere ghosts,
I want to enter there and probe your dreams.
But of my dreams I've hidden all from you,
just as from me you've hidden all your truths.

Two heads, two chests—oh, let them nestle close!
Two manes of hair—mix locks both short and long.
Around both shoulders let the arms entwine.
Let love, all of it, surge up in the eyes.
And let them grapple fast, two pairs of lips,
so I can hear the clashing of our teeth,
and wild with rapture, I shall tell you this:
"Come closer yet—you're still too far from me!"

218. The dress of Hà-đông silk

Nguyên Sa

In Saigon heat I suddenly felt so cool
because you wore a dress of Hà-đông silk.
I've always loved that color in a dress—
my poems are still made of raw white silk.

I still recall you sitting there, short-haired,
while all around me autumn seemed so long.
My mind's eye drew your portrait there and then,
and opening doors, displayed it in my soul.

Meeting you once, I found it a sheer joy—
meeting you twice was heaven for my soul.
My student poems, like a hill, piled up—
your eyes became the wine to make me drunk.

You spoke no word: I heard a melody.
You cast no glance: I saw a vast blue sky.

Upward I looked to you, with prayerful eyes,
and in pure poems reached for your white sleeve.

You came, you went—no warning. Yes, I know
that it will shine or rain with no excuse.

But why take off without a word? I'm left
to call you in sad poems, echoed sounds.

I'm left to curse my eyes which failed to speak,
to curse my poems which said futile words.

You're gone—remorse now whispers on my lips,
and on my shoulders days weigh heavier yet.

Where are you now, my autumn with short hair?
For me please keep the dress of Hà-đông silk.

I've always loved that color in a dress—
please keep it, my love poem of white silk.

219. If in a future life we meet again

Bàng Bá Lân

> To Phạm Kim Thuần, my lifemate

I shan't forget that winter in Bắc-giang:
I went to see you there and seek your hand.

I loved you for your smile, your winsome smile;
I loved you for your sweet, endearing ways.

You were fifteen, the age of a full moon—
so small and young, the bride came home with me.

In all your acts you proved a model wife,
a gentle soul—who could help loving you?

You had some wishes, nursed some little dreams,
and fondly hoped that I'd make them come true.

Alas, I've let them all go up in smoke,
for I was born a muddled, feckless man.

The livelong day, bemused and lost, my mind

keeps wandering back and forth in neverland.
We are no paupers, but our modest means
cannot afford a private house, a car.
Yet never will you utter one regret,
contented with your garden and your field.
Some broods of piglets ramble on the loose
while in the barnyard, ducks and chickens play.
You do what you enjoy—you grow fruit trees,
raise silkworms, harvest green mulberry leaves.
Your two white hands, so soft and pretty once,
now show those swollen streaks, a few blue veins.
Often I've thought about you, and contrite,
I've tried to shoulder functions in the world
so you'd acquire some leisure of your own
and on your lips would bloom a carefree smile.
But poetry won't let go of me, alas,
and this disease has worsened day by day.
I take delight in simple, rustic joys
and tire of that mad race for gain and fame.
Besides, my multifarious love affairs
have further tangled up our family life.
Damsels with powdered cheeks and crimson lips
have often interloped between us two.
At times, the china rattles, dishes crash,
as wife and husband bandy jibes and taunts.
You've known much woe and trouble, thanks to me,
but still you hold me dear. When I ask you,
"You've wed a poet—don't you curse your fate?"
you speak no word and only shake your head.
You've borne a hundred griefs, a thousand pains—
why haven't you breathed one complaint, my love?

If in a future life we meet again,
again I'll marry you ... and her, the muse!

(May 13, 1957)

220. Like leaves

Lâm thị Mỹ Dạ

Look at the leaves:

you'll think that they taste sweet,

so young and luscious they all seem.

Young tender leaves drive cold and winter off:

oh, are my kisses like the leaves or not?

I walk amid a season of new growth,

numbed and bewildered in a flush of leaves.

I yearn for someone so—

to heaven let me send a kiss.

When humans want for love,

they're like an earth all bare of leaves.

The soil can't do without the breath of life—

O mellow leaves out of my very depths!

If I could draw my kisses on the sky,

I'd cause them all to look like leaves.

221. Her story

Diên Nghị

But where is she? At the seaside? On some hill?

The highlands and the plains,

all suburbs and the city's heart—

I've searched the whole wide world for her.

I've asked the dawn, I've talked to dusk—

at sunset I've felt all forlorn.

The groves in mourning will not welcome me—

cold strangers, they all avert their gaze.

I've roamed the west, I've wandered in the east.

Rivers have scowled—I've grieved within.

They've tightly shut their mansions' doors.
Flowers and willows all have shied away.

What does she wear? A purple gown,
or some brown tunic stained with mold?
Does she have silk-soft fingers? Toil-worn hands?
She has a soul—I cherish her.

I've gone in quest of her on moonlit nights.
I've listened to sea winds, spied mountain clouds.
I've found a desert everywhere I've looked—
her story how am I to tell?

The cosmos pulses with my cries for her.
The moon and stars cast shadows on my path.
Through mists in space I walk toward nothingness—
taking each step, I haul a leaden weight.

My soul keeps drifting back and forth in dreams—
quite lost, it knows not where to go.
Is she a vision, or does she exist?
Somewhere too far away from earth?

222. Waves

Xuân Quỳnh

They rage and rave, caress and soothe;
they shout and roar, lie still or hushed.
The stream can't understand its waves—
they leave and find their way to sea.

Oh, waves of yesterdays and waves
of afteryears! They're all alike.
The tides of thirst and lust for love
arouse such turmoil in young breasts.

Before those waves which stir the sea,
I think of you, think of myself.

I muse upon the boundless sea:
where did those billows all arise?

"It was with winds that waves began."
But where did they begin, the winds?
Neither do I remember now:
when did it all begin, our love?

Waves in the bowels of the sea,
waves on the surface of the sea—
all waves are homesick for their shore,
so sleep eludes them day and night.
My heart just longs for you, my love,
and while it dreams stays wide-awake.

I may set off and head straight north
or face about and move down south—
no matter where I go, my thoughts
all turn in one direction: you.

Far, far out there, upon the sea,
behold them all, those waves and waves:
which ones will flinch from that broad space
and fail to reach their shore?

Though life's a long, long haul,
the months and years do pass away.
However vast that sea may be,
the clouds will cross it going home.

Oh, how to make the heart dissolve
and be a hundred little waves
that borne upon the sea of love,
forever lap against the shore.

(December 29, 1967)

223. Beauties in white

Kiên Giang

When still unmarried, I recall,
as a mere stripling of a man,
I felt so awkward, ill at ease,
walking beside a maternity dress.

Among the girls, I feared, might spread   5
the rumor that I'd wedded young.
It would make them feel rather sad—
their interest in me would wane.

One day, I saw my mother sitting there
and making such a dress as dusk came on.   10
My older sister would receive the gift—
in February she had wedded, months ago.

When she got it, she laughed, eyes filled with tears—
before a mirror, quick she put it on:
"O mother, I shall be a mother soon,   15
and yet I feel just like a new-wed bride!"

A gentle man, her husband coddled her.
He'd hold her, help her on and off the bus.
Inside a theatre, out in the street,
he'd stroke her hand like some love-smitten boy.   20

He was a poet, too—
he wrote a long, long ode
and set to music his own hymn
to her maternity dress.

A woman's girlhood is all gone,   25
but on her hair still blossom nuptial flowers.

When in her womb the baby kicks,
the mother feels a wrench and smiles.

In dreams she sees a budding flower—
inside the fetus buds a mother's love.   30

And slowly, hope grows up in that white dress
to bear the fruit, the baby's flesh and blood.
A girl today, a mother the next day—
she'll be the selfsame beauty, fit for love.

If after childbirth she grows thin and pale,   35
her baby's need and love
will be her rouge, her powder,
will gush in her own flow of milk.

And if they wither up, her lips,
her husband will embellish them   40
with kisses, fond and warm—
a good wife's lips feel fresh again.

Now that I'm past my teens,
I don't feel awkward anymore,
walking beside a maternity dress   45
when she, my darling, has it on.

I lost my shyness when I fell for her.
I dreamed that from the lamp a soft, cool light
would radiate sheer love all through the bed
as man and wife would lie in close embrace.   50

Please bow and pay respects to that white dress
when you pass by a gate, walk through a shop,
when you call at a clinic, stroll along a street,
visit a village—anywhere at all.

For all those beauties, clad in white,   55
are virtuous wives, will be good mothers soon.
They are humanity's eternal flowers,
pure blossoms all in their maternity garb.

(1960)

6. Life and Art

224. The lyre of myriad tunes
Thế Lữ

I am a wanderer roaming back and forth
along the paths or high roads of the world,
seeking my thrills from laughter and from tears,
in hours of mirth, at moments of distress,
when striving or while dreaming idle dreams.
I cherish life with all its woes and joys,
its heartbreaks and its horrors, its delights
and glories, its fierce passions, love or hate.
You tell me I am fickle, take to heart
no purpose, lack a doctrine—but who cares?
I'm just a man who desperately loves,
who craves for beauty's myriad shapes and forms.
I borrow from the muse her fairy brush,
her wondrous lyre—with both I'll paint, I'll sing
all beauty—quiet, delicate, naïve,
or noble, grandiose, heroic, proud,
the splendor of wild nature, poetry, thought,
a woman's lovely grace, bewitching charm,
the dance of light, the vivid sun of spring,
the gloom and hush on days of dismal rain,
the furor of the waves, of waterfalls,
the frailty of a petal on the wind,
the squalor of those spots where mud collects,
the bliss of hovering in pipe dreams and mists,
the zest for battle on the field of life:
I love it all and spellbound, grasp it all.
I want to mourn, on hearing cries of grief,
to feel inflamed by verses breathing fire.

I sing high praise and lift the spirit up,

or for some lovelorn girl I sigh and moan.

I echo that glad warble of a flute

or comfort with a bell's miraculous voice.

The muse lends me her lyre of myriad tunes,

her brush of myriad tints—I want to play

a wizard working wonders, magic tricks

with all the sounds and colors of the earth.

225. Feelings and emotions

Xuân Diệu

To be a poet is to hum with winds,

to ride the moon and dream, to roam with clouds,

to have one's soul involved in myriad ties

and share one's heart among a hundred loves.

Here is a home where all the world may lodge,

a vase that gathers minds of every hue,

a garden birds will sow with every seed,

where honeyflowers jostle poison fruits.

His eyes, two wells, contain the skies above;

his ears erect no barrier, stop no sound:

he can perceive each whisper out of space

and of the blue can catch the faintest hint.

With hand on breast, he feels the tide of blood

and tears for all men's hearts within one heart.

He penetrates the murmur of a brook,

birdcalls, the howl of storms, a sunbeam's cheer.

Born wingless, he takes off and roams the sky;

walking on earth, he visits heaven's heights.

His minute can enfold a thousand years;

he sees all nature in one blade of grass.

I'm just a little pin—a million things
are all a million magnets drawing me.
Night scents, entrancing, rise with the full moon—
why blame the poet for his throes of love?

226. Magic
Xuân Diệu

Listen, my love, to music's fragrant tune.
It thrills like wine drunk on the nuptial night,
it seeps like incense through the bone and pith—
its magic euphony invades the soul.

Surrender now—let music's rose-hued tune
lead you to Melody, to fairyland.
Please hold your breath—discover there a world
abloom with flowers, redolent of scents.

You'll hear a symphony—the voice of brooks,
the speech of birds, the human cry of grief.
Drink up the wine, the poetry in those notes,
which sweetly moan and yearn for times long gone.

And when the music's fallen silent, hushed,
still hold your breath and listen to your heart:
it still keeps throbbing, trembling like a leaf
after the gust of wind has long died down.

227. Casting fragrance to the winds
Xuân Diệu

How many beautiful flowers in the wilds
have cast their scent to ingrates, all those winds!
They have misspent their lives in dells and nooks
where no wayfarer ever once sets foot.

A flower casting fragrance to the winds
sends its own message forth—it offers love.
Lonesome, it waits in vain for some response:
its wind-borne scent will fade as sunlight dims.

The dumbstruck wind keeps roaming woods and hills,
as in the wilds sweet fragrance goes unloved.
Those beautiful flowers drop on barren stone,
and dusk will spread dark silence over all.

A flower's scent means love, eternal love.
How many hearts that bloomed along the way
have loved and lost by trusting fickle winds!
The loved ones know not who their lovers are.

The thoughtless world receives a gift of dreams—
such dreams, such poems it won't understand.
Forever lovers are wild mountain flowers,
wasting their scent on those who do not care.

228. Foreword to a book of poems

Xuân Diệu

I am a bird from mountains you don't know.
My throat feels itchy—so I start to chirp
when sings the morning wind among the leaves,
when dreams the moon at midnight in the blue.

Perched on a branch, the bird longs for its brook—   5
it will break into song and not know why.
Its ditties cannot make the fruits grow ripe;
its carols cannot help the flowers bloom.

It's profitless to sing, and yet the bird
will burst its throat and heart to sing its best.   10
It's sung of light while dripping with red blood,
and someday it will fall amid the dawn.

I trill and warble—Heaven bids me sing.

My heart, a boat, will move as flows the stream.

The wind is blowing—up the sails must hoist. 15

My soul must drift and wander—blame the clouds!

The world once teemed with artists in past lives—

they've left me their bequest of too much love.

I grieve for furrows on care-laden brows

and mourn the tears that sorrow sheds all night. 20

To pick and choose some words—a children's game!

I offset lines of gloom with lines of cheer.

All mists and shadows—nothing makes clear sense.

But don't you laugh! Does life make any sense?

My song will make nobody grow and thrive, 25

but to this book I've trusted my whole heart.

Open with caution—don't disturb my heart.

And gently close—a lover's soul's so frail!

Daylight has faded, yet my heart still keeps

each golden sunset with its rainbow hues. 30

Spring's hurried off—whatever scent is left

I've reached for with both hands and hold in here.

If something seems to stir the pure-white page

and sway to music, that's my living soul.

Restless and anguished, it still haunts the book: 35

within your hands, you see it breathe again.

I should have kept these poems to myself.

They give no joy—why put them on display?

It's rather strange, but sorrows I once felt

I'm not content to save as private griefs. 40

Well, let me speak and get them off my chest.

Reader, if you love me, have my thanks.

If you loathe me, I'll take it with a smile:
I cannot hold against you what's my fault.

On second thought I'd rather live than die.   45
Better stay close together—love tastes sweet!
So, I'll confess my hope that many friends
will read me and remember me for long.

But you may think, "Who ever is so sad?
Where can one hear so sorrowful a voice?"   50
I'll ask, "Who's never shed a tear or two?"
We all have grieved—let's comfort one and all.

And love me, friends, for just an hour, please.
Or even for a minute—love a bit.
I sing my sorrows—humankind, give ear.   55
Young sister, listen! Brother, stop and heed!

The wind will blow my poems here and there
and bid you, readers, share what's in my heart.
If I see my strong wine warm all your lips,
I shall rejoice to have a heart that grieves.   60

I am a bird from mountains you don't know.
My throat feels itchy—so I start to chirp.
Please listen—as to reasons for my song,
why ask me? I just don't know what to say.

Note: This is the prefatory poem to the collection Xuân Diệu published in
1945, *Gửi hương cho gió (Casting Fragrance to the Winds).*

229. Beauty and the poet

Nam Trân

A bobbing boat behind the phoenix trees:
a lovely Kim Luông girl was rowing it.
I went aboard—she did not know,
but poets, seeing Beauty, must give chase.

Reaching the pier, the girl rowed back—
she swung the oar, and water splashed.
I gazed and gazed upon her oar
as it was churning up the clear blue stream.

But do you know, O Beauty, do you know
your oar's still stirring ripples in my heart?

230. Against tunes in a minor key
Nam Trân

Stop singing motley tales of broken love—
musician, rise and take the road with me.
I loathe your passion for lugubrious tunes,
for baring all your dissipated soul.

Stand up and rid your lyre of doleful airs.
I need to hear strong tunes that shout and set
the horses galloping on tireless legs,
that shine like swords unsheathed, that rage like storms.

Musician, how effete a man can be!
Why dote upon those lurid melodies,
those songs devoid of charm and poetry, sung
by sluts who wallow in the mire of lust?

To crones and dotards, with a bow, give back
ditties that breathe no spirit, no ideal.
Come out—hear breakers crash, watch clouds roll on,
and then compose for me some brave new tunes.

231. To be a poet
Sóng Hồng

To be a poet—if it means "to hum with winds,
to ride the moon and dream, to roam with clouds,"
to hang your heart inverted on a branch

or, languid, with the willow swing and sway,

to pull wry faces, threatening to weep,   5

or beg for pity from the Lord on high,

to let your soul go wandering like a waif,

to whine cicadalike in summertime;

if it just means that planted at your desk,

you sweat to show how love helps two hearts beat,   10

take life and make some neverland of dreams

and revel in delights dubbed "jade and flowers";

if it just means you weave some fine brocade

and spread it over ruin and decay,

you hum sweet ditties, drowning out the groans   15

of humans who must toil and writhe in pain,

then such a poet, truth to tell, my friends,

is for the people just a bane, a curse,

who wears his heartstrings out and wastes his youth

to praise injustice, sing of tyranny,   20

who bows before harsh power as he hopes

to pick up crumbs of favor day by day

while fellowmen are drowning in dire woes

or suffering agonies beneath their yoke.

No! That can't be! O artists of the pen!   25

O poets loved by all throughout the land,

poets for all that's clean and clear and pure,

flowers of our spring garden on Việt soil!

A poet has a soul that soars to heights,

a will of steel, a noble mission too.   30

He writes and sings of freedom, progress, love

(love for peace, justice, and humanity).

He lifts his voice intoning hymns to praise

heroes who loved our land and risked their lives,

like Phan Đình Phùng, Đề Thám, and Phan Chu Trinh,[1]   35

men of Bãi Sậy, of Thái-Nguyên, of Yên-báy.[2]

A poet is to follow winds of change,

look for ideas on the Bạch-đằng's waves,[3]

enthrall his soul to glory at Chi-lăng,[4]

immortalize the battle of Đồng-đa,[5]   40

pour out his fervor, all his zeal and fire,

and warm the wintry souls of fellowmen,

let his heart beat at one with Đô-lương,[6]

with our Six Provinces, Bắc-sơn, Đình-cả.[7]

To be a poet is to sing and laud   45

the greatest struggle ever fought on earth,

resist aggressive forces in the world,

and raise aloft the democratic flag.

His pen, a lever, turns the system round;

each rhyme, a bomb, blasts power—if need be,   50

he'll toss his pen aside and grab a sword.

O poets, all spring to your feet, stand up!

The time of wine and roses is long past.

No longer moan with winds and weep with clouds—

along the road of progress take brisk steps.   55

Make poems, and with poems shed cold light

on social sores that fester everywhere.

With workers sow and grow tomorrow's world—

in Soviet Russia it has budded forth.

(1944)

Note: Sóng Hồng ("Red Wave") is one of the pen names Trường Chinh used
when he wrote about literary and cultural matters. This poem pointedly
rebuts those sentiments expressed by Xuân Diệu in "Feelings and emotions"
(Poem 225).

1. Phan Đình Phùng (1847–1895) led the anti-French struggle from 1885
until his death, in the woods and hills of Nghệ-an and Hà-tĩnh. Đề Thám (or
Hoàng Hoa Thám) organized and led rebels against the French for twenty-five
years in the rugged region of Yên-thế (Bắc-giang Province, in northern Vietnam), until he was betrayed by a Chinese bandit and killed in 1913. Phan Chu
Trinh (1872–1926) symbolized nonviolent opposition to French rule in the
twentieth century, in contrast to other nationalists such as Phan Bội Châu,
who advocated armed resistance.

2. Bãi sậy ("Swamp of Reeds") is an area of Hưng-yên Province in northern Vietnam, where Nguyễn Thiện Thuật established the main base of resistance to the French between 1885 and 1889. Thái-nguyên is a province in northern Vietnam where Hồ Chí Minh set up his command post in 1944. Yên-báy is the principal city in the province of the same name in northern Vietnam. There Nguyễn Thái Học and other members of the Việt Nam Quốc Dân Đảng fomented an ill-fated mutiny among Vietnamese soldiers at a French garrison on the night of February 9, 1930. Read Poem 131, "The day of mourning at Yên-báy," by Đằng Phương.

3. Bạch-đằng: see the note to Poem 2, "The Bạch-đằng River," by King Trần Minh-tông.

4. Chi-lăng: a mountain pass in Lạng-sơn Province, northern Vietnam, the site of several Vietnamese victories over Mongol and Chinese troops, during the Earlier Lê, the Trần, and the Later Lê dynasties.

5. Đống-đa: a site near Hanoi where Nguyễn Huệ, the Tây Sơn leader who proclaimed himself King Quang Trung in 1788, caught the Chinese general Ts'en Yi-tung (Sầm Nghi Đống) off guard and defeated him in a New Year's day attack in 1789. See Poem 186, "The shrine of Ts'en Yi-tung" by Hồ Xuân Hương.

6. Đô-lương: an area in central Vietnam where the Communists provoked a mutiny among Vietnamese soldiers on November 11, 1941.

7. The Six Provinces (Lục Tỉnh) were the western provinces of southern Vietnam where the Communists staged uprisings in 1939. Bắc-sơn: a mountainous area of northern Vietnam where the Communists organized an insurrection in September 1939 and used guerrilla tactics for the first time. Đình-cả: a locality in Thái-nguyên province where an uprising took place in 1940.

232. In a garret
Nguyễn Nhược Pháp

A lane with mud and moss—a garret flat.

Writers and artists number just fifteen.

A lamp keeps flickering there all through the night,

near heaven—where all poets make their home.

High in the air, they gladly live on dreams.

They're out at elbows since they write too much.

Their manes of hair will waggle with their hands
when, giving praise, they nod and say, "That's good!"

Though artists may go broke for beauty's sake,
they'll gobble up beef noodles—two cents' worth.
Often, with empty stomachs and full brains,
they must retire to bed and eat asleep.

But they believe the world's in love with them—
thousands who read their verse are their soul mates.
They sit there conjuring up some fairyland
and visit their old pawnshop afterward.

When they wake up, they hear rain pit-a-pat,
and helter-skelter fly the wind-blown clouds.
With threadbare elbows, hollow-bellied still,
they gaze at heaven, nibbling on their rhymes.

233. Buying a dress for my love

Đông Hồ

"My dress of many years is all worn out—
I really cannot wear it anymore.
So when you go and sell your poems, dear,
stop at a shop and buy me a new dress."

"You love blue fabric with plum blossoms, right?
Which cloth or hue do you want me to choose?
But you neglect to tell your measurements!
What is the width? And how long is the flap?"

"That's fine of you to ask me all these things!
Need you inquire about my measurements?
You've held me in your arms—you know the width!
And we've stood cheek to cheek—you know the length!"

Note: This whimsical poem alludes to the advent of the "new poetry" *(thơ mới)* in the 1930s.

234. The poem of humankind

Đông Hồ

The World Poetry Congress at Knokke-Le-Zoute, September 7–11, 1961

What else have we? We need not know. We know
that we have us—together, we are here.
We have our poems—poems never die,
embracing both the present and the past.

Our poetry, a spaceship, carries space aboard
and breaks through time, ignoring day and night.
Our sun and moon will whirl among the stars,
not rising over there, not setting here.

The earth keeps spinning round and round—one globe:
why split it up and sunder East from West?
For poetry has just one source, humankind,
and poetry permeates the seven seas.

Let's scoop and drink cool water from one brook.
Let's dip into one ocean of sweet scents.
Let's look into one glass—the silver moon:
we poets stand out clear against the clouds.

Let's sing in just one tongue, hum just one tune,
and let's speak nature's speech to birds and winds.
With love and friendship's ties may poetry join
all peoples and all poets, hand in hand.

235. To Nguyễn Du

Đằng Phương

Nguyễn Du, a poet towering over all!
From your own heart you squeezed out blood and tears
to fashion pearls—on golden threads of silk
you then embroidered them and made brocade.

Nguyễn Du, a poet living for all times! 5
You plucked your heartstrings playing that sad tune
to mourn a gifted beauty cursed by fate
and mourn your self, which dust and storm had stained.
You dipped your pen in pools of bitter tears
and drew a life that jolted down rough roads. 10
You sang a melody the gods might sing,
speaking for all unfortunates like you
(all those whose hair so early grays with woe),
unburdening hearts of woes the world ignored,
venting a rage that nothing could appease, 15
as someone born at odds with his own times.

Nguyễn Du! If somehow you can hear these words,
stop brooding—rest in peace among the shades.
Though you once grieved and suffered much on earth,
some crumbs of solace you did once enjoy. 20
You could escape the field of dust and storm
when with the muse and on her golden wings
you soared and entered that elysian sphere,
far from a world where honors mixed with shame.
You did not know the plight of common men. 25
They swallow anger rolling in the dirt,
dragging their wretchedness across the earth,
finding no words to utter their complaints.
To all your gifts you gave the fullest scope—
you need not ever blush to be a man. 30
A man will do what he, a man, must do—
what matter if he fails or he succeeds?

You did not feel the grief of some brave soul,
endowed with talent, powered by strong will,
who wants to sweep the ground quite clean of thorns 35
and to the fatherland acquit his debt.
Ill-fated, he gets captured and confined

to waste away, forgotten, in the wilds
and nurse a silent wrath all through his life,
because the world won't nurture gallant men.   40

You've been well understood by many men
and as a poet loved by many men.
Not a few loyalists have shared your plight—
on hearing your lament, they have shed tears.
You have not known the torment and despair   45
of men who live forlorn, deserted lives,
without a friend or any kin, despised,
abandoned by their countrymen, their race,
whose chilly souls have nothing but the sun,
whom no faint echo answers when they call,   50
who let their hearts, which flow with love and trust,
slowly run dry and wither in the dark.
You have not known the anguish many feel,
those luckless ones who're human—nothing more.
While life is quietly, coldly streaming past,   55
their bodies tire beneath the load of years—
they panic as they stagger at death's door
and in despair hark back to their lost youth.
Before bright pictures conjured in their minds,
they feel their zest for life aroused again.   60
They wish to live, live on, defying death,
but twilight's falling—what are they to do?
To think they'll be no more beneath the blue!
To think that under those green trees they'll rot!
Oh, they shall die—to think that they shall die   65
and leave behind them nothing in the world!

Alas for those, untalented, unskilled,
who must stand there and stare beyond death's door.
Unlike a poet of eternal fame,
unlike you, minstrel for all times, Nguyễn Du,   70

they cannot hope they will be missed and mourned

by men on earth three centuries from now.[1]

(Spring 1945)

Note: Nguyễn Du (1765–1820), who also called himself Tố Như and Thanh
Hiên, wrote, among other works, *The Tale of Kiều*, a long poem generally
considered the supreme masterpiece of Vietnamese literature. Lines 6 through
16 here allude to it.

1. The last two lines refer to a poem in classical Chinese by Nguyễn Du,
"On reading Hsiao-ch'ing's extant poems." Some three hundred years before
his time, Hsiao-ch'ing (or Wen Chi), a Chinese woman poet, was the concubine
of a man whose wife ill-used her. Hsiao-ch'ing left a sheaf of poems when she
died; some survived, although the jealous wife burned most of them. Nguyễn
Du's poem reads: "The gardens on West Lake have gone to waste. / Beside a
window I peruse old sheets. / Fate's favored rough and powder—she's still
wept. / A poet's cursed—why care for what fire spared? / Heaven keeps mum
on past and present wrongs— / I feel a kindred bond with all her grief. / Who
knows if after some three hundred years / anyone will shed tears and mourn
Tố Như?"

236. More thoughts on Nguyễn

Chế Lan Viên

Born into those foul times of dusk and dust,
you reached and touched no soul mate by your side.
Your sorrow matched the fate of humankind:
Kiều spoke your thoughts and crystallized your life.

Kings rose and fell—the poem still abides.
You fought and won your feats on waves of words.
You planted stakes in the Bạch-đằng of time:[1]
our language and the moon forever shine.

Tấm raised her goby fish in a dark well—[2]
you nursed and loved the idiom scholars scorned.
But let a reader call: some line of *Kiều*
will from the well rise like a drop of blood.

All storms of life created you—their pearl.

Alas, a pearl is wont to shun the world.

You ushered in the age through your strait gate:

the crushing of Ch'ing troops you left outside.

Why borrow foreign scenes? Our land flows not

with one Ch'ien-t'ang but many fateful streams.[3]

Why split yourself? Nguyễn Du, Tố Như, Thanh Hiên:[4]

the tears in Kiều merge all three into one.

Need we one century more to feel for Nguyễn?[5]

Mourning our nightfalls, we soon grieve for his.

We love kings' calls to arms, yet we shall not[6]

forget those frost-white reeds along Kiều's road.[7]

Note: Nguyễn: Nguyễn Du. See the note to Poem 235, "To Nguyễn Du" by Đằng Phương.

1. Bạch-đằng: see the note to Poem 2, "The Bạch-đằng River," by King Trần Minh-tông.

2. In secret, Tấm (the Vietnamese Cinderella) raised a goby in a well to be her pet and friend. Every day she would save some cooked rice for the fish: dropping a handful of grains into the well, she would call the fish and it would come up to eat the rice. But Tấm's stepmother and stepsister, when they learned her secret, lured the goby to the surface and killed it. When Tấm summoned it for its daily meal, no fish, but a glob of blood emerged from the well.

3. The Ch'ien-t'ang (Tiền-đường) River (which flows through what was once known as the subprefecture of Ch'ien-t'ang in Chekiang Province, China) carries a symbolic significance in *The Tale of Kiều.* When her life reached its lowest ebb of despair, Kiều tried to end it by throwing herself into the Ch'ien-t'ang. But she was rescued, and the cycle of her woes was broken.

4. See the introductory note to Poem 235, "To Nguyễn Du," by Đằng Phương.

5. See the note 1 to Poem 235.

6. "Kings' calls to arms:" literally, official "calls to arms and proclamations of victory over the Wu." The Wu were the Chinese viewed as aggressors and invaders.

7. The allusion to "those frost-white reeds along Kiều's roads" recalls a particularly painful episode in the heroine's life. Sold by mistake as a concubine to a pimp, Scholar Mã, Kiều was taken by him to Lin-tzu. Some of the best-loved lines in Nguyễn Du's poem describe how Kiều's career of shame

and grief began: "She traveled far, far into the unknown. / Bridges stark white with frost, woods dark with clouds. / Reeds huddling close while blew the cold north wind: / an autumn sky for her and her alone. / A road that stretched far off in hushed, still night: / she saw the moon, felt shame at her love vows. / Fall woods—green tiers all interlaid with red: / bird cries reminded her of her old folks. / She crossed unheard-of streams, climbed nameless hills— / the moon waxed full again: Lin-tzu was reached" (lines 911–920 in *The Tale of Kiều*, Huỳnh Sanh Thông's translation, Yale University Press, 1983).

237. The Beau Ideal

Vũ Hoàng Chương

Today, the painter tossed his brush away
because Reality and Dream don't match.
Those vaporous strokes just shimmer in his soul:
his paltry art can't bring them onto silk.

In truth, he cannot blame it on the paint;
the silk's pure white, the canvas smooth as silk;
the brush obeys each motion of his hand.
His fingers, though, are human—that's their fault.

Musicians and we poets share one fate:
they snap strings off, we crumple pages up.
Plain rhymes and rhythms mar the splendid thought,
and it's betrayed when set to notes and tones.

Music and poetry may delight the ear,
yet they cannot escape terrestrial bounds.
Their sound still bears the weight of earthly dust:
how could it faithfully speak the Absolute?

Oh, how a passionate man rues his mean art!
He gives one woman fair his love, his all.
His dream of beauty soars above the earth:
huge wings beat at Reality, the cage.

Mingle with wine the many tears you've shed,
musicians, poets, painters, artists all!

life and art   312

Let all the sorrow that pervades your soul
sink in your cup and drown, you love-struck fools!

Smash your guitar to bits, discard your pen,
tear up your canvas, paper, sheets of silk.
Don't force pure jade to wed your filth, your mud:
what's dust and dirt give back to dust and dirt.

An artist's soul has always lacked for depth—
he'll love with fervor and won't hide his love.
He's vainly tried to air ethereal thoughts
on wood and silk, on what's inert as steel.

Please drain your bitter goblet to the dregs;
drink and get drunk, and drink some more—go mad.
Then, hand in hand, you'll follow Wine, your nymph,
to bathe in dreams, the Absolute's cool springs.

A clumsy brush, an awkward lute cannot
give shape to what transcends, the stuff of dreams.
But she's still here, Liu Ling's own widow, Wine:[1]
she'll lead each drunkard toward his Beau Ideal.

> 1. Liu Ling: see note 49 to Poem 209, "The marvelous encounter at Blue Creek."

238. Selling my soul
Minh Đức Hoài Trinh

To market I take my own soul,
but it's too late, past market time.
Where have the customers all gone?
Well, I'll just lug my soul back home.

A whore will peddle her good looks—
I wish to hawk my very soul.
People give praise but will not buy.
Night falls and sows such loneliness.

All rouged and powdered, gussied up,
she waits for men who'll buy her charms—
I stoop my back and scribble on:
who's better off and who's worse off?

The whore endures her body's pains,
dreads her good looks will someday fade—
I sit here staring at the night,
seek topics, chewing on my pen.

Both she and I feel frazzled now,
as night recedes and morning dawns.
In sorrow we both ask ourselves:
"But what am I now headed for?"

People will sneer at how she looks.
People will scoff at how I write.
She, feeling hurt, locks herself in—
I'll throw away my pen and quit.

Red lips, white paper—it's the same:
the whore and I are kith and kin.
We share a common bitterness,
a low regard for humankind.

I feel so sad in these long nights.
I sit here gazing at the page—
the ink holds back and will not flow
because the soul feels like a waif.

In slices I cut up my soul
and offer it to those who read.
But gimcracks are what people prize.
... At nightfall dewdrops are like tears.

239. My poetry is no poetry

Nguyễn Chí Thiện

My poetry is no poetry, no,

but it's the sound of sobbing from a life,

the din of doors in a dark jail,

the wheeze of two poor wasted lungs,

the thud of earth tossed down to bury dreams,

the clank of hoes that dig up memories,

the clash to teeth all chattering from cold,

the cry of hunger from a stomach clenching up,

the throb-throb of a heart that grieves, forlorn,

the helpless voice before so many wrecks.

All sounds of life half lived,

of death half died—no poetry, no.

(1970)

7. The Passage of Time

240. The rich look grand, the poor seem cheap and mean

Nguyễn Bỉnh Khiêm

The rich look grand, the poor seem cheap and mean.

But wealth belongs to none—it goes around.

These swamps can still dry into banks of sand.

Those plains may vanish under piles of rocks.

Wise men must know a rise precedes a fall.

A fool should learn that little will grow big.

They who now bow shall someday rear their heads.

The vast design of Heaven never errs.

241. Men jostle and men fight with labored breath

Nguyễn Bỉnh Khiêm

Men jostle and men fight with labored breath.

Their life is but a sojourn—don't they know?

Those shuttles, sun and moon, keep flashing past.

The world of wealth and tinsel soon fades out.

When flowers have blossomed forth, they're bound to wilt.

As waters reach full tide, they're due to ebb.

Succeed or fail—your fate's already sealed.

Who ever can depart from Heaven's Way?

242. My hair has thinned, my teeth have worn away

Nguyễn Bỉnh Khiêm

My hair has thinned, my teeth have worn away.

I've left the household to my children's care.

A chessboard and wine cups among bamboos;

A bunch of twigs, a fish pole in the hills.
Leisure enhanced by pleasure brings sheer joy.
Rice flavored with sea salt tastes good and fresh.
At ninety, I would say it's late in spring.
Let this spring go—another spring will come!

243. Self-reflection
Nguyễn Bỉnh Khiêm

From past to present, year has followed year.
Heaven ordains your fate, both life and death.
Down winding streams, a boat submits to oars.
Up rocky trails, a horse obeys the whip.
Nature's design will not unfold through words:
the joy of poetry leaps and rides the clouds.
Wild roots and garden greens feed you enough—
with simple wants and tastes, old age feels young.

244. Looking forward to retirement
Nguyễn Công Trứ

You're loathed by some, but then by some you're loved.
Where can you choose a way to please them all?
Fate makes you poor or wealthy—hold no grudge.
By nature wise or foolish, dare you change?
Explore the sea of learning for the young.
On days of leisure, banter with old friends.
Shake off all contrasts of nonself and self.
Had you enough of pleasures in the world?

245. A wasted life

Nguyễn Công Trứ

Thirty-six thousand days—the human span.
Some sixteen thousand I've already spent.
I'll ask the Maker, "Please turn time around
and give a man more scope wherein to play!"

246. Remembering the past in the City of the Soaring Dragon

(Lady) Thanh Quan

Why did the Maker stage such drama here?
Since then, how many stars have spun and fled!
Old horse and carriage paths—faint autumn grass.
Once-splendid towers and mansions—setting sun.
Rocks stand stock-still, unawed by time and change.
Waters lie rippling, grieved at ebb and flow.
From age to age, a mirror of things past:
the scene from here can break the viewer's heart.

Note: Hanoi was once known as the City of the Soaring Dragon *(Thăng-long)*.

247. A scholar-laureate in retirement

Nguyễn Khuyến

Between some god and Buddha, here am I!
Buddhas and gods all dwell within the heart.
Is Indra needed for a human guide?
Amida teaches nothing sons live by.
I'll leave red halls of state to younger men:
blue streams, green hills are friends for us old folks.
"Where is the scholar-laureate?" you may ask.
Between some god and Buddha, here am I!

248. Self-portrayal

Nguyễn Khuyến

The months and days, like birds, are flying off.
Look back on your old self—how strange it is!
When was that silver sprinkled on your hair?
Your set of wobbly teeth still dangles there.
Have they improved your rhymes? You answer Yes!
When in your cups, you say, "But I'm not drunk!"
Throughout the world, all worry—you don't care.
I'm just amazed at you, my grand old man!

249. Old age

Nguyễn Khuyến

Remember that raw youth, some years ago?
Now out of nowhere has arrived old age!
A thatch of hair, part black, part streaked with white.
Two rows of teeth, half loose, half fallen out.
Four blurry eyes—can I tell light from dark?
Three tottering legs—am I awake or drunk?
I lug about a set of dreary things:
mortar and pestle for my betel quids.[1]

1. Old people grink their betel quid in a little mortar before chewing it.

250. Fleeting time

Anonymous

Flowers drift downstream—a dismal thing, this world!
Days flee, months fly, like shuttles hurtling past.
An hour's a twinkling—off there goes the colt.[1]
Swallows urge change—the seasons last short spans.
No holding back—green spring must rush ahead.
With wisps of silver hair, you'll nod and watch.

While you're still young, remember this advice:
apply yourself to study, lose no time.

1. See note 36 to Poem 44, "A song of sorrow inside the royal harem," by
Nguyễn Gia Thiều.

251. Our hearts are ancient citadels
Vũ Đình Liên

Rise up, O boat, asleep there in the port,
for we'll set sail again tonight and go.
With our dream oars we'll let you drift toward climes
where in the small hours moonlight seeps through clouds.

No wind—the river flows, an ice-cold stream.
The vessel drifts in shadows of old walls.
They suddenly come to life, as on a tower
a horn moans faintly under that pale moon.

After so long, the past's dead soul wakes up.
The horn's faint voice stirs moonlight for a while.
But soon, again, falls silence all around:
the past lies hushed and still beneath the moon.

Drift on, O boat, keep drifting farther yet!
As moonlight splashes, row, row on, dream oars!
Our hearts are ancient citadels and ring
with that faint cry of horns from days long gone.

252. The old calligrapher
Vũ Đình Liên

Each year when peach trees blossomed forth,
you'd see the scholar, an old man,
set out red paper and black ink
beside a street where many passed.

The people who hired him to write
would cluck their tongues and offer praise:
"His hand can draw such splendid strokes!
A phoenix flies! A dragon soars!"

But fewer came, year after year—
where were the ones who'd hire his skill?
Red paper, fading, lay untouched.
His black ink caked inside the well.

The aged scholar sat there still;
the passers-by paid him no heed.
Upon the paper dropped gold leaves,
and from the sky a dust of rain.

This year peach blossoms bloom again—
no longer is the scholar seen.
Those people graced a bygone age—
where is their spirit dwelling now?

(1936)

253. Speaking to my photo
Tản Đà

But who are you? A lover like myself?
I thought you someone else, O you of mine!

Though you and I are two, we two are one.
Why, being one, are I and you still two?
So you flashed into being just this year—
my birth came over twenty years ago.

Laughter and tears make up my human world.
To earn a living, I run right and left.
Still young, my head's already streaked with frost—
I fear, I blush, I worry, and I grieve.

We two look like one person, share one face:
why do you seem as happy as a god?
Your mien and airs breathe nature pure, unspoiled:
no grief, no fear, no worry, and no care.

Eternal spring is heaven's gift to you—
a mirror, bright and clear, to capture love.
After a hundred years, I'll leave this world.
Forever keep your spirit—never fade.

254. Still at play

Tản Đà

Who claims your servant's wearied of the world?
Of me the world's not wearied—I still play.
I'll play till both the world and I get sick—
when it gets sick of me, then I shall quit.

I may say so, but why ought I to quit?   5
While I'm still in the world, I shall still play.
People will play until a ripe old age—
this year, my life's just reached the halfway mark.

I'm at midlife—the prime of serious play.
To play at will is paradise on earth.   10
Who in the world has played as I have played?
I've always played with words and won't soon quit.

What bliss it is to play with words! Why quit?
A young new moon is shining on the world—
our realm of letters faces this new age,   15
and like the young new moon, I'm still at play.

No lack of playboys in the realm of words,
and who has loved the world as I have loved?
I've always loved, shall always love the world:
the world won't let me if I wish to quit.   20

The world, still loving me, won't let me quit—
dare I take off and disappoint the world?
When I once stayed away, the world missed me—
I missed the world and rushed right back to play.

Half of my life or more I'll play away—   25
until I've played that much, I shall not quit.
If I quit now, I'd find it sad for me
and sadder for the world where no one plays.

Now let's hear from all lovers of the world.
Why have you left and not come back to play?   30
I've waited long for you—where have you fled?
Well, have you wearied of the world and quit?

If I, like you, got tired of the world,
who in the world would then be left to play?
Let's not get tired of the world as yet—   35
if tired of the world, I would have quit.

Yes, I once got half sickened with the world.
I thought it over—back I came to play.
I've loved to play so much that I've got hooked:
the world may let me quit, but I shall not.   40

I think of my own self, then of the world:
when thinking of the world, how dare I quit?
The world's still here—I'll still be here and play:
I'll play and give a playmate to the world.

All through my lifetime I'm to play and play: 45
until I'm through with life I shall not quit.
I wonder: will my life be long or short?
But, short or long, my life I'll play away.

I'll live to be a hundred years—that's all.
After a million years the world won't quit.   50
The time shall come when me the world will mourn.
The world's not mourned me yet—I'm still at play.

Of my own hundred years not much is left.

About my afterlife let me say this:

ages from now the world will think of me—   55

after I've quit I will be playing yet!

Note: Throughout the poem these three rhyme words are used together in each
stanza: *chơi* ("to play"), *đời* ("the world, life"), and *thôi* ("to stop, quit;
that's all"). Nguyễn Vỹ professed disapproval of such frivolous sentiments and
rebuked Tản Đà with a similar poem titled *Hết chơi* ("No more play"), using
the same rhyme words.

255. Nothingness

Xuân Diệu

And yet I, too, shall someday die, alas,

I who dig in my teeth and grip the sun,

I with a heart where flows the earth's own blood,

I who with fingernails cling on to life!

I who have lapped up love and bruised my lips,

and yet I, too, shall someday die, alas!

My sparkling eyes will someday lose their sparks

behind dry lids, as ugly grows my face.

Last night, alone, I was awake and sick,

hearing with heavy heart the hours tramp past.

My sole companion—with a feeble glow,

the lamp fought off the dark all through the night.

And winter-gray, I trembled like a leaf—

sweat soaked my brow, tears welled up in my eyes.

The months and years had pushed me, hustled me

toward this, the chilly brink of nothingness.

256. Come on, make haste

Xuân Diệu

Come on, make haste—please, won't you hurry up?
O darling, our young love is aging fast!
My little heart, wild goose, take wing and fly—
make haste, for time will not stand still and wait.
Love's colors shimmer, riding wisps of air—
a few days hence, new love will have grown old.
Without fair warning, flowers bloom and droop:
love comes and goes at pleasure—who can tell?
People sow seeds of parting as they meet—
from ancient gardens, footprints are long gone.
Please hurry up—tomorrow I so dread,
for life is flux: our feelings will not last.

The pillow, shifted, kills a golden dream;
alter a single feature—beauty's marred.
There's splendor, gold and crimson, in the blue—
you turn around, the sunset mansion's crashed:
a cloud will let the wind hurl it away.
Can we afford to shilly-shally, dear?
This morning, fogs on the horizon stir,
urging wild geese to leave and fly up north—
who can predict I shall not play you false,
that your own heart will stay as firm as rock?
Let's pluck our flowers in the flush of spring,
let's burn a million candles, light our sun:
sooner a flash of glory, then dark night,
than tedium flickering for a hundred years.
Enjoy—your teeth reflect the full moon's gleam:
I'll suck the nectar from each hour of love.
Come on, make haste—please, won't you hurry up?
O darling, our young love will soon grow old!

257. Spring out of season

Xuân Diệu

Some flecks of sun, some drops of chilly dew,
a few green branches, smatters of fresh tints:
that's spring enough—I shall not ask for more,
since spring already overflows my heart.
It's not just three fair months out of the year.
It's spring when sunshine takes me by surprise
and birds on trees read poems as they chirp.
It's spring when breezes blow, though un-hoped for.
During cold winter, suddenly one day
the clouds will part to bare a patch of sky:
it's springtime then—the day will feel some warmth,
like holding in my hand a girl's fresh hand.

Spring comes in winter when some sunshine gleams,
in summer after rain, when heaven's blue,
in autumn when a morning breeze will waft
chance bits of color onto my loose gown.
If bellerics don't shed all their withered leaves,
and blooms, though sparse, glow redder than before,
if in some garden longans give off scent,
it's springtime then—what else should I await?

It's glorious dawn when love is pledged each time—
O spring, forever live within my breast
as two young people meet out on the road
and locking eyes, exchange a bashful smile!
It's spring when, says my blood, my heart's about
to bloom once more, though wilted in the past.
It's spring when I hurl forth my soul through space
to net therein new promises of love,
when wings inside my bosom gently flap,
arousing as caresses that delight.
It's spring when in my hand a letter throbs.

It's spring again when out of days long gone,
a voice one morning softly echoes now.
Let skies stay clear, let ripples stir my heart:
that's spring aplenty—need I birds and flowers?
Ignoring seasons, weather, and mere youth,
it's ageless love, it's spring outside of time.

258. In a hurry
Xuân Diệu

I want the sun snuffed out
so color will not fade.
I want the wind tied up
so fragrance won't grow faint.

For bees and butterflies a honeymoon—
here are the blooms in meadows splashed with green,
the leaves on branches lilting, lithe as silk;
for lovebirds here's a rhapsody of love,
and through closed eyelids comes a gleam of light.
Each morning, Joy comes knocking at the door.
This second moon—a pair of lips up close.
I'm happy, but I'm also in a rush:
I fear for spring, though summer's far away.

Spring's coming on—that means it's passing, too;
if spring's still young, that means it will grow old,
and when spring dies, that will mean my own death.
My heart is big—small measures God doles out,
loath to prolong the youth of humankind.
Why say that spring in cycles will return
if youth is doomed to blossom once, not twice?
Heaven and earth endure—I'm not to last:
in anguish I mourn earth and heaven, too.
They smack of parting grief, all months and years;

the streams and hills keep whispering, "Good-bye!"
A balmy breeze is sighing through green leaves:
is it because it grieves to blow away?
A lively bird, while singing, just stops short:
does it so dread the coming wilt of flowers?
Oh, nevermore, it shall be nevermore!

Let's hurry up—the sun has not yet dipped.
I want to hug
all life on earth in its first flush of youth,
I want to grasp fleet winds and flying clouds
and, love-mad, ride on wings of butterflies,
I want to gather in a single kiss
the hills and streams, the sparkling grass and trees,
so I'll get drunk on fragrance, drenched with light,
and overfilled with vernal sights and sounds.
O luscious spring, I'll grab your flesh and bite!

259. Forever

Xuân Diệu

Forever, yes, forever I'll love you—
forever means a moment all too brief.
The color red forever lives today—
wild myrtle flowers riot on the hills.

To me you whisper, "Man I cherish so,
love me forever, always, will you, please?"
And in my rapture, I too ask my love:
"Forever, darling, love me, please, won't you?"

For ages morning glories want to bloom:
the mortal heart expects a thousand years.
In silence rivers flow and hills wear down:
the world rolls on—how can it be held back?

Forever we shall love each other, though—

forever means a moment all too brief.

What's the long run? Sheer shadows, mists, the kiss

of chance-met lips, the clasp of random arms.

Forever lies in promises and vows,

in hopes and wishes nurtured every day.

No, time does not at all belong to us—

why reckon love's eternity by months and years?

Forever, yes, forever I'll love you

in this brief moment that's to last and last.

Tomorrow, though we'll go our separate ways,

we'll have forever, side by side, sat here.

260. A geologist and millions of years

Xuân Diệu

I think of how geologists must love.

When they love someone, it's for real, for keeps.

Unbounded time pervades their soul—

it's no long stretch, three hundred million years.

Geologist, I see your soul   5

as swept by winds from dawn to dusk.

It sees birds in and out, lets clouds float through.

The mountains keep you company morn and eve.

Your feet have crossed and then recrossed blue streams.

The earth you study opens wide   10

her book of stone and turns each page for you.

You're telling me her history from way back,

reckoned in epochs of a million years.

An instant has become eternity—

your hand holds bits of rock   15

that somehow have survived, erasing time.

A million years ago, there was a bird
that hopped and skipped beside the purple sea.
A little wave came up and gently licked
the bird's fine footprints, spellbound as it were,   20
declaring love. After the bird flew off,
another ripple brought a cast of mud.
Beneath the brooding layers of months and years,
mud turned to stone. The sea's receded now,
yet they've stayed on, those footprints of the bird . . .   25

About a hundred million years ago,
some raindrops fell and quickly soaked away
or soon evaporated—yet on stone
there still remain fresh traces of those drops.
And wings of dragonflies, which in folk speech   30
mean frailty, glimmer still in limestone here,
reminders of those days when they could fly,
about three hundred million years ago . . .

And ancient pollen's still astir in stone.
Three hundred million years—one sniff, and I   35
inhale again all fragrant seasons past.
Those giant trees whose stamens smelled so strong
released their pollen in the golden sun.
There was no man,
but nature had her spring—   40
stalking and stomping, dinosaurs wooed, made love . . .

Geologist,
your bits and chips of rock
enclose prehistory, that primeval age
which seems like yesterday. The newborn earth   45
was just a baby uttering its first whines,
cries you still hear at present, loud and clear.
You go prospecting day and night:
friend, if you yearn for someone in your heart,

far off she must feel quite a glow of warmth   50

as though she were still snuggling at your side.

When you love someone, it's for real, for keeps.

Unbounded time pervades your soul—

it's no long stretch, three hundred million years.

261. An orange with the rind still green
Xuân Diệu

Whenever autumn comes,

I love the scent of orange rind.

Still green beneath the fingers peeling it,

it smells yet fresher then.

The golden pulp then tastes so sweet.

But in no hurry is the rind.

It will infuse my nostrils with the zest

of perfume, wave by wave.

It is as if along that path my youth

comes back and hovers somewhere here.

It's like that autumn once again,

when I was drunk on my first love.

I wish somebody's hand,

amid remembrance of love past,

would, trembling, peel

an orange with the rind still green.

262. The body
Huy Cận

O God! Look, you gave us a vessel made

of flesh and bone to hold the soul.

You gave us hands like blooming flowers
and legs like shoots from strong young trees,
collected winds to make our breath,
put in our eyes the gleam of stars.

Deep eyes light up to see the universe,
and vibrant ears catch music from the spheres.
The silk of hair smells fragrant with all scents,
and to a perfect rhythm throbs the chest.

The neck stands upright like a tree's firm trunk.
Shoulders spread out like rivers flowing forth.
O God, our body you took pains to build—
but in your masterpiece lurk worms and germs.

For life's a trail of frailties, on and on—
tomorrow's steps will cover today's tracks.
The body is an urn filled up with sins—
its primal soil goes back to dirt and mud.

Do blood and body ever know relief?
Since when have mouths let go of bitter breasts?
The body smarts, the lungs breathe pain—one arm
enfolds the body, one hugs tight the grave.

God, pity wilted buds and addled eggs.
Forgive and love these selves all withered up.
The heavy body has dragged down the soul:
don't blame on us the loss of paradise.

How many hearts have grieved in black despair
and tumbled down like bats with broken wings!
How many streams of acrid tears have gushed
and left all sorrows in the world uncleansed!

How many souls are damned and lost because
they've lifted to their lips the urn of fire!
God, if you knew, you'd feel remorse and shame
that you ordained and sealed the human fate.

263. A dirge

Huy Cận

Who died? Why does the music speak such grief?
An orphaned afternoon—chill roams the streets.
A dull, gray town, the color of old stone
spattered with dew—or is it dust and grime?
The fall of teardrops on some withered dream.
Can birds be happy? Branches have snapped off.
Bleak afternoon—those sunrays seem so frail!
Pale lips are wilting—have they ever smiled?

Who died? The axles turn, the wheels push on—
what region is the hearse now heading for?
A winter dusk is falling from the skies—
unwarmed by fire, the soul is shivering so.
So great a sorrow—how can you accept
to leave the earth? For here's the town you've known,
yet soon the hearse will take you far away
to some lone spot—how chilly you will feel!
Horse carriage, please move at a gentle pace—
don't jolt a body used to life's soft bed.
And mourners, see the cortege to the grave—
don't follow it halfway and turn around,
distressing that dead soul. A few bowed heads,
condolent hearts beside the grave will let
the soul, about to sink to nothingness,
catch one last glimpse, on faces that show love,
of this our world, henceforward pushed far off.
The hearse is rolling: streets, spare it your bumps. `
O space, I beg, contract your vast expanse!
How doleful is an evening of goodbyes!
You too, O winds who're whining, howling so,
please hush and help allay the loneliness.

All those black flags are ravens flapping wings—

they bear ill tidings, guide extinguished souls ...

Who died? Why does the music speak such grief?

264. Talking with the pyramid
Huy Cận

Blue heavens have supplanted grass and trees.

The far-flung desert's sands fill up the days

and nights; the moon here basks in sands.

What are those speckles? Stars or dancing sands?

Pharaohs would not be buried by mere sands—   5

a hundred tombs of stone would scale the skies.

They've scorned the desert for five thousand years

and thought they held eternity in their clutch.

"O Pyramid! What have you seen since then?"

"All seasons I have watched winds blow the sands   10

and hurtling sands claw at the face of time."

"O Pyramid! Do you still sport your sneer

at months and years or taunt the centuries?"

"At first, drunk with my sense of power, I bade

that days not wane—I stuck the zenith sun   15

above my summit like a glorious gem,

a diamond sparkling in the sovereign's crown."

"Millennial Pyramid, what happened next?"

"While in my bowels lay the Pharaoh's corpse,

ten thousand subjects languished at my feet.   20

He wished to triumph over towering time

and rest untroubled in a sleep of stone.

He lived through life preparing his own grave,

clasped death and hoped to slowly vanquish death:

let time's winds blow—his soul would feel no chill.   25

The sun spun round, but I stood still, unworn.
The king slept undisturbed—I stayed awake:
by violent fits rose sands and yet more sands,
blasting my body, causing stings and burns.
I tried to rouse the king and let him know   30
that his eternity under the stars was doomed:
'Pharaoh, wake up! How could you fence out death
with death?' The king slept on, but stones broke down:
along the skyline many friends in ruin
had from eternity thrown kings' mummies out.   35
I felt my feet were shivering, touched by time."
"What else have you beheld, O Pyramid?"
"From age to age I've watched herds of bowed men
plod at my feet and vanish in the mists.
But sometimes one with pensive forehead would   40
fix piercing eyes on me and ask me this:
'You've lifted death on tiers and tiers of rocks:
has one inch stirred to life again so far,
after five thousand years, O lonesome tower?'
I froze inside my heart and ever since,   45
I, petrified, have died a little more
in each cold fiber of my frame of stone ..."

"O Pyramid, what more have you beheld?"
"Amid these windswept wastes, I've also watched
some signs that death will resurrect to life.   50
The sands have cried a cry of desperate faith,
wanting to change what's stone-dead back to cells,
fresh, fluid cells of flesh, of leaves and flowers,
and see life fight to spring from dust and rock."

In the blue dusk, beside the desert's sands,   55
early cornstalks have sprouted tassels forth.

The pyramid's shadow cools the riverbank.
(Notes taken at the site where sandstorms gust.)

(Egypt, July 1962)

265. Graves
Chê Lan Viên

Bury it deep, the smile on your red lips,
and choke it dead, the song inside your throat.
Stop looking for the fresh, bright hues of flowers
and listening for the silver tones of birds,

Because each joy now only brings to mind
those crazy dreams once smoldering in the soul,
those sorrows festering in the heart's dark jail;
inside sad eyes, all images of youth.

The past is one long row of tomb on tomb.
The future is a row of graves unfilled.
And do you know, my friend? The present, too,
is silently interring all our days.

In summer heat the lush, green leaves grow dim
to set the stage for autumn soon to come.
And one by one our days of youth fade out
to weave the graveclothes that will shroud our soul.

266. Silk threads of memory
Chê Lan Viên

I want the world to stop and spin no more,
cease gushing forth the flow of days and months.
Spring, don't come back; and summer, snuff out fire.
Autumn and winter, quit distressing me.

The earth stirs my silk heartstrings as it turns.
My private grief soaks in all nothingness.
Cham bricks keep falling as the months flee past.[1]
Cham towers keep crumbling under their wan moon.

When summer lights its fire, my rage flares up.
The autumn wind cuts through my soul with chill.
After a winter eve, a bright spring morn
only adds gloom to grief already felt.

Creator, send me back to Champaland!
Take me away, far from the world of men.
All scenes of life offend and hurt my eyes.
All fresh, bright hues remind me of decay.

Give me a planet full of frost and ice,
a star that shines alone where ends the blue.
There, living out my days and months, I'll hide
from all the pain and anguish I have known.

1. The Cham people had a flourishing kingdom until the eleventh century,
when the Vietnamese began the southward expansion that eventually
destroyed Champa as a political entity. The Vietnamese poet (who gave himself a Cham name) apparently used the Champa metaphor to mourn the loss
under the French of national independence.

267. The waning night
Chê Lan Viên

We two look at each other, still and hushed,
lest a lament should shatter our deep night.
Two breaths that seek to mingle in the dark;
two souls that plunge and drown in sorrow's sea.

"Cham maiden, force yourself to smile, my love,
and give my heart a respite from all care.
Why gaze on that horizon so far off?
Why brood and mourn our Champa's past of woe?

Look out, look out, a star is falling down!

Please lean away and dodge the star, my love.

Perhaps my spirit shook the heavens loose

as it rushed back to Champa's streams and hills."

I am still speaking—vanished is the night.

Before we have made love, we're split apart.

On earth the sun has risen over there

to wrest the maiden's soul away from mine.

Note: See the note to Poem 266, "Silk threads of memory," by Chế Lan Viên.

268. On the way home
Chế Lan Viên

One day, I left the city and went back

to see the hills and streams of my Cham race.

Worn thin with longing, here are my Cham towers.

Old temples crushed beneath the weight of time.

Deserted rivers crawling through the night.

Cham statues moaning their foul sores of rust.

Here are deep woods where treetops droop—Cham ghosts

prowl them together, groping in the dark.

In that dense jungle, twilight lurks and slinks,

alive with scents and sounds; the sun dips low.

Often, both sides joined battle on this field.

Dead fighters' souls roam all forlorn and howl.

Cham blood still churns with anger as time flows.

Cham bones still carry memories of hate.

Here are the sights of Champaland at peace.

Lone hamlets bathed in streams of sunset gold.

Cham lasses nimbly sauntering, homeward bound,

and gaily chatting, wrapped in brown red smocks.

Here are resplendent mansions in the sun
and gorgeous palaces beneath blue skies,
proud warboats sleeping on the quiet stream,
huge elephants calmly walking by a wall.

In the ethereal glow of pearls, here are
Cham kings and courtiers drunk on ivory flesh,
Cham beauties lulled to dream by songs of flutes,
swaying in rhythm, bodies fair as flowers.

I'll see them all, those scenes, on my way home.
They've haunted me as days and months pass by.
And ever since, my heart has overflown
with sorrow and regret for my Cham race.

Note: See the note to Poem 266, "Silk threads of memory," by Chê Lan Viên.

269. The war elephant
Chê Lan Viên

Birds hush. The evening twilight dare not stir.
Those golden leaves, fear-frozen, cease to fall.
The silver brook stops babbling in the woods.
The trees choke their gay chatter, terror-struck.

On that leaf mat stained with the blood of beasts   5
someone is tramping—all the jungle shakes.
Or is it silence crashing on spilt blood?
Or sorrow sobbing through the wilderness?

Amid the maze of huddled trees and leaves
walks the mute elephant, inspiring awe.   10
Under his feet all tremble, woods and hills.
Under his feet all groan, leaves green and gold.

Uttering no sound, he walks, eyes blurred by tears,
as grief and longing coil around his legs.

On his old back the empty howdah sits,   15
agleam with pearls and fringes, red or blue.

By a deserted stream the elephant stops
to let his soul flow with the waves and reach
those far-off shores where golden breezes waft
past halls and mansions slumbering under mists;   20

those far-off shores where he, a soldier, marched
that evening at the curfew drum's behest,
when in the dark, red banners slowly drooped,
when waves at sunset glowed all pink with haze;

where Vijaya, one morning, rang with songs[1]   25
as Chams in triumph were returning home,
as their war elephants walked in stately files
and incense swirled amid the awesome hush;

where on the battleground, one night, blood howled,
horns brayed, steeds neighed while heads were falling off;   30
and they, Cham elephants, wildly charged ahead
as burned in them the fire of their Cham race;

where once, for centuries, in splendor rose
high walls and ramparts, palaces and shrines,
where horses' neighs in triumph rode the wind,   35
where rang the hymn of all the Chams on earth ...

Those sights and sounds flash through the elephant's mind—
with pounding heart, he stares and listens, rapt.
The river drawls along as sunshine fades—
the past, or so it seems, is flowing here.   40

And wading through the stream, he leaps to hail
those days of yore the current brings his way.
The dream dissolves in water—he wakes up
and sees a realm all drenched in dusk and gloom.

In the cold wind the old war elephant roars,   45

and echoes carry tremors through the wilds,

rumbling like claps of thunder up in space,

and stars all shudder in the cloudless sky.

Note: See the note to Poem 266, "Silk threads of memory," by Chê Lan Viên.
    1. Vijaya: the capital of Champa between 1000 and 1471.

270. The human skull
Chê Lan Viên

O skull, a human creature owned you once!

Beneath all that thin crust of bone on top,

what do you still remember in the dark?

What hopes or wishes do you entertain?

Do you think of the execution grounds

where one by one, ten thousand heads did fall?

Or of those ghastly nights when your own soul

flew to and fro amid will-o'-the-wisps?

Do you still look, on windless afternoons,

for traces of your body, now decayed?

Do you remember it, your anguished soul,

now wandering in the far-off world of death?

O skull, I must have gone stark mad! I want

to clasp you in my arms, with all my strength,

and let that blood still clinging there infuse

my soul and in sad poems run again.

I want to bite you, tear you to small bits

and swallow you, a hunk of dried-up bone,

and taste again an era vanished now,

a stream of months and years that's flowed away.

271. The river

Đông Hồ

Men err and idly mourn a fallen flower.
If flowers fall, they'll bloom again next spring.
But it's a river that you should bemoan.
It leaves and won't come back—a life flows past.

272. Shilly-shally

Hồ Dzênh

Promise to come, my love, but don't you come.
Grief-struck, I'll pace the courtyard as I watch
the cigarette burn slowly in my hand.
I'll say so softly, "Oh, how I miss you!"

Promise to come, my love, but don't you come.
O darling mine, can love make any sense
after its early stage, when it's so frail,
more fragile than a sunbeam, than sheer silk?

They shilly-shally, flowers and butterflies,
hoping tomorrow will bring joy and cheer.
Happiness is tomorrow, not today—
promise to come, my love, but don't you come.

I'll shun you—silently I'll slip away.
If you do come, please turn around and leave,
for love will lose its flavor once fulfilled—
the very best is life you've yet to live.

Finish no letter, land no boat—between
the past and future leave them dangling there . . .

273. A falling leaf

Trần Gia Thoại

The sky, a deep blue sea.
A golden boat,
wind-driven, lists and tilts—
unmoored, it sinks.
And coldly time flows on.

274. The night train

Trần Gia Thoại

Its whistle shrieks and rips the veil of mists,
and from afar it comes, with dots of fire.
So toward the platform, jostling folks will rush
to meet some friend or see some loved one off.
All eyes will watch the train that's drawing near,
that will unload so many fervent hopes
and take aboard so many wondrous dreams:
the night will shine, resplendent as the dawn.
The train will stop for just a moment, though:
its wheels will turn and pull its freight away
to vanish slowly into that black space
and leave behind disquiet, grief, regrets.
And, on reflection, what is life if not
the image of a train traversing night?
Compare a man's existence to that train:
the station is his sojourn on this earth,
and night is time in all its dismal gloom.
Life's drifting toward the sea of nothingness:
this bubble, bobbling up and down on waves,
will leave behind a whisper, muffled, hushed.

275. Tall trees

Phạm Hổ

I've now forgotten when it started, but
I've liked to linger gazing at tall trees . . .

Those age-old trees stand where I find raw youth,
primeval nature, green and cool as jade,
where mornings bathe in rose-red sunshine first,
where evenings welcome crystal dewdrops first,
where dust cannot rise high enough to cling.
They're splendid rhymes, they're songs of epic life:
they're pure and lofty souls that will not bow—
souls of the past, the present, future times . . .
Nor can I remember for what cause
I've liked to linger gazing at tall trees,
where things at moonrise stir when breezes waft,
where earth and sky loom vaster when birds sing,
just as our hearts—when they love life too much—
will throb and throb for joy with other hearts,
where sap will flow the farthest when least heard,
to feed a tree and help it reach its height,
where young green tops do not forget their roots,
where what's near heaven owes great debts to earth . . .

I've liked to linger gazing at tall trees,
and all through life I've never quite known why . . .

276. Forty

Hoàng Trinh

A blink, a twinkling—I'll be forty soon!
Will flowers still look fresh, the sun still shine?
Those dreams I dreamed in youth I now recall,
lying awake at night, and blush for shame.

But I am I as ever, am I not?
Disheveled hair, a lonesome home, few friends.
Along with liquor, poetry has gone stale.
Now spring's come back—I'm at a loss for words.

What can I say to you, my self of yore?
I'd be a hundred and still young, I thought.
The present I, like the old I, won't weep—
why is my handkerchief then wet with tears?

I thought I'd still be I, but I'm not I.
Witness the girl who's always lived next door.
She bowed and called me "Uncle" yesterday.
There I stood stunned as she went walking past.

The girl went walking past; thus passed my spring.
O spring, so you too wither and grow old!
Today, I see how beautiful you are,
with all your flowers, all your butterflies.

277. To the Black Nymph

Vũ Hoàng Chương

A tryst with you—I shall nurse no regret;
from my past life I shall not mourn a thing.
Blow closer here your coils of pale blue hair;
bring closer to my lips your brown gray lips.

It's cold tonight—I seek you in the dark,
and in your hands I'll leave the wasted years.
Why would my spirit choose the path that leads
right back to sorrows felt in autumns past?

For as you know, it was along this path
that love once wilted, dreams once broke to bits.
Along this path, from many graves would rise
fond memories to pull me by the feet.

Oh no, dear lady, I've no courage left—
it has gone dry, the well of love and tears.
Inside your fiery eyes, burn up for me
some crumbs of grief still clinging to my lips.

Blow closer here your coils of tousled hair;
bring closer to my lips your drowsy lips.
Then, gently lift me on your wings of smoke
and in oblivion's limbo drown my soul.

278. No more anxiety

Vũ Hoàng Chương

The question mark surrounds a human life:
the snail gnaws on the heart—hushed drops of blood.
Today, the final exclamation point:
the answer's nailed—it's in the coffin now.

Note: The poet wrote this quatrain on the day of his mother's death.

279. Soap bubbles

Bùi Khải Nguyên

My darling, won't you try this little game?
Roll up a sheet of paper and make sure
it looks just like the flute you used to play
on evenings of blue skies and gentle winds.

Blow bubbles with soap water and have fun—
let three or five of them soar heavenward.
They're orange, violet, blue, and red—what else?
You clap your hands and, laughing, shriek with joy.

All those soap bubbles rise and rise aloft—
they keep ascending toward the higher spheres.

A sudden gust of wind bursts them apart—
and clutching tight my hand, you claim amends.

But you're unjust, for I am not to blame!
Come near and let me quickly dry your tears.
My darling, carried off by winds of change,
what now exists will turn to nothing soon.

Alas for all soap bubbles blown in sport!
They're glimpses of some splendid dream, far off.
They're hints of happiness that flutter past
to flee and vanish with the winds of life.

280. Getting well

Ngân Giang

This morning, that dread ghost, disease, has fled.
Before my mirror, I can't help but smile.
The eyes still harbor stars that twinkled there.
The face yet shows a moon, both soft and bright.
Red lips have blossomed, flowers tinged with rouge.
Dark hair lets go, strands loosened on the wind.
I thought black earth would bury my white cheeks.
Who'd have thought life would keep a grip on me?

281. A retired mandarin's wife complains

Ưng Bình

Ah, all those scores of years! Love's labor lost!
It was my luck to hit upon this man.
He boasts a scholar's fame, a mandarin's rank—
he doesn't own one dime, one inch of land.
Word-crazy, he keeps hugging his few books—
rose-fancier, he hangs around those beds.

His monthly pension? But he spends it all!
I never can squeeze one cent out of him.

282. Congratulating a friend on his new dentures
Tô Giang Tử

Gums hurt, teeth ache—the ills and woes of age!
If Heaven grants longevity, why complain?
You gnashed bones hard as stone—out fell worn teeth.
You chewed hot spices—seasoned gums would smart.
A beautician has repaired those sunken cheeks.
A dental doc's replaced those wobbly jaws.
Look in the mirror—see again your youth,
boasting a brand-new set of teeth, milk-white.

283. A gaffer in love
Y Vân Tử

An idler's busy, for he loves the Muse.
The lady, as she's wont, plays hard to get.
He pampers her, scrubs rhymes to lend them gloss.
He coddles her, shuns thoughts that show coarse taste.
He whispers passion—music fires the words.
He sings in rhythm—melody conjures dreams.
As cries the crane, his poems soar aloft.
The white-haired bird still feels his oats—surprise!

284. Mother's faith
Thừa Phong

Mother, throughout her life, took pride in me,
setting great store by all those old wives' tales.

You'll shrug them off as nothing more than myths—
to Mother they portended glorious deeds.

A crimson caul! Rare omen, she believed:
I should grow up to tower over men.
The newborn baby, though, was hard to please:
for three full days he sulked and would not suck.

The tiny body withered in plain sight:
our village quack, at his wits' end, gave up.
Mother bought drugs, called doctors, begged the gods:
her money was misspent, love's labor lost.

But, miracle! Heaven would not doom a babe:
the brat felt sudden pangs and craved for food.
Those days and nights, he'd staged a hunger strike:
with gusto, now, he grabbed his mother's breast.

Then, eating well, he promptly grew and grew—
he went to school, learned schoolboys' tricks and pranks.
With his first whine he'd proved a wayward child—
still, Mother thought, "He's meant for something great!"

He entered life's wide world and pushed ahead,
vying for his own share of wealth and rank.
He had his ups and downs, he tripped and fell—
he knew few joys, but many pains and griefs.

And, often, through hard luck or some mistake,
his whole career collapsed and washed downstream.
Mother would gaze at him and say again:
"One day, my son, you will surpass your peers!"

Honors and profits—I've now quit that race
with empty hands and hair long since turned white.
Mother, if still on earth, would yet keep faith,
watching her son kill time and scribble verse.

(Birmingham, Alabama, 1982)

285. Where have *they* gone?

Võ Phiên

Those times, recaptured in a flash:
eighteen and twenty, You and I.
Entwined together, two were one.
Remember—earth and heaven dwindled then.
We wrapped life's meaning up in one word—love!
We censused humankind and counted two!
Space shrank to let the shoulders touch,
let chest press chest, let lips kiss cheek.
At their right season, girl and boy once met—
merged *yin* and *yang* in their full flush.
Heaven and earth—oh, how they matched and fit!
Spring sunshine heated, while spring breezes stirred.

You think of that young couple, You and I—
wistful, you ask: "Where have *they* gone?"
I give a start, embarrassed, ill at ease.
The noonday sun feels like some intimate heat.
Your question pokes those ardors that burned once,
and hereabout there wafts a smell of flesh.
So close, they thought! And they've pulled far away . . .
Where have *they* gone? But who can tell?

Where have *they* gone—that couple, You and I?
We miss them as green waters miss blue skies.
All things on earth must perish as they live:
day at the zenith starts to sink and die.
What's motionless will never cease to move—
from us *they* parted who knows when!
The past took off without a by-your-leave—
we've longed and languished ever since.
We count the months and years and ask ourselves,
"Where have *they* gone?" We're left alone,
shriveled and wrinkled, quite forlorn.

286. Coaxing my illness
Mai Thảo

Each time my body threatens and acts up,
I talk with it again and smooth things out.
I coax it lest it cause some big to-do—
on second thought it somehow gives me grace.

Inside, my illness has become my mate:
after a long, long while it's part of me.
Pillowed on what ails me, I sprawl at ease:
illness and I are now two bosom friends.

287. All come to me
Nguyễn Chí Thiện

All you who would, of your whole life,
reduce to ashes months and years,
whose hearts bear wounds that burn like fire,
scorching each minute of your time!

All you whose dreams have shriveled up,
who've tramped the world on played-out legs,
whose hearts are graves where you've interred
bruised memories still streaked with scars!

All come to me, for I am Death.
All come to me like rivers to the sea.
My bosom opens, deep, immense.
Sorrows and agonies on earth
all turn to nothing in my breast.

(1965)

8. Peasants, Merchants, and Scholars

288. *The well*

Nguyễn Thiên Túng

The sparkling light of heaven fills the well.
From it ten thousand homes forever draw.
Oh, how to hurl its water through the air
and sprinkle all parched fields to grow good crops!

289. How blessed is a middle rank in life!

Nguyễn Trãi

How blessed is a middle rank in life!
Between high plane and low, days smoothly glide.
Enjoying peace, remember times of war—
eating your rice, thank those who plow and plant.
With learning, goods and riches can't compare:
love men who work, and free your hands from toil.
Kind Heaven keeps exhaustless stores of wealth:
your heirs won't have to borrow for their needs.

290. A round shape water takes inside the gourd

Nguyễn Trãi

A round shape water takes inside the gourd.[1]
For good or ill, all fit some frame or mold.
Live near the rich—you'll munch on crackly rice.
Fall in with thieves—you'll rue it and eat stick.[2]
Befriend a fool—you'll join the pack of fools.
Meet clever men—you'll learn some clever tricks.

Mix with low folk—you'll stoop to their low plane.

Get black near ink, get red near cinnabar.[3]

Note: This poem is virtually made up of folk sayings.

1. "In a gourd, [water] is round; in a tube, [it] takes a long [shape]."
(*Ở bầu thì tròn, ở ống thì dài.*)

2. "Live near the rich and your teeth will ache eating crackly rice; live
near thieves and your back will hurt getting thrashed." *(Gần nhà giàu đau
răng ăn cốm, gần kẻ trộm ôm lưng chịu đòn.)*

3. "Near ink you get black, near a lamp you get bright." *(Gần mực thì
đen, gần đèn thì sáng.)*

291. Merchants

(King) Lê Thánh-tông

They bustle on sand beaches, day and night,

to haul back goods that cram their houses full.

A lizard's heart will scheme to snitch and snatch;

a viper's tongue can speak and spit fine words.

They gain their ill-got wealth throughout the land—

their venal motives serve as butts of songs.

Compare—how do they differ from mere cheats?

It's strange that men could sell to fellowmen!

292. Scholars and soldiers

Nguyễn Công Trứ

Scholars and soldiers marshaled in two files!

Scholars rank high, soldiers not far below.

Red sunshades and blue hammocks—scholars' pride.[1]

Gold swords and silver badges—soldiers' power.

Scholars flap phoenix-wings and keep the peace.[2]

Soldiers roar tigers' roars and quell all strife.

To scholars soldiers must defer in peace:

with men of letters warriors can't compare.

1. Scholars successful at civil service examinations were granted ceremonial parasols and hammocks or palanquins (on which they were carried in
triumph back to their native villages).

2. The mythical phoenix is a symbol of Confucian virtue and wisdom.

293. To a watering scoop

Bùi Dương Lịch

Perk up, bend down—you toil and don't complain.

You work to save the crops from parching drought.

On earth, who ever knows how to make rain?

By the rice field, you stand all set to help.

Let plowlands, deep and shallow, lie in flood—

a single splash of water earns our thanks.

It seldom rains when rain is needed most;

you can be proud you draw on your own strength.

294. Summer drought

Phạm Quý Thích

Last summer, harvests washed away with floods.

This summer, harvests wilt with burning drought.

Fields, high and low, are rigged with water scoops.

Roots, at midday and at night, replace the rice.

Rainbows and clouds deceive all farmers' hopes.

Grasses and trees can't bear the sixth-moon frost.

Men gather in the village, mourning crops:

they see the tax collector—off they run.

295. Fishermen and cormorants

Phan Thanh Giản

These fisherfolk own just a barge.

Eight mouths to feed—all live afloat.

To hunt the depths they weave no nets;

for catching fish they set no traps:

they merely hire some cormorants.

They moor where fast the river flows.

Cormorants move in groups and teams—

together, big and small, they flock.

All day, their masters let them loose

to swim about and dive for fish.

No kin to fish are cormorants,

yet they can tell where fish resort.

Big cormorants catch bigger fish;

small cormorants catch smaller fry.

The fish, once caught, stick in their craws—

all, big and small, lodge snugly there.

Enough big fish to fill a creel;

enough small fish to heap a tray.

The birds don't gorge themselves alone,

nor do their masters wolf it all.

The masters eat the bigger fish—

the smaller fry are for the birds.

296. To some students caught nodding in class

Nguyễn Khuyến

My students, you? What students I must teach!

The way your heads keep waggling makes me laugh.

Your voice, so thick with sleep, can't breathe a word.

Your eyes, half drowned in slumber, hardly see.

You rock and roll—are you by fiends possessed?

You reel and sway—has wine bewitched your soul?

Perhaps you ape Ou-yang Hsiu's man in red:

you read some deathless line and nod forthwith![1]

1. According to legend, whenever the Sung scholar Ou-yang Hsui (Âu
Dương Tu, 1007–1072) was engaged in grading papers for some civil service

examination, he had a vision of a man in a red gown standing nearby; from time to time, the man would nod his head to indicate approval of some line of verse or prose in the paper Ou-yang was reading.

297. Grains of rice

Phan Văn Trị

They leave rice fields to travel far and wide:
who doesn't count on them for sustenance?
Doffing their golden coats, they bask in sun;
displayed in every place, they shine like jade.
Time after time, their forebears saved the realm—
for centuries their breed has fed our folk.
By fire and water they'll forsake their lives:
is anyone aware of what they do?

Note: This poem is a tribute to Vietnamese peasants not only as growers of rice but also as soldiers defending their homeland against foreign aggressors.

298. Harvesting at sunset

Anh Thơ

The sun is setting—clouds still glow with red.
Storks in white flocks fly over far-off fields.
A whistle-kite plays music with the wind
while sings a lass who picks mulberry leaves.

In the rice field, stalks sag with golden ears—
young lads in joyous teams all reap the grain.
Meanwhile, an old man under his cone hat
sits smoking, puff by puff, at the far end.

Along the dike wave wind-borne tufts of hair:
small children, busy chasing after kites,
leave buffalo in peace there on the grass—
eyes dream and gaze at ripples of the breeze.

299. The country road

Tê Hanh

An alley once, I dragged my idleness
throughout the village, loitering, bored, and sad.
I reached that hamlet, caught the breath of grass,
the field's sweet scent—there, I burst out in song.

Over my body, grass has grown since then.
My bosom smells so fragrant with wildflowers.
I hug a paddy field, clasp manioc plots,
enfold a pond of algae and dark mud.

On joyous mornings, sunshine shoots afar—
my soul lies glittering in the light of day.
On quiet evenings I ramble on,
just like some farmer sauntering, homeward bound.

I've often suffered much in summer heat—
my skin, all dried and shriveled up, has cracked.
I've often gone through hell in rains and floods—
they've riddled me with sores, torn me to shreds.

I share the happiness of village folks
when they bring in good crops, their cares and woes
when harvests fail. I even feel the thrills
of country boys and girls at their love trysts.

So gloom and tedium haunt my life no more—
in my poor village, well content, I stay.
With rapture I absorb through all my pores
aromas exhaled from the fields, the earth.

300. Bamboos of Vietnam

Nguyễn Duy

"Since when have you existed, green bamboos
that figured in the tales of long ago?

peasants, merchants, and scholars 357

With meager stems and flimsy leaves, how come
you've built those walls and ramparts for defense?
You've stayed so green and fresh, no matter where,
and even thrived in barren grit or lime."

"It's no big deal! Keep hoarding bits of fat
and in due time they will amount to much.
Our bamboo roots don't balk at such poor soil:
so many toilers are our many roots.

As the wind blows, our branches swing aloft:
despite hard times, we hum and lull the leaves.
We love the golden sun and heaven's blue:
a green bamboo won't cower in the shade.

We will protect each other in a storm
and closer cling together with our arms.
All bound by love, bamboos don't live alone:
that's how we've built our walls and forts, O men!

If by misfortune breaks a stem or branch,
our rootstock will pass life on to our shoots.
The bamboo breed will never stoop and bow:
a sapling thrusts its points as sharp as spikes.

We adults bare our backs to sun or dew
and for our children save the curtailed shirts.
Mere shoots, just peeping out, already boast
the straightness and round form of tall bamboos.
Let months pass by and years go on their way:
bamboos grow old, and up will spring young shoots.

Tomorrow and forevermore, our land
shall keep its green, the green of green bamboos."

301. The bamboo hedgerow

Nam Xuyên

The bamboo hedgerow cut a dark-green swath
across the autumn field of golden rice.
Over the blue of hills that mists blurred out,
the azure skies, a few white clouds above.

Screened by bamboos, the village did not stir,
yet something brewed and smoldered, live, inside.
It had the farmers' simple thatch-roofed huts;
it had those people who'd brave rain and sun,
all forces quiet but persistent, tough,
those buffalo, shy and gentle, also fierce,
a life at one with nature, flowing on
as slowly months and years or seasons flow,
a clean, plain world of toil with decent dreams
nursed in the shadow of those tall bamboos,
with joys from caring for the green rice shoots
while gladly feet tramped mud and hands touched soil.

Those tall bamboos once shielded good, full lives
with plantains lush amidst areca palms,
with ponds in which fish swarmed, with plots of greens
and yellow flowers speckling mustard beds.
At daybreak, roosters crowed and hailed the dawn—
the age-old chime of peasants' clocks,
the soul of life that sang a triumphant hymn,
the friendly call that woke the village up.

The bamboo hedgerow! Once, behind it all,
when autumn breezes brought a hint of grief,
when rice sent fragrance wafting through the house,
I suddenly felt so sad for no real cause.
The cherished scene my heart could not let go
lies now beyond the seas, beyond the clouds.

From that green bamboo hedgerow I still see

a swirl of autumn leaves all through my soul.

302. The quarrel of the six beasts (*Lục súc tranh công*)
Anonymous

Heaven creates all things;

earth nurtures every kind.

What breed or species wants for skills?

How can a man dispense with beasts?

The Dragon mends the sky and bathes the sun;[1]   5

The Unicorn assists all gods and saints;[2]

the Tortoise sees the future, good or ill;[3]

the Phoenix can tell weal from woe and rise from fall.[4]

Within the orb of three thousandfold worlds,[5]

they're called the Four Most Holy Animals.   10

And then there are six sacrificial beasts

that Heaven sent to succor men below.

All aches and sores, the Buffalo laments:

"I bear the brunt of many tasks alone.

The Cock no sooner crows night's end   15

than summoning the herdboy up,

the Master tells him, 'Drive the Buffalo

to pasture now and let him graze a bit.'

But all too soon the east glows red—

it's time to toil, to labor hard.   20

In front two ropes coil round my neck;

behind I have to pull a plow.

A bridle ties my mouth, a rope my nose.

Flies swarm my body, leeches prick my legs.

When, tired to death, I pant and puff,   25

the man will curse me right and left.

When at high noon he lets me off,

worn out and hungry, I can hardly budge.
While others rest, may I just idle too?
When I'm exhausted, who will take my place?   30
I plow them all, both deep and shallow fields;
I till the beds for pulse and sesame.
At work I don't have time to breathe;
at meals I don't have time to chew.
Do I complain of rain or wind?   35
Do I rebel at dew or frost?
I, Buffalo, give them their grains, their silks—
without me, Buffalo, no fruits, no nuts!
It's I who'll haul the stalks of rice they've cut;
it's I who'll thrash the sheaves they're piling up.   40
From the first moon until the last,
from spring to winter, all year round,
as soon as farming work is done,
I cart all things, enjoying not one break.
Branches for hedges, wood for fuel,   45
twigs, thatch, bamboo, manure—
take anything that must be moved:
it falls on me to carry all.
Am I to balk at hills and heights?
Am I to flinch from brooks and streams?   50
I hunch my back and drag my load
while scathing words are hurled at me.
Dry hay and weeds, that's all I eat;
can I reject their nasty stall?
I, Buffalo, have set up this or that,   55
established bins or garners, high and low.
Were I to get my full deserts,
I should be clad in silk, no less.
I'd settle, though, for hemp or cotton pants,
or even for a cloth around the loins.   60
I should be given rice and fish to eat—

or, short of that, thin gruel mixed with greens.
When someday I grow old and fail in strength,
I should be nursed as payment for my pains,
Instead of offering me no sacrifice, 65
they should feed me in death just as in life.
Men close their hearts to me while I'm alive—
they will mistreat my spirit when I'm dead.
They'll hand each other baskets and sharp knives;
they'll fetch grass kindling and dry wood for fire. 70
They'll say, 'The Buffalo was Buddha once.[6]
Let's set the brute aflame and speed his soul
to Paradise!' About my poor remains,
they all will huddle and decide.
One man suggests, 'I'll take the head!' 75
Another cries, "The dewlap!" They'll fight to get
the bowels and bladder—pillows for their heads.
They'll fashion combs and shuttles with the horns
or turn them into earrings and fan ribs,
measuring bowls and cups for wine, 80
fine bugles you can blow quite loud
or chessmen you bang hard upon the board,
a clapper or a box,
handles of fans and knives.
My legs they'll share among themselves 85
to make some salads with raw meat.
All said and done, we buffalo are beasts
condemned by fate without appeal.
When dead, I'll be brushed off like so much dust.
While still alive, I'll tell the Master this. 90
Remember? At blood-smearing rites for bells[7]
the king of Ch'i reprieved an innocent.
When old and feeble, I shall bless T'ien-tzu
who bade his children not to sell their beasts.[8]
Have you forgotten it, my lord, 95

this timeless precept from the past?
'By your own virtue act upon the world!'
Instead, you've rendered evil for good deeds!
Must I keep spinning matters out?
My lord, let me butt in and say a word.   100
No looks, no skills—why take such pains
to rear the Dog and all his breed?
They stuff themselves quite nice and plump
only to play and wreck your home, your grounds.
They hang around for their three meals   105
and sidle off when work's at hand.
Before it's cold, they show how cold they feel,
curl up and tuck their tails between their legs,
or paw the straw and ashes on the hearth,
knock topsy-turvy all three kitchen gods.[9]   110
Before it's hot, they sprawl around and gasp
while lolling out their span-long tongues.
When you don't watch but look the other way,
they filch your food—that's one thing they do best.
If only they knew how to till the land,   115
ah, they would claim all credit in the world!
They gorge on well-cooked rice and gruel
while I must chew tough hay and straw.
And when they die, you'll bury them
with votive gifts, in solemn rites.   120
The lord is inhumane—he favors curs
while he mistreats one who deserves much more!"

The Dog has heard those words—his bosom smarts.
Quick he runs out and yelps a shrill retort:
"Heaven endows each kind with its own skills—   125
big beasts get harder tasks, small beasts light chores.
Because you boast huge shoulders and huge thighs,
you are assigned to plow-and-harrow work.
I, Dog, though weak of limb from birth,[10]

still do my best to guard the house.   130
So smart, you blow on hair and look for scars;
meddling, you part the leaves and grope for worms.[11]
We share the same condition, you and I—
both serve the Master with a single heart.
Some act one part, some play another role;   135
some tend the outside world, some watch home grounds.
My eyes are kept wide open through the night—
burglars, fear-stricken, all stay out of sight.
My eardrums, all day long, are on alert—
knaves panic when they catch a glimpse of me.   140
When men's ancestral spirits must be fed,
I go out hunting squirrels, chasing foxes.
Do I mind wriggling through sharp thorns?
Do I complain when muzzling into holes?
How come you feel no sorrow for my plight?   145
Instead, you draw such envious parallels!
I swallow crumbs of rice and dregs of soup,
when it's not rotten taro, wormy yam.
At mealtime I don't care how much I get—
if there's an empty bowl, that has to do!   150
You say you're fed coarse straw and grass—
but then you have a boy to wait on you.
He costs not only clothes and food,
but wages, too, and bonus gifts.
He's paid twice yearly at the least—   155
a herdboy's pay is worth one buffalo.
You claim your labor makes the Master rich:
just earn your keep and you'll have done enough!
To me the Master trusts his family wealth,
and I cost him no penny for a boy.   160
And yet, without my watchful eyes and ears,
that wealth would vanish into burglars' hands.
You, Buffalo, can talk but cannot think

and see how much I, Dog, perform.

The goods and chattels I protect on earth—   165

in death I'll guard that bridge to the Dark World.[12]

I'll help the virtuous ones escape from hell—

the mean and wicked I shall not let pass!

Mindful of past and future services,

the lord will bury me with cash and rice.   170

If he grants me great favors and large boons,

how shall I fail to welcome him down there?

I see you don't yet know the roots of things—

I'm telling you lest you think me a fool!"

As Buffalo and Dog lodge their complaint,   175

the Master's at a loss whose side to take:

"Enough comparison twixt Me and Thee!

I bid you two make peace—it's past all price."

Once reconciled, together, those two beasts

bow low before their lord and speak these words: 180

"If you're to judge by what we both perform,

we are beset with worries day and night.

Excuse us—is he such a prize, the Horse,

that you take pains to house him in such style?

For nourishment you feed him green bean soup;   185

you lodge him in a stable roofed with tile.

Each day he gets spruced up, then takes a stroll;

each day you pare his hoofs, you clip his mane.

You've gone to such expenses for his sake—

just reckon up the hundreds you've disbursed.   190

You've bought a saddle, bells, caparison,

stirrups, a bit, and reins;

fringes of gilt that hang from head to tail;

under the belly, silver-coated bands and straps.

But on reflection, that's a giddy breed—   195

their temper's full of whims and quirks.

Though they put on such pompous airs,
home matters leave them in a daze.
At the plow or harrow they will horse around,
and on a hunt they can trot out no skill.   200
They're not aware who raises them,
can't find their way and go back home.[13]
They do not qualify as fools,
nor should their wisdom be proclaimed.[14]
They scurry round like snails with borrowed souls[15]—   205
why ask for trouble rearing them?"

Those spiteful words arouse the Horse's bile—
he rushes out and whinnies his rebuke:
"Hey, let me tell you blokes some facts!
Now, who can boast a face as long as mine?   210
We all are beasts, but there are beasts and beasts:
of all known animals who rivals me?
I've roamed the empire's length and breadth;
I've raced to many battles north and south.
My knees have labored for the public good;   215
my back has buckled under kings and lords.
Each day I wait upon the dragon throne;
each day I must escort the phoenix coach.[16]
Kao-tsu waged war on horseback for five years
until he won the empire for the Liu.[17]   220
Kuan Yü once fought through all six border gates
with his Green Dragon sword, on his Red Hare.[18]
I've rescued strongholds and defended towns;
I've braved keen arrows and defied sharp shots.
Over a thousand miles, through hills and heights,   225
I've galloped at a stretch from post to post.
You little guys can eat and sleep your fill
because I've kept relentless watch.
With zeal I guard the country's peace—
glad farmers everywhere can farm.   230

peasants, merchants, and scholars **366**

You dogs just snuggle up in kitchen nooks;
you buffalo shine only in the fields.
Stop spouting gibberish; hold back your urge
to plunge headfirst and criticize.
Without my presence, who protects the realm?   235
If bandits come, will they leave you alone?
You know a thing or two, but not enough—
don't glory in your little skills and knacks."

The Horse harangues at length and makes his point—
to heal the breach, the Master says some words: 240
"You're big and small, but talents each can claim,
so cease to fight among yourselves."

And so all three, Horse, Buffalo, and Dog,
pay homage to their lord and make to leave.
But as he bears the Goat no love, the Horse   245
stays on a while and enters his own suit:
"The Goat is just a beast like me—
we both are kept and fed by you.
But you allow him time to frisk and play
while you ride me and run me off my legs.   250
Yet what's a goat? A head without a tail!
A bloated body on a stunted trunk!
He waddles like a chap whose testes hurt;
he skips and scampers like a bandit's kid.
He looks so awkward when he tries to trot   255
and cuts a sorry figure at the plow.
When someone hovers by his side,
he gapes his mouth and cries, 'Baa-baa!' "

The Goat has heard the Horse disparage him—
his beard perked up, he prances out and says: 260
"Let us compare your bulk and mine—
which one is bigger, Horse or Goat?
You've visited all towns and capitals—

why waste your notice on a country clod?
A stronger beast, you've served the Master's realm,   265
yet don't you act so high and mighty, Horse!
The Master will reward those with rare skills,
but let the rest work too and earn their keep.
I, Goat, don't dare to touch his rice and yam;
I never tamper with his greens and beans.   270
Let me advise you—cease your bumptious talk
and take less pride in your much-vaunted strength.
Who doesn't know that horses have long tails?
Long tails can flap at gadflies and mosquitoes.
But though my tail is short and clipped,   275
no, thanks—I shan't add yours to mine!
You brag you can breeze through a thousand miles—
I jump and clear three knolls: that's work enough.
I, Goat, cut capers as I wish—
you, Horse, go through your paces and cavort.   280
For plow and harrow some are born;
others exist to trot and run.
We goats by nature go with sacraments—
yes, we come in when scholars hold their rites,
when men must plead with saints or gods,   285
ask them for peace and happiness.
At such grave times we're granted precedence—
men offer goats before they kneel and pray.
You look impressive both in bulk and height,
but who considers horsemeat fit for gods?   290
If humans build a shrine, a market shed,
they immolate a goat, then break the ground.
On days when generals go off to war,
they slaughter one of us, then sally forth.
About the new-moon feast Confucius said: 295
'Begrudge a goat, Tzu-kung, and lose a rite?'[19]
You speak at random and don't think—

in merit are we goats so wanting, Horse?

Talk straight and to the point—

don't slander and malign.   300

Though short of tail and small of head,

I'm titled Registrar with a Long Beard![20]

What beast outranks your humble Goat?

Your lowly Goat ranks high in all the world!

Since you have moved among the great,   305

what title have they granted you?

O Master, judge the Horse and me, the Goat!

Please weigh our work—whose service tips the scale?"

The Horse has listened, learned some truths—

who'd think the little goat a big, big shot?   310

The Goat replies and shows a serpent's guile;

the Horse protests and struts a dragon's strength.

The Master thus decrees: "You two are peers—

let each mind his own business and concern."

Once Horse and Goat have come to terms,   315

the Goat sets on the Rooster thus:

"We goats and horses do the realm much good—

you raise those chickens and receive no thanks.

Sow beds with mustard or coriander seeds—

clucking, they will all scratch and pull up roots.   320

Lay down some rows of manioc or peas—

they all will trample leaves and blooms to shreds.

Just when you thatch your roof, up there they'll hop

to peck at straws and strew them to the winds.

Feed them—they'll wipe their beaks and turn their backs; [21] 325

before night falls, they're ready for their roost.[22]

They never leave a heap of trash alone;

they never give the greens a chance to root.

They pester you, bedevil you all day—

what does it profit you to raise their tribe?"   330

The Rooster's lungs and liver burn with rage—
wings flapping, head a-cocking, he jumps out:
"Come, now! Five virtues roosters all possess—
kind, brave, and loyal, skilled at war and peace.[23]
A mandarin's cap adorns our brow;   335
our claws display two lethal spears.
Time and again, I've served on battlefields
and there performed resounding feats of arms.
As drums beat fast the third watch in Lung-hsi,
I crowed three crows before day broke.   340
The first one said, 'O sun, arise betimes!'
The second said, 'Long live and thrive our king!'
The third one said, 'Let joy prevail on earth!'
Somebody feigned my voice and saved Meng Ch'ang;[24]
my call aroused two gallant men of Tsin.[25]   345
Whoever wants to change his evil ways
wakes up at cockcrow, bent on doing good.[26]
The rising destiny of Chou
was augured by a rooster's leg. [27]
I sing and soothe all those with sleepless nights;   350
I crow and cheer all those who wait for dawn.
Now that you ponder such home truths,
do you perceive the sense of things?
You angered me as you kept talking grub
or trying to pick holes and point at flaws.   355
We roosters know the rites as well as goats—
you're Registrar, I'm Herald of the Morn!
Just those few facts prove I'm your match—
I've left unmentioned all my healing arts.
I wonder who's the slugabed!   360
I wonder who's the villain of the piece!
Since none is hired to wach me come and go,
at times I scratch and claw where I should not.
There's always someone looking after goats,

yet ten times more destruction you have wrought.   365
Does chicken feed cost overmuch each day?
You make such picayune comparisons
I have to teach you, Goat, a thing or two
or you'd think me a feckless chap on earth.
Have you forgotten? Roosters chime the dawn   370
to make all husbands cherish virtuous wives,[28]
to bid all Shun's disciples do good works.[29]
I'll yield to you in this, your toady's beard,[30]
which serves no purpose, come to think of it.
Comparing us, why should I envy you?   375
To my sound reasons lend an ear."
After he's heard the Rooster's case,
the Goat begins to see both sides:
"Enough! One word is plenty to the wise—
I'll gladly sign a compact and make peace!"   380

The Rooster's wrath still smolders in his breast—
he lets the Master know as he speaks out:
"I, Rooster, serve you faithfully and well—
I'm always last to bed and first to rise.
You once took care of me, a chick—   385
grown up, I shift now for myself.
If I scratch hard I'll fill my craw;
if I don't peck but loaf, I'll starve.
I should feel sorry for myself, I think:
I slave, yet I get nothing in return.   390
The Pig just stuffs, then settles down to snore;
he plays the fool and shirks all work for you.
In countenance he looks so odd:
outlandish, yes, so foreign to this earth!
Though he's no pet, he's pampered like a pet;   395
his fodder costs as much as lawsuits cost.
When fattened up, he merely romps and sports;
hungry, he sprawls around and gnaws the sty.

Religiously, he eats three times a day—
I've yet to see him miss a single meal!   400
Is he some gem to love and treasure, or
some stone-blind cripple, ripe for alms?"

"You, Cockalorum, wag your beak no more
or someday I, Pig, shall bite out your throat!
The Master treats us as it pleases him—   405
don't you sneak up to him and tell on me.
If life manhandles you, it serves you right—
please leave me free to take my own sweet ease.
Which one of all six household beasts
outshines me, Pig, in gorgeous fat?   410
When kings officiate at the Southern Shrine,[31]
I'm needed for the triple sacrifice.[32]
Leave off your way of gabbling tommyrot—
stop sneering at the way pigs eat or sleep.
Look at betrothal vows or marriage rites—   415
could they occur without a feast of pork?
You go and beg the world upon your knees:
without me, no one would approach your door!
To settle feuds I play a foremost role—
all hatreds melt in sight of my plump snout.   420
A couple—the benighted man and wife—
may come to blows and bash each other's heads.
The neighbors helter-skelter rush in there,
but nobody can disembroil the two.
Now bring me in, make me the centerpiece: 425
all tangled webs will come unsnarled at once!
But is that not the truth?
Consider it and see.
At weddings, funerals, all formal rites,
I, Pig, boast pride of place and lead the way.   430
You little bantam, you talk big,
compelling me to straighten out some facts.

But far be it from me to brag—
I only strive to do what's right.
Pigs, too, repay their debts of gratitude;   435
pigs, too, cast out all evils and all woes.
Do we complain when they tear up our flesh?
Do we lament when they grind down our bones?
We shine in fealty to our lord—
and we account at nothing our own lives.   440
You, Rooster, crowed such bunk
that you provoked this wrangle, this dispute."

The Master thereupon decides the case
with utmost sense and sentiment:
"The Rooster will accept a righteous death.   445
The Pig will give his life for humankind.
No more comparison twixt Me and Thee—
together live in peace and multiply!"

The tale, at leisure, is penned down
to show the world in its true light.   450
But still all this is said in jest—
please read it if you wish, for fun and laughs.

Note: Lục súc tranh công ("The quarrel of the six beasts") was possibly
written by some scholar-official living in the Huê area of central Vietnam
during the first half of the nineteenth century. This narrative poem is cast in
the unusual form and style of a comic playlet rather than in six-eight *(lục-bát)*
verse. In the guise of six domestic animals (the water buffalo, the dog, the
horse, the goat, the rooster, and the pig), representatives of various social
classes are allowed to speak for themselves and against one another, with the
Master—the feudal lord or king—acting as an impartial moderator. The six-
way debate ends on an inconclusive note, with an appeal from the Master for
mutual tolerance and harmony. In giving the longest and most eloquent speech
to the water buffalo, however, the author appears to show special sympathy
for the poor peasant farmer, who, now as in the past, has given the most and
received the least in return. Though this fable is a valid document of conflict
and unrest in traditional Vietnam, it can also be understood and enjoyed as a
satirical broadside aimed at certain dominant groups in society and as a witty

interweaving of folklore with classical erudition. The vivid portrayal of each beast both by itself and by another is particularly faithful to animal characteristics. While the account mirrors some features of rural life in Vietnam, it reflects with humor or sarcasm on human behavior that can be observed among peasants, officials, law enforcement officers, professional soldiers, intellectuals, bureaucrats, and priests.

1. The dragon *(long)*, controlling water and making rain, represents the most beneficent force in nature and is worshiped as the highest of all four supernatural creatures or "sacred animals" *(tứ linh)*, the other three being the unicorn, the tortoise, and the phoenix.

2. The unicorn *(lân)* is a gentle creature that appears only under the reigns of wise rulers, as an augur of prosperity and peace.

3. The tortoise *(qui)* is associated with divination. In ancient China, questions were incised on a tortoise shell, and a hole was bored partway through the shell, which was then subjected to heat; cracks would form that could be interpreted by an oracle as answers to the questions asked.

4. The phoenix *(phượng)*, the highest of all birds, stands for the acme of moral virtue, and its decline portends an era of political and social upheaval.

5. In *A Dictionary of Chinese Buddhist Terms*, compiled by William Edward Soothill and Lewis Hodous, the concept of "three thousandfold worlds" *(san ch'ien shih chieh* or, in Sino-Vietnamese, *tam thiên thế giới)* is defined as follows: "Mt. Sumeru and its seven surrounding continents, eight seas and ring of iron mountains form one small world; 1,000 of these form a small chiliocosm *(hsiao ch'ien shih chieh)*; 1,000 of these small chiliocosms form a medium chiliocosm *(chung ch'ien shih chieh)*; 1,000 of these form a great chiliocosm *(ta ch'ien shih chieh)*, which thus consists of 1,000,000,000 small worlds. The *san ch'ien* indicated the above three kinds of thousands."

6. According to Buddhist lore, there was in India a species of holy oxen (or buffalo) whose blood was drunk for longevity: they were called Buddha-oxen.

7. According to a story in the *Mencius*, a Confucian classic, King Ch'i Hsüan once saw an ox (or buffalo) being led off to be slaughtered for the ritual anointment with blood of a newly cast bell. Taking pity on the beast, he ordered that it be spared and replaced for the sacrifice with a sheep (or goat).

8. In ancient China, T'ien-tzu Fang was admired for his kindness to animals.

9. The name *ba ông táo* (the "three kitchen gods"), given by the Vietnamese to the three stones or blocks of baked clay that support a cooking pot on the hearth, comes from a folktale about the proverbial triangle. (The story also makes clear that those three kitchen gods are really a triad consisting of one strong female and two subordinate males.) According to a well-known version, an incense merchant often traveled and left his wife at home. On one trip, he failed to reappear after many years; assuming him dead, she married

another man. One day, while the latter was out on a hunt, the former husband turned up. When the new master of the house was about to come back, the woman told the unexpected visitor to hide in a heap of straw, where he fell asleep. The hunter now returned with a deer, which he proceeded to roast, setting fire to the heap of straw. Thus, unintentionally, he killed the former husband. Because she blamed herself for the tragedy, the woman leaped into the fire and died. The second husband, who could not live without her, followed her example. The King of Hell, moved by the mutual fidelity of the three, allowed them to stay together by changing them into the three stones on the hearth, which people have come to worship as the so-called three kitchen gods.

10. The alleged weakness of a dog's limbs is explained by a Vietnamese folktale about the creation of the canine species. Heaven created the dog in a moment of absentmindedness and equipped it with only three legs—three not very strong ones, at that. As it complained of its infirmity, the compassionate Buddha gave it a fourth leg magically made with a hair plucked from his armpit. Whenever a dog passes water, it gingerly lifts the leg that the Buddha bestowed on it, which it takes care not to soil.

11. See note 14 to Poem 37 "Catfish and Toad," for a discussion of the provervbial phrases "to blow on hair and look for scars" and "to part the leaves and grope for worms."

12. East Asian mythology has an equivalent of the Greek and Roman Cerberus.

13. A Vietnamese proverb says: "When you've lost your way, follow your dog; when you've strayed from your path, follow your buffalo." *(Lạc đàng theo đuôi chó, lạc ngõ theo đuôi trâu.)* Those two beasts, able to find their way home, symbolize a servant's steadfast devotion to his master. By contrast, horses do not know who raises them and can't find their way back home: they stand for military men, unreliable and potentially treacherous. Although another Vietnamese proverb asserts that "a horse gets used to the same old path" *(ngựa quen đường cũ)*, this has to do with inveterate habit, not with staunch loyalty.

14. The proverbial phrase "neither quite foolish not quite wise" *(dại chẳng ra dại, khôn chẳng ra khôn)* ironically characterizes unremarkable people of very average intelligence. As applied to horses in this fable, it reflects the low esteem in which the mental endowments of career soldiers were held in traditional Vietnam. This phrase also suggests that rather ordinary individuals may entertain an exaggerated opinion of their own worth and importance and behave accordingly, thus making nuisances of themselves. That connotation is spelled out in the following proverb: "If smart, be really smart, and people will respect you; if dumb, be really dumb, and people will feel sorry for you; but if you're just in between, you'll only make people hate

you." *(Khôn cho người ta rái, dại cho người ta thương, dở dở ương ương chỉ tổ người ta ghét.)*

15. In Vietnamese, hermit crabs are called "snails with borrowed souls" *(ốc mượn hồn)*: they are contemptuously dismissed as inconsequential busybodies.

16. The dragon, as the holiest of all beasts, and the phoenix, as the highest of all birds, are both symbols of kingship, ideally the source of all virtues and all powers for good on earth.

17. After the downfall of the Ch'in dynasty, two strong men fought for control of China: Hsiang Yü and Liu Pang. Eventually Liu triumphed to found the Han dynasty in 206 BCE and became known as Emperor Han Kao-tsu.

18. In an exciting and edifying episode of *The Romance of the Three Kingdoms*, the brave Kuan Yü became a prisoner of the wily Ts'ao Ts'ao after the fall of a city. Though treated with respect by this captor, who wished to woo him away from his lord and friend Liu Pei, Kuan Yü wanted to escape. Riding a horse named Red Hare over enemy territory and through six well-guarded border gates, and wielding a sword named Green Dragon, he succeeded in rejoining Liu. Kuan Yü, the epitome of loyalty unto death, became deified as the Chinese god of war. This incident is here cited by the horse as a pointed rejoinder to anyone who doubts the allegiance of military men. It is to be noted that the color red—both for Kuan Yü's horse and for his face as represented in folk art—indicates constancy in one's devotion to a person or cause.

19. In a passage of *The Analects*, Tzu-kung, a disciple of Confucius, wanted to do away with the presentation of a sacrificial sheep (or goat) at the ceremonial announcement of each new moon. The Master disapproved of the idea, saying: "You begrudge a sheep, Tzu-kung, but I begrudge a ritual."

20. A Sung scholar once jokingly gave the title "Registrar in Chief with a Long Beard" to the goat, perhaps poking gentle fun at the bureaucratic passion for titles and ranks.

21. The phrase "to eat, then wipe one's beak" *(ăn rồi quẹt mỏ)* is a description of rank ingratitude, here compounded by the phrase "to turn one's back" *(sấp lưng)*.

22. Chickens are noted for their regular sleeping habits. The phrase "to sleep like a chicken" *(ngủ như gà)* means "to go to bed early and on time."

23. The rooster can claim five virtues or qualities: kindness *(nhân)*, because it calls other chickens whenever it finds some grain; bravery *(dũng)*, because it loves to fight; loyalty *(tín)*, because it never fails to crow on time; military skill *(vũ)*, because it is armed with two sharp spurs; and literary talent *(văn)*, because a cock's comb looks like a scholar-official's cap. Thus this bird represents the model mandarin who faithfully and efficiently serves his king and his people in war and peace.

24. In ancient China, Prince Meng Ch'ang, chief minister of Ch'i, was captured and held hostage by the king of Ch'in. He tried to flee but had to cross a border long before dawn. One of his retainers imitated the cry of a rooster so well that all roosters in the area started a crowing chorus. The guards opened the border gate, and the prince could escape.

25. Under the Tsin dynasty, Liu Kun and Tsu T'i always slept with their weapons under their heads and woke up at cockcrow, ready to pursue the enemy.

26. The phrase "to do good at cockcrow" is attributed to Mencius. See note 29.

27. K'ang Tzu-ya examined a rooster's leg to predict the fall of Shang and the rise of Chou.

28. Mencius allegedly said that virtuous wives "awake their men at cockcrow."

29. Shun, to whom Yao gave the throne, was one of the two legendary sage-kings of China. This is another allusion to a saying by Mencius: "Shun's disciples rise at cockcrow to do good."

30. In traditional opera, the goatee is a feature that conventionally marks the man who wears it as a sycophant or potential traitor.

31. Every three yeas, Vietnamese kings offered sacrifices to Heaven at an open-air altar south of the capital; the ceremony was called Sacrifice at the Southern Shrine *(Nam-giao)*.

32. At state sacrifices to Heaven, three beasts were slaughtered: an ox (or buffalo), a sheep (or goat), and a pig. Compare this with the Roman *Suovetaurilia*, the sacrifice of a boar, a ram, and a bull.

9. War and Peace

303. War

Đông Hồ

Cool earth, calm heaven—smoothly waters flow.
Soft moon, sweet rainfall—gently winds caress.
Life looks on you with love, a velvet smile.
All nature slumbers in a golden dream.

Hot earth, grim heaven—sullen waters stand.
Sad moon, sour rainfall—tempests whine and wail.
Life looks askance at you and tartly sneers.
All nature's heading for the battlefield.

Skewed earth, tipped heaven—wildly waters churn.
Mad moon, fierce rainstorm—tempests howl and shriek.
Life glares at you with hatred, bares its fangs.
All nature struggles, squandering blood and flesh.

Afraid to die, they fight so they may live—
they struggle for some perfect way of life.
As they love life, they slaughter, scorning death—
they vie for that grand prize: to die like men.

Oh, when will war and conflict ever end?
A futile question that you need not ask.
And why complain at all? A world of strife
creation has ordained since time began.

304. The string of pearls

Đông Hồ

You picked up fallen stars on some clear night,
fished iridescent gleams out of the depths,
caught drops of morning dew from every leaf—
you gave me this to keep: a string of pearls.

Sheer light was trembling in your joyous hands
as on ten fingertips you offered love.
And tender feelings blossomed in your breast
as you put it on me, around my neck.

I hid the pearls inside my heart of hearts—
I wore it near my bosom, white and pure.
And on that day, yes, somehow on that day,
I thought they'd stay with me all through my life.

How could I then suspect that war would come
and dash the string of pearls to bits and shreds?
O pearls, you're like the poet's fallen flowers:
"They hit the ground and uttered not one cry."

The string of pearls you gave me once is lost.
There's left a string of sorrows and regrets.
And, hoarded in my heart, here are some pearls:
pearls of true love are dropping from my eyes.

Lost stars will not come back—the heavens grieve.
Those glints of light have drowned—the ocean mourns.
Dew melts and grasses wilt—the spirit yearns.
The pearls are gone; you're far away—tears brim.

(1946)

305. Who?

Tương Phổ

Who is that soldier, hero of my heart?
May he get rid of war and save our land,
discard Sun Wu's great treatise with a smile[1]
and let no bloodshed stain our hills and streams.

Who is that champion with a noble soul?
May his goodwill and skill convert our foes
and roll all streams and mountains into one,
with no life squandered on the battleground.

Who is that saint who'll reconcile the world?
May he stop men from killing fellowmen,
restore tranquillity and peace to earth
and make our ancient homeland glow afresh.

The glorious man—will he appear or not?
All through our far-flung land, on dusty paths,
I've roamed in search of him these months and years.
Oh, may the time bring forth their hero—who?

1. Sun Wu, who lived in the sixth century BCE, wrote *The Art of War*.

306. The Red Cross

Mộng Tuyết

To a young sister with beautiful hands

There are some hands so beautiful, so soft,
hands boasting not one line of haughty pride,
embellished with no varnish red or pink,
yet all aglow and full of tender grace.

Brushing aside all personal concerns,
those hands have vowed to get involved, to care.

They will bring balm assuaging aches and pains,
will bind and bandage, healing hurts and wounds.

They're treasures lavished on the battleground.
They're treasures spent to praise a fighter's pluck.
They're treasures symbolized by this one sign:
a cross bright red beneath the golden sun.

Compassion here enfolds the field of war.
Here they sustain and nurse a hero's will.
Here soldiers, stricken down, for comfort lie
in arms that bear a sign: the bright red cross.

307. Elephants

Tô Hữu

O elephants, elephants all!
Elephants we cherish so!
Elephants, lie down and rest.
Elephants, relax and play.

O elephants, elephants all!
Your heads are made of steel.
You crook your legs and strut.
You raise your trunks and laugh.

O elephants, elephants all!
Both mothers and your babes,
all elephants big and small,
go now—the hour is late.

O elephants, elephants all,
go off to war, won't you?
Elephants, you'll roar and scream.
Elephants, you'll rip and tear.

We hug you, cuddle you.
Get up—we'll carry you.

We all have iron backs;
we all have legs of stone.

Through jungles we all march,
rustling bamboos and reeds.
O elephants, hear us sing
and make the mountains ring.

Let's climb and cross the pass;
let's up and scale the slope.
O elephants, it's quite steep—
what's steep we'll overcome.

The rocky, rugged path
is what we soldiers tread.
Climbing each slope, each pass,
we shout and cheer you on.

O elephants, elephants all!
The path lies long ahead.
It's strewn with thorns—so what?
We're of good cheer and laugh.

Try harder just a bit,
and look down on our foe.
Let's hurry and get there—
O elephants, we have arrived!

Bravo, good elephants all!
Bravo, artillerymen!
Dear elephants, we'll strip you,
give you a wipe, a wash.

All elephants and all men,
we're of one mind, one heart.

O elephants, fight your best—
this battle we shall win.

(1948)

Note: "Elephants" are heavy artillery pieces in Vietnamese Communist slang.

308. A drinking song
Trần Dạ Từ

We have two arms—
what good, though, are two arms?
What can they hug today?

We have two legs—
what good, though, are two legs?
Our homeland is no longer home.

We have two ears—
what good, though, are two ears?
Bullets and bombs are shrieking now.

We have two eyes—
what good, though, are two eyes?
Night follows night, drags on and on.

We have two nostrils—
what good, though, are two nostrils?
Flowers and leaves have withered up.

We have a throat—
what good, though, is a throat?
Our breath has lost all warmth.

We have a mouth—
what good, though, is a mouth?
We can no longer give a cry.

The liquor's going flat—
please raise your cup, my friends.

309. The new lullaby

Trần Dạ Từ

Sleep well, my child—a shadow, not mama,
will tuck you snug in bed and help you sleep.
A tombstone is your pillow—let the sky
spread over you a blanket, keep you warm.
To shield you as a curtain, there's the rain.
A tree will be your fan, its leaves your roof.
The stars will twinkle as your mother's eyes.
The battlefield will be your romping ground.
Sleep well and smile, with blood upon your lips.
Bullets and bombs will sing your lullaby.

310. Gifts as tokens of love

Trần Dạ Từ

To you I'll give a coil of wire, barbed wire,
the climbing vine of all this modern age—
it's coiling tight around our soul today.
Take it as my love token—don't ask why.

To you I'll give a car of plastic bombs
that will explode amidst some crowded street—
they will explode and shatter flesh to shreds.
This is the way we live—you understand?

To you I'll give the war that's killing now,
killing our homeland, many mothers' land,
where people dine on bullets and on bombs,
where cloth runs short for children's mourning bands.

To you I'll give the gift of twenty years
or seven thousand nights of cannon fire.
For seven thousand nights it's sung to you—
have you dozed off or are you still awake?

I want to give you many other things.

Enough—take just one more: a tear gas bomb.

With neither grief nor joy, my own tear glands

are gushing as I just sit here and wait.

311. The hand

Phạm Hổ

The day he was to leave,

he clasped his son with both his hands:

one held the boy, the other stroked his cheeks.

The child was still so young,

a fragile sprout of life

amid a village wreathed in smokes from bombs.

When he bent down and kissed the child,

his cheeks smelled of sweet milk

and of gun powder, too.

"My son, your dad must go to war.

At home stay healthy and grow up."

The boy blinked both his eyes and smiled,

his dimpled cheeks like two young moons.

Now peace.

He's now back in his village home.

To hold his child he only has one hand—

the hand that stroked the cheeks

is here no more.

His body, briefly, tilts aside:

for the first time, he misses it, the hand.

Suddenly his cheek feels cool, magically cool:

the child's small hand has just stroked it.

He looks at it, the pretty hand,

so round and white and pure.

It smells of flowers and of fruits—
life's fragrance has dispelled the stench of death.

The child's small hand,
close up against his cheek,
laid skin to skin, becomes a part of him,
transfusion of the sap of youth.
He feels he's not lost it, his hand.

312. The sea
Phạm Hổ

When I gave my first cry,
I had my mom, my dad—
I also had the sea.
Who says the sea lies far beyond our ken,
the sea that sprawls to heaven's rim?   5
She snuggles up inside my heart
with skies and clouds, with winds and waves.

Those afternoons when sands feel hot,
the sea will softly sing a lullaby—
the fishing village with its nets,   10
the grove of firs,
the bunch of islands far away,
all slumber, eyes half-shut.

At times the sea will scowl in wrath—
chasing the wind and rain, she howls, she screams,   15
and turmoil shakes the vault above,
while down below, the waves all roar.
The rain is beaten back, the wind has fled—
the sea will raise a mother's gentle voice,
calling those anglers' boats   20
that hide along some beach, behind some rock,
telling each fleet of sails:

"Come out, far out!
Head toward the welcoming sun."

I lived beside the sea,   25
just as I lived beside my mom, my dad.
I loved the sea
just as I loved my grandmother, my grandfather.
"For generations," he told me,
"the sea has fed us, kept us alive."   30
The shrimp at midnight gleamed
as if the moon and stars
had dropped out of the sky.
The fish would shimmer in the boat,
glistening with reflections from the sun.   35
To market went the fish, the shrimp, and men
to trade for rice and feed the fisherfolk.

A fighting man, eight years ago,
I'd left the sea for hills and woods.
When late at night, the brooks would sing,   40
I missed the sea, I missed my mom, my dad—
would any drop from all these brooks
be flowing out to sea?
Before my eyes the sea loomed stark and clear,
with all her boats,   45
with all her fishing nets spread out to dry.

Our village suffered hell,
fighting the enemy over each small wave
to get a perch, a shrimp, a jellyfish . . .
Thinking of home, I felt my heart on fire.   50
Today I'm back—
I let my eyes embrace the sea.
She is still here, but not my dad, my mom.
The day I left she told me with a kiss:

"We shall be here as long as our blue sea.   55
When you watch her, you watch your mom, your dad."

The sea, our mother, leads those fishing boats
and steers them one by one to shore.
Our village, smeared with ash and soot,
is building huts, new houses of bamboo.   60
Black pelicans that warned of coming foes
have left long since.
The morning waves are like young tots
learning to swim—
gingerly, they spread themselves out on the beach.   65
Father and mother, I've come home,
older but in good health.

I've now come home to stay
by our blue sea, near both of you.
Wearing a crown of clouds,   70
the sun in glorious red is rising over there,
beyond the sea.
I watch the motherland, feel deeply stirred—
both skies and waters glitter in the dawn.
O sea, how rich and beautiful you are!   75
Your blue lights up a native heart come home.

313. A letter to my future child
Trần Đức Uyển

When, dragging hideous crutches, war
is harrowing your land
and tearing up your country like a rag,
when paddy fields lack days to sprout young shoots
and there's no time for grass to grow,
I'm writing you this letter now
while I've no family yet.

Who will she be, your mother? I don't know.
But I believe you'll come into our world.
You'll enter it not while the curfew's on,
not stillborn and not writhing in an ambulance
like the second child of Aunt and Uncle Vinh,
or like many other children in these times.
Your father hopes you'll come into our world
with robust body and stout limbs.
You'll enter like a rising sun,
the Eastern sun, the summer sun.
You shall grow up amid the sounds of joy.
Along with vast green fields of rice,
along with grass and trees you'll live.
Hearing no plane by day, no gun at night,
you'll sleep untroubled sleep—
the sleep of radiant innocence.
Each morning, leaving home, I shall kiss you
beside the cradle fragrant with your mother's milk.
On your red lips shall bloom a smile,
a wholesome smile.
The greatest dreams on earth
I trust to you, my child.
You are the seed of humankind,
the hope, the future of the world.

314. Words of comfort
Đỗ Tấn

I want to mourn the stream,
I want to mourn the road,
I want to call the sun—
they all break down and weep.

Now weep no more, O river of farewells.

Now weep no more, O road of sad goodbyes.

Now weep no more, O hungry, tattered sun.

I'm nothing—don't blame me.

I'm just an orphan left distraught.

I'm just a lover, sorrow-crazed.

I'm just a widow numb with pain.

I'm nothing in the world today.

315. Peace! Peace!

Đỗ Tân

A vagrant whistles in the street.

An aging strumpet slinks through mists.

A mongrel roams the sidewalk, all alone.

A rat pokes its foul muzzle in the ditch.

I have lived all those lives.

I have grown up in shame.

I'm slowly wilting in the night.

I'm looking now at rain.

The rain can only soak the tramp.

The rain can only soak the cur.

The rain can only soak the prowling whore.

The rain can only soak the nervous rat.

My breath has weakened day by day.

My faith has cracked and chipped.

My heart has withered bit by bit.

My tears may soon dry up.

Yet in tomorrow I still put some hope.

Yet on the future I still pin some faith.

Heaven forbid that I should cry tonight—

Heaven grant me a good, long sleep.

316. Yearning

Nguyễn Đình Thi

Whom do the stars yearn for? They blink and gleam,
lighting the path of soldiers through the clouds.
Cold night: whom does the fire yearn for? It glows
and warms the soldiers' hearts beneath dense trees.

I love you, darling, as I love our land,
suffering and wretched, yet so beautiful.
I miss you so, at each step of my way,
at mealtime every day, each night in bed.

The stars that light the dark will never dim:
loving each other, we'll struggle till we win.
The campfire in the forest flares bright red:
loving each other, proudly we'll live life.

(1951)

317. My mother's son

Trần Huiền Ân

My mother, from the first, I was your son.
My baby hands reached out for your kind breasts—
delicious milk, the soft-sung lullaby
once coaxed me into sound, untroubled sleep.

At six, one morning bright as in a tale,
I clung on to your dress and walked to school.
That autumn sky shone with rare hues of jade—
my months and years at school were love affairs.

On silent evenings, by a fitful light,
I'd study, do my homework, while you sewed.
The heavens seemed to glimmer in your eyes—
you'd gaze on me and gently stroke my head.

With tender care, with fragrant rice, clean clothes,
you taught me I should love my fellowmen.
I'd be a man—you died in that belief,
a happy smile on your two frozen lips.

I always thought I was my mother's child
and I forever would remain your son.
Alas, he's small and weak, as is our breed—
and foreign gold's poured sorrow on our soil.

The world wants me to hate and only hate:
blood flows and bones heap up—I look away.
Now what you taught me dawns on me once more—
but that's a pack of nonsense, says the world.

Our bloodline I have tried to carry on,
yet from the mirror stares an alien face.
Am I your son, or someone else's child?
You're gone—now whose forgiveness can I ask?

(1965)

318. The old vow
Trần Huiền Ân

We were then waging war against the French.
I put on coarse, gray clothes and went to school,
night school, by torchlight flickering in the wind
and quickly doused whenever planes were heard.

We sat there, huddling in the village hall.
The teacher's shadow danced on wattle walls.
Heads of cropped hair, long tresses held by clasps—
bright-eyed, we looked up, drinking in each word.

Pen nibs were sharpened tips of old bamboo.
Rough-grained rice paper still showed specks of straw.

The teacher marked with some red-yellow dye—
I practiced writing, coddling each slant stroke.

Outside of school, I cut the hay, chased birds,
gleaned paddies, tended oxen, watched the fields.
My parents, worn with age, still worked so hard:
their tears ran down—back to their hearts flowed blood.

That was how I spent the early years at school—
out of dry, barren soil there bloomed fresh flowers.
So used to hardships, I felt them no more,
embraced dreams with both arms, smile on my lips.

We hated them, our cruel enemies—
they burned our books, killed teachers, tore down schools.
Their bayonets, which stank of blameless blood,
would not spare children at their ABCs.

We vowed that when grown up, we all would build
an independent country, one at peace,
so schools would proudly rise, and every dawn,
schoolchildren's songs would gaily hail the sun.

And then, along with passing days and months,
my schoolmates slowly drifted from my mind.
Uncertain, I embraced a soldier's life—
it's jolted me, recalling our old vow.

Day after day, when marching with the troops,
bathing in sweat and sunshine on drill grounds,
I've watched young children—pictures from my youth—
who hawk sweet rice or cakes along the roads.

Their hawking cry will rise and then choke up,
followed by no ingratiating drawl.
Bodies with scrawny arms that look like bones
walk barefoot, hobbling on and panting hard.

Sell off your stuff, run quickly back to school,
herd buffalo, hold babies, watch your house.
I've searched my soul and judged myself at fault—
we've erred, and as your elders, we've failed you.

So, waifs, you still go hungry, wear foul rags,
and early toil for half a bowl of rice.
At five, you can't still wipe your noses clean,
yet you are left to sink or swim in life.

I call myself a soldier—do I wish
the young to carry forward our great dream,
or should I help those gloating, while blood sheds
to fatten even more on fratricide?

(1966)

319. The man who sleeps out in the fields
Bùi Khải Nguyên

The field, bright green, laps sunshine up.
The weeds and grasses choke with scents.
In clear-blue heavens, clouds stand still.
Grief settles in the soul, deep down.

Cool winds come fanning from the sea—
leaves fair as jade wave to and fro.
That spirit which the tropics breathe
is clinging to the coconuts.

His head lies pillowed on soft grass—
he's sleeping, sleeping quite at peace.
His soul flies off and rides the wind
to soar and visit with the gods.

The helmet lies beside his head,
seemingly quite lost in slumber, too.

A kerchief covers up his eyes—
O sun, don't you disturb his rest!

An inconsiderate fly, a boor,
comes flying out of nowhere now.
It pokes its head inside his ear,
its wings aflutter, all abuzz.

Wait, wait, don't leave—it's early yet.
His lips, ajar, bare ivory teeth.
The butterfly feels thrilled at heart—
it thinks it's perching on a flower.

Wait, wait, don't hurry people so!
It's still too young, the far-off dream.
The great adventure's in full swing—
fold up your wings and stay, O time!

The kerchief stirs a little bit
as gently blows a breath of air.
Upon the barrel of his gun
the dragonfly lies sound asleep.

Over his chest, bare as a beach,
fire ants enjoy their leisured stroll.
They swarm together, then disperse
along the streaks of fetid blood.

The bullet went clear through his lung,
leaving a hollow gap, quite round.
You should believe it, O my heart!
It was for Freedom that he died.

320. The buffalo boy on a field of corpses
Phổ Đức

The sun is going down behind the hills—
he looks around, sees not a single roof.

He asks himself: "What land begot me once?
I'm standing here, but where did I come from?"
He tries, tries hard, but can't recall   5
a relative, a friend or foe.
He still has eyes and yet can't see.
He still has ears and yet is deaf.
He howls so all the world can hear:
"I am not mute! I can still speak.   10
I'm one who has survived—
I'm looking for my land, my home."

Now he stops shouting, out of breath—
he knows he's talking to himself.
Around him no one's left—the field   15
beneath his feet's all lined with corpses.
He makes his way through puddles of foul blood,
while looking for his herd of buffalo.
He only finds more bodies, heaps and heaps.
Reeking miasmas blur together   20
winners and losers in the body count.
Among them he hopes he won't find his beasts.
His stupid brain asks all those lying there:
"You shot and slaughtered one another—why?
My buffalo locked horns at times   25
but cared for one another, led by me.
As humans, you were civilized, advanced—
why kill each other, strewing fields with flesh
and watering soil with blood?
Where's grass left for the buffalo to eat?   30
You're covering all my land—
where shall I plow and plant?
The buffalo, my herd, are gone—
where shall I look for them?
I tend live buffalo—   35

your corpses I don't tend.
Give back to me my meadows lush and green;
give back to me the bufflao
I've loved and lost.
The war has wolfed my parents down.   40
Bullets and bombs have robbed me of my friends.
I'm dumb, can only live with buffalo:
I've lost them all—
where shall I go from here?
I tend live buffalo—   45
dead people I don't tend."
The field remains quite hushed,
stinking of blood.
He still stands there,
without his herd of buffalo—   50
only dead bodies lie beneath his feet.
He screams till he is out of breath,
then he looks back.
The bodies still lie there,
with skin of every hue: 55
they're yellow, ruddy, white, and black.
They all still lie unstirring there.
They all have spilled and mixed their blood.
They all lie now in chill repose.
They all have trunks and limbs like his.   60

The afternoon is gone,
and dusk is drawing on.
Death vapors rise—
he still stands there and waits.
While looking for his herd, he never thought   65
he'd end up standing there
and guarding those dead bodies in night mist.
The corpses still lie stirless there
upon the windswept field.

Again he moans: 70
"Where shall I find my meadowland
whose edge looks like a vivid S?"
Upon that field of corpses lie
humans who wear skins like his.
Amid the yellow of their skins,   75
amid the color of the homeland's blood,
he gropes and walks—
the bodies block his path.
The night has fallen, deep and thick—
a voice comes like some echo out of space: 80
"Stop and stand still.
Watch over all those fields—
your friends lie there, you know?"
Again he howls:
"I tend live buffalo—   85
dead people I don't tend.
I too came from the yellow race,
but I'm no longer Vietnamese."

321. My home
Yên Thao

I'm standing on this side—
across the stream, that's enemy land.
My hamlet's over there,
dark gray, the hue of clotted blood.
Those gaunt bamboos and betel palms   5
whose drooping hair is drenched with dew and rain.
Whitewashed with lime,
the bare, stark walls
of that old village hall.
O folks, what's there to cheer about?   10
I am a soldier waging war,

who left his home when blood began to flow.
I swung my bone-thin arms and went,
reliving that heroic age
when we crushed Mongol troops—   15
I clasped my gun and dreamed about V-Day.
My feet are travel-worn
after they've walked a thousand miles.
A faded uniform
still gives off sparks of pride.   20
Now I am back—a chilly night.
The river welcomes me,
atwinkle with some scattered stars.
I have a wife, so young, as beautiful as song.
She's in her early twenties—I wed her,   25
and then I joined the flag.
Her cheeks were white and soft,
so fragrant with ripe rice.
Who could then wrench himself away?
I left my love and felt no joy.   30
At parting, hushed and still, she simply stared.
As I marched off, tears dripped inside my soul.

I have a mother, too,
whose hair's turned cotton-white.
Almost a century old,   35
her scrawny back
has warped beneath the load of life.
She's struggled since she lost her man—
the silkworm's ever spun its thread
while shrinks and wilts its heart.   40
Alas, I went away—
with eyes all dimmed by tears,
she's gazed far off and waited for her son.
I've wakened up on rainy nights—
hearing the roar of guns,   45

I've thought about the day I left.

Mother, I chose to leave—

the enemy gone,

I would come home

and you could smile again.   50

Now I am back—a chilly night.

The river welcomes me,

atwinkle with some scattered stars.

My trousers' legs are patched-up rags, dirt-brown.

But I still clutch my gun,   55

and dream of Nguyễn Huệ.[1]

My hamlet's over there,

forlorn beside the enemy camp—

it seems as quiet as a grave.   60

Are they still there, my aged mother and my wife,

dear ones who, when I left, all wept?

I am a soldier waging war,

who, following his troops,

has come back here   65

to liberate the fatherland.

Our callow heads have gathered dust

from everywhere,

and our bare feet

have trampled enemy posts.   70

Hey, fellow soldiers there!

Hey, my artillery friends!

Has the fateful hour struck,

when we shall tear the enemy camp to shreds?

Just lob on target, please,   75

and do not hit my home.

West Hamlet's farther end—

there stands my home.

It has a trellis with some flowering vines.

It holds some people whom I love.   80

1. Nguyễn Huệ (1752–1792), peasant leader of the Tây Sơn rebellion who proclaimed himself King Quang Trung in 1788, won a decisive battle against the Chinese invaders by launching a surprise New Year's Day attack at Đống-đa, near Hanoi, in 1789.

322. The song of a soldier's wife (Chinh phụ ngâm)
Đặng Trần Côn and Phan Huy Ích

When all through earth and heaven dust storms rise,
how hard and rough, the road a woman walks!
O those who rule in yonder blue above,
who is the cause and maker of this woe?

In our Ch'ang-an drums beat and moonlight throbs.[1]   5
On Mount Kan-ch'üan fires burn and clouds glow red.[2]
The emperor, leaning on his precious sword,
at midnight calls for war and sets the day.

The realm has known three hundred years of peace—
now soldiers don their battle dress once more.   10
At daybreak, heralds speed them through the mists—
the law outweighs what they may feel inside.

Full armed with bows and arrows, they fare forth,
from wives and children wrenching their numb hearts.
As banners wave and drums resound far off,   15
grief spreads from chamber door to mountain pass.

Born to a race of heroes, you, my love,
discard your brush and ink for tools of war.
You vow to capture citadels for the throne—
your sword will spare no foe of Heaven's sway.   20

A man will win a horse skin for his shroud;[3]
his life he'll drop in battle like goose down.[4]

In war attire, you leave and cross the Wei,[5]
cracking your whip while roars the autumn wind.

Beneath the bridge the brook flows crystal-clear.   25
Along the nearby path thrives grass, still young.
I see you off and sorrow—oh, to be
your horse on land, your vessel on the stream!

The water flows, yet grief won't wash away.
The grass smells sweet, yet hearts won't feel assuaged.   30
We say goodbye, then we hold hands again—
we try to part, keep halting at each step.

My heart pursues you like the moon on high.
Through space leaps your heart, bound for Thousand Peaks.[6]
The wine once drained, you wave the Lung-ch'üan sword[7]   35
and thrust it toward the lair of those wild beasts.

You'll tread in Chieh-tzu's steps and seize Lou-lan.[8]
You'll reach Man-hsi, discussing old Fu-po.[9]
Your coat is red like sunglow from the clouds;
your horse is white as if all cloaked in snow.   40

A jumbled din of drums and horses' bells—
we huddle face to face, then have to part.
Here at this bridge we'll go our separate ways—
forlorn beside the road, I watch flags fly.

Carts form the van, approaching Willow Camp.   45
Horsemen bring up the rear at Poplar Field.
In haste the troops escort you on your way—
do willows and poplars know I ache inside?

Flutes pipe and send faint echoes from afar.
Flags file and stir vague shadows to and fro.   50
Your tracks pursue the trail of clouds on clouds—
I watch the mountain range and mourn our home.

Your way leads you to lands of rain and wind—
mine takes me back to our old room, our bed.

We turn and look, but all has come between—   55
green mountains and blue clouds roll on and on.

You in Han-yang still turn your head and gaze.[10]
Here at Hsiao-hsiang I still stare after you.[11]
Between, the Hsiao-hsiang mists shut off Han-yang.
Between, the Han-yang trees shut off Hsiao-hsiang.   60

We look to find each other but cannot—
we only see those green mulberry groves.
Mulberry groves all share one shade of green—
of your own grief and mine, which hurts the more?

Since you left for the realm of wind and sand,   65
where are you resting on this moonlit night?
Of old and now, such are all battlegrounds,
those endless wastes the elements assault.

Men's faces shrivel under raw wind blasts,
and horses' knees will buckle fording streams.   70
For pillows all hug saddles or clasp drums—
they lie asleep on white sand or green moss.

Today Han troops pitch camp inside Pai-teng,
tomorrow Huns will watch from their Blue Sea.[12]
A scene of streams and mountains, near and far—   75
they roll on and break off, they rise and fall.

From mountain peaks, dew falls, like rain at dusk,
and down in streams the fords still lie waist-deep.
Pity those who've long worn their coats of mail—
their homesick faces bear a world of gloom.   80

Inside brocaded curtains, does He know?
A soldier's portrait who could paint for Him?
I think of you who've wandered all these years,
from the Vast Desert to the Lonesome Pass.[13]

You've braved the wilds where snakes and tigers lurk;   85
you've shivered, dwelling with chill dew and wind.

I climb up high and watch the pall of clouds—
whose heart can stay unstirred by longing-pangs?

You left and traveled toward the far Southeast—
who knows where you are fighting at this hour?   90
All those who for so long have gone to war
have learned to treat their lives like leaves of grass.

With valiant spirit they'll pay off great debts—
how many, courting peril, will die old?
The moon shines, dangling over hushed Mount Ch'i.[14]   95
Winds blow on lonesome tombs along the Fei.[15]

Winds howl and howl at ghosts of those war's killed—
on soldiers' faces shines the stalking moon.
O men, alive or dead, has anyone
portrayed your faces or invoked your souls?   100

The brand of war has marked old streams and hills—
a traveler, passing by, feels sore of heart.
A man must spend his prime on battlegrounds:
his hair all streaked with frost, Pan Ch'ao came home.[16]

I think of you as you bear pains and hurts—   105
armed with a sword, a saddle, you rush past
the windswept shores, the moonlit woods, as arrows whiz
past horses' heads and spears attack the walls.

A hundred dangers strew the path of fame—
you toil and struggle, never taking rest.   110
To whom can you confide what moves your heart?
I'm here at home, you're there at heaven's edge.

Inside this door I live my fated life,
but were you born to roam at heaven's edge?
We hoped to join like fish and water once: 115
instead, we're split apart—a stream, a cloud.

I never thought I'd be a soldier's wife;
you never aped rich playboys touring far.[17]

war and peace   404

Why are those streams and hills dividing us
and causing us to sorrow day and night?   120

Endowed with grace and charm in youthful bloom,
we formed a couple bound by ties of love.
Who has the heart to break young lovers up
and build a mountain wall between the two?

No orioles yet on willows—you set out   125
and promised you'd come back when cuckoos sang.
Cuckoos have followed orioles grown old—
before the house some swallows chirp and peep.

Plum trees were wind-shy still when you went forth
and promised you'd come back as peaches bloomed.   130
Peach blossoms now have fled with their east wind—
beside the river, roses fall to shreds.

You told me once you'd meet me in Lung-hsi—[18]
from dawn I looked for you but saw no trace.
I choked back tears as leaves fell on my hair—   135
at noon the village woke to birds' shrill cries.

You pledged to meet me by the Han-yang bridge—
till nightfall I awaited you in vain.
I choked back tears as winds lashed at my gown—
the evening tide was surging on the shore.   140

I've sent you word but haven't seen you back—
the poplar's catkins, wilted, strew green moss.
Green moss in many patches spreads around—
I pace the courtyard, turmoil in my heart.

Your letters have come home, but you're not home—   145
the sun sends tilted beams through my thin blinds.
The sun keeps shining through day after day—
why have you failed nine pledges out of ten?

Let's reckon—ever since you went away
the lotus leaves like coins have thrice peeped forth.   150

Pity those who must man such distant posts,
with shelter far from home, near Mount Huang-hua.[19]

Who has no kin or family to love?
All long for, miss old parents or young wives.
Your mother's hair is covered now with frost—   155
your son who's still at suck needs tender care.

The mother waits heart-weary at the door.
The child in hunger cries for his chewed rice.
I feed your mother, serving as her son,
and like a father teach your child to read.   160

Alone, I feed the old and teach the young—
I bear all burdens, yearning for my man.
I long for you while stars will whirl away
as spring's passed by and winter's drawing near.

Let's count those years of parting—three or four.   165
My heart has grown a thousand more snarled threads.
If only I could nestle by your side,
revealing all the bitterness I've felt!

This hairpin from the Han, your wedding gift,
and that Ch'in looking glass we two looked in—   170
by whom could I transmit both there to you
and let you know how much I'm missing you?

The ring my finger wears I've so admired,
the emerald comb I toyed with as a child—
by whom could I dispatch both there to you   175
as tender keepsakes from the one you love?

For many springs news traveled back and forth—
this spring's devoid of any sign from you.
In vain I've hoped for letters, seeing geese—
in vain I've made a quilt at the first frost.   180

The wester thwarts the path of geese in flight.
Alas, out there you're drenched by snow and rain.

You live with rain as screen, with snow as tent—
I think of you and feel your cold out there.

My message on brocade I seal, unseal.[20]   185
I toss the coins and dread what they portend.
At dusk I stand beneath the eaves, forlorn—
the midnight moon lights pillowed hair, unkempt.

Have I a mind gone crazy, addled wits?
Bedazed, I drift and wander in a void.   190
With shame I set my hairpin, don my skirt—
my raveled hair's awry, my waistband's loose.

In staggering steps I pace the lonesome porch.
I often raise and drop a diaphanous shade.
Outside the shade no magpie brings glad news—   195
inside, perhaps, the lamp knows how I feel.

The lamp may know, but nothing can it do—
my heart must bear its anguish all alone.
Its sorrow finds no utterance in words—
pity the shadow by the lamp's bright flame.   200

Cocks crow the night's fifth watch as dewdrops fall.
Sophoras flutter, tossing shadows down.
An hour of waiting drags and seems a year—
my grief lies deep and sullen like the sea.

Incense I burn—my soul, enraptured, roams.   205
The mirror I look in—my tears stream forth.
I try to pluck the lute, but I so dread
to break its strings or disarray its frets.

If with the easter I could send this heart,
I'd pay pure gold and send it to Mount Yen.[21]   210
It grieves me that Mount Yen cannot be reached—
in thought I search for you through vast, vast skies.

The sky's too vast to search from end to end—
my yearning love for you will never cease.

war and peace **407**

As nature mourns, a human heart knows grief—   215
hoarfrost soaks trees, rain mutes grasshoppers' cries.

Frost hammers willows, wearing them away.
Rain saws plane trees, destroying withered boughs.
On high, birds chill their wings amid dense mists.
Insects on walls lament—bells toll far off.   220

A cricket's chirps, with moonbeams, strew the yard.
Outside the porch, winds blast at plantain leaves.
A sudden gust bursts through—the curtain stirs.
The moon casts shades of flowers on the blind.

In floods of moonlight smooth as silk bask flowers—   225
the moon enfolds and sets aglow each flower.
A play of moon and flower, of flower and moon—
watching the moon, the flower, I ache within.

How can I tell of all the pain I feel?
A woman's skills I have neglected since.   230
I've shunned the sewing needle, spurned the loom—
I've stopped embroidering orioles in pairs.

I loathe to paint my face, I hate to talk,
leaning against the window morn and eve.
Against the window, brooding, I just lean.   235
You're gone—whom would my rouge and powder please?

I groom myself no more—grief fills my heart.
I grieve for you, who're rambling far from home.
I'm like Ch'ang O who pines there in the moon,[22]
the Weaver Maid who sobs by Heaven's Stream.[23]   240

Who'd make a pillow, heaping grief on grief?
Who'd cook a dinner boiling gloom with gloom?
I would allay my pain with flowers and wine,
but sorrow sours the wine and wilts the flowers.

I clap jade castanets—they give no sound.   245
I clasp the zither—frets fall from my hand.

war and peace   408

I grieve for you whom duty sent away
to tread long trails with hunger in your bag.

The mocking cuckoo's song makes me shed tears.
The watchman's drumbeats tug at my heartstrings.   250
My lovely looks have changed, turned drawn and pale.
How bitter parting is! I know the taste.

I taste of bitterness and know my heart.
Who's given it to me, this bitter taste?
Because of you, tears flow in two long streams.   255
Because of you, I shiver all alone.

I'm not to join you there inside your tent—
my tears are not to wet your battle cap.
I can come near you only in a dream—
at night I prowl all riverbanks for you.   260

I look for you on the road to Yang Tower.[24]
I find you at the harbor of the Hsiang.[25]
When happy chance brings us together thus,
we share an hour of love, a spring night's dream.

I curse my lot unequal to my dream,   265
each time I meet you there in Lung or Han.
How I regret each dream on waking up!
All love amounts to nothing, in a dream.

My heart cannot be torn away from you—
it ever follows you, each day, each hour.   270
It follows you, yet nowhere are you seen,
when on a height I peer for your cart's wheels.

Southward I look, but duckweeds hide the stream.[26]
Grass jasper blue, mulberry leaves bright green.[27]
Some village huts that totter in the wind.   275
Below the twilit cliff, a flock of storks.

Northward I look—a knot of travelers' inns.
Clouds, flush with trees, block out the soaring hills.

Wild rice grows scattered at the ramparts' foot.
Rain sprinkles—in a chamber sighs a flute.   280

On eastern hills I see but leaves and leaves.
A pheasant flaps its wings, plum branches dance.
Thick mists like billows surge above the woods—
a wind-blown bird, astray, gives piteous cries.

Westward the river turns and twists its course.   285
Geese sail on high, waves steer an angler's boat.
Reed swamps lie snugly tucked among the pines—
across the stream, some man is going home.

I look around, exploring earth and sky—
I often go upstairs, come down again.   290
Cloud rises after cloud to halt my gaze—
where is Jade Pass, the field of men at war?[28]

How could I get that wand and shrink the earth,[29]
or find that magic scarf and bridge far shores?[30]
I'd turn to stone, but then I'd have no tears   295
to weep for you, awaiting you upstairs.[31]

When I gaze back at willows, how I wish
I'd counseled you to spurn a noble's rank.[32]
I wonder—while you're traveling your long road,
does your heart also feel what my heart feels?   300

If only it would feel that way, your heart!
Then I'd not let my mind pursue wild thoughts.
My heart turns toward the sun just like the flower—
as your heart roams, I dread the sun will set.

The sun has spurned his flower and let her wilt.   305
The flower's wilted, as the sun won't shine.
Wilted, she drops her petals by the wall—
I've often watched them drop on dew-cold nights.

The garden's orchids all have been plucked off—
now duckweeds near the bank are breathing scent.   310

war and peace   410

Clad in my robe, I stroll before the house,
my languid gaze on heaven's glorious vault.

The Silver River gleams and dims by fits.
The Strider will appear and disappear.[33]
The clouds now glow quite bright, now turn quite pale.   315
The Dipper's handle shifts from east to west.

My looks and charms keep fading year by year,
and still my man keeps wandering far away.
We were a body and its shadow once—
now we stand worlds apart like Shen and Shang.[34]   320

Your horse is galloping on cloud-wrapped trails—
My slippers shuffle on moss-covered paths.
Day after day the spring wind's brought no news—
how many happy seasons we have missed!

They come to mind, those flowers of Yao and Wei,[35]   325
wedding their gold and crimson on spring winds.
And lo, the Herdboy and his Weaver Maid
who cross the Stream beneath the autumn moon.

I mourn the wife inside an empty room
who lets her finest seasons go to waste.   330
The days and months like shuttles hurtle by,
and youth is springtide ebbing in a flash.

In spring I brood, in fall I seethe with rage—
I've known more grief of parting than shared joy.
Anger and grief entangle all their threads—   335
how can a reed, a willow stop spring's flight?

There was Wen-chün, a beauty in the past:
afraid that age would gray her head, she grieved.[36]
And there was P'an whose face shone like a flower:
as he feared frost would mar his hair, he wept.[37]   340

I mourn my looks, a flower in full bloom,
and mourn fleet time, which slides and slips away.

war and peace   411

I mourn a thankless fate, mourn blossom years—
a fresh young maiden turns a matron soon.

Upon this moonlit tower I see your face.   345
Inside that flower-decked room scents waft about.
On Heaven I must blame our life gone wrong—
I grieve and grieve for you, for my own self.

Haven't you seen those mandarin ducks afield?
They go in pairs as mates and won't soon split.   350
Haven't you watched those swallows on a roof?
United, they can't part till hoary age.

Two *ch'iung-ch'iung* beasts stay close, head touching head.[38]
Two *chien-chien* birds fly jointly, wing to wing.[39]
The willow and the lotus are mere plants,   355
yet each boasts wedded leaves and coupled flowers.

That's how in nature ties of love will bind—
why keep two humans severed, here and there?
May we in future lives become two birds
that join their wings, two trees that twine their boughs![40]   360

No doubt, a thousand lifetimes love shall last,
but life together here and now is best.
To silver may age never turn your hair!
And may I ever keep the looks of youth!

Oh, let me be your shadow, follow you!   365
Where you're to go you'll find me by your side.
I wish you will remain out in the sun
as you perform the duties of a man.

Serve well your country with a true-red heart.
Defend your people with an iron will.   370
The Chun-yü's blood and Jou-chih heads will sate
your thirst and hunger, as your drink and meat.

Time after time you rush at swords and spears,
but Heaven will protect a loyal man.

war and peace   412

You'll win all battles, and from our north pass   375
to our west hills all arms will be laid down.

Banners and flags will leave the border posts—
bound for the city, men will sing of triumph.
Mount Yen will bear your name in stone-writ odes.
Your trophies you will offer to the throne.   380

You'll wash your weapons in the Silver Stream.[41]
They will make music and intone your praise.
In merit you'll compare with Ch'in and Huo[42]—
your fame will grace Mist Tower, Unicorn Hall.[43]

A state grandee, you'll shine in sash and cap—   385
on monuments, public joy will be engraved.
Your son will share in bounty from above—
with you, your wife will bask in Heaven's grace.

I'm not a foolish woman like Su's wife,[44]
and you're as clever as those Lo-yang men.[45]   390
When you come home and bear that seal of gold,
will I stay at the loom and show disdain?

I'll take from you the soldier's coat of mail.
I'll shake from you the wanderer's dust and dew.
For you I'll fill a golden cup with wine;   395
for you I'll wear enchanting scent and powder.

You'll view my tear-stained kerchiefs one by one.
You'll read my song of grief line after line.
We'll substitute gay lines for doleful lines—
while sipping wine, we'll tell each other all.   400

We'll slowly fill and drain cup after cup;
we'll softly sing one stanza, then the next.
We'll hum linked verse and face to face we'll drink,
staying together till a ripe old age.

This parting grief—we'll make up for it all: 405
we'll have and hold each other, blessing peace.

war and peace 413

I sing and with my love send you this wish:

thus may you act and live, a gallant man!

Note: Đặng Trần Côn was born between 1710 and 1720 in the village of
Nhân-mục (popularly known as Làng Mộc), west of Thăng-long (present-day
Hanoi), the capital under the Later Lê dynasty. He died around 1745, in his
late thirties. In his youth, Đặng was already celebrated for his fanatical
devotion to his studies. Legend has it that when a strict curfew was being
enforced, he would dig himself an underground shelter where he could read
and write, undetected from the outside, until the small hours. He passed the
regional examinations *(hương-thí)* and as a *hương-cống,* qualified for the
examinations in the capital *(hội-thí).* But he failed that crucial test and as a
result, was never to rise high on the mandarin ladder. Successively, he served
as a provincial education officer *(huấn-đạo),* as the subprefect *(tri-huyện)* of
Thanh-oai, and as a censor *(ngự-sử).*

According to his contemporary Phạm Đình Hổ (in the *Tang thương ngẫu
lục* or "Random notes of flux and change"), Đặng Trần Côn was admired as a
free spirit, fond of wine. He excelled at writing poetry and rhythmic prose and
was particularly adept in the use of classical allusions. His writings became
models for students and scholars of his time. His most famous work, destined
to remain a beacon in the history of Vietnamese literature, was a poem written
in classical Chinese: the *Chinh phụ ngâm* or "The Song of a Soldier's Wife."
The work can be best described as an extraordinarily astute pastiche of bits
and pieces from Han and T'ang verse on a theme close to many hearts in Đặng
Trần Côn's lifetime as well as throughout Vietnam's turbulent history: war
and the sorrows caused by war. The poem must have created a sensation
among his fellow scholars and poets, for quite a few undertook to translate it
into Vietnamese verse and make it available to the general public.

Of the seven such versions that have survived, the best known and best
loved is used as the basis for this English rendition. For a long time, it was
attributed to the woman poet Đoàn Thị Điểm (1705–1748). Now, however,
more and more scholars have come to accept Hoàng Xuân Hãn's carefully
documented thesis that it was in fact the work of Phan Huy Ích. Phan Huy Ích
was born in 1749 or 1750 and died in 1822. He graduated with top honors at
the Nghệ-an examinations in 1771 and was found so brilliant that he at once
was offered an appointment in Sơn-nam. But he preferred to pursue his
academic career and won the doctorate *(tiến-sĩ)* in 1775. In the main he
enjoyed the high regard and trust of successive rulers, the Trịnh lords and
the Tây Sơn sovereigns, and even King Gia Long, the founder of the Nguyễn
dynasty. Even though Phan had served the latter's enemies, the king revered
him as an unusually gifted man of letters, more motivated by the spirit of
public service than by partisanship.

Đặng Trần Côn is not known to have composed anything in Vietnamese. Phan Huy Ích, on the contrary, wrote both in classical Chinese and in Vietnamese. After he completed his adaptation of Đặng Trần Côn's *Chinh phụ ngâm*, Phan celebrated the event with the following poem in Chinese: "The Nhân-mục master wrote *The song of a soldier's wife*. / The Grove of Letters sings his hymn to love. / Many have prized it as their meat and drink; / not few have toiled to tell it in our speech. / A poem's essence can't be rendered whole— / in melody the lyric comes to life. / At leisure I created this new song: / I hope I saw clear through the poet's heart."

Phan Huy Ích's version was composed in the "double-seven six-eight" *(song-thất lục-bát)* meter like the other masterpiece of Vietnamese lyricism, the *Cung oán ngâm khúc* ("A song of sorrow inside the royal harem," Poem 44) by Nguyễn Gia Thiều. In contrast to the latter poem, though, "The song of a soldier's wife" vividly and sensitively treats a topic of universal relevance without digression into philosophical musings: through the voice of a wife deploring the absence of her husband, who is away fighting on some far-off battlefield, the poem expresses the yearning of average people for peace, for simple joys that, having been sacrificed to the "higher" goals of the state, have turned into unaffordable luxuries. In particular, Phan Huy Ích's Vietnamese version, with its natural grace and spellbinding music, has raised translation of poetry to high art and enjoyed a wide audience among all segments of the population, whereas the original is now known only to a few specialists. Most Vietnamese will feel a pang of recognition when they hear the opening line of the vernacular adaptation: "When all through earth and heaven dust storms rise. *"(Thuở trời đất nổi cơn gió bụi)*.

1. Ch'ang-an (Trường-an): the main city in Shensi and capital of the Chinese empire under several dynasties, the T'ang in particular; now known as Sian.

2. Mount Kan-ch'üan (Cam-toàn): a mountain in Shensi, about two hundred miles northwest of Ch'ang-an, halfway between the ancient capital and the Great Wall. Beacon fires were lit there and smoke signals sent up to warn the capital of impending attacks by barbarians.

3. "A man will win a horse skin for his shroud": the proverb runs, "A man's purpose [is to go fighting] thousands of miles [away, die, and be buried in] a horse skin." The following lines have been attributed to the Chinese marshal Ma Yüan (Mã Viện, 14 BCE–49 CE): "A valiant man gets a horse skin for his shroud. / Why settle for death in the arms of your wife and children?"

4. "His life "[he'll] drop in battle like goose down": the expression comes from a proverb, "he'll drop Mount T'ai as lightly as goose down." Mount T'ai (Thái-sơn), in Shantung, was one of the five sacred mountains of China. Ssu-ma Ch'ien remarked: "Of course, a man must die, but sometimes he thinks it as heavy as Mount T'ai, and sometimes he treats it lightly as if it were goose

down"; and Li Po wrote: "There are in Yennan heroes from the Wu family who will drop Mount T'ai as easily as if it were goose down."

5. The Wei (Vị): a river flowing through Shensi—it was crossed by Chinese troops in their expeditions against barbarians.

6. Thousand Peaks: Ch'ien-shan (Thiên-sơn), a mountain in Manchuria, near the Korean border.

7. The Lung-chüan (Long-tuyền) sword: the "Dragon Stream" sword—a magic weapon of Chinese antiquity, the East Asian equivalent of Excalibur.

8. "You'll tread in Chieh-tzu's steps and seize Lou-lan," or "Hunting down [the ruler of] Lou-lan, [you] say [you'll] follow [the example of] Chieh-tzu. "Fu Chieh-tzu (Phó Giới Tử, first century BCE), a famous general under Emperor Chao-ti of the Han dynasty, volunteered to go and punish the ruler of Lou-lan who had ordered the execution of some Chinese envoys. He came back to announce that he had captured the rebellious vassal. When asked for some proof, he produced the barbarian's head.

9. "You'll reach Man-hsi, discussing old Fu-po," or "[You'll] reach Man-hsi [and] discuss matters [about] the Tamer of Waves." Man-hsi ("Wild Mountain Stream") once referred to the area south of China and peopled by tribes like the Vietnamese who still resisted Chinese control. Ma Yüan (Mã Viện) led an army into what was then northern Vietnam in 43 CE and put down an attempt by the two Trưng sisters to throw off the Chinese yoke. For his military services, he was given the title "Fu-po Chiang-chun" (Phục-Ba Tướng-Quân), or the "General Who Tamed the Waves."

10. Han-yang: located in Shensi, it was the capital under the Ch'in dynasty and stood about five miles north of Ch'ang-an, on the left bank of the Wei.

11. Hsiao-hsiang: the place in Hunan where the Hsiao and Hsiang rivers meet.

12. Pai-teng: a fortress in Shansi were Emperor Han Kao-tsu was besieged for seven days by Tartars in 200 BCE. The Blue Sea (Ch'ing-hai): the Kokonor.

13. The Vast Desert: the Gobi; the Lonesome Pass: Hsiao-kuan, in Kansu.

14. Mount Ch'i: Mount Ch'i-lien in Kansu. Here the Han general Huo Chu-ping (Hoặc Khứ Bình) won a great victory over the Tartars in 121 BCE.

15. The Fei (Phì): a river that flows through Anhwei. On the banks of the Fei, Fu Chien (Phù Kiên), a Ch'in lord who led an expedition against the Eastern Tsin, suffered a crushing defeat in 384 CE.

16. Pan Ch'ao (Ban Siêu, 31–101) spent thirty-one years in central Asia fighting against various tribes. He returned to China only to die soon afterwards.

17. "Rich playboys touring far" is "grandsons of princes" (lũ vương-tôn).

18. Lung-hsi (Lũng-tây): a district in Kansu.

19. Mount Huang-hua (Hoàng-hoa): a mountain in Shansi, the site of a T'ang victory over barbarian invaders.

20. "My message on brocade": Su Hui (Tô Huệ) embroidered a poem on brocade and sent it to her husband, Tou T'ao (Đậu Thao), who had been fighting against barbarians for many years in the Gobi Desert. The sovereign, moved by her love for her man, allowed him to come home.

21. Mount Yen: Mount Yen-jan (Yên-nhiên) in Outer Mongolia.

22. According to Chinese myth, Ch'ang O (Hằng Nga) stole the drug of immortality from her husband, the sun god Shen Yi (the Divine Archer), and fled to the moon, where she has reigned as its celibate goddess ever since.

23. The Weaver Maid: see note 30 to Poem 44, "A song of sorrow inside the royal harem," by Nguyễn Gia Thiều.

24. Yang Tower (Dương-đài): see note 2 to Poem 209, "The marvelous encounter at Blue Creek."

25. The Hsiang (Tương) River: see note 38 to Poem 209, "The marvelous encounter at Blue Creek.

26. In the classical tradition, floating ferns and duckweeds symbolize longing and homesickness.

27. This is a quotation from "Spring grief," a poem by Li Po about a woman's yearning for her absent man.

28. Jade Pass: Yü-men-kuan (Ngọc-môn-quan) in Kansu—it commanded the road to central Asia.

29. This is a reference to the magic bamboo walking staff—a dragon, really—on which Fei Ch'ang-fang (Phí Trường Phòng) rode to travel long distances in a few moments.

30. A man named Tsui married a nymph who had a magic scarf; it could serve as a bridge in an emergency.

31. According to a well-known folk myth, a woman stood waiting for her absent husband until she turned to stone.

32. This alludes to the quatrain titled "A young wife's lament" by the T'ang poet Wang Ch'ang-ling: "The young woman has never once known grief. / Face rouged and powdered, she climbs the tower. / She sees spring willows in their green and sobs: / for rank and fame she sent her man to war."

33. The Strider: the K'uei constellation, which symbolizes manly ambition.

34. Shen (Sâm), a constellation which includes some stars in Orion, and Shang (Thương), Lucifer, a morning star, never see each other: they represent lovers separated by insurmountable obstacles.

35. In ancient China, Yao (Diêu) and Wei (Nguy) were two aristocratic clans that adopted the yellow and red peonies, respectively, for their heraldic emblems.

36. Cho Wen-chün (Trác Văn Quân) was a young widow whom the Han writer Ssu-ma Hsiang-ju (Tư Mã Tương Như, 179–117 BCE) courted by play-

ing the tune "A phoenix woos his mate" on the lute or zither. He succeeded in persuading her to elope with him against her rich father's wishes. Later, tired of his aging wife with faded looks, Ssu-ma wanted to take a young concubine. Cho wrote a poem titled "White hair" that moved him to give up that unfaithful course.

37. Under the Tsin dynasty, P'an Yo (Phan Nhạc) was renowned for his looks in youth.

38. According to Chinese myth, *ch'iung-ch'iung* are white creatures that look like horses. The male and the female, together, can run for a hundred miles at a stretch.

39. *Chien-chien* are fabulous birds: each has only one wing, and two must join their wings in order to fly.

40. This is an allusion to the love affair between Emperor T'ang Minghuang (Đường Minh-Hoàng) and Lady Yang (Dương Quí-phi), as described by Po Chü-i in "A song of everlasting sorrow."

41. This refers to a line in an antiwar poem by the T'ang poet Tu Fu.

42. Ch'in: Ch'in Ch'iung (Tần Quỳnh), a famous general under the T'ang dynasty. Huo: Huo Chu-ping (see note 14).

43. Mist Tower (Lang-yên-các): Emperor T'ang T'ai-tsung had the portraits of twenty-four meritorious ministers and generals displayed in Mist Tower. Unicorn Hall (Kỳ-lân-đài): Emperor Han Hsüan-ti honored eleven heroes in the same manner at Unicorn Hall.

44. Su Ch'in (Tô Tần), still a poor, unknown scholar, was despised by his wife, who would deliberately snub him, refusing to leave her loom when she saw him come home. But later he gained fame and fortune as a wandering diplomat who succeeded in forging a league of six states against the dominant kingdom of Ch'in during the Warring States period (403–221 BCE).

45. Lo-yang (Lạc-dương), as the capital of China, attracted the best and the brightest. Su Ch'in himself was a native of that celebrated city.

Index of Poets and Poems

The name of a woman poet is followed by the letter **W**. The title of a work originally written in Chinese appears in *italics*, and that of a long traditional poem in **boldface**.

Anonymous poets
- 18. The village crier
- 19. In praise of the hat
- 20. In praise of the broom
- 30. Exhortation to learning
- 35. The bird in a cage
- 36. Last words
- 37. **Catfish and Toad** *(Trê Cóc)*
- 43. Stepping out of the world
- 79. The Lake of the Returned Sword
- 80. Flood
- 119. The Fourteenth of July
- 208. Trương Chi, the lovelorn boatman
- 209. **The marvelous encounter at Blue Creek** *(Bích Câu kỳ ngộ)*
- 210. **The constant mouse** *(Trinh thử)*
- 250. Fleeting time
- 302. **The quarrel of the six beasts** *(Lục súc tranh công)*

Ái Lan (W; real name: Lê Liễu Huê; b. 1910)
- 128. A deathless autumn

Anh Thơ (W; real name: Vương Kiều Ân; b. 1919)
- 298. Harvesting at sunset

Bàng Bá Lân (b. 1913)
- 126. They starved, they starved . . .

- 183. Mother, I am still here with you
- 219. If in a future life we meet again

Bùi Công Trừng (b. 1905)
- 154. A fallen fruit

Bùi Dương Lịch (1757–1827)
- 293. *To a watering scoop*

Bùi Khải Nguyễn (twentieth century)
- 279. Soap bubbles
- 319. The man who sleeps out in the fields

Cao Bá Quát (1809–1853)
- 33. Drink and drown your cares
- 34. Good luck, bad luck

Cao Tần (real name: Lê Tất Điểu; b. 1942)
- 177. Our friend would board the *Thương-Tín* and go home
- 178. Five crackpots got together
- 179. The booby had a little sack

Chế Lan Viên (real name: Phan Ngọc Hoan; b. 1920)
- 236. More thoughts on Nguyễn
- 265. Graves
- 266. Silk threads of memory
- 267. The waning night
- 268. On the way home
- 269. The war elephant
- 270. The human skull

Diên Nghị
   221. Her story
Du Tử Lê (real name: Lê Cự Phách)
   174. The dawn of a new
      humankind
Dương Bá Trạc (1884–1944)
   81. Prison life
Đào Duy Kỳ (b. 1916)
   153. At Condore Port
Đào Duy Từ (1572–1634)
   41. Where gather mists and
      clouds
Đằng Phương (real name: Nguyễn
      Ngọc Huy; b. 1924)
   131. The day of mourning at
      Yên-báy
   235. To Nguyễn Du
Đặng Thái Thuyên (1897–1931)
   135. Contrasts
Đặng Trần Côn (1710–1745) and
      Phan Huy Ích (1750–1822)
   322. The song of a soldier's wife
      (Chinh phụ ngâm)
Định An (real name unknown)
   182. Visiting an old friend
Đỗ Tấn (full name: Đỗ Tấn Xuân)
   314. Words of comfort
   315. Peace! Peace!
Đông Hồ (real name: Lâm Tấn Phác;
      1906–1969)
   233. Buying a dress for my love
   234. The poem of humankind
   271. The river
   303. War
   304. The string of pearls

H. H. T. (twentieth century)
   185. The sea and the sands
Hà Huyền Chi (real name: Đặng Trí
      Hoàn; b. 1935)
   169. The sea, the world, and
      the boat people

Hải Âu Tử (real name unknown;
      twentieth century)
   121. Zoo cages
Hậu Điền (real name: Nguyễn Dậu;
      twentieth century)
   176. Biding our time
Hoàng Trinh (twentieth century)
   276. Forty
Hồ Chí Minh (real name: Nguyễn
      Sinh Cung; 1890–1969)
   148. The song of a cotton yarn
Hồ Dzếnh (real name: Hà Triệu Anh;
      b. 1919)
   272. Shilly-shally
Hồ Văn Hảo (b. 1917)
   127. Revolutionary youth
Hồ Xuân Hương (W; eighteenth and
      nineteenth centuries)
   186. The shrine of Ts'en
      Yi-tung
   187. Snail
   188. The cake-that-drifts-in-
      water
   189. Jackfruit
   190. Scolding some dunces
   191. Confession
   192. Elegy for the prefect of
      Vĩnh-tường
   193. On being a concubine
   194. The girl without a sex
   195. The Man-and-Wife
      Mountain
   196. Swinging
   197. On hearing a woman
      mourn her husband
   198. A woman lies alone
   199. A girl caught napping by
      day
   200. The Threefold Pass
   201. The Funny Grotto
   202. Ode to the fan
   203. On picking flowers

204. An unwed mother

205. Poking fun at a bonze

206. The bonze got stung by a
bee

Hồng Chương (real name unknown;
b. 1921)

155. It's me, your son

*The Hồng Đức Anthology of Verse in
the National Language*
(fifteenth century)

5. The Bạch-đằng River

6. Homage to the Trưng
queens

11. King and subjects

12. Staffs and hats

13. Ode to the toad

14. Ode to the watermelon

15. Ode to the betel palm

16. Ode to the sewing needle

39. The monastery on Mount
Hill-and-Stream

Huy Cận (full name: Cù Huy Cận; b.
1919)

157. The two wooden men

262. The body

263. A dirge

264. Talking with the pyramid

Huỳnh Mẫn Đạt (1807–1883)

54. The old hound

55. The old whore becomes a
nun

Huỳnh Phú Sổ (?–1947?)

125. Bread

Huỳnh Thúc Kháng (real name:
Huỳnh Hanh; 1876–1947)

105. The comedy of the world

106. A farewell song

Kiên Giang (real name: Trương
Khuông Trinh; b. 1929)

132. The hero of our times

223. Beauties in white

Lâm thị Mỹ Dạ (W; b. 1949)

220. Like leaves

Lê Đức Thọ (real name: Phan Đình
Khải; b. 1911)

156. A fighter's thoughts of
spring

Lê Thánh-tông (King) (1442–1497)

9. The conduct of kings

10. A king's portrait

291. Merchants

Luân Hoán (real name: Lê Ngọc
Châu; b. 1941)

180. Washing my wife's
clothes

Lưu Văn Vong (real name: Trần Văn
Bảng; twentieth century)

165. Run! Run!

166. Paradise

Lý Thường Kiệt (1019–1105)

1. *The Southern emperor
rules the Southern land*

Mạc Thiên Tích (?–1780)

42. *The morning bell at Tiêu
Monastery*

Mai Thảo (real name: Nguyễn Đăng
Quý; b. 1927)

170. Island

286. Coaxing my illness

Minh Đức Hoài Trinh (W; real
name: Võ thị Hoài Trinh;
b. 1930)

238. Selling my soul

Mộng Tuyết (W; real name: Lâm
Thái Úc; b. 1918)

306. The Red Cross

Nam Trân (real name: Nguyễn Học
Sỹ; 1907–1967)

229. Beauty and the poet

230. Against tunes in a minor
key

Nam Xuyên (real name: Phan Ngọc
    Châu; b. 1909)
    301. The bamboo hedgerow
Ngân Giang (W; real name unknown;
    twentieth century)
    280. Getting well
Nguyên Sa (real name: Trần Bích
    Lan; b. 1932)
    218. The dress of Hà-đông silk
Nguyễn Bính (full name: Nguyễn
    Bính Thuyết; 1917–1966)
    211. Two hearts
    212. The girl next door
Nguyễn Bỉnh Khiêm (1491–1585)
    17. Three ranks of men, three
        grades of things
    26. Clouds float through
        dreams
    27. Time and again you've
        seen them win or lose
    28. Before the world of power
        you'll fold your arms
    40. On reading the Buddha's
        scriptures
    240. The rich look grand, the
        poor seem cheap and mean
    241. Men jostle and men fight
        with labored breath
    242. My hair has thinned, my
        teeth have worn away
    243. Self-reflection
Nguyễn Chí Thiện (b. 1933)
    162. The Party left me in the
        wilds
    239. My poetry is no poetry
    287. All come to me
Nguyễn Công Trứ (1778–1858)
    31. Officialdom
    32. A hero's will
    207. Ode to all flowers
    244. Looking forward to
        retirement

245. A wasted life
292. Scholars and soldiers
Nguyễn Du (1765–1820)
    45. Calling all souls (Chiêu
        hồn)
Nguyễn Duy (full name: Nguyễn Duy
    Nhuệ; b. 1948)
    300. Bamboos of Vietnam
Nguyễn Đình Chiểu (1822–1888)
    47. Fleeing from bandits
    48. The storm
    49. Elegy for Trương Định
    50. Waiting for the east wind
    51. The loyal horse
    52. A fisherman speaks his
        mind
    53. A blind poet looks at the
        world outside
Nguyễn Đình Kiên (?–1942)
    87. Prison impromptu
    88. Back in prison
Nguyễn Đình Thi (b. 1924)
    316. Yearning
Nguyễn Gia Thiều (1741–1798)
    44. A song of sorrow inside the
        royal harem (Cung oán
        ngâm khúc)
Nguyễn Hữu Chu (twentieth century)
    86. Neither fish nor fowl
Nguyễn Hữu Huân (?–1875)
    46. Carrying a cangue around
        the neck
Nguyễn Khuyên (1835–1909)
    59. On hearing the rail cry
    60. To a statue
    61. The French national
        holiday
    62. At an exposition
    63. The comedian gets a
        curtain lecture
    64. The widow's reply to a
        matchmaker

65. *To a discarded fan*

247. A scholar-laureate in
retirement

248. Self-portrayal

249. Old age

296. To some students caught
nodding in class

Nguyễn Ngọc Thuận (twentieth
century)

163. A prisoner's funeral.

Nguyễn Nhược Pháp (1914–1938)

232. In a garret

Nguyễn Tất Nhiên (real name:
Nguyễn Hoàng Hải; 1952–
1992)

167. Folk songs for today.

Nguyễn Thiên Túng (fifteenth
century)

288. *The well*

Nguyễn Trãi (1380–1442)

4. A womb's own flesh and
bone—strong brotherhood

7. The old banyan tree

8. He tends the tree who
wants to eat the fruit

21. Ask to be put in charge of
streams and hills

22. For years you wallowed in
the scholar's world

23. Among the great, no
smooth and open world

24. Tired legs won't climb the
high road of blue clouds

25. Both favor and disgrace
you have full known

38. The hibiscus

289. How blessed is a middle
rank in life!

290. A round shape water takes
inside the gourd

Nguyễn Văn Lạc (1842–1915)

66. Shrimp

67. To a dead dog in the river

Nguyễn Văn Năng (1902–1968)

146. A prison cell

147. I shall not die

Nguyễn Ý Thuần (b. 1953)

168. Homecoming

Nhật Tiến (full name: Bùi Nhật Tiến;
b. 1936)

171. Two eyes

Nhượng Tống (real name: Hoàng
Phạm Trân; 1897–1948)

108. A sense of history

109. Mourning a hero

Phạm Hổ (b. 1926)

275. Tall trees

311. The hand

312. The sea

Phạm Quý Thích (1760–1825)

294. *Summer drought*

Phan Bội Châu (real name: Phan
Văn San; 1867–1940)

89. In a Canton jail

90. Mourning Nguyễn Thái
Học and Nguyễn thị Giang

91. The alarm clock

92. To a cuckoo

93. Human nature

94. Character

95. Rights

96. You eat the figs, so sit
beneath the tree

97. Epitaph for my dog

98. My shadow and I

Phan Chu Trinh (1872–1926)

99. Impromptu

100. Ode to the candle

101. Breaking rocks on Poulo
Condore

102. A game of chess

103. Opera actors

104. Dogs in the loft

Phan Huy Ích See: Đặng Trần Côn
and Phan Huy Ích
Phan Thanh Giản (1796–1867)
    295. *Fishermen and*
        cormorants
Phan Trọng Bình (twentieth century)
    130. Independence Day
    136. International solidarity
Phan Trọng Quảng (twentieth
        century)
    107. A ricksha man's
        impromptu
Phan Văn Hy (twentieth century)
    120. The ricksha man
Phan Văn Trị (1830–1910)
    56. The rice mill
    57. The mosquito
    58. Opera actors
    297. Grains of rice
Phổ Đức (real name: Lê Phước Đại;
        b. 1939)
    320. The buffalo boy on a field
        of corpses
Phùng Khắc Khoan (1528–1613)
    29. *Advice to students*
Phùng Quán (1932–1995)
    159. What Mother told me once

Sóng Hồng (better known as Trường
        Chinh; real name: Đặng
        Xuân Khu; 1907–1988)
    231. To be a poet

T. P. (Trần Phong?; twentieth
        century)
    133. Verses for the end of an
        era
Tạ Hữu Thiện (twentieth century)
    160. Looking for her
Tản Đà (real name: Nguyễn Khắc
        Hiếu; 1888–1939)
    110. The tattered map

111. The ship An-Nam
112. The barber
113. Dark night
114. The rail and the bullfrog
115. The canary in a cage
116. To a scarecrow
117. The state of the world
118. The troth between the hill
    and the stream
253. Speaking to my photo
254. Still at play
Tê Hanh (full name: Trần Tê Hanh;
        b. 1921)
    164. Mother
    299. The country road
Thanh Quan (Lady) (real name:
        Nguyễn thị Hinh;
        nineteenth century)
    246. Remembering the past in
        the City of the Soaring
        Dragon
Thế Lữ (real name: Nguyễn Thứ Lễ;
        b. 1907)
    123. Opium
    224. The lyre of myriad tunes
Thiên Thê (real name unknown;
        twentieth century)
    129. Wrecking the statue of
        Paul Bert
Thừa Phong (real name: Lê Văn Cư;
        b. 1914)
    284. Mother's faith
Tô Giang Tử (real name: Nguyễn
        Quang Nhạ; b. 1908)
    282. Congratulating a friend on
        his new dentures
Tô Hữu (real name: Nguyễn Kim
        Thành; b. 1920)
    138. Orphans
    139. Since then
    140. The song on the River of
        Perfumes

141. Three sounds

142. A cradlesong

143. Prison thoughts

144. The cuckoo calls its flock

307. Elephants

Tôn Thất Diệm (twentieth century)

85. To a piggy bank

Trần Cao Vân (1866–1916)

82. On Poulo Condore

83. It's mere child's play to
die

Trần Dạ Từ (real name: Lê Hà Vĩnh;
b. 1940)

308. A drinking song

309. The new lullaby

310. Gifts as tokens of love

Trần Đức Uyển (b. 1941)

313. A letter to my future child

Trần Gia Thoại (twentieth century)

273. A falling leaf

274. The night train

Trần Huiền Ân (real name: Trần Sĩ
Huệ; b. 1937)

317. My mother's son

318. The old vow

Trần Huy Liệu (1901–1969)

149. What's my crime?

150. A down-and-out fighter
and the spring nymph

151. Dropping by the guava
graveyard in Sơn-la

Trần Minh-tông (King) (1300–1357)

2. The Bạch-đằng River

3. Farewell to two envoys
from the Yüan court

Trần Minh Tước (b. 1913)

152. Prison dreams

Trần Mộng Tú (W; twentieth
century)

175. A New Year's wish for a
little refugee

Trần Tế Xương (1870–1907)

68. Tomorrow, should I
fail . . .

69. New-style examinations

70. No, thank you!

71. What earthly use are these
Confucian graphs?

72. Lamenting the state of
Confucian scholarship

73. Actors

74. Poor and happy

75. Looking far ahead

76. Drought

77. A man has lost his way

78. Best wishes for the New
Year

Trần Tuấn Khải (1894–1983)

122. Our land, our home

Trinh Tiên (W; real name unknown;
twentieth century)

134. A woman writes to her
daughter who's studying
overseas

Trương Anh Thụy (W; twentieth
century)

181. The first day of school

Từ Diễn Đồng (1866–1918)

84. The long night

Tương Phố (W; real name: Đỗ thị
Đàm; b. 1900)

305. Who?

Ưng Bình (courtesy name: Thúc Giạ
Thị; 1877–1961)

281. A retired mandarin's wife
complains

Viên Linh (real name: Nguyễn Nam;
b. 1938)

172. Cold season

173. A hundred tongues

Việt Phương (real name unknown;
b. 1928)

161. O life I love and cherish like my wife!

Võ Liêm Sơn (1888–1949)
137. Paradise and hell

Võ Phiến (real name: Đoàn Thế Nhơn; b. 1925)
285. Where have *they* gone?

Vũ Đình Liên (b. 1913)
251. Our hearts are ancient citadels
252. The old calligrapher

Vũ Hoàng Chương (1916–1976)
124. Far away
237. The Beau Ideal
277. To the Black Nymph
278. No more anxiety

Xuân Diệu (full name: Ngô Xuân Diệu; 1917–1985)
158. New tiles
213. To love
214. A fool in love
215. It's all in the heart
216. You must say it
217. Distance
225. Feelings and emotions
226. Magic
227. Casting fragrance to the winds
228. Foreword to a book of poems

255. Nothingness
256. Come on, make haste
257. Spring out of season
258. In a hurry
259. Forever
260. A geologist and millions of years
261. An orange with the rind still green

Xuân Quỳnh (W; full name: Nguyễn thị Xuân Quỳnh; 1942–1988)
222. Waves

Xuân Thủy (real name unknown; b. 1912)
145. You cannot lock up the mind

Y Vân Tử (real name: Nguyễn Trung Ẩn; b. 1909)
283. A gaffer in love

Yên Ba (real name unknown; twentieth century)
184. Twenty-eight lines for my wife

Yên Thao (real name unknown; twentieth century)
321. My home

Bibliography

Anthologie de la poésie vietnamienne. Paris: Les Editeurs Français Réunis, 1969.

Buttinger, Joseph. *The Smaller Dragon: A Political History of Vietnam.* New York: Praeger, 1958.

————. *Viet-Nam: The Dragon Embattled.* New York: Praeger, 1967.

Cima, Ronald J., ed. *Vietnam: A Country Study.* Washington, D.C.: Federal Research Division, Library of Congress, 1989.

Duiker, William J. *The Communist Road to Power in Vietnam.* Boulder, Colo.: Westview Press, 1981.

————. *The Rise of Nationalism in Vietnam, 1900–1941.* Ithaca, N.Y.: Cornell University Press, 1976.

Durand, Maurice, and Nguyễn Trần Huân. *Introduction à la littérature vietnamienne.* Paris: G. P. Maisonneuve and Larose, 1969.

Dương Đình Khuê. *Les Chefs d'oeuvre de la littérature vietnamienne.* Saigon: Kim Lai Ấn Quán, 1966.

Đặng Trần Côn and Phan Huy Ích. *Chinh phụ ngâm / The Song of a Soldier's Wife.* Edited and translated by Huỳnh Sanh Thông. New Haven, Conn.: Lạc-Việt Series, no. 3, Council on Southeast Asia Studies, Yale University, 1986.

Echols, John M. "Vietnamese Poetry." In *Princeton Encyclopedia of Poetry and Poetics,* edited by Alex Preminger. Princeton, N.J.: Princeton University Press, 1965.

Fall, Bernard B. *The Two Viet-Nams: A Political and Military Analysis.* New York: Praeger, 1967.

FitzGerald, Frances. *Fire in the Lake: The Vietnamese and the Americans in Vietnam.* Boston: Little, Brown, 1972.

Glimpses of Vietnamese Classical Literature. Hanoi: Foreign Languages Publishing House, 1972.

Halberstam, David. *The Making of a Quagmire.* New York: Random House, 1964.

Hammer, Ellen J. *The Struggle for Indochina.* Stanford, Calif.: Stanford University Press, 1954.

Hickey, Gerald C. *Village in Viet-Nam.* New Haven, Conn.: Yale University Press, 1964.

Hoàng Văn Chí. *From Colonialism to Communism.* New Delhi: Allied Publishers, 1966.

Hồ Huệ Tâm *see:* Tai, Hue-Tam H.

Huỳnh Kim Khánh. *Vietnamese Communism, 1925–1945.* Ithaca, N.Y.:
Cornell University Press, 1982.

Huỳnh Sanh Thông. *The Heritage of Vietnamese Poetry.* New Haven, Conn.:
Yale University Press, 1979.

Karnow, Stanley. *Vietnam: A History.* New York: Viking Press, 1983.

Lục súc tranh công / The Quarrel of the Six Beasts. Edited and translated by
Huỳnh Sanh Thông (with an introduction by Nguyễn Ngọc Huy). New
Haven, Conn.: Lạc-Việt Series, no. 4, Council on Southeast Asia Studies,
Yale University, 1987.

Lý Chánh Trung. *Introduction to Vietnamese Poetry.* Translated by Kenneth
Filshie. Saigon: Ministry of National Education, 1960.

McAlister, John T. *Viet Nam: The Origins of Revolution.* New York: Knopf,
1969.

Marr, David G. *Vietnamese Anticolonialism, 1885–1925.* Berkeley: University
of California Press, 1971.

———. *Vietnamese Tradition on Trial, 1920–1945.* Berkeley: University of
California Press, 1981.

Nguyễn Chí Thiện. *Hoa địa-ngục / Flowers from Hell.* Edited and translated
by Huỳnh Sanh Thông. New Haven, Conn.: Lạc-Việt Series, no. 1,
Council on Southeast Asia Studies, Yale University, 1984.

Nguyễn Du. *The Tale of Kiều.* A bilingual edition, translated and annotated
by Huỳnh Sanh Thông. New Haven, Conn.: Yale University, 1983.

Nguyễn Đình Hòa. *Vietnamese Literature: A Brief Survey.* San Diego, Calif.:
College of Education, San Diego State University, 1994.

Nguyễn Khắc Kham. *An Introduction to Vietnamese Culture.* Tokyo: The
Centre for East Asian Cultural Studies, 1967.

Nguyễn Khắc Viện et al., eds., and trans. *Anthologie de la littérature
vietnamienne.* 2 vols. Hanoi: Editions en Langues Etrangères, 1972–73.

Nguyễn Khắc Viện and Hữu Ngọc. *Littérature vietnamienne: historique et
textes.* Hanoi: Fleuve Rouge, Editions en Langues Etrangères, 1979.

Nguyễn Ngọc Bích (ed.). *A Thousand Years of Vietnamese Poetry.* Translated
by Nguyễn Ngọc Bích with Burton Raffel and W. S. Merwin. New York:
Knopf, 1975.

Schonberg, André. *Social Structure and Political Order: Traditional and
Modern Vietnam.* Jerusalem: The Hebrew University, Magness Press,
1979.

Shaplen, Robert. *The Lost Revolution.* New York: Harper and Row, 1965.

Smith, Ralph. *Viet-Nam and the West.* London: Heinemann, 1968.

Sully, François, ed. *We the Vietnamese: Voices from Vietnam.* New York:
Praeger, 1971.

Tai, Hue-Tam H. *Millenarianism and Peasant Politics in Vietnam.*
Cambridge: Harvard University Press, 1983.

————. *Radicalism and the Origins of the Vietnamese Revolution.*
Cambridge: Harvard University Press, 1992.

Taylor, Keith Weller. *The Birth of Vietnam.* Berkeley: University of
California Press, 1983.

Trương Bửu Lâm. *Patterns of Vietnamese Response to Foreign Intervention,
1858–1900.* New Haven, Conn.: Southeast Asia Studies, Yale University
Monograph Series 11, 1967.

Whitfield, Danny J. *Historical and Cultural Dictionary of Vietnam.*
Metuchen, N.J.: Scarecrow Press, 1976.

Woodside, Alexander Barton. *Community and Revolution in Modern
Vietnam.* Boston: Houghton Mifflin, 1976.

————. *Vietnam and the Chinese Model.* Cambridge: Harvard University
Press, 1971.